Organizational Ethnography

Organizational Ethnography

Studying the Complexities of Everyday Life

Edited by
Sierk Ybema, Dvora Yanow, Harry Wels
& Frans Kamsteeg

Los Angeles | London | New Delhi
Singapore | Washington DC

Introduction and editorial arrangement © Sierk Ybema, Dvora Yanow, Harry Wels and Frans Kamsteeg

Chapter 1 © Kees van der Waal 2009
Chapter 2 © Michael Humphreys and Tony Watson 2009
Chapter 3 © Peregrine Schwartz-Shea and Dvora Yanow 2009
Chapter 4 © Simon Down and Michael Hughes 2009
Chapter 5 © Sierk Ybema and Frans Kamsteeg 2009
Chapter 6 © Davide Nicolini 2009
Chapter 7 © Brian Moeran 2009
Chapter 8 © Mats Alvesson 2009

Chapter 9 © Gary Alan Fine and David Shulman 2009
Chapter 10 © Nic Beech, Paul Hibbert, Robert MacIntosh and Peter McInnes 2009
Chapter 11 © Chris Sykes and Lesley Treleaven 2009
Chapter 12 © Halleh Ghorashi and Harry Wels 2009
Annotated Bibliography – Defining 'Organizational Ethnography' © Dvora Yanow and Karin Geuijen 2009
Bibliography © Sierk Ybema, Dvora Yanow, Harry Wels and Frans Kamsteeg 2009

First published 2009
Reprinted 2010

SAGE Publications Ltd
1 Oliver's Yard
55 City Road
London EC1Y 1SP

SAGE Publications Inc.
2455 Teller Road
Thousand Oaks, California 91320

SAGE Publications India Pvt Ltd
B 1/I 1 Mohan Cooperative Industrial Area
Mathura Road
New Delhi 110 044

SAGE Publications Asia-Pacific Pte Ltd
33 Pekin Street #02-01
Far East Square
Singapore 048763

Library of Congress Control Number: 2008938550

British Library Cataloguing in Publication data

A catalogue record for this book is available from the British Library

ISBN 978-1-84787-045-2
ISBN 978-1-84787-046-9 (pbk)

Typeset by C&M Digitals (P) Ltd, Chennai, India
Printed in Great Britain by the MPG Books Group
Printed on paper from sustainable resources

Mixed Sources
Product group from well-managed forests and other controlled sources
www.fsc.org Cert no. SA-COC-1565
© 1996 Forest Stewardship Council
FSC

Contents

About the Contributors

Mats Alvesson is Professor of Business Administration at the University of Lund, Sweden. He is also affiliated with the University of Queensland Business School. He has previously held positions in Montreal, Turku, Linkoping, Stockholm and Goteborg, and has been a visiting academic at the universities of Cambridge, Melbourne, Colorado and Oxford. He received his PhD from the University of Lund in 1984. Research interests include critical theory, gender, power, the management of professional service (knowledge intensive) organizations, organizational culture and symbolism, qualitative methods and the philosophy of science. Recent books include *Reflexive methodology, 2nd edition* (Sage, 2009, with Kaj Sköldberg), *Postmodernism and social research* (Open University Press, 2002), *Understanding organizational culture* (Sage, 2002) , *Knowledge work and knowledge-intensive firms* (Oxford University Press, 2004) and *Changing organizational culture* (Routledge, 2008, with Stefan Sveningsson).

Nic Beech is Professor of Management at St Andrews University, Scotland. His research is mainly focused on the social dynamics of organizational life – the intertwining of people's identities, relationships and practices. He has a particular interest in cultural industries and the health sector. Nic is the founding chair of the British Academy of Management's special interest group on identity.

Simon Down is a Senior Lecturer in Management at the University of Newcastle Business School, UK, and Deputy Director of the Centre for Knowledge, Innovation, Technology and Enterprise (KITE). Beginning his working life as an entrepreneur in the independent music sector, he has published articles on small firm policy, entrepreneurial self-identity, management history and ethnographic methodology. He is the author of *Narratives of enterprise: Crafting entrepreneurial self-identity in a small firm* (2006), an ethnographic study of a small firm in the UK. He has also conducted ethnographic research in an Australian steel plant on the topic of culture change and self-identity. It is this experience that is discussed in his chapter here.

Gary Alan Fine is the John Evans Professor of Sociology at Northwestern University. He received his PhD in Social Psychology from Harvard University. For the past 30 years he has conducted a series of ethnographic studies of leisure domains and workplaces, examining the development of small group cultures. These sites include Little League baseball, fantasy role-play gaming, restaurant kitchens, mushroom hunters, art collectors, and government meteorologists. His current ethnographic research examines the social worlds of chess.

Karin Geuijen teaches Public Management at the Utrecht School of Governance. Her research focuses on European policy networks and on (transnational) discourse coalitions, especially on issues of migration and human rights. Her research focuses on transnational discourse conditions especially in the field of migration and human rights. Her dissertation was on shifting asylum policy within the Netherlands, in comparison with Germany and the United Kingdom. Recent publications include 'Dutch Eurocrats at work: Getting things done in Europe' (with Paul 't Hart and Kutsal Yesilkagit), in R.A.W. Rhodes, Paul 't Hart & Mirko Noordegraaf (eds), *Observing government elites: Up close and personal* (Palgrave MacMillan, 2007) and *The new Eurocrats: National civil servants in EU policy making* (with P. 't Hart, S. Princen and K. Yesilkagit (Amsterdam University Press, 2008).

Halleh Ghorashi holds the chair in Management of Diversity and Integration in the Department of Culture, Organization, and Management at the VU University Amsterdam the Netherlands. She is the author of *Ways to Survive, Battles to Win: Iranian Women Exiles in the Netherlands and the United States* (Nova Science Publishers, 2003). She has published several articles on topics such as identity, diasporic positioning, cultural diversity, and emancipation issues. As an active participant in the Dutch public debates on diversity and integration issues, she has received several awards. Her present research focus is on the narratives of identity and belonging of migrants, along with the processes of exclusion and inclusion in the context of growing culturalism.

Paul Hibbert is Lecturer in Management at the University of Strathclyde. He is developing a research focus on knowledge, learning and reflexive practice, combined with a continuing interest in inter-organizational collaboration. Paul has published his work in leading international journals, books and practice-oriented publications. His research has received best paper awards from: the Research Methods Division of the British Academy of Management (2008, with co-authors Christine Coupland and Robert MacIntosh); the Critical Management Studies Group of the Academy of Management (2007); and the Identity Division of the British Academy of Management (2006). In addition he received the Academy of Management's Organization, Development and Change Division Rupert F. Chisholm award for the best theory-to-practice article (2005, with co-author Chris Huxham).

Michael Hughes is a Team Leader at a steelmaking plant in Australia. Initially trained in the hospitality industry, he began working in the steelmaking industry in the early 1990s as an operator. He has taken an active part in major departmental workplace change processes in the late 1990s and in his particular section's initial and continuing workplace change. Michael attended the 2003 Asia Pacific Researchers in Organization Studies (APROS) Conference in Oaxaca, Mexico, where he presented an earlier version of this chapter.

Michael Humphreys is Professor of Organization Studies at Nottingham University Business School. His current research interests include studies of organizational identity, narrative and change; innovation and improvisation in teams; public sector management and qualitative research methodology. He has published in a wide range of journals, including *Journal of Applied Behavioral Science*, *Journal of Management Studies*, *Journal of Organizational Change Management*, *Organization*, *Organization Studies*, and *Public Administration*.

Frans Kamsteeg is Associate Professor in Organization Studies and Anthropology at the Faculty of Social Sciences of the VU University Amsterdam. His research focuses on the question of how ideology and religion shape discourses in (Dutch) civil society organizations. He has published several articles and book chapters on culture and identity problems in non-profit organizations, as well as on the value of organizational anthropology and discourse analysis to management (in *Intervention*, *Journal of Culture, Organization & Management*, 2004, 2005). His methodological interest involves the contribution of ethnographic analysis to organizational change processes, and the special position of the anthropologist as change agent. He received a PhD in cultural politics and religion in Chile.

Robert MacIntosh holds a chair in strategic management at the University of Glasgow's Business School. He completed his PhD in engineering management and his research focuses on strategy development and organizational change. He is also interested in the process of doing research with managers and co-chairs the Action Research SWG of the European Group for Organization Studies. At the moment he is working on a range of projects with the National Health Service and Her Majesty's Revenue and Customs in the UK. He also delivers consultancy and executive education to a range of public and private sector organizations. Undermining his credibility as a management researcher, however, is his status as a shareholder in Aberdeen Football Club – not the wisest investment decision, but one filled with hope!

Peter McInnes is a Lecturer in Management at the University of Strathclyde. Peter's research interests lie in exploring the impact of identity dynamics upon the way in which people understand themselves, each other and the organizations that they are part of. This has seen Peter undertake studies in a number of organizations within both the public and private sectors. His research has been published in such journals as the *International Journal of Public Administration* and *The International Journal of Public Sector Management*.

Brian Moeran is Professor of Business Anthropology in the Department of Intercultural Communication and Management at the Copenhagen Business School and Director of the ©*reative Encounters* research programme. A social anthropologist by training, he has spent more than 15 years in Japan where he has conducted research on advertising, art marketing, media, popular culture, women's fashion magazines, and fragrance culture. He has published widely in the fields of economic anthropology, media studies, and creative industries.

Davide Nicolini is Assistant Professor and RCUK Fellow at IKON, the research unit on Innovation Knowledge and Organizational Networks of Warwick Business School. Prior to joining the University of Warwick, he was researching and lecturing at the University of Trento and Bergamo (Italy) and held the position of Senior Social Scientist at the Tavistock Institute of Human Relations in London. His recent work focuses on the development of a practice-based approach to the study of organizational phenomena and its implications for the understanding of knowing, collaboration, and change in organizations. Other areas of interest include the advancement of action-methodologies, the development and use of reflection practices, and their application to learning from accident, safety, and inter-organizational relations. Although these days most of his field work is carried out in healthcare, he has also studied construction sites, factories, public organizations, and scientific labs.

Peregrine Schwartz-Shea is Professor of Political Science at the University of Utah. Her research on doctoral curricula in methodology has appeared in *PS: Political Science and Politics* and *Perestroika! The raucous rebellion in political science* (ed. Kristen Renwick Monroe, Yale University Press, 2005). She is co-editor with Dvora Yanow of *Interpretation and method: Empirical research methods and the 'interpretive turn'* (M. E. Sharpe, 2006). Her current research, also with Yanow, examines US institutional review board policy.

David Shulman is Associate Professor of Anthropology and Sociology at Lafayette College. He received his PhD in Sociology from Northwestern University. He has published ethnographic research on deception and impression management in the workplace, culminating in *From hire to liar: The role of deception in the workplace* (Cornell University Press, 2007). He has also published articles on research methods and symbolic interactionism in general and on ethnographic methods in particular. He is presently working on a research study of themed environments.

Chris Sykes is a Lecturer in the School of Management and Marketing in the Faculty of Commerce at the University of Wollongong. Chris's research interests are in the areas of organizational discourses, practices and knowing. His dissertation and a number of recent publications examine the effects of changing organizational discourse and organizational knowledge in Australian community services organizations. He is a committed action researcher and is currently co-ordinating three learning and teaching projects working with the Australian Business Deans' Council Learning and Teaching Network.

Lesley Treleaven is a Senior Lecturer in the Faculty of Economics and Business at the University of Sydney, with extensive experience in business education and organizational studies. For over 20 years she has employed various forms of participatory action research with people wanting to inquire collaboratively into everyday organizational life to improve situations. Her work is published in both the *Handbook of action research* (eds. Bradbury and Reason, 2006) and *Participation in human inquiry* (ed. Reason, 1994). Her current research interests in organizational practices, change and discourse are informed by applications of feminist poststructuralist theory. She is currently chief investigator on an Australian Research Council Linkage Grant exploring practice-based knowing in community organizations. She is a member of two nationally-funded Australian Learning and Teaching Council grants: 'Embedding the Development of Intercultural Competence in Business Education' and 'Facilitating Staff and Student Engagement with Graduate Attribute Development, Assessment and Standards in Business Faculties'. Details of her publications and research interests are available from her home page http://www.econ.usyd.edu.au/15854.html

Kees van der Waal was born in the Netherlands and grew up in South Africa. He studied anthropology at the Pretoria and Rand Afrikaans universities. He worked as a museum anthropologist in Pretoria and then taught at Pretoria, Rand Afrikaans and recently Stellenbosch University, where he is a Professor in Social Anthropology. His research has mainly been done in the Limpopo Province of South Africa and has focused on the following topics: the use of space in Venda, crafts in the informal sector, development intervention in a rural settlement, household dynamics and violence, and local law. He has also worked on the transformation in Afrikaans *volkekunde* (anthropology) and the various approaches to diversity at Stellenbosch University. His current research focuses on organizational interactions in the context of development interventions in the Dwars River Valley, outside Stellenbosch.

Tony Watson is Professor of Organizational Behaviour at Nottingham University Business School. He teaches, researches and writes about industrial sociology, organizations, and managerial and entrepreneurial work. Ethnographic research is a special interest. His books include *In search of management* (revised edition, 2001) and *Sociology, work and industry* (5th edition, 2008). His current research is in deploying ethnography and using concepts of identity work, narrative, culture and entrepreneurship to study aspects of the beer and public house industries.

Harry Wels is Associate Professor in the Department of Culture, Organization, and Management, VU University Amsterdam. His research interest is focused on structures of organizational cooperation between often-antagonistic stakeholders in the field of nature conservation and natural resource management in southern Africa. His recent publications include *Competing jurisdictions: Settling land claims in Africa* (Brill, 2005, with Sandra Evers and Marja Spierenburg) and '"Securing space": Mapping and fencing in transfrontier conservation in southern Africa' (2006, *Space and Culture*, with Marja Spierenburg). He is also Director of South Africa-Vrije Universiteit-Strategic Alliances (SAVUSA), which coordinates the Desmond Tutu Programme of VU University Amsterdam and is aimed at generating academic publications on issues relating to South and southern Africa.

Dvora Yanow holds the Strategic Chair in Meaning and Method at the VU University Amsterdam. Her research has been shaped by an overall interest in the communication of meaning in organizational and policy settings. She is the author of an organizational and policy ethnography, *How does a policy mean? Interpreting policy and organizational actions* (Georgetown University Press, 1996) and two other books, *Conducting interpretive policy analysis* (Sage, 2000); and *Constructing 'race' and 'ethnicity' in America: Category-making in public policy and administration* (M.E. Sharpe, 2003); and co-editor of *Knowing in organizations: A practice-based approach* (M. E. Sharpe, 2003) and *Interpretation and method: Empirical research methods and the interpretive turn* (M. E. Sharpe, 2006). Her published articles treat the role of built space in communicating policy and organizational meanings, organizational learning from an interpretive-cultural perspective, the role of improvisation in methods and management, public policies as collective identity stories, and interpretive philosophies and research methods.

Sierk Ybema is Assistant Professor in Organization Science in the department of Culture, Organization, and Management at the VU University Amsterdam. His research revolves around processes of politics, identity and sensemaking. He conducted ethnographic research within an amusement park and within the editorial staffs of two newspapers. He has widely published on a variety of issues, including relational and temporal identity talk, managerial discourse and postalgia, culture and 'symbolism', intercultural communications, interorganizational relationships, and organizational change and crisis.

Studying everyday organizational life

Sierk Ybema, Dvora Yanow, Harry Wels and Frans Kamsteeg

Just as newspapers do not, typically, engage the ordinary experiences of people's daily lives, organizational studies has also tended largely to ignore the humdrum, everyday experiences of people working in organizations. The most central discussions and debates in organizational studies textbooks are often remarkably remote from these commonplaces, as if organizations are not inhabited and embodied by individuals who go to work. There is, as Fineman, Sims and Gabriel (2005: ix) note, 'a gulf between the lived experience of organizing and being organized by others, with its uncertainty and confusion, and the tidy, rather sanitized, texts on organizational behaviour'. Here is where organizational ethnography makes its contribution.

Although the quotidian experiences of people working in organizations may, to some, hardly seem exciting, for organizational ethnographers much of the intriguing 'mystery' of organizational life is hidden in the ordinary exchanges of ordinary people on an ordinary sort of day. From this perspective, the intricacies of everyday organizational life can be better grasped not through questionnaires developed and analysed while sitting in an office, but by going out into the organizational 'field' – shadowing managers, joining street cops on motorbikes, attending (un)eventful meetings, working as a midwife's assistant, and so forth; in short, by 'hanging out,' where and when one can closely monitor 'up close and in person' how work is organized and how that organizing organizes people.

Organizational ethnographers strive for an appreciation of the complexities of the everyday in organizational settings (Koot, 1995), which we chose to illustrate, metaphorically, on the cover of this book by using Evert Thielen's way of painting everyday organizational settings. This may seem an oxymoron, as complexity may not come immediately to mind when thinking about mundaneity. After all, daily occurrences appear readily enough observable: plain to the eye, and hence, one might argue, rather uncomplicated and perhaps even self-evident and unremarkable. Where here is complexity?

Yet clarity about everyday commonplaces often comes only with hindsight. The very 'ordinariness' of normality often prevents us from seeing it: we tend to have a blind spot for what is usual, ordinary, routine. Moreover, immersion in the particular settings of our daily lives often leads to a rather poor awareness of the social processes that contextualize them. Because the everyday tends so often to be overlooked, we might well speak of the *sub*mundane rather than the mundane, what French novelist Georges Perec (1989) called the 'infra-ordinary' by contrast with the extraordinary. Like Perec, the ethnographic researcher explores the details of everyday life which otherwise go unnoticed, trying to read the tacitly known scripts and schemas that organize ordinary activities. Ethnographers hold that an appreciation of the extraordinary-in-the-ordinary may help to understand the ambiguities and obscurities of social life.

The authors of this book's chapters engage the ways in which ethnographic methods, by attending to the extraordinary in the mundane, day-to-day aspects of organizing, can lead to a fuller, more grounded, practice-based understanding of organizational life. Through detailed accounts of organizational life, organizational ethnography has made a substantial contribution over the years toward obtaining an understanding of organizations and organizing. But despite its growing popularity in organizational studies, the field has, on the whole, been without methods texts (other than a short 1993 volume by Schwartzman in the Sage 'blue book series') that treat organizational ethnography's distinctive features and particular problematics. Recently, books by Kostera (2007) and Neyland (2008) have put the field on the organizational methods' radar screen, emphasizing ethnography's sophisticated tools for depicting daily meaning-making in organizations. Both of these volumes convey something of the 'how to' of ethnographic research, with introductory chapters on culture, ethnography, and organizations (Kostera's volume) and treatments of the whole research process amply illustrated by various organizational ethnographies (Neyland's textbook).

The chapters in the book you are holding extend the discussion by problematizing the practice of organizational ethnography and tackling key challenges and problematics that arise in the doing and writing of organizational ethnography. Getting out into the organizational field, being there, and writing about what one observes and experiences – in short, doing organizational ethnography – presents its own methodological, analytical, (re)presentational, ethical, and social challenges for researchers. The chapters in this book have been written by organizational studies scholars grappling with these issues in various forms and in various settings. They research and write with an 'ethnographic sensibility' that informs their work, and they engage some of the central concerns of organizational studies scholarship today.

The chapters introduce an ethnographic approach to the study of organizations and organizing through engaging methodological issues particular to its writing practices (Part 1), raising questions about closeness, closure, and distance in fieldwork and deskwork (Part 2), giving voice to critical perspectives and exploring new methodological considerations and challenges (Part 3), and providing a guided overview of the world of organizational ethnographies (the Appendix, an annotated bibliography). The authors argue for the advantages an ethnographic approach brings to these concerns, at the same time as they explore the special problematics faced by organizational ethnographers, ranging from accessing research sites to writing texts, from acquiring local knowledge to maintaining a 'stranger's' perspective, from meeting accepted standards of scientific detachment to intervening for organizational action or social justice. Taken together, the chapters engage specific problems of, provide new thoughts for, or provoke established ways of thinking about organizational ethnography.

In the rest of the introduction, we set the stage for the book's engagement with organizational ethnography by briefly exploring the emergence and growth of the tradition of ethnographic studies of organizations and organizational life, by discussing 'organizational ethnography' itself and describing its key characteristics, and, finally, by identifying some of the conceptual issues we encountered in putting the book together. In describing various ways in which ethnographic researchers access the intricacies of organizational life, we outline some of the characteristics of 'ethnographying' as a method and introduce the chapters of the book.

a heritage of long standing

Writing detailed accounts of organizational life is a long-standing tradition, as others have also remarked (e.g., Morrill and Fine, 1997). Notable among these accounts are the Hawthorne studies of the 1920s and 1930s and Elton Mayo's adoption of anthropological field methods (for example, Mayo, 1933), as well as ground-breaking, in-depth analyses published from the late 1940s to the early 1960s of the 'informal organization' and the bureaucratic 'underlife' (Goffman, 1961). Among the latter are classic studies by Whyte (1948), Selznick (1949), Gouldner (1954), Blau (1955), Dalton (1959), Goffman (1983/1959), Kaufman (1960), and Roy (1960). These authors enriched the field of organizational studies by showing some of the limitations of theories depicting formal bureaucratic organizational forms as efficiently functioning machines, bringing into view the 'irrationalities' of behind-the-scenes politics and other practices taking place in organizational 'back regions' (Goffman 1983/1959).

With the development from the 1950s on of survey research, statistical science, mainframe computers, and behavioralist theories, research aiming to measure organizational structures, contingencies, and behaviours through quantitative means came to dominate the organizational studies field, and ethnographic studies of organizations fell into decline. However, toward the end of the 1970s and into the 1980s, a renewed appreciation for qualitative methods (e.g., Van Maanen, 1979), processes of institutionalisation (e.g., Meyer and Rowan, 1977), and organizational symbolism and cultures (e.g., Smircich, 1983) brought a social-cultural approach back into the field. As alternatives to the then-mainstream research, these newer streams began to drive a 'methodological renewal,' drawing attention to ethnographic methods and associated theoretical ideas (see, for example, Bate, 1997; Czarniawska-Joerges, 1992,

1997; Koot, 1995; Koot et al., 1996; Linstead, 1996; Morey and Luthans, 1987; A. Prasad and P. Prasad, 2002; Rosen 1991a; Tennekes, 1995; Wright 1994), and ethnographic research returned once again to the organizational studies kitbag. Moreover, some of this research began to reshape various fields of study, from strategy to leadership, organizational design to implementation, organizational change to ethics and normative behaviour (see, for instance, Barley, 1983, 1986; Collinson, 1992; Delbridge, 1998; Dubinskas, 1988; Gregory, 1983; Ingersoll and Adams, 1992; Jackall, 1988; Kondo, 1990; Kunda, 1992; Moeran, 2006; Morrill, 1995; Orr, 1996; Rosen, 1991b; Watson, 1994; Yanow, 1996; Ybema 1996; Young 1989).

This methodological renewal has been led by some key theorists, notable among them John Van Maanen (e.g., 1979, 1988, 1995), who, in empirical as well as methodological work, has both demonstrated and theorized the place of ethnography in studies of the organizational. Similarly, David Silverman's methodological writings (e.g., 2007) have done much to make qualitative research, including ethnography, more acceptable within the organizational studies discipline. Barbara Czarniawska has argued for ethnographically informed approaches as the ones 'best suited for grasping the essence of organizational action – the inherent dialectics of matter and ideas' (Czarniawska-Joerges, 1992: 44). Others, among them Paul Bate (1997), Stephen Linstead (1996), Calvin Morrill and Gary Fine (1997), and Tony Watson (1994), sounded similar notes, remarking on the advantages of ethnographic methods and approaches for locating the study of organizations within historically and culturally sensitive contexts. The call has been picked up more recently by other organizational studies scholars, chiefly Anshuman Prasad and Pushkala Prasad (A. Prasad and P. Prasad, 2002; P. Prasad, 2005; P. Prasad and A. Prasad, 2002), along with Kostera (2007) and Neyland (2008), as well as by anthropologists David Gellner and Eric Hirsch (2001) and Brian Moeran (2005). This is the tradition and the methodological community which our book joins.

organizational ethnography

But what is organizational ethnography, as practised within this heritage and community? At its simplest and most self-evident, organizational ethnography is the ethnographic study, and its dissemination, of organizations and their organizing processes. This subject of study takes its place alongside ethnographies of religion, of a city or neighbourhood or ethnic community, of gang life, homeless people, professions and occupations (such as doctors and waitresses), fashion design, social movements, and many other aspects of human life.

Were we attempting with this book to distinguish organizational ethnography from one of these other forms of ethnography, we might point to the setting, or 'field', which is the focus of analysis as the distinguishing feature defining *organizational* ethnography (a term that itself needs ever more problematizing given the changes in organizational forms; see the introduction to the annotated bibliography, this volume). We might also point to challenges posed to ethnographers by the particularities of organizational life. Among these are the greater frequency with which research participants also become readers of the monograph, leading to issues of informational privacy versus scientific norms for the public dissemination of findings (see, for example, Mosse, 2006); the extent to which some organizations draw more attention than others, leading their members to feel 'over-researched', itself leading to problems with access (Moeran, Chapter 7, this volume); the monetary temptations of being better paid (and perhaps more appreciated) as a consultant, rather than as a marginalized academic researcher (Chapman, 2001); or the complicated and politicized complexion that may colour researcher-researched relationships (see, e.g., Beech et al., Chapter 10, and Fine and Schulman, Chapter 9, this volume).

Even more importantly, we might point to what to us appears an increasingly salient feature of the ways in which ethnography is being done in the field of organizations. Rather than trying to grasp the entire gestalt of the organizational 'village', organizational ethnographers seem increasingly oriented toward following the person (for example, the CEO or other employee; see, for instance, Koot and Sabelis, 2002) or a specific organizational practice (for example, the corporate culture coordinator in Kunda's (1992) study; see also Nicolini, Chapter 6, this volume) or an object or 'fact' (for example, Harper's (1998) study of IMF documents; on this, see Latour, 1988). This 'following' can take place at any level of the organizational hierarchy – studying up or studying down – or across departmental and organizational boundaries; it can be done within a clearly demarcated organizational 'space' or in more fragmented, diffuse, and even 'virtual' organizations.

Our efforts are, however, more focused on essaying to mark what is distinctive about 'ethnographying' (Tota, 2004) in organizational settings – to set organizational *ethnography* apart from other approaches to the study of organizations and to delineate what it can contribute to their understanding. Attempting to detail its special character has led some to coin new terms for this enterprise, in no small part because the etymology of 'ethnography' (θνος, *ethnos* = people and γράφειν, *graphein* = writing) suggests that *ethnos* might not be the most accurate denotation for ethnographic research into *organizations*. Czarniawska (1997: 202; 2007: 108), for example, advanced the neologism 'ergonography'. We find this term problematic as it is meant, etymologically, to designate the ethnography of work, whereas we see organizational ethnography as having a broader focus – on organizing and its materializations: organizations. 'Organography' might have seemed a closer fit, at least in its orthography and sound, but as it is used in the medical and biological sciences to refer to the scientific description of the organs of plants and animals, we have not adopted it, either. Instead, we retain the double designation, organizational ethnography, which enables us to attend to both its aspects.

In the following pages, we describe seven key characteristics of (interpretive) organizational ethnography.

1 *Combined fieldwork methods* It is its conduct – undertaken to grasp complex organizational processes at their fullest through an equally complex set of methods – that gives organizational ethnography its specific flavour. As is commonly done, we characterize ethnographic *methods* in organizational settings as the combined field research 'tools' of observing (with whatever degree of participation), conversing (including formal interviewing), and the close reading of documentary sources. These methods rest upon action ('talking, laughing, working, doing') and proactive perception ('observing, listening, reading, smelling'). This distinctive set of methods for accessing or generating data (discussed by Van der Waal, Chapter 1, this volume) distinguishes ethnography from other approaches to the study of organizations (see also Denzin and Lincoln, 2000, and, for a critical reflection, Alvesson and Deetz, 2000). Through the use of these different methods of generating data over an extended period of time, ethnographers are able to describe various aspects of organizational life: organizational actors' sensemaking practices across different situations, engaging with what people do and what they say they do; routine patterns as well as dynamic processes of organizing; frontstage appearances and backstage activities; the minutiae of actors' lifeworlds as well as the wider social and historical contexts in which these lifeworlds unfold.

2 *At the scene* Organizational ethnographers do not describe the complexities of everyday organizational life in the abstract, but instead through reporting on their first-hand, field-based observations and experiences. Starting from an empathic perspective (although the empathy may not last; see Down, Garrety, and Badham 2006; Fine and Shulman, Chapter 9, this volume) and looking closely into the doings and dealings of organizational actors enables organizational ethnographers to describe the lived realities of flesh and blood people in their everyday organizational lives. Ethnographers go out into the field of study to participate in organizational members' lifeworlds, establishing working relationships with them, immersing themselves in the circumstances of members' situations, and giving voice to participants' own interpretations of these. In this fashion, as Van Maanen put it with reference to the dissemination of this research, ethnographic texts achieve 'a kind of documentary status on the basis that someone actually goes "out there", draws close to people and events, and then writes about what was learned in situ' (1995: 3). By providing all manner of detail on everyday organizational life, organizational ethnographers place both author and reader at the scene, in the thick of things, thereby conveying a sense of 'being there' to the reader (Bate 1997). Detailed renderings of objects, actors, events, language, and interactions open a window onto some of the everyday processes of organizational actors' meaning making.

3 *Hidden and harsh dimensions: Power and emotions* In drawing close to subjects and situations, organizational ethnography has the potential to make explicit the often-overlooked, tacitly known and/or concealed dimensions of meaning-making, including its emotional and political aspects. Such ethnographies can, at times, have a somewhat critical, even 'raw' – direct, unpolished, and sometimes shocking – quality, laying bare harsh and/or hidden social realities and exposing the entanglement of culture with power. Looking at the world 'with a skeptical and unflinching eye, with a characteristic passionate dispassion' (Jackall, 1988: ix), ethnographers may highlight the politics of sensemaking practices as they take into account the relative power of organizational actors, the interests at stake, and the strategies pursued (Tennekes, 1990). To organizational members, descriptions of routine, taken-for-granted ways of thinking and acting can often be both familiar and surprising, and even confronting, as they see themselves through someone else's eyes. In revealing otherwise covert aspects of organizational life, ethnographies may at times even fly in the face of what organizational actors would like to hear or read about themselves and their organizations.

4 *Context-sensitive and actor-centered analysis* Organizational ethnography also combines an orientation toward subjective experience and individual agency in everyday life with sensitivity to the broader social settings and the historical and institutional dynamics in which these emerge or are embedded (Bate, 1997; Fetterman, 1998; Geertz, 1973; Prasad, 2005; Rosen 1991a; Yanow and Schwartz-Shea, 2006). Like Sergio Leone's acclaimed style of filming in *Once upon a time in the West*, ethnographic texts tend to alternate 'extreme close-ups' that show detail by portraying persons with particular facial expressions, talk, gestures, and clothes with 'wide-angle' or 'long shots' that show panoramic views of the institutional context, the historical background, power relations, and societal discourses. Ethnography's strength is thus to 'see the world in a grain of sand' (slightly paraphrasing William Blake), exploring and exemplifying the general through the local and the particular. As the structure versus agency debates in the social sciences continue to carve up the field of organizational studies (Reed, 2006), the combination of contextual analysis with an actor-centered approach promises to remedy the apolitical reading of organizing and what Andrew Pettigrew critiqued as the 'ahistorical, acontextual and aprocessual' qualities of most organizational studies (quoted in Bate, 1997: 1155).

interpretivist organizational ethnography

Ethnographic research and writing can be informed by different ontological and epistemological presuppositions. These range from a realist (or 'naturalist') perspective that positions the ethnographer as an objective observer and 'knower' of naturally-occurring social phenomena, to a more interpretivist perspective that sees social realities as being socially constructed, with the ethnographer as fully part of these constructivist processes (for more theoretical-philosophical treatments of these differences, see, e.g., Bernstein, 1976, 1983; for more social scientific treatments tied to research methods, see, e.g., Polkinghorne, 1983, 1988; Prasad 2005; Yanow and Schwartz-Shea, 2006). In this volume, chapter authors on the whole articulate a constructivist ontological and interpretive epistemological perspective on organizations and organizational research. They treat organizational and other social realities as socially – collectively, intersubjectively – constructed in an ongoing interplay between individual agency and social structure, in and through which individuals and structures mutually constitute each other (Berger and Luckmann, 1991/1966; Giddens, 1984; Jenkins, 2004).

5   *Meaning-making* What this means in practice is, first, that ethnographers work to make sense of organizational actors' sensemaking, usually through the latter's own language and concepts, although these may be cast in the language of 'culture', 'identity', 'scripts and schemas', 'values, feelings, and beliefs', 'interpretive models of and prescriptive models for reality', and the like – in short, as 'meaning-making'. Analysis presents the symbolic representations of actors' meanings – that is, the specific language, acts, and/or objects that carry and transmit human sensemaking as those actors create, experience, and attribute meaning to social realities (Dandridge et al., 1980; Jones, 1996; Kamsteeg and Wels, 2004; Yanow, 1996). These symbols are studied by focusing on, among other things, such theoretical categories as narratives, discourses, stories, metaphors, myths, slogans, jargon, jokes, gossip, rumours, and anecdotes found in everyday talk and text (symbolic language); rites and rituals, practices, customs, routines (symbolic acts); or built spaces, architectural design, clothing, and other physical artefacts (symbolic objects). In describing meaning-making processes, ethnographic research challenges readers as well as researchers to question their taken-for-granted beliefs about the organizational aspects being studied and (re)presented.

6   *Multivocality* An interpretivist ethnographic approach, grounded in a hermeneutic-phenomenological perspective on social realities, also calls on the researcher to be alert to the potential multiplicity of voices and interpretations that create and recreate the stages and stories of organizational life. Such an approach breaks away from a 'fixed-stage', univocal account that holds out the promise of mirroring organizational reality (see Rorty 1979) in favour of richly describing many different situations and events and 'the polyphony, though more usually cacophony, of voices' (Bate 1997: 1166) in the organizational arena. Such ethnographies describe tensions and discrepancies between official pronouncements and unofficial practices, formal design and informal wheeling and dealing, front regions and back regions (Goffman, 1959), what people do and what people say about what they do (Brunsson, 1985), the managed and the 'unmanaged' organization (Gabriel, 1995), espoused theories and theories-in-use (Argyris and Schön, 1974). Von Holdt's (2003) description of South African steelworkers' struggles for changes in the violent workplace regime during the apartheid years, for instance, provides an interesting example. Von Holdt conveys these struggles not simply in the sense

of a one-dimensional contestation between 'good' (steelworkers) and 'evil' (white management), but as a complex, intertwined configuration of multiple voices, multiple interests, multiple ideals, all of this contextualized within broader societal developments in South Africa in general and the trade unions' role in the fight against apartheid, in particular. Ethnographic narratives of whatever methodological orientation may thus create in the reader the almost visceral sense of being part of organizational life's ups and downs.

7 **Reflexivity and positionality** Finally, and importantly, what an interpretive organizational ethnography offers is the understanding that we, as researchers, '*call* it [the world that we study] a grain of sand' (Pachirat, 2006, after poets Blake and Wisława Szymborska). That world, in other words, does not arrive pre-labeled and pre-theorized. An interpretive approach brings into play a self-conscious awareness of the researcher's role in what Nelson Goodman (1978) called 'worldmaking' – creating sense during fieldwork, deskwork, *and* textwork (Yanow 2000) out of the settings, events, and actors we are studying. A constructivist-interpretive perspective means that ethnographers need to inquire into their own meaning-making processes. This calls for a heightened self-awareness – a 'reflexivity' – of the ways in which their own persons (from education and training to experience to personalities to demographic characteristics) might be shaping the knowledge claims researchers advance with respect to their research topic: their 'positionality'. For some, especially those working from a more critical theoretical perspective, this means inquiring into issues of power in the researcher-researched relationship and the links between knowledge and power. Most interpretive ethnographers, then, think of ethnographic knowledge as being 'generated' in research, rather than as data being 'collected' or even 'accessed', and some treat research participants as co-generators of ethnographic knowledge. In this view, research knowledge (or 'truth claims') is situational, co-constructed through interactions with others in organizational settings, reflective of researchers' and others' positionality with respect to subjects and settings.

The texture of the organizational ethnographic approach just described is delineated in the book in terms of three themes that constitute its overall structure: issues of expressive power, plausibility, and authorship in deskwork and textwork (Part I); tensions between a deep familiarity with the field of study and problems of closeness and closure during and after fieldwork (Part II); and particular ethical, social, and political problems arising in relationships between researcher and researched throughout the research process (Part III).

Part I. ethnographic doing and writing

Kees van der Waal starts the book off with the story of his own professional conversion from an 'innocent' South African ethnologist to a critical organizational ethnographer, inviting the reader to join him in the various steps of organizational ethnography and offering an interesting account of his positionality.

In Chapter 1 he briefly describes these steps, constantly reminding us that it is the ethnographer's reflections on his/her positionality and context, including power, that constitute the stepping-stones of mastering the craft of organizational ethnography, whether it is in accessing or generating data, using theory in analyzing those data, or writing the research narrative. This chapter, in addition to engaging some of the central problematics encountered in doing organizational ethnography, can also serve as a methodological baseline for those just now beginning to think about this form of research.

The next three chapters engage 'ethnography' as a genre of writing. While fieldwork generates the basis for the descriptive aspects of a study of organizational life and deskwork works through the analytic relationships between descriptive material and theoretical concerns, ethnographic textwork aims to convey the researcher's field experiences and theoretically-informed analysis to a reader (or listener or viewer, in the case of an oral report or perhaps even an ethnographic film). For ethnographers, the expressivity of the narrative and plausibility of the argument, as well as the style and 'richness' of the writing, are crucial to creating a compelling text. However, what these texts are to look like – how they 'read', how they 'feel' – is not so self-evident. Discerning four different styles of writing ethnography, ranging from a straightforward realist style to fictionalised or semi-fictionalised styles, Michael Humphreys and Tony Watson (Chapter 2) offer an overview of options intended to help organizational ethnographers choose, develop, and reflect on their own writing styles. The chapter underlines the importance of the expressive character of ethnographic writing, at the same time that it considers stretching the boundaries of what traditional scholars might consider acceptable writing in the field of organizational studies.

Peregrine Schwartz-Shea and Dvora Yanow (Chapter 3) describe the ethnographic genre 'from within', so to speak, engaging the variety of different characteristics it entails. They note, among other things, that ethnography as a form of narrative reporting values the 'being there' quality established by empirical detail. More crucially, through various textual tools, including theoretical refinement and citation practices, the ethnographer-as-author signals membership in a specific academic community – in our case here, the community of organizational studies scholarship – and within that, membership in a particular epistemic community. Although organizational ethnographies are also written from realist ontological perspectives, the authors' primary concern in this chapter is with the written forms of methodological devices that ethnographer-writers use to signal membership in the epistemic community of constructivist ontological and interpretivist epistemological scholarship (in keeping with the orientation of this volume). They are equally concerned with how reviewers or other readers of ethnographic manuscripts might recognize those signals and evaluate research accordingly, rather than holding it to standards more appropriate to other epistemic communities (for example, that of survey researchers).

Lastly, in Chapter 4, Simon Down and Michael Hughes challenge academic ethnographers to put their pens where their self-proclaimed strengths and methodological values and beliefs are, so to speak, by asking ourselves why, when we claim to give voice to organizational members and understand 'from within', we insist on holding power over the keyboard. Based on their experience co-writing a paper reporting on Down's ethnographic research at Hughes' organization, the authors advance an argument for co-generated ethnographic texts in which organizational members narrate their own stories in their own voices. The chapter raises questions concerning authorial power as it reflects on organizational ethnographers' inclinations to reclaim and retain a puppeteer-like authority in relation to the researched when the writing process starts.

Part II. familiarity and 'stranger-ness'

Organizational ethnographers work at becoming as knowledgeable about the organization they are studying as its members are, while at the same time holding on to a stranger's perspective. Establishing distance and 'stranger-ness' enables ethnographers to see 'new' things more clearly, keeping what is familiar to members from becoming commonplace in their own eyes and sustaining an inquisitive stance with respect to its reasons and rationales, while developing an intimate familiarity enables them to grasp the import of that which they are seeing and/or experiencing. In this way they combine *emic* understanding with *etic* analysis (Headland, Pike and Harris, 1990), interpreting their own experiences and observations and structuring the interpretations of organizational members in light of contextual factors and the theoretical concerns of their disciplines (Crang and Cook, 2007; Lofland and Lofland, 1995). The chapters in Part II of this volume explore problems and challenges around several contradictory pairs that characterize various aspects of this research process: immersion and distance (Chapter 5), zooming in and zooming out (Chapter 6), participating and observing (Chapter 7), and closeness and closure (Chapter 8).

Balancing immersion and distance requires fieldworkers to get close to organizational members' working lives and gain an understanding of the latter's everyday lifeworld 'from within' at the same time as researchers strive to preserve some of the surprise they experienced initially as newcomers to the organization. Arguing that ethnography's traditional emphasis on making the strange familiar through immersion in the field has deflected attention away from the importance of distancing and defamiliarizing in ethnographic research, Sierk Ybema and Frans Kamsteeg (Chapter 5) describe different observational fieldwork roles and theoretically informed interpretive strategies that organizational ethnographers might use to yield such surprise and make the familiar strange once more.

Playing off the interplay between proximity and distance, Davide Nicolini (Chapter 6) argues that researchers studying organizational practices should alternate getting close to the field with creating distance throughout the research process. The iterative process of 'zooming in' and 'zooming out' which he describes can lead the researcher to follow the spreading branches of practices, tracing organizing activities that cross organizational boundaries. His work anticipates an argument that ethnographic methods need to change in order to meet newer organizational forms that do not fit the traditional, anthropologically-derived model of a single, bounded field setting (a point taken up in the Appendix). In addition, whether 'newly' positioned in places foreign to them or more 'naturally' placed in more familiar ones, fieldworkers at some point need to climb out from under copious amounts of often disorganized data – observational field notes, interview notes, notes on documents, notes on methods – and turn those data into thickly described texts which link to their epistemic community's theoretical concerns. One way in which ethnographers might hold on to their outsider positions, as Nicolini notes in passing, is through their membership in their academic-epistemic communities and their interest in sharing their insights with those members through theorizing about their field research.

Notwithstanding the importance of distancing or zooming out, gaining a 'deep familiarity' (Goffman, quoted in Lofland 1995: 45) with subjects and situations is crucial for gaining information, rapport, and access in the field, something Brian Moeran (Chapter 7) illustrates in detail. Rather than actively contributing to work activities and climbing the formal or informal hierarchical ladder in organizations, Moeran argues, organizational ethnographers often remain relatively marginal players in the field, preferring to adopt the role of observer rather than participant. As organizational ethnographers often research at the lower end of the organizational hierarchy and organizational members put up formal, friendly or unfriendly façades, it can be difficult to establish close connections to higher echelons and gain access to inner circles within organizations. Moeran suggests that organizational ethnographers need to join in the work activities of organizational members in order to become respected and incorporated into the closed and confidential circuits of the organization.

Stranger-ness is more or less given in foreign settings – those at a cultural, and often geographic, distance from one's community of origins. But there are numerous 'strange' and different settings in one's own society that provide such challenges as well – life spheres that are completely alien to the organizational ethnographer's own experience, background or social milieu. Imagine, for instance, the organizational ethnographer doing research in an abattoir in his own home country and society, participating actively in different occupational positions in relation to the process of slaughtering and processing animals on their way to becoming steaks and lamb chops on sale in the supermarket (Pachirat, 2008). Moeran's argument for 'observant participation' rather than 'participant observation' can be seen as a radical version of ethnography's traditional predilection for researcher immersion in settings and circumstances different from their own 'natural' ones. If, however, ethnographers expect themselves to learn to think, see, feel, and act as a regular or ordinary member of a setting and its culture, why not conduct research in one's own 'home' organization? Mats Alvesson (Chapter 8) argues at length for the utility of doing such 'at-home ethnography', precisely for the natural familiarity and lack of strangeness of its setting. In his view, the advantages of researching an organization with which one is already familiar far outweigh the problems potentially posed by such familiarity. Alvesson also discusses how to avoid 'closeness and closure', as he puts it, and a possibly myopic gaze.

Part III. researcher-researched relationships

Because ethnographic research rests on a close engagement with the people and processes studied, it tends to place particular demands on organizational ethnographers' ethical, social, political, and methodological sensibilities, in ways that do not arise in survey and other non-fieldwork forms of research. In the field as well as in the deskwork process of engaging theoretical concerns and textwork processes of disseminating the research, scholars encounter some of the key methodological challenges confronting ethnography today: questions concerning its ethical practices, political impact(s), and scientific standing. What the chapters in Part III make clear is that one's ethical commitments shape the conduct of the research, as well as the manuscripts through which it is reported. These chapters call on ethnographers to engage, explicitly, with what might be called the truth-stretching 'lies' built in to ethnographic research (Chapter 9), the role of friendship in research relationships (Chapter 10), the challenges of moving beyond research toward engaged action (Chapter 11), and their own potential complicity in social injustice, even when they do not take on a more engaged role (Chapter 12).

When organizational research is ethnographic, becoming embroiled in the daily lives of organizational members and directly reporting on relationships between the ethnographer and the 'ethnographied', ethical acts, or their absence, come to the fore. Rather than discussing research ethics in the abstract through articulating ideal norms or moral codes of ethnographic conduct, Gary Alan Fine and David Shulman (Chapter 9) explore ethical boundaries by detailing the kinds of violations of commonly accepted behaviours that can arise out of the messiness of doing and writing organizational ethnography. They argue that organizational ethnographers often present an idealized vision of how they work, concealing the ethical compromises that belie the public face of the kind, honest, friendly, observant, candid, and fair ethnographer. Theirs is an ethnographic account of research ethics offered through a backstage narrative of *un*ethical conduct both in the field and behind the desk.

Ethnographic and other interpretive methodologists are increasingly emphasizing the relational character of the ties developed between researchers and those they research. In some cases, the researched can become more than just 'information providers' to the researcher. Prolonged involvement can lead to the formation of research friendships, at times leading researchers to treat the researched as co-constructors of interpretations (see, e.g., Behar 1993) or even as co-authors (as Down and Hughes discuss in Chapter 4). Some of these friendships may outlast the research relationship itself, whereas others may be severed at various turns in the research. Research relationships pose all manner of challenges to ethnographic processes and ethnographers' abilities, as Nic Beech, Paul Hibbert, Robert MacIntosh, and Peter McInnes observe (Chapter 10), demanding social skills in approaching strangers, dealing with the 'troubles' of research relationships, and traversing a lifecycle of relationship and concomitant emotions.

The centrality of research participants to ethnographic research also raises questions about what the researcher is giving back to the field. Should organizational ethnographers make more of their claim to give voice to their organizational partners by fostering collaboration in the writing of ethnographic texts, as Down and Hughes (Chapter 4) suggest? Or still more, as Chris Sykes and Lesley Treleaven (Chapter 11) assert, should research itself be designed in collaboration with members of the research setting, such that the research engages with what is of concern to them, rather than (only) to the researcher? Putting the needs of the setting's members first stands to benefit the researched (in the form, for example, of better running organizations or more livable workplaces) and not just the researcher (in the form of yet another publication). Sykes and Treleaven question less the absence of the researched in the work of the ethnographer, but rather the latter's inclination to eschew contributing to organizational practices. Ethnographers' participation in work processes usually does not involve doing research to inform organizational action, unless this happens more typically through a consulting role or as an accidental byproduct of the research contract (on the latter, see Moeran, Chapter 7). Sykes and Treleaven describe some similarities and differences between action research and ethnography, challenging ethnographers to see their role, and the role of their research, in a different light.

Organizational ethnographies do not always entail studying 'down,' yet when studying 'up' raises political or other power issues, the role of the ethnographer can become problematic. Halleh Ghorashi and Harry Wels (Chapter 12) argue that ethnographers, despite – and even counter to – their often explicitly stated goal and quest for (more) social justice, actually cannot escape straightforward complicity in oppressing and marginalizing those in relatively powerless positions within existing power structures. Ghorashi and Wels explore possible ways for organizational ethnographers to reach beyond complicity in the situations they study.

ethnographic sensibilities

Suffusing all of the chapters in this book is an appreciation for another dimension of ethnographic research that informs all of its aspects. Organizational ethnographers bring with them to the field, as well as to their texts, an attitude of wonder, an openness to the potential for the unfolding of surprises there (Ybema and Kamsteeg, Chapter 5, this volume), a talent for improvising as observational or interview circumstances demand and for being less reliant on interview schedules and closed-ended questions, and a theoretical imagination that links observations to interpretations (Humphreys, Brown and Hatch 2003). More than mere method or tool, organizational ethnography embodies a special kind of orientation to the organizational world and its exploration.

Ethnographic fieldwork, analysis, and writing are imbued with an ethno-graphic 'sensibility' (Pader, 2006) that is known tacitly and therefore rather difficult to render in words. It refers to the ethnographer's way of being in, looking at, and moving through the research setting that also informs and suffuses the way she writes about that setting. This sensibility entails an acute 'attunement' to the spatiality of research settings and the things, persons, language, and acts they contain. It combines an awareness of detail – for instance, the ritualistic features of a company's annual Christmas breakfast, the nostalgic evocations of the former boss in everyday talk, or, at an even smaller level of detail, the architectural design of organizational office build-ings, the gestures of the CEO giving his annual speech at the breakfast party, the boss's tone of voice when he recalls what it was like to lead the firm – with an orientation to the meaning(s) of those details within their particular context. It is the expectation that things, acts, events, words, clothing, gestures, and other nonverbal forms of expression might *be* meaningful, depending on the circumstance. That expectation leads the ethnographer to move about with a questioning attitude and a meaning-focused eye in all manner of settings and circumstances – 'antennae', so to speak, whose working permeates everyday activity and that, in our experience, can be hard to turn off when one is 'off the job'. It is this ethnographic sensibility that creates a family resemblance among ethnographic research and ethnogra-phies across the different kinds of settings and disciplinary hooks in and with which they have been conducted, and that sets organizational ethnography apart from other methodological approaches to organizational research.

our aims for this book

Our imagined audience for this book is readers interested in organizational studies as a field, ranging from advanced undergraduate and graduate students to organizational scholars, researchers, consultants, and analysts, both those who are new to such research and those who have been practising and/or teaching it for a while but who are open to exploring new avenues and issues within it. We have assumed academic readers in the wide range of schools and departments where courses in organizational studies are taught: not only business and management, but also public administration, educational studies, health care administration, planning, social work, and legal studies (law and society programmes), along with sociology, political science, anthropology, and interdisciplinary programmes such as our own Department of Culture, Organization, and Management (COM) at the Vrije Universiteit in Amsterdam, a programme with a background and focus on organizational ethnographic research (Dahles, 2004; Koot, 1995). While written in a scholarly fashion, the chapters are, we hope, accessible to researchers who are new to the field as well as to those pursuing organizational analyses outside of the academy.

Although the approach described in these pages has gained increasing numbers of adherents over the years, the close analysis of everyday practices is not the commonly accepted starting point for organizational studies and has not been so for quite a long time. As our students do not hesitate to tell us, it is as 'deviant' as it is difficult. Ethnographic research does not have predetermined, prespecified routes to access, gather or generate interesting data and make sense of them – nor will it. There is no programmed procedure or fixed set of rules for doing ethnography, nor are there ready-made answers or prescribed pathways for interpreting the vast amounts of data that one amasses, typically in the form of field notes. In our experience, and as noted in this introduction, ethnographic research demands a lively imagination, well-developed social and analytical skills, a degree of comfort with ambiguity, and an openness to improvising, together with a firm methodological and theoretical base. This book does not pretend to take away the moments of uncertainty, ambiguity, and obscurity that accompany this type of research, nor can it. Our hope is to lay some groundwork for those who would embark on such undertakings, sketching some of organizational ethnography's key issues and reflecting upon some of the challenges in its practice and its chances for enriching organizational analyses.

acknowledgements

This book fulfils a long-standing wish of the editors and their colleagues for a book they could use in teaching organizational studies students. It had its beginnings in conversations on the VU University campus in Amsterdam, where the Department of Culture, Organization, and Management is located within the Faculty of Social Sciences. The department's research and curriculum have, since its formal inception in 1989, been focused on analysing cultural processes in and between organizations, starting from an interpretation of managing practices and organizing processes as cultural phenomena. That curriculum carries the imprimatur of the work and inspiration of the department's founders, Hans Tennekes, Allard Willemier Westra and Harry Wels, and Tennekes' successor, Willem Koot, hallmarks which are also manifest in the pages of this book.

We are tremendously grateful to our chapter authors for being so cooperative and efficient in meeting our requests for ever clearer texts and looming deadlines. We would like to acknowledge the continuous support, good humour and tolerance displayed throughout this project by Patrick Brindle, Kate Wood, Anna Coatman and Wendy Scott at Sage in London. Closer to home, our COM colleagues provided a pleasant working environment by offering their ideas, support and humour, and we thank in particular Heidi Dahles, Alfons van Marrewijk, and Marcel Veenswijk for sharing their thoughts with us throughout the project, and Saskia Stehouwer for her patient manuscript preparation. Finally, we also extend our thanks to Evert Thielen for permission to use his multi-panelled painting 'Unified' (1993–1996) for the cover of the book. We have selected a detail from the workaday section of the painting that so wonderfully portrays the complexities of everyday organizational life.

references

Alvesson, M. and Deetz, S. (2000) *Doing critical management research.* Thousand Oaks, CA: Sage.

Argyris, C. and Schön, D. (1974) *Theory in practice.* San Francisco, CA: Jossey-Bass.

Barley, S. (1983) Semiotics and the study of occupational and organizational cultures. *Administrative Science Quarterly* 28(3): 393–413.

Barley, S.R. (1986) Technology as an occasion for structuring: Evidence from observations of CT Scanners and the social order of radiology departments. *Administrative Science Quarterly* 31(3): 78–108.

Bate, S.P. (1997) Whatever happened to organizational anthropology? A review of the field of organizational ethnography and anthropological studies. *Human Relations* 50(9): 1147–71.

Behar, R. (1993) *Translated woman.* Boston, MA: Beacon Press.

Berger, P. and Luckmann, T. (1991/1966) *The social construction of reality. A treatise in the sociology of knowledge.* London: Penguin.

Bernstein, R.J. (1976) *The restructuring of social and political theory.* Philadelphia: University of Pennsylvania Press.

Bernstein, R.J. (1983) *Beyond objectivism and relativism.* Philadelphia: University of Pennsylvania Press.

Blau, P. (1955) *The dynamics of bureaucracy: A study of interpersonal relations in two government agencies.* Chicago: University of Chicago Press.

Brunsson, N. (1985) *The irrational organization.* New York: Wiley.

Chapman, M. (2001) Social anthropology and business studies: Some considerations of method. In D.N. Gellner and E. Hirsch (eds), *Inside organizations: Anthropologists at work*, pp. 19–33. Oxford: Berg.

Collinson, D.L. (1992) *Managing the shopfloor: Subjectivity, masculinity and workplace culture.* Berlin: De Gruyter.

Crang, M. and Cook, I. (2007) *Doing ethnographies.* London: Sage.

Czarniawska, B. (1997) *Narrating the organization: Dramas of institutional identity.* Chicago: University of Chicago Press.

Czarniawska, B. (2007) *Shadowing: And other techniques for doing fieldwork in modern societies.* Copenhagen: Copenhagen Business School Press.

Czarniawska-Joerges, B. (1992) *Exploring complex organizations: A cultural perspective.* London: Sage.

Dahles, H. (2004) *McBusiness versus Confucius? Anthropological perspectives on transnational organizations and networks.* Inaugural lecture, Amsterdam: Vrije Universiteit.

Dalton, M. (1959) *Men who manage.* New York: Wiley.

Dandridge, T.C., Mitroff, I. and Joyce, W.F. (1980) Organizational symbolism: A topic to expand organizational analysis. *Academy of Management Review* 5: 77–82.

Delbridge, R. (1998) *Life on the line in contemporary manufacturing: The workplace experience of lean production and the 'Japanese' model.* Oxford: Oxford University Press.

Denzin, N. and Lincoln, Y. (eds) (2000) *Handbook of qualitative research* (2nd edn). Thousand Oaks, CA: Sage.

Down, S., Garrety, K., and Badham, R. (2006) Fear and loathing in the field: Emotional dissonance and identity work in ethnographic research. *M@n@gement* 9(3): 87–107.

Dubinskas, F.A. (ed.) (1988) *Making time: Ethnographies of high technology organizations.* Philadelphia, PA: Temple University Press.

Fetterman, D. (1998) *Ethnography* (2nd edn). London: Sage.

Fineman, S., Sims, D. and Gabriel, Y. (2005) *Organizing & Organizations* (3rd edn). London: Sage.

Gabriel, Y. (1995) The unmanaged organization: Stories, fantasies and subjectivity. *Organization Studies* 16(3): 477–501.

Geertz, C. (1973) *The interpretation of cultures.* New York: Basic Books.

Gellner, D.N. and Hirsch, E. (eds) (2001) *Inside organisations: Anthropologists at work.* Oxford: Berg.

Giddens, A. (1984) *The constitution of society.* Cambridge: Polity.

Goffman, E. (1959) *The presentation of self in everyday life.* New York: Doubleday.

Goffman, E. (1961) *Asylums: Essays on the social situation of mental patients and other inmates.* Harmondsworth: Pelican.

Goffman. E. (1983/1959) *De dramaturgie van het dagelijks leven [The presentation of self in everyday life].* Utrecht: Bijleveld.

Goodman, N. (1978) *Ways of worldmaking.* Indianapolis, IN: Hackett Publishing.

Gouldner, A.W. (1954) *Patterns of industrial bureaucracy.* New York: Free Press.

Gregory, K. L. (1983) Native-view paradigms: Multiple cultures and culture conflicts in organizations. *Administrative Science Quarterly* 28(1): 359–76.

Harper, R.P. (1998) *Inside the IMF: An ethnography of documents, technology and action.* London: Academic Press.

Headland, T.N., Pike, K.L., and Harris, M., (eds) (1990) *Emics and etics: The insider/outsider debate.* Newbury Park, CA: Sage.

Humphreys, M., Brown, A.D. and Hatch, M.J. (2003) Is ethnography jazz? *Organization* 10(1): 5–31.

Ingersoll, V. H. and Adams, G. (1992) *The tacit organization.* Greenwich, CT: JAI Press.

Jackall, R. (1988) *Moral mazes: The world of corporate managers.* Oxford: Oxford University Press.

Jenkins, R. (2004) *Social identity* (2nd edn). London: Routledge.

Jones, M.O. (1996) *Studying organizational symbolism.* Thousand Oaks, CA: Sage.

Kamsteeg, F. and Wels, H. (2004) Anthropology, organizations and interventions: New territory or quicksand? *Intervention Research* 1(1): 7–25.

Kaufman, H. (1960) *The forest ranger: A study in administrative behavior.* Baltimore, MD: Johns Hopkins Press.

Kondo, D. (1990) *Crafting selves: Power, gender and discourses of identity in a Japanese workplace.* Chicago, IL: University of Chicago Press.

Koot, W.C.J. (1995) *De complexiteit van het alledaagse: Een antropologisch perspectief op organisaties [The complexity of the everyday: An anthropological perspective on organizations].* Bussum: Coutinho.

Koot, W. and Sabelis, I. (2002) *Beyond complexity. Paradoxes and coping strategies in managerial life.* Amsterdam: Rozenberg.

Koot, W., Sabelis, I. and Ybema, S. (1996) *Contradictions in context: Puzzling over paradoxes in contemporary organizations.* Amsterdam: VU University Press.

Kostera, M. (2007) *Organisational ethnography: Methods and inspirations.* Lund: Studentlitteratur AB.

Kunda, G. (1992) *Engineering culture: Control and commitment in a high-tech corporation.* Philadelphia: Temple University Press.

Latour, B. (1988) *Science in action: How to follow scientists and engineers through society.* Cambridge, MA: Harvard University Press.

Linstead, S. (1996) Understanding management: Culture, critique and change. In S. Linstead, R. Grafton Small and P. Jeffcutt (eds), *Understanding management,* pp. 11–33. London: Sage.

Lofland, J. (1995) Analytical ethnography: Features, failures, futures. *Journal of Contemporary Ethnography* 24(1): 25–40.

Lofland, J. and Lofland, L. (1995) *Analyzing social settings: A guide to qualitative observation and analysis.* Belmont, CA: Wadsworth.

Mayo, E. (1933) *The human problems of industrial civilization.* New York: Macmillan.

Meyer, J.W. and Rowan, B. (1977) Institutionalized organisations: Formal structures as myth and ceremony. *American Journal of Sociology* 83(2): 340–63.

Moeran, B. (2005) *The business of ethnography.* Oxford: Berg.

Moeran, B. (2006) *Ethnography at work.* Oxford: Berg.

Morey, N. and Luthans, F. (1987) Anthropology: The forgotten behavioral science in management history. In F. Hoy (ed.), *Best Papers Proceedings of the 47th Annual Meeting of the Academy of Management,* pp. 128–32. Athens: University of Georgia.

Morrill, C. (1995) *The executive way. Conflict management in corporations.* Chicago: Chicago University Press.

Morrill, C. and Fine, G.A. (1997) Ethnographic contributions to organizational sociology. *Sociological Methods & Research* 25(4): 424–51.

Mosse, D. (2006) Anti-social anthropology? Objectivity, objection and the ethnography of public policy and professional communities. *Journal of the Royal Anthropological Institute* 12(4): 935–56.

Neyland, D. (2008) *Organizational ethnography.* London: Sage.

Orr, J. (1996) *Talking about machines: An ethnography of a modern job.* New York: Cornell University Press.

Pachirat, T. (2006) We call it a grain of sand: The interpretive orientation and a human social science. In D. Yanow and P. Schwartz-Shea (eds), *Interpretation and method: Empirical research methods and the interpretive turn,* pp. 373–79. Armonk, NY: M. E. Sharpe.

Pachirat, Timothy S. (2008) *Repugnance and confinement: Dividing space, labor, and bodies on the kill floor of an industrialized slaughterhouse.* Unpublished PhD dissertation, Department of Political Science, Yale University.

Pader, E. (2006) Seeing with an ethnographic sensibility: Explorations beneath the surface of public policies. In D. Yanow and P. Schwartz-Shea (eds), *Interpretation and method: Empirical research methods and the interpretive turn,* pp. 161–75. Armonk, NY: M. E. Sharpe.

Perec, G. (1989) *L'infra-ordinaire [The infra-ordinary].* Paris: Editions du Seuil.

Polkinghorne, D. E. (1983) *Methodology for the human sciences.* Albany, NY: SUNY Press.

Polkinghorne, D. E. (1988) *Narrative knowing and the human sciences.* Albany, NY: SUNY Press.

Prasad, A. and Prasad, P. (2002) The coming of age of interpretive organizational research. *Organizational Research Methods* 5(1): 4–11.

Prasad, P. (2005) *Crafting qualitative research: Working in the postpositivist traditions.* Armonk, NY: M.E. Sharpe.

Prasad, P. and Prasad, A. (2002) Casting the native subject: Ethnographic practice and the (re)production of difference. In B. Czarniawska and H. Höpfl (eds), *Casting the other,* pp. 185–204. London: Routledge.

Reed, M. (2006) Organizational theorizing: A historically contested terrain. In S.R. Clegg, C. Hardy, T.B. Lawrence & W.R. Nord (eds), *The Sage handbook of organization studies* (2nd edn), pp. 19–54. London: Sage.

Rosen, M. (1991a) Coming to terms with the field: Understanding and doing organizational ethnography. *Journal of Management Studies* 28(1): 1–24.

Rosen, M. (1991b) Breakfast at Spiro's: Dramaturgy and dominance. In P. Frost, L.F. Moore, M.R. Louis, C.C. Lundberg and J. Martin (eds), *Reframing organizational culture*, pp. 77–89. Newbury Park, CA: Sage.

Rorty, R. (1979) *Philosophy and the mirror of nature*. Princeton: Princeton University Press.

Roy, D. (1960) Banana time: Job satisfaction and informal interaction. *Human Organization* 18: 156–68.

Schwartzman, H.B. (1993) *Ethnography in organizations. Qualitative Research Methods* Volume 27. Newbury Park: Sage.

Selznick, P. (1949) *TVA and the grass roots: A study in the sociology of formal organization*. Berkeley: University of California Press.

Silverman, D. (2007) *A very short, fairly interesting and reasonably cheap book about qualitative research*. London: Sage.

Smircich, L. (1983) Concepts of culture and organizational analysis. *Administrative Science Quarterly* 28: 339–58.

Tennekes, J. (1990) *De onbekende dimensie: Over cultuur, cultuurverschillen en macht. [The unknown dimension: On culture, cultural differences and power]*. Apeldoorn: Garant.

Tennekes, J. (1995) *Organisatiecultuur: Een antropologische visie [Organizational culture: An anthropological perspective]*. Apeldoorn: Garant.

Tota, A.L. (2004) Ethnographying public memory: The commemorative genre for the victims of terrorism in Italy. *Qualitative Research* 4: 131–59.

Van Maanen, J. (1979) The fact of fiction in organizational ethnography. *Administrative Science Quarterly* 24: 539–50.

Van Maanen, J. (1988) *Tales of the field: On writing ethnography*. Chicago: University of Chicago Press.

Van Maanen, J. (1995) An end to innocence: The ethnography of ethnography. In J. Van Maanen (ed.), *Representation in ethnography*, pp. 1–35. Thousand Oaks, CA: Sage.

Von Holdt, K. (2003) *Transition from below: Forging trade unionism and workplace change in South Africa*. Pietermaritzburg: University of Natal Press.

Watson, T. (1994) *In search of management: Culture, chaos and control in managerial work*. London: Routledge.

Whyte, W.F. (1948) *Human relations in the restaurant industry*. New York: McGraw-Hill.

Wright, S. (ed.) (1994) *Anthropology of organizations*. London: Routledge.

Yanow, D. (1996) *How does a policy mean? Interpreting policy and organizational actions*. Washington, DC: Georgetown University Press.

Yanow, D. (2000) *Conducting interpretive policy analysis*. Newbury Park, CA: Sage.

Yanow, D. and Schwartz-Shea, P. (eds) (2006) *Interpretation and method: Empirical research methods and the interpretive turn*. Armonk, NY: M.E. Sharpe.

Ybema, S. (1996) A duck-billed platypus in the theory and analysis of organizations: combinations of consensus and dissensus. In W. Koot, I. Sabelis and S. Ybema (eds) *Contradictions in context: Puzzling over paradoxes in contemporary organizations*, pp. 39–61. Amsterdam: VU University Press.

Young, E. (1989) On the naming of the rose: Interests and multiple meanings as elements of organizational culture. *Organization Studies* 10(2): 187–206.

Part I

Ethnographic Doing and Writing

1

Getting going: Organizing ethnographic fieldwork

Kees van der Waal

introduction

The work of ethnography is to make the exotic familiar and the familiar exotic, to problematize what is taken for granted, to 'suggest in writing what it is like to be someone else' (Van Maanen, 2001: 235). A characteristic of ethnography is its criticality, its radical challenge to received ideas about people and society (Bate, 1997: 1153). In this book, the core question is: what is the contribution of the ethnographic approach to the study of organizations in both familiar and exotic settings? Organizational processes dominate our lives more markedly than ever before over large parts of the globe, given the articulation of complex production and consumption processes that connect us to more people in larger networks, demanding more streamlining, efficient coordination and precise planning in shorter time periods. While this book focuses on the complexities of organizations fundamental to everyday work and economic life, this thematic focus should not prevent us from keeping an eye on the many interconnections between various sites and between symbols of home and workplace.

Ethnographic fieldwork can be defined as the 'firsthand experience and exploration of a particular social or cultural setting on the basis of (though not exclusively by) participant observation' (Atkinson et al., 2007: 4). It makes use of field research tools in the interpretative tradition of social science in which participant observation, conversational interviewing and the close reading and analysis of documents are key. In this chapter, I look at the way in which doing ethnography in organizational settings has been represented in the literature and how this relates to my own research experience. How is ethnography in organizations actually done? What are the characteristics of different approaches to organizational ethnography? I will refer to my ethnographic experiences in the following inter- and intra-organizational settings in South Africa: local development planning processes in two rural areas (a tribal hierarchy and a development committee in Limpopo Province, a housing planning project in the Western Cape), as well as two university settings (university labour relations in Johannesburg and higher education language planning in Stellenbosch). I write from the perspective and preoccupations of an anthropologist although I attempt to present the ethnographic process here in more general social science terms. I refer to 'ethnography' as a generic research approach and 'anthropology' as a specific social research field.

The core idea within this chapter is that the ethnography of organizations has characteristics and challenges that reflect crucial current methodological and theoretical concerns in ethnography in general. These have to do with the nature of the object of study and the relationship between the ethnographer and this object. Specific issues that surface in organizational ethnography are the problematics of access and intervention. The focus in the most insightful work in this field is on organizations as symbolic and social processes as discourses and practices in specific contexts, rather than as institutions. The implications of this choice are apparent in the delimitation of 'unit of observation' and 'unit of analysis' as well as in the emphasis on power relations. This chapter is organized around issues that often emerge in an organizational study: choosing a research question, choosing a research site, how to gain access, what ethnographic fieldwork entails, the significance of various types of data and the importance of issues of power and ethics. I argue against a narrow, purely inductive and empiricist approach to ethnography in view of the important role of the ethnographer's life experience and prior cognition for the research process. As the personal and subjective dimension is so central to the ethnographer's being, this needs to be recognized and reflected upon. Ethnographic research, I maintain, benefits from the awareness of it being an open and contingent process.

choosing a research question: the importance of theory and prior assumptions

Although ethnographic research is celebrated for its closeness to experiential knowledge, the importance of theory and other prior knowledge for ethnographic research should not be obscured. My own trajectory from a more conservative and closed perspective on ethnography, to a more critical and open perspective proves this point for me. My training in anthropology occurred within the conservative framework of the Afrikaans-speaking academic environment of Pretoria University in the late 1960s and 1970s in which *volkekunde* (the study of 'peoples') was the accepted theoretical approach. The task set by this paradigm was to understand human life in terms of separate traditional cultures that were supposed to be stable and homogeneous ethnic forms, such as 'tribes'. This academic knowledge confirmed popular fantasies in white South Africa about the incommensurability of 'races'. *Volkekunde* studies, like most older ethnographies, were characterized by several exclusions: of the ethnographer's position, of 'modern' or 'powerful' social subjects and of the wider social context (Macdonald, 2007: 71). My own work for a master's degree (Van der Waal, 1977) fitted into this paradigm by focusing on the use of space in Venda (an area on the border with Zimbabwe) as mainly a cultural phenomenon that needed description in terms of widely shared cultural patterns. In line with our training, my methodological approach did not include participant observation, as this would have overstepped the apartheid taboo on social interaction between 'races', but it also rested upon the wrong assumption that one could gain sufficient insight into cultural life primarily by asking questions during ethnographic interviews.

Some years later, I was fortunate to experience a paradigm shift towards a more critical and Marxian informed position when I moved to the anthropology department of Rand Afrikaans University (now Johannesburg University). This was sociologically an exciting period during the run-up to the South African political transformation. The members of the department started to ask new research questions (Kotzé, 1982) and to initiate fieldwork among the black population based on participant observation, something that we had not done before because of the apartheid ban on cross-racial social intimacy. Apart from discarding bounded notions of cultural and social entities, we also began to foreground social process and context as important theoretical and analytical concepts with important implications for the way we were doing ethnographic fieldwork.

This account of my personal trajectory illustrates how theory informs the choice of research questions as well as the methods used in the field. In my *volkekunde* period the research questions I pursued were mainly descriptive, restricted to issues within bounded cultural entities and with no attention to organizational issues. In my later work (Van der Waal, 2001; 2003a), informed by the anthropologies of development and of organization, I started to give more attention to issues of interpretation (what caused these particular forms of organization, in this specific setting, in this exact context?), looked at relationships across cultural and social boundaries and included managers and political figures in my analyses – studying up. Since the publication of *Writing culture* (Clifford and Marcus, 1986), ethnographic writing has become more of a focus among researchers, leading to increased self-awareness, an emphasis on the biographical dimension of fieldwork and a questioning of the legitimating claims of ethnographers (Atkinson et al., 2007: 3, 4). This orientation to theory and method also affected my work in its later phase, for instance, in the ways in which I framed research questions. The above illustrates the dialectical relationship between the theory that one employs and the way one does research.

There is, however, a theoretical approach, known as 'grounded theory', which advocates an a-theoretical position when entering the field (Charmaz and Mitchell, 2007). It is true that much that occurs during ethnographic work is unpredictable (Van Maanen, 2001: 253), meaning that there are always experiences in the field unforeseen in one's theoretical preparation. A strong grounded theory position would argue that one cannot know the questions to be addressed in a research setting in advance; therefore one needs to reflect on such questions while in the field and to test one's insights continuously. It is indeed important to prioritize the issues that are central to the people among whom one is doing ethnographic research – above one's own theoretical preoccupations – in order to discover local knowledge (Hirsch and Gellner, 2001: 8). While acknowledging the importance of theory, it is sobering to relativize all knowledge, including social theory, by regarding all voices as equal and problematic, following the insights of Foucault and Latour (Abram, 2001: 200).

Although I prefer to go into the field with an open mind and would also agree that theoretical interpretation needs to be built on empirical research, I do not think one can escape the reality that theoretical conceptions inform ethnographic fieldwork. Social theory is the ethnocentric burden of the ethnographer, although it is, after all, the best set of interpretations that one can take along into the field. There is value in an open-ended approach, but there is also a need for an initial theoretical disposition or at least for having a set of carefully formulated possible interpretations as a starting point for ethnographic work, while constantly testing these insights and retaining a flexible research approach (Burawoy, 1998). In the end, ethnographic work aims not only at describing and interpreting, but also at contributing to theoretical understanding, based on new fieldwork-based insight (Bate, 1997; Hirsch and Gellner, 2001: 9). The implication is that both social scientific theory and local frameworks of thinking need to take their place in the ethnographic work of making sense of organizational process.

As my argument suggests, a merely descriptive study will not suffice when choosing a research question for an organizational ethnography. It may add to our knowledge to know the 'what', 'how' and 'who' of an organizational setting, but in order to progress beyond taxonomy and description, the 'why' (or 'criticality') question also needs to be engaged with. In order to answer the question of why a set of relationships or symbolic understandings is the way it is, it needs to be set against the background of other factors and processes. In other words, it needs to be contextualized. A lasting contribution of a Marxian theoretical approach in social science is its emphasis on forces (especially historical and political economic factors) that impact on small-scale relationships and cultural forms. One should therefore not study an organization per se as an isolated entity. Additionally, the main point of interest would not so much be the form and function of an organization, but rather the organizational process as it unfolds between sets of actors, including other organizations. Core to the organizing process is the tendency to set up a governing ethos (organizational culture), rules for interaction and resource allocation, and the necessity to monitor these (Hirsch and Gellner, 2001: 3, 4). In choosing a research question the boundaries of organizations and other social settings should not be taken as given and homogeneity in the research setting should not be assumed.

As such, some possible research questions in the ethnographic study of organizations might include the following:

- What are the relationships between different actors in a specific organizational process?

- What form does the organizing process that is studied take and how does it change?

- Why does this particular form of organizational interaction occur in this specific context?

- How do relations of power and contestation emerge in organizational processes, and how are these related to meaning (symbols and cultural forms)?

- What are the effects of a specific organizational process on particular socio-economic relationships?

situating oneself and gaining access

Organizational ethnography potentially ranges from the very local to the global, from a village development committee setting in its interaction with the local offices of the national state to a United Nations agency in Geneva or a multinational headquarters in a metropolis. It may encompass several organizational levels and follow the relationships between and among them. Mostly, however, due to the constraints of time and location, researchers will choose a local setting as the primary research site and follow the connections between that site and other sites as far as is feasible and to the extent that these connections are relevant to a research project. Organizational ethnography often tends to be done in a specific site, within the boundaries of the organization selected as the unit of observation. However, the possibility of multi-sited organizational research work is very promising. In this way important connections between organizations and their interactions can be followed from local to global levels (Hirsch and Gellner, 2001: 4). In choosing a research site, one will be led by the theoretical understanding one has of the issues to be studied. It makes sense to develop several possible lines of approach to the main research questions and then decide on a specific approach in light of its viability.

Ethnographic research sites have often been characterized by large differences in class between researcher and researched. This used to be the case in colonial contexts and is still the norm in development situations. Class differences often meant relatively easy access for a researcher to settings where her or his social position was socially powerful. But many organizational settings are now very challenging in terms of access. Organizations' gatekeepers in industrial, urbanized settings tend to be more assertive and less accessible than those in community settings in rural areas. One reason for this difference is that organizations that are publicly active in economic and political realms tend to be very vulnerable regarding their reputation (Chapman, 2001: 31). Despite legislation promoting transparency and a commitment to free flows of information, many gatekeepers are well aware of the damage that can be done by the publication of 'misinterpretations' by social scientists. Therefore, it is quite common to experience problems in gaining access to organizations, or even to be denied access. In many cases trust has to be established before intensive research work on the ground can begin. The initial contact, the way in with the help of a contact person, and the nature of first meetings are all very important, but difficult to control. Much of the success of the 'way in' depends on the impression you make and the time that you take to establish social contact with decision-makers or brokers who can facilitate or block access to a research setting. Even where access is denied, it may, nevertheless, be possible to study an organization through the available literature, through informal contacts with people involved in the organization and through the study of the effects of the organization.

Ethnographic research is time-intensive, and the first stage – that of reconnaissance – should not be rushed. Time should be taken to find out which organizational setting would be most useful to study in terms of its role in the organizational process and to develop a sense of possible alternatives. Spending time in alternative research settings, getting to know local role-players informally and establishing contact with gatekeepers is absolutely essential, preceding the formal process of requesting permission to spend time in an organization or to peruse its records. It is quite important to point out the need for and the benefits of the research project without making unrealistic claims or promises. One of the main issues in this regard is that the emphasis in ethnographic work and in presenting the proposed research plan to gatekeepers should not be on scrutinizing specific role-players or conflictual relationships, but on the understanding of organizational processes. In the negotiations about access, especially if there are fears about possible harm from the publication of research results, it may be wise to offer the draft publication for comment. By the time that the research has been written up, it will be of great value to have established dialogical relationships with persons in the organizational settings that were studied, in order to be able to discuss a draft publication, settle factual questions, and corroborate one's understanding of the social processes studied. Such an exchange can, however, lead to difficulties, of which researchers should be aware ahead of time. These may include issues of interpretation and emphasis. Workshopping these differences in meetings with role-players from the ethnographic setting may lead to new insights. However, what should be avoided at all costs is to be tied to obligations to obtain approval of one's work in order to publish it, as this will compromise the necessary independence of the researcher. In some cases it may, however, be unavoidable to have to submit a report for approval by the management of an organization, especially where research is done in the organization where one is employed (see also Chapter 8 by Alvesson, this volume). Hilhorst (2003) gives a fascinating account of her study of a women's movement in the Philippines and how her conclusions were ultimately rejected by the women she studied. Despite the breakdown in relationships, she felt sufficiently justified in her social scientific analysis to proceed with publication.

Gaining access to an organizational research situation, similar to other ethnographic work, is an ongoing process (Smith, 2007: 226). Getting in for the first time may be the most daunting step, but in multi-sited fieldwork it may be necessary to renegotiate access several times. Getting access should neither be underestimated nor overestimated. Being aware of the openness of ethnographic research and making the most of this flexibility is the best preparation for turning unexpected difficulties into fascinating opportunities (compare Chapter 7 by Moeran in this volume). The basic requirements for participant observation – being open to opportunity, maximizing social relationships and building on shared social experience – should be optimized for gaining access while one gets to know the field. Making use of oneself as the basic research instrument, through one's social skills, honest self-presentation and genuine interest, is usually a sufficient guarantee for developing new social relationships that lead to mutually beneficial partnerships and opportunities for research. A measure of assertiveness is needed. However, too much pressure on people with busy schedules, or a lack of conviction in the value of your research project, may inhibit entry. Above all, a sensitivity to social situations and lots of patience are needed.

Instead of going against the flow of resistance to a research project in a reactionary way, it is advisable to use the tension that is generated creatively in order to make sense of the underlying forces that may throw light on the reasons for resistance (possibly arising from a sense of vulnerability felt initially by some role-players). One may reflect on the situation and develop alternative strategies (including the use of a developing network of contacts). Don't give up too easily. It may be possible to adapt a research proposal to accommodate the sensitivities of the organizational players and to integrate the needs of these players into the research project. These tensions and one's efforts to overcome them are heuristic tools for understanding the methodological path of a research project at the analytical stage of writing. It is, therefore, advisable to document the phases of the research process, including one's reflection on initial assumptions and experiences, in order to make sense of crucial periods in the research project at a later stage.

My own recent research experience has proved to be a learning curve in terms of gaining access. After arriving in Stellenbosch in 2002, I decided to do an organizational ethnography of inter-organizational interaction concerning local development in the Dwars River Valley (Van der Waal, 2005). This is a historical and scenic rural landscape in the Cape Winelands, just outside Stellenbosch, where white-owned wine farms exist side by side with a mainly 'coloured' population in several settlements, going back to the days of the emancipation of slaves in 1834–38. Interesting processes of change in governance and land-use are occurring in the valley.

First, under the old political order the settlements were part of Coloured Rural Areas with their own form of local and national government. They became part of the Stellenbosch municipality when rural areas were integrated into municipalities in South Africa after 2000. Second, agricultural land-use has shifted from intensive viticulture and deciduous fruit farming to luxury rural estate development in combination with agriculture. The genealogy of land ownership of a large part of the valley goes back to the seventeenth century French Huguenots and their descendants, then to Cecil John Rhodes, the Cape tycoon and prime minister at the end of the nineteenth century, and more recently in the twentieth century, to Anglo American, the largest multinational corporation in the country. In 2003 this corporation sold its land to Boschendal, a new company with a strong black economic empowerment component. The farm worker population was moved off the farms into a newly established farm worker village, Lanquedoc, where they gained home ownership.

To follow inter-organizational interaction around these processes, I had to gain access to the villages and organizations, each uniquely different in this regard. As I was new to the area, I decided to make contact with one of the local municipal councillors. She was willing to see me, immediately sensed my interest in historical processes, and took me to meet a retired headmaster. After a long discussion and a quick tour of the area, I met several of his friends and contacts to whom I could return from time to time for interviews and for pointers about other people to see and meetings to attend. In contrast, getting access to the staff of the multinational and the new owners of Boschendal proved to be more difficult. Emails and telephone calls were often ignored, and some individuals proved well nigh to inaccessible.

As my previous research had been mostly done in rural areas with easy access, I found these difficulties unsettling, interpreting them as a refusal to let me into the organizations, only to learn that this was not the case at all. It merely proved necessary to work step by step, taking sufficient time to get to know the right people and to build on an emerging network of contacts. At a certain point I started to receive documentation about the public participation process concerning the development plans for the estate development and its associated social development plan. This happened because I had put my name on a list at a public meeting, thereby becoming one of the 'interested and affected parties' in the planning process.

I now have a much more realistic understanding of the accessibility of people involved in complex and highly structured processes. One has to nourish a network of contacts, follow processes over time and be prepared to wait for new opportunities to arise. In following the unfolding process of the institutionalization of development-oriented processes, the most efficient ways to strengthen my research network were to be present at events when those opportunities presented themselves and to build on existing contacts. This has involved me attending church meetings, bazaars, meetings of ward committees, neighbourhood watch groups, etc., depending on the opportunity and research focus. What seemed to be inaccessible corporate environments at the outset proved to be much more open once my students and I became known in the area. For instance, documents that I did not even consider asking the companies for were handed to me by villagers who had been summoned to court for occupying houses or who had served on development committees. I have learned to become much more opportunistic and to let things unfold, rather than pressing for information. In that way access has become less of a preoccupation and more of an opportunity, although I do remain eager to find out more about unfolding processes.

fieldwork – getting it going

Once all the preliminaries are done (usually including the production and approval of a final research proposal, getting the financial and time resources in place, selecting a research site or sites, and obtaining initial access), it is time to start doing 'real fieldwork'. At this stage the researcher may experience strong feelings of anxiety, due, for instance, to the lack of control one typically has over the unfolding process, the challenge of identifying unknown factors that influence the way the research may develop, the lack of local knowledge, and the sense of having to prove oneself academically. It is important to reflect on one's experiences and feelings and to record them – they may be useful indicators of the initial reception of the research process. The assumptions and research strategies that one brings to the field will be tested by the realities one encounters, especially in the initial process of getting to know the 'lay of the land'. Ethnographic research needs time, often entailing a year or more of fieldwork and a writing process that may take equally long (depending on what other work is competing for one's time) to produce a book or a series of academic articles.

Spatial exploration is often a good strategy for getting going (see Jordan, 2003: 21–4). It may be very enlightening to spend time getting to know the layout of a research site and its immediate physical context. When an insider comments on the use of space, for example parts of a building, sites of production or places in a neighbourhood, it helps to understand important aspects of relationships, processes and social categories that make local sense. Discussing these spatial connections and divisions with local experts, as reflected in maps, organizational charts and photographs, can be extremely useful for getting a sense of how relationships between social roles and spatial arrangements are organized and conceptualized. The spatial is an expression of the social and can therefore be used as a heuristic tool for making sense of underlying social frameworks. The use of space is often expressive of social status, as in the relative location and size allocated to different offices, and of the social values that underlie organizational processes. For example, the presence and use of meeting-places might indicate that value is placed on participatory decision-making, and signage of offices and socially relevant space often reveals perceptions of status (Jordan, 2003; Tilley, 2007).

Apart from mapping the socio-spatial, another approach that reveals much of the organizational process is to follow events. This may include attending meetings, or shadowing people willing to take the researcher along, focusing on specific issues that happen to occupy the hearts and minds of an organization's members at the time of the research. An example of this approach would be to follow decision-making about a development project during the different stages of its implementation in order to assess forms of exclusion and inclusion.

While it is important to get going by focusing on specific events and the use of space and symbols, the whole picture needs to be explored as well in as far as it is practically possible. Information relating to many other key issues in one's research setting may be available in various kinds of documentation or in oral narratives. Of course, what is said and what is available as text are only partial reflections of much more complex social interactions. One has to continuously interpret these (often idealized) narratives in terms of one's understanding of local social differentiation and broader processes, while exploring other possible interpretations (often derived from theoretical literature) in terms of their heuristic fertility. Organizational processes are rich in symbols that reveal important meanings and relationships, such as status differences, local values and a sense of heritage. Such symbols provide condensed indications of socially relevant knowledge. These are indicated in the nomenclature and self-presentation of organizations, but also in the actual use of space, time, speech and writing (as employed by individual agents) (see Kamsteeg and Wels, 2004).

During ethnographic fieldwork the danger of essentialism (Fuchs, 2001) must be recognized and prevented. Due to the small-scale settings in which much ethnographic work has historically been done, ethnographers have often been trapped by the boundaries of their research contexts, e.g., the village, tribe, neighbourhood or organization studied. Seeing the local setting or the cultural context or a prominent aspect of either of these as a 'thing' or essence easily leads to taking the part for the whole. For example, the researcher might take the totalizing accounts of one social category (for example, men) as the complete narrative about local relationships, thereby assuming homogeneity where differentiation and contestation may be cardinal, if not necessarily immediately apparent. Generalizing beyond what is justified essentializes specific characteristics.

It should be our aim to go beyond the limitation of idealized images presented to the researcher as an outsider to the ethnographic situation. Also, it should be our aim to go beyond the static impression gained from studying organizational settings only at specific points in time. One can, indeed, follow multiple actors in their wheelings and dealings, the organizational process in its different forms, complexities and settings, the pathways of materials and things in organized trade and consumption, the meanings and models being pursued or attached to organizational relationships, and so forth (see for example, Appadurai, 1996; Van Maanen, 2001).

In my research on inter-organizational interaction around local development in the Dwars River Valley, it was important to get an introductory overview of the setting. As mentioned, this was initially provided by a local retired headmaster whose valuable introductions opened many doors. Driving around with him and later with the chairperson of a housing association gave me a direct introduction to the local setting. I trekked along parts of the valley in the company of a local expert in the archaeology and local planning of the area, using routes onto private land that local people still regarded as their right of way into the mountain area. In addition, I found very useful written overviews of the area on tourist websites, economic and demographic data on the local government website, and an extensive spatial and development planning document that came from the office of a prominent local planning company (Dennis Moss Partnership, 2005). The guided tours and documentation afforded a quick entry into the rich and complex ways of naming and claiming that accompany historical and current engagements with land, social identity and economic development (Van der Waal, 2005).

Another benefit to be gained from following people was the insight it provided into the border between frontstage and backstage settings. I got to know the difference between meetings that were open to researchers and those regarded – at least by some – as private. When I asked about meetings that I could attend in the local setting, villagers told me about a meeting arranged by the municipality for discussing the budget in the local municipal ward. I could listen there to how development objectives were phrased by representatives of the municipality as well as to the questioning of these budget items by villagers. However, when members of a housing association said I could come along to a meeting with officials of the District Council, I was taken by surprise when the senior official chairing the discussion ruled that my presence was unacceptable. I was chaperoned to his office, where I was told that the sensitivity of the matter (involving the clarification of responsibilities for infrastructure provision and the contractual obligations of contractors) made my presence problematic – this was to be a private meeting. Of course I left, but I had learned a valuable lesson in terms of naively accompanying people to their meetings, while at the same time getting an immediate indication of what were regarded as sensitive issues in housing development implementation. I also learned, from visits with students to the research area, that when leaders in the local setting can tell the story of their organization or of a development initiative to a captive audience, the event often becomes an energetic public performance. The emphases intended for public consumption are then much more formally and clearly communicated than in the subdued setting of one-on-one interviews. In a personal meeting, on the other hand, there is often more chance for 'off the record' comments.

Being present when events unfold during fieldwork means sensitivities, local meanings and strategic alliances can be witnessed first hand. In the Dwars River Valley the identity of the oldest village, Pniel, goes back to the early 1840s when it was established as a labour pool around a church for emancipated slaves. Social identity in the village has recently become more strongly tied to the former slave history and the symbolism it generated for heritage purposes, especially since the democratic transition made it more valuable to relate back to an early non-white and oppressed origin.

In 2004, in the public space in front of the church (*die werf*), a monument was erected to celebrate the freedom from slavery granted 170 years earlier. The bell that had been used by the first missionary in the early days of the settlement to indicate the evening curfew was remembered as a 'slave bell'. In the 1940s this bell was damaged in a storm and then hung in the office grounds of the large, local company, Rhodes Fruit Farms. In recent years the bell had become a focus for restoration as it had strong symbolic value tied up with slavery's past in Pniel. This was realized by the company, which responded to the claims made on the bell by having it repaired and officially handing it back to Pniel. A big celebration was arranged on Heritage Day in September 2006, where the links between the church, as representative of the Pniel community, big business and the South African Heritage Resources Authority, were reinforced. This helped patch up relations that had become strained because of the resistance that leading residents from Pniel had initially shown to real estate development plans involving the immediate environment around the village. These forms of symbolism – and the sensitivities related to them – only became evident in the course of my fieldwork, as the available documents did not allude to them.

types of data

When studying organizations and their interactions, a variety of types and sources of data, apart from published organizational or industry-related literature, are important. First, many organizations will have websites containing useful information, such as annual reports and links to other important sites.

A second important source of information is the range of documents mostly available at the organizations themselves. These can take the form of minutes, reports with limited distribution and files of correspondence and other 'gray' (unpublished) literature that may be of great significance. Often one may need to negotiate with representatives of an organization about the use of these documents. In my experience, once a researcher has become established in a relationship of trust, he or she may be given access to sets of files and even sometimes may get to take these home. This, of course, places a responsibility on the researcher to use their contents with great care – and to return them, if borrowed! Of course, you may be denied access to internal documents and will have to rely only on whatever materials are available.

Third, as with other forms of ethnography (Bernard, 1995; Hirsch and Gellner, 2001: 13), organizational ethnography requires a close attention to detail at events and interactions. This entails participant observation: immersing oneself in the social context that is being studied and being open to the events and interactions taking place. In organizational ethnography this research strategy often means using fragmented bits of immersion wherever this seems viable, for instance, attending a meeting, having lunch with someone involved in the everyday running of an organization, and attending to small talk. One of the core features of participant observation is that it is meant to reduce reactivity during ethnographic fieldwork, to the extent that this is possible (Van Maanen, 2001: 240). Limited or full participation needs to be accompanied by the documentation of one's observations – that is, the writing of field notes – on a regular basis, and preferably daily, in order to build up a record of the flows of events witnessed, the people talked to and any documents read during the research period.

Fourth, interviews are part of the research methodology that could be employed during participant observation for organizational ethnography. Although more formal than informal discussions during participant observation, most interviews should (preferably) remain semi-structured rather than structured, thereby allowing maximally for the organization of knowledge from the inside perspective (Chapman, 2001). Much of the material gathered during interviews or recorded during public events will be in the form of 'official' narratives that can strengthen and reproduce an identity, or that can structure experience. But a great deal is also less structured and informal, requiring the researcher to be perceptive and open to all kinds of unofficial knowledge. At the other end of the spectrum, some highly structured interviews in the form of surveys may be needed for representative or comparative samples.

Key to recording 'data' during participant observation is to cultivate your ability to listen and observe carefully. You may need to put your list of questions aside at times or let a discussion develop naturally. Many pieces of information, moreover, will only be revealed when you interact informally with people who know the local conditions. Listening closely to these cues is essential for developing an awareness of the complexity and multi-layered character of meanings and relationships.

The growing body of information that emerges in daily notes about events, interviews and other interactions needs to be systematically organized in order to find specific detail easily and to see the emerging patterns in the information. Fieldnotes should already be used as a resource while in the field to make sense of the mass of detail collected. Reading and re-reading notes is a sure way of allowing different parts of the body of information to come together and lead to a range of insights, while still in the field. As indicated in the section on choosing a research question, some of the benefit that grounded theory offers, namely to let theoretical insight emerge from an intensive engagement with the data, can be gained during fieldwork and analysis. While this process of sense-making remains somewhat intuitive in nature it is not a 'black box', but is based instead on logical and disciplined thought processes. These are informed by your training in the craft of ethnography, by reading extensively, by comparing field notes with anothers, contextualizing them, and looking for answers to the recurring basic questions: What? Who? Why?

A system of recording is necessary for each research project. This could consist of chronological fieldnotes, sets of interviews, survey results, etc.

Much of this material can nowadays be stored on a computer but can also often be handwritten and printed. One characteristic of fieldnotes is that they are contemporaneous with the events recorded. Another is that they can reduce and represent events selectively, rather than accurately describe them (Emerson, Fretz and Shaw, 2007: 353). Not everything that is consciously and unconsciously experienced can be noted in a physical, written record. When finally writing an ethnographic text, much of what becomes relevant in the analysis will be that broader set of intuitive understandings of the field-work situation that remain hidden until the formulation of ideas in the process of creating a written account.

For my work in the Limpopo Province I wrote notes during field visits in quarterly holiday breaks and also collected texts written by research assistants in those periods when I was not present in the field. In the Dwars River Valley project, I was able to follow much more of the local dialogue (mostly in Afrikaans) and could therefore pick up local meanings as expressed in everyday discourse more easily. As I live close to the research area, I am less dependent on research assistants living in the local settlements, although I still use such texts written by local people with some success. Fieldnotes and analytic notes are best stored in both a hard (paper) and soft (electronic) copy format. Computer database programs are also available that will help record and analytically process materials. Examples are Ethnograph, NUD*IST and Inmagic.

power and ethics in fieldwork relationships

Ethnographers have focused on 'local-level politics' (Swartz, 1969) as struggles for power and resources that take place in villages, organizations and other micro-settings. Ethnographic fieldwork itself is such a setting in which the reflex-ive ethnographer appreciates that he or she is part of a field of asymmetric relations of power. Ethnographic fieldwork requires great care in managing relation-ships as these may acquire privileged dimensions with ethical implications. While entry into an organization may be gained on the basis of initial, formal negoti-ations, much depends on your social skills in making progress towards long-term relationships conducive to open dialogue. Being yourself, showing genuine interest in other people, and giving time and patience to research relationships will usually lead to unexpected opportunities. As far as possible, try to encour-age and work at a strong relationship of trust with anyone you interact with. There are, of course, people who might remain sceptical of a stranger who is nosing around in other people's business, and sometimes access to information will be denied. Here it is important to strive towards a more informal relation-ship in order to build trust and thus overcome the resistance that might accom-pany any doubts about your motivations. Again, time will be needed to establish relationships (and some of these may become friendship relation-ships), although these might retain many of the utilitarian and instrumental characteristics that will accompany the search for information. To a large extent the participant observation mode of doing research facilitates relationships that are less instrumental and more open to non-utilitarian aspects than in other modes of research, although the predatory character of all social research needs to be recognized and resisted (Rock, 2007: 36).

Relationships in fieldwork have important ethical implications. Ethnographic research can harm those studied, especially in the publication of accounts of their lives (Murphy and Dingwall, 2007: 341). Therefore, ethical guidelines have been developed (e.g. Anthropology Southern Africa, 2005) that especially emphasize the protection of research participants' interests, for example by keeping their identities confidential, where necessary. Other interests that need to be protected are those of colleagues and collaborators. The ethnographic method differs from many other field research approaches in that informed consent cannot be obtained from every individual during participant observation, for example when working in a dense social context.

Two of my research experiences illustrate different researcher roles in organizational research and their ethical implications. At Stellenbosch University, I started to do research on diversity politics in the institution, against the background of the 'language debate' regarding the position of Afrikaans in South Africa (Van der Waal, 2003b). I had access to information as a member of staff that I could not use directly in my research, but which helped me to make sense of the material that I was collecting. Newspaper reports and letters to the editor in an Afrikaans daily, *Die Burger*, reflected various positions taken during the 'debate' on how the university should transform itself. The material also consisted of official public documents and press releases made by the university. The university had to comply with the demands of the state for the improved representation of the whole population in terms of student and staff profiles, which would lead to more communication in English. On the other hand, a large part of the staff, students, their parents and other white Afrikaans-speakers wished to retain Afrikaans as the main teaching medium. I had to be careful not to let my own bias towards inclusivity obscure my understanding of the positions taken by conservative colleagues and alumni.

In contrast, when I did ethnographic fieldwork in the Limpopo Province in the early 1990s on development initiatives involving a village development committee and external actors, I had a totally different role profile. My local role there was more than that of a researcher as I had maintained friendship links with several people and had been able to arrange bursaries for senior learners. I had a house in the village to which I periodically returned for fieldwork. I had access to many snippets of private information that helped me understand local relationships, but which had to be treated with care. I managed this situation by avoiding identifying specific persons in my writing. The two research contexts, Stellenbosch University and the rural village in Limpopo Province, had different implications for the way I did research and used information, due to the different ways in which I was embedded in these situations as more than a researcher.

conclusion

In this chapter, organizational ethnography was unpacked in terms of 'getting going', the crucial points in starting an ethnographic project both conceptually and practically. Basic questions were addressed with regard to theoretical and methodological assumptions and points of departure. These issues were related to my own fieldwork experiences. Interestingly, while organizational complexity seemed to be greater in the urban setting and organizational interactions more intense, organizational identities were important in both settings, whether tribal or academic. Such similarities indicate that studies of organizations can build on classical ethnographic analyses and social theory. Core questions around essentialism, culture and power emerge in all ethnographies, whether focused on organizational or other social settings. An approach that values complexity and processual fluidity was proposed.

In terms of methodology, the challenges around getting access, tracing relationships and following events in organizational ethnography may be high, due to efficient gatekeeping, the multi-sited or de-localized nature of organizational processes and the fluidity of complex interactions. Fieldwork and analysis, as basic and dialectical processes in the course of ethnographic work, were addressed in terms of strategies and ethics. Core issues for any fertile interpretation of organizational process were identified as differentiation, process, power, agency, structure and context.

references

Abram, S. (2001) 'Among professionals: Working with pressure groups and local authorities', in D.N. Gellner and E. Hirsch (eds), *Inside organizations*. Oxford: Berg. pp.183–203.

Anthropology Southern Africa (2005) 'Special number on ethics', *Anthropology Southern Africa*, 28(3&4).

Appadurai, A. (1996) 'Disjuncture and difference in the global cultural economy', in J.X. Inda and R. Rosaldo (eds), *The anthropology of globalization: A reader*. Oxford: Blackwell. pp. 46–64.

Atkinson, P., Coffey, A.J., Delamont, S., Lofland, J. and Lofland, L.H. (eds) (2007) *Handbook of ethnography*. Los Angeles, CA: Sage.

Bate, S.P. (1997) 'Whatever happened to organizational anthropology? A review of the field of organizational ethnography and anthropological studies', *Human Relations*, 50(9): 1147–75.

Bernard, H.R. (1995) *Research methods in anthropology*. Walnut Creek: Altamira.

Burawoy, M. (1998) 'Extended case method', *Sociological Theory*, 16(1): 16–25.

Chapman, M. (2001) 'Social anthropology and business studies: Some considerations of method', in D.N. Gellner and E. Hirsch (eds), *Inside organizations*. Oxford: Berg. pp.19–33.

Charmaz, K. and Mitchell, R.G. (2007) 'Grounded theory in ethnography', in P. Atkinson, A.J. Coffey, S. Delamont, J. Lofland and L.H. Lofland (eds), *Handbook of ethnography*. Los Angeles, CA: Sage. pp. 160–74.

Clifford, J. and Marcus, G.E. (1986) *Writing culture: The poetics and politics of ethnography*. Berkeley: University of California Press.

Dennis Moss Partnership (2005) Boschendal Sustainable Development Initiative. Planning policy and development strategy. Inception phase report, consultative draft on CD.

Emerson, R.M., Fretz, R.I. and Shaw, L.L. (2007) 'Participant observation and fieldnotes', in P. Atkinson, A.J. Coffey, S. Delamont, J. Lofland and L.H. Lofland (eds), *Handbook of ethnography*. Los Angeles, CA: Sage. pp. 352–68.

Fuchs, S. (2001) *Against essentialism: A theory of culture and society*. Cambridge: Harvard University Press.

Hilhorst, D. (2003) *The real world of NGOs: Discourses, diversity and development*. London: Zed.

Hirsch, E. and Gellner, D.N. (2001) 'Introduction: Ethnography of organizations and organizations of ethnography', in D.N. Gellner and E. Hirsch (eds), *Inside organizations*. Oxford: Berg. pp.1–15.

Jordan, A.T. (2003) *Business anthropology*. Prospect Heights: Waveland.

Kamsteeg, F. and Wels, H. (2004) 'Anthropology, organizations and interventions: new territory or quicksand?', *Intervention Research*, 1(1): 7–25.

Kotzé, J.C. (1982) *Volkekunde en grense*. Inaugural lecture. Publication Series of Rand Afrikaans University A142. Johannesburg: Rand Afrikaans University.

Macdonald, S. (2007) 'British social anthropology', in P. Atkinson, A.J. Coffey, S. Delamont, J. Lofland and L.H. Lofland (eds), *Handbook of ethnography*. Los Angeles, CA: Sage. pp. 60–79.

Murphy, E. and Dingwall, R. (2007) 'The ethics of ethnography', in P. Atkinson, A.J. Coffey, S. Delamont, J. Lofland and L.H. Lofland (eds), *Handbook of ethnography*. Los Angeles, CA: Sage. pp. 339–51.

Rock, P. (2007) 'Symbolic interactionism and ethnography', in P. Atkinson, A.J. Coffey, S. Delamont, J. Lofland and L.H. Lofland (eds), *Handbook of ethnography*. Los Angeles, CA: Sage. pp. 26–38.

Smith, V. (2007) 'Ethnographies of work and the work of ethnographers', in P. Atkinson, A.J. Coffey, S. Delamont, J. Lofland and L.H. Lofland (eds), *Handbook of ethnography*. Los Angeles, CA: Sage. pp. 220–33.

Swartz, M.J. (ed.) (1969) *Local-level politics: Social and cultural perspectives*. London: University of London Press.

Tilley, C. (2007) 'Ethnography and material culture', in P. Atkinson, A.J. Coffey, S. Delamont, J. Lofland and L.H. Lofland (eds), *Handbook of ethnography*. Los Angeles, CA: Sage. pp. 258–72.

Van der Waal, C.S. (1977) *Die woning en woonwyse onder die Venda*. MA thesis, University of Pretoria.

Van der Waal, C.S. (2001) 'Participation in development: South African rhetoric and practice', in H.C. Marais, Y. Muthien, N.S. Jansen van Rensburg, M.P. Maaga, G.F. de Wet and C.J. Coetzee (eds), *Sustainable social development*. Menlo Park: Network. pp. 115–22.

Van der Waal, C.S. (2003a) *Culture, power and inequality in South Africa: The relevance of the anthropology of development and organisations*. Inaugural lecture, Stellenbosch University.

Van der Waal, C.S. (2003b) 'Diverse approaches in a South African debate on language and diversity in higher education', *Anthropology Southern Africa*, 25(3&4): 86–95.

Van der Waal, C.S. (2005) 'Spatial and organizational complexity in the Dwars River Valley, Western Cape', *Anthropology Southern Africa*, 28(1&2): 8–21.

Van Maanen, J. (2001) 'Afterword. Natives 'r' us: Some notes on the ethnography of organizations', in D.N. Gellner and E. Hirsch (eds), *Inside organizations*. Oxford: Berg. pp. 233–61.

2

Ethnographic practices: From 'writing-up ethnographic research' to 'writing ethnography'

Michael Humphreys and Tony Watson

introduction

When we were asked to write this chapter we talked about our experiences of writing ethnographically which each of us have had over the years. We felt that we had something useful to pass on to others and we agreed with the suggestion made by Wright Mills, when writing about 'intellectual craftsmanship' in his classic *The sociological imagination*, that it is by engaging with 'conversations in which experienced thinkers exchange information about their actual ways of working' that emerging researchers can best be helped to develop their craft (1959: 215). We therefore decided to write in this spirit. The two of us would have a series of conversations about the various ways in which we have written ethnographic accounts and then 'write them up' in book-chapter form. In effect, this is what we have done. But we were somewhat troubled by this notion of 'writing up' at first. We were tempted, instead, to try to write a mini-ethnography in which the reader would see Michael and Tony sitting at a table in an office in their lakeside university building, passing thoughts back and forth, occasionally standing up to write notes and typologies on the office whiteboard. Why were we so tempted by this idea? It was because of the main message we wanted to put across in the chapter: that ethnography is not something one 'does' out in the field before returning to one's study to 'write it up'. To us, ethnography is writing.

What do we mean by saying that we see ethnography as writing? The answer to that question is that we think it is helpful to separate out the intensive *fieldwork* that ethnographers need to do from the written ethnographic *account* that follows from it. The ethnography is the account. Hence we are working here with a formal definition of ethnography as 'a written account of the cultural life of a social group, organisation or community which may focus on a particular aspect of life in that setting' (Watson, 2008a: 100). We see the written ethnography as 'wrapping up' any specific concerns within a broader attention to what Baszanger and Dodier (2004: 13) call 'a cultural whole'. So, for example, when one of us focused on managerial work within a large company for the *In search of management* (Watson, 2001) study, it was not to 'do' *an* ethnography of that organization but to set the analysis of the managers within the 'cultural whole' of the business and the factory. We can say similar things about Casey's (1995) exploration of change in a US-based multinational and Delbridge's (1998) study of new manufacturing techniques and worker experience in two factories, as Bryman and Bell (2003) recognize. And although we reluctantly acknowledge the value of the broad term 'ethnographic approach' to characterize work which we might not accept as 'full ethnographies' (see Smith, 2001), we think it is best to reserve the 'ethnography' label for work characterized by what Geertz called 'thick description'. We tend to sympathize with Bate in his polemic against the 'quick description' that he feels too many would-be ethnographers produce in place of 'thick description, after they have undertaken a "journey into the organizational bush [which is] often little more than a safe and closely chaperoned form of anthropological tourism"' (1997: 1150).

It follows from all this that writing ethnography is a big challenge. It is true that, as the editors of a large handbook of ethnography say, ethnography 'does not always mean exactly the same to all social scientists at all times or under all circumstances' (Atkinson et al., 2001: 5). We think, however, that it is important to retain, in any characterization of the genre, the 'cultural whole' dimension. We are troubled by the fact that, as Tedlock correctly observes, 'thousands of works written in many languages and genres have been encoded as "ethnographic"' (2000: 459), covering a huge range from doctoral theses converted into extended monographs to short stories, plays and poems.

In the light of our rather demanding criteria for calling work ethnographic, we decided that we could not, after all, write this chapter as a mini-ethnography. There simply would not be space to set the two characters in the 'cultural whole' of university business-school life. Nevertheless, we wanted to retain an element of the dialogic, which would have characterized an ethnographic account, had we embarked on such a venture. In writing what follows we have followed the procedure described by Humphreys et al., where

> [s]tarting with the basic structure of the article the lead was passed back and forth between the *performers* ... to facilitate a process not unlike *trading fours* in jazz. Each *performer* read (listened to) the words (voice) of the other, restructuring, embellishing, commenting and adding new material before passing the manuscript on to be reworked in the next iteration. (2003: 23)

But this is a 'writing up' process. Analysis of our experiences as academic writers has occurred prior to our constructing a written document. It is our experience of doing 'real' ethnography, unlike on the present occasion, that as much or more of the analysis or the interpretation of the fieldwork experience occurs in the process of writing as occurs in the preparation for writing.

The analysis that emerged from our dialogue about our ethnographic writing experiences came to take the form of a four-fold typography of ethnographic forms: the *plain*, the *enhanced*, the *semi-fictionalized* and the *fictionalized*.

writing ethnography: a typology and a continuum

As we examined the different pieces of ethnographic writing we have done we found ourselves locating different pieces of 'output' along a continuum from minimally manipulated written accounts to highly manipulated or 'fictionalized' accounts. And to 'tighten' this analysis we were able to construct four ideal type ethnographic forms, which could be located at various points along this continuum. These, we must stress, are not recipes for ethnographic writing; they are indications of the range of options that any particular ethnographer may choose from. Within this, we have found, like Van Maanen (who produced his own invaluable typologies of ethnographic forms of writing in 1988 and 1995), that the ethnographer is 'flying by the seat of [their] pants much of the time' (1988: 120).

Our key injunction to the new ethnographer would be, in Mills's words again, 'be a good craftsman. Avoid any rigid set of procedures ... Avoid the fetishism of method and technique ... let theory and method again become part of the practice of the craft' (1959: 224). But no craftworker learns the trade without having looked closely at what more experienced workers have done. This is the spirit in which we wish our illustrations of writing in the four ideal type forms to be read.

It is at the mid-point of the continuum in Table 2.1 that we move significantly away from the conventions of traditional social science. The key shift is epistemological; the basis of the claim for truth or validity is no longer in what philosophers call 'correspondence' terms. The ethnography is not true any more in terms of 'this is exactly what happened'. Certain 'facts', we might say, have been altered by the writer, for a variety of reasons, the most obvious one being the protection of the research subjects. But the key truths about processes – about 'how things happen' or 'how things work' – are retained. And the test for this is the one suggested by the Pragmatist epistemologists: how well would any individual, regardless of what their personal projects are, cope in the situations covered by the ethnography if they were informed in their actions by their reading of this account, rather than another? There is here no concept of an ultimate or final truth. No research account can ever be totally 'true' but that some accounts are truer than others. And the truer ones are those that would better prepare someone entering the area of life being studied to cope (or 'fulfil projects') in that sphere than would another account. As Joas expresses it, 'the guiding principle of Pragmatism changes the relationship between cognition and reality'. Truth is no longer to do with getting a correct 'representation of reality in cognition'; 'rather, it expresses an increase of the power to act in relation to an environment' (1993: 21).

Table 2.1 Four ideal type forms of ethnographic writing, located on a continuum from minimum to maximum manipulation of research 'materials'

A. Plain Ethnography	B. Enhanced Ethnography	C. Semi-fictionalized Ethnography	D. Fictionalized Ethnography
A traditional social science account of events occurring within the investigation of a single case	An account of events occurring within the investigation of a single case which uses the presentational techniques of the novelist: descriptive scene-setting; use of dialogues; author as a character in the narrative; inclusion of emotional responses by author and subjects; attention to the perspectives and stories of subjects	A restructuring of events occurring within one or more ethnographic investigations into a single narrative (incorporating B form features) This is an invaluable of using research 'data' that is highly sensitive or confidential and which would not be publishable without very heavy disguising	A drawing on ethnographic and related experiences from the author's life to construct an entertaining and edifying narrative (incorporating B and C form features). Characters and events may be 'created' out of materials gathered over the authors personal and scientific life
Theory: the investigation and the writing are informed by theory and contributions to existing theory are drawn out in the written account	**Theory**: as A	**Theory**: as A	**Theory**: the writing is informed by social science theories but may not deal with these explicitly account
Truth claims mainly in *correspondence* terms: 'this is as close as I can get to a straight "witness-statement" report of wha happened'	**Truth claims** mainly in *correspondence* terms: 'this is more-or-less what happened, but as a novelist might report it'	**Truth claims** mainly in *pragmatist* terms: 'this account is truer than other accounts to the extent to which it better informs human practices than do those other accounts'	**Truth**: as C
See Entering the faculty (p. 44–5)	See Crossing the bridge (p. 46–7)	See Charity begins at home (p. 49–50)	See Scrimshaw scrimshanks (p. 52)

Minimum 'manipulation' ←——————→ Maximum 'manipulation'

The first two ethnographic forms that we are now going to look at are closer to more traditional epistemological positions. Michael, with his example of *plain* ethnography, was anxious in this piece of work to give an account that corresponded, as closely as possible, with what he saw and experienced 'in the field'. And Tony's example of *enhanced* ethnography is almost like a film sequence. He is trying give the reader a feeling of actually 'being there' watching the two researchers and their activities in the pub. Let us begin, however, with Michael's example of a piece of plain ethnographic writing.

plain ethnographic writing: Michael's 'entering the faculty'

When I was doing my first ethnographic study I needed to somehow represent for my readers how it felt living, working and collecting data in Turkey. I felt that I had been immersed in another culture, that I had been a 'stranger in a strange land' (Heinlein, 1961) and that I needed to express this in some appropriate way. At the time I felt that I was taking an ethnographic approach in using descriptive scene-setting vignettes in the style of Van Maanen (1988: 136), who described them as 'personalised accounts of fleeting moments of fieldwork in dramatic form' (see also Barter and Renold, 2000; Ellis, 1998; Erickson, 1986). I think, in retrospect, that this style of writing could justifiably be labelled as 'naive realism' (see for example Denzin, 2001; Hammersley, 1992). Let me show you what I mean with an extract from a vignette.

Entering the faculty

The taxi turns right out of the honking traffic through the main gate set within a forbidding, three-metre-high, spiked wrought iron fence.[1] The taxi driver jokingly asks us, in English, whether the fence is there to keep students in, or others out. Students mill about in the yard, between the fence and the dull grey concrete buildings. They are nearly all female, and there seem to be two styles of dress. Some wear very short skirts or tight jeans, sweaters, shirts, boots and long hair. In contrast to this there are some in Islamic dress, their hair and head fully covered by the *hijab* or scarf and only the skin of the face and hands visible. We enter the main door, and are greeted by the caretakers, all brown-suited middle-aged men with moustaches, leaning against grey unadorned walls. We pass the student common room and tobacco smoke billows from the door. We walk along a tile-floored corridor past a large black bust of Atatürk, a Turkish National flag, tall glass cabinets with examples of costumes and embroidery, and continue onto a grimy stone floor, passing hundreds of students along the way. Glancing right we see a 'kitchen' lined with large steaming urns of boiling water. In here there are five or six middle-aged men in blue overall jackets making glasses of tea and coffee and carrying them away, one handed, on silvery metal trays. We walk up a wide uncarpeted staircase, into the main administration and management area where the floor is carpeted and each office door has a brass plate with the occupant's name and title. Each of the offices has an outer office with a secretary.[2] As we enter the Vice-Dean's rooms her secretary, a woman in her forties wearing a dark skirt and white blouse, welcomes us with a formal and deferential '*Guneydin*', shakes our hands and shows us into the main office. The room is about four metres square, with a blue/grey plain carpet, high windows across one wall and a piece of flat modern sculpture on the wall opposite. There is a large, very tidy, dark wooden desk. Everything on it is neatly arranged including pens, pencil, scissors, a jar of sweets, a television remote control, and two telephones. At the front of the desk is a black ceramic nameplate with 'Prof. Dr -------' in gold lettering. The desk has a padded black leather chair behind it. On the right of the chair is a Turkish flag furled on a pole topped by a golden crescent. Next to the flag there is a blue and

---

white circular enamel charm against the evil eye. On the wall directly above the chair is a severe black and white portrait of Atatürk looking down into the room. An IBM computer sits on a small table to the left of the desk, and behind this is a television. There are three houseplants in the corner, and two armchairs facing each other across a low coffee table, on which there is a notepad from the Manchester Museum of Science and Industry and a prospectus from Purdue University. The inside of the office door is covered in quilted leather padding. The secretary, through our interpreter, apologizes for the absence of the Vice-Dean, giving us a choice of tea, apple tea, coffee, or a sage herbal drink. We order apple tea and sit waiting. After about five minutes the Vice-Dean arrives, breathlessly explaining that she had been to a meeting to substitute for the Dean who was ill. She is wearing a blue and black striped suit and a white sweater and we notice a small gold Atatürk's-head lapel badge. She sits behind her desk under the portrait of Mustafa Kemal and immediately telephones her secretary to order more refreshments.

In the final version of my work I justified my use of this representational device by claiming that it 'enhance(s) the understanding of the "story", in each of the two case-studies' (Humphreys, 1999: 100) Reflecting on this some nine years after it was written I think that despite the lack of any explicit reflexive ethnographer's voice it is still possible to draw inferences about researchers and their relationships with the researched. I am trying to describe the experience of physically entering this Turkish university's women's faculty building. The focus on small details that catch my attention suggests that these stood out for me as unusual. Why were these things unusual? Well, this is in large part because I was a 'stranger' here in several different ways: an English male in an all female Turkish faculty; a European in Asia; a Westerner in the East, and (nominally) a Christian in a secular state with an Islamic population.

I think that things were taken too far by the style of critique of ethnography that was exemplified in the Clifford and Marcus (1986) collection of essays, which encourages us to worry about becoming patronizing neo-colonial mis-representers of 'the other'. I very much like the line taken by Peter Manning (2001) on this kind of thing, although he was focusing more on the Denzin and Lincoln (1992) view that the writing style of ethnography is 'the reality of interest', and not the 'data' or the 'empirical basis'. Manning suggests that most social scientists do not go this far and, instead, look for a compromise. They seek 'some fit between the subjective, psychic reality as experienced and the shared social reality in part captured by symbols and linguistically conveyed representations' (2001: 157).

enhanced ethnographic writing: Tony's 'crossing the bridge'

At first, the piece of writing that I am presenting here to illustrate the 'enhanced' style of ethnographic writing does not look radically different from what Michael called his 'vignette', especially with regard to the 'descriptive scene-setting' which is being done. But this excerpt is rather more than a vignette. It is actually the opening of an ethnographic study and, in addition to setting the scene, it introduces the researchers and actually gets the narrative rolling by introducing the characters and some plot issues.

I wrote this for the present chapter, while pretending that I was writing the opening pages of a book about what is, in fact, a research study that is still ongoing. In fact I have built into this piece of writing some points which I would otherwise be putting into the main text of the present chapter. The account has built into it some thoughts about the nature of ethnographic investigation, analysis and writing.

Crossing the bridge

As we approached the steps down from the footbridge which had taken us over the railway line we looked down at people eating and drinking in the garden of the public house which was part of the business that Diane and I were currently studying. Tynemill, a business running a couple of dozen pubs and bars, had moved its base to the upper floor of *The Victoria*, a late nineteenth century former railway hotel.

We entered *The Vic* and, after pushing our way through the group of customers who were crowding the main bar, found ourselves being greeted by Neil, a director of Tynemill who was currently spending most of his time in *The Victoria* and, it would seem, taking charge of activities in the pub.

'Perhaps you ought to get round this side of the bar and help us out', he suggested to Diane, who had learned how to serve pints, take food orders and all the rest at this bar as part of the 'ethnographic fieldwork' component of the Tynemill study.

Neil looked a little more askance at Tony, 'Fancy seeing you here, stranger'.

'Yes, it's no good asking me to help out, Neil. I'd be no better that side of the bar than I am at this'.

Neil rolled his eyes upward, jokingly acknowledging his awareness of Tony's well-known discomfort at struggling to get served at crowded bars. But he was also aware, from earlier conversations, that Tony tended to associate going into *The Victoria* with some unhappy experiences when he was working as a participant observer in the large company across the railway line. These were experiences of 'going for a goodbye drink' with managerial colleagues who had found themselves made redundant by the company to which they had given years of highly committed service. Yet, as Neil had pointed out on an earlier occasion, *The Victoria* in pre-Tynemill times was a 'very different place'.

'*The Vic*, as it was then', Neil had argued, was 'precisely what Tynemill had come into existence to provide an alternative to. It had been a scruffy, unwelcoming dump offering one brand of keg beer (imposed on it by the brewery) and two flavours of crisps if you were lucky'.

'But look what you've got now', he went on. 'There's a proper choice of real ales, bottled beers and excellent wines. You've got full food menus in the bar and the restaurant. And you've got the chance of good conversation, without jukeboxes or

---

games machines. And all of this is in a comfortable physical environment, inside or out in the garden, without any kind of pretentiousness ...'

'Except perhaps on the part of some of the regulars who tend to block the bar,' interrupted Tony, 'and some of the old brewery posters are a bit ...'.

'Well, if you came in here a bit more often ...', Neil started to respond before being called away to deal with a problem that had arisen in the kitchen, an area of his territory that he was especially proud to rule over.

'I'd better go and see what's happening in the kitchen', Neil explained, 'and I'm expecting to see Chris at any time now. We've some rather big things to discuss'.

With Neil away in his beloved kitchen, Tasha came over and served us with our pint of Hemlock (brewed in Tynemill's own Castle Rock brewery) and a glass of red wine. Diane and Tasha had a quick conversation about recent developments among the *Victoria*'s bar staff but nothing was said about what the issues might be that Neil was going to be discussing with Chris, the managing director of Tynemill. This was something we would need to find out about later. Meanwhile, however, we took our drinks over to the one empty table, which was next to the door of the bar. This was a slightly uncomfortable place to sit but, as Diane pointed out, it provided with the still uneasy Tony with quite a good vantage point for people who took their ethnographic research seriously. Suitably chastized, Tony sipped his Hemlock and turned to see how the customers who had newly arrived in the pub were managing to navigate through the now even more crowded space in front of the bar.

In this piece of writing, I am deliberately using techniques we usually associate with the novel. I need to stress that this is a matter of *technique* and *presentation* as opposed to a shift towards fiction, in the sense of trying to be a 'creative writer'. The distinction I am making here was implicit in Rose's interesting suggestion some years ago that 'the novel has been transforming the scientific monograph' (1990: 55). The transformation he refers to is, to quote him directly, not 'through the use of fiction particularly, but through the descriptive setting of the scene, the narration of the local people's own stories, the use of dialogue, the privileging of the objects of inquiry along with the subject or author who writes, and the notation by the author of emotions, subjective reactions, and involvement in ongoing activities' (1990: 55). All of these techniques are used in the above excerpt. It certainly uses the fiction-writer's techniques, but it is as close as memory and field notes would allow to 'what actually happened' that day. All the same, the piece is doing more than just reporting an event for the sake of reporting an event. It is simultaneously setting up the rest of the ethnographic writing which is to follow.

The extracted narrative begins with two characters, the researchers, in the specific physical location of a railway bridge. After a very simple sketch of the pub garden below the bridge, we are told what the study is about. The company being studied is named and the nature of the business it is in is explained. In the second paragraph, we are given a quick impression of the inside of the public house and are introduced to one of the 'subject' characters of the study. The use of the phrase 'it would seem' is a device intended to 'hook' the reader who is invited to reflect 'Aha, what is going on here?', with the implication that they had better stay with the story to see what might be going on. We then get some direct dialogue which, when built upon with the description of rolled eyes and the story of the researcher's earlier experiences in the pub, establishes that emotions are playing quite a strong part on the researcher's behalf (as we gather later these are with Neil, when we hear the reference to his 'much loved kitchen'). There is then further banter between the two men, in which we learn that Neil thinks that Tony does not come into the pub often enough. This is setting up some issues that are to be explored later in the study, about my serious unease with the heavy masculinity that is prevalent in parts of the organization. But woven into this interactional material is a strand of the pub's history. This has considerable significance, we should note, because it introduces us to the 'foundational myth' of the business (providing an alternative to bad old pubs like the bad old *Vic*).

As the excerpt unfolds, we see more of this careful interweaving of novel-like detailed descriptions of natural-sounding events with information about the business. And an attempt is made to whet the reader's appetite for an interesting business-story-to-come with the indication that important discussions are to take place between Neil and Chris (the company's managing director).

At one level this short piece of writing is simply a plain-sounding accessible narrative of events that happened over 30 minutes or so in an English public house. But at another level it is an artfully crafted piece, which sets out to achieve a great deal more than simply report events. And at the heart of the rhetorical work I am doing here is an attempt to persuade the readers that the whole study is one worth reading (Golden-Biddle and Locke, 1993; Watson, 1995). The promise of 'a good-story-to-come' is one of the most important things that any writer needs to establish, as early as possible in the 'pitch' they are putting to their readers. These are readers whose attention is sought by hundreds if not thousands of rival researcher/writers who have something to say about the nature of organizations, business, entrepreneurship, management and, yes, the nature of advantages of ethnography itself.

semi-fictionalized ethnographic writing: Michael's 'charity begins at home'

The next piece of ethnographic writing is derived from research that I carried out in the USA Bank *Credit Line*'s headquarters in the UK, where I was investigating the identity of the organization via the narratives of the employees (Humphreys and Brown, 2008). One of my primary research interests is in the multiple, often changing, occasionally consonant, sometimes overlapping, but often competing narratives that participants will tell about their organization

(Humphreys and Brown, 2002a; 2002b). One pervasive corporate narrative was *Credit Line*'s stance on corporate social responsibility represented in accounts of its environmental and social activities both internally, with its own employees, and externally, with the local community. This position is encapsulated in an extract from the bank's website:

> At *Credit Line* we believe that a great company must hold itself to the highest standard, so we take our role as a corporate citizen seriously. We believe true corporate success is measured not simply in the ledger but rather in a company's positive impact, both in the community and in the workplace. (*Credit Line* website)

As I spent more time within the bank I gradually came to realize that although members of the organization publicly extolled the bank's community and green credentials, in private their views were very different. This presented me with an ethical problem. In order to represent these contrasting public and private stories I needed to express the opinions of individuals but also maintain their anonymity. I did this by writing an 'ethnographic' account of a composite person, who could not be identified as any single employee.

Charity begins at home

Soon after I started research work at the bank *Credit Line* I met Charity, who was in charge of community relations. She was a great research subject, bubbling with infectious energy, enthusiasm and drive – all of which were reflected in her office hours, work rate and speed of conversation. She was happy to tell me all about her background in a poor Catholic working class family in Yorkshire, where her parents still lived. Leaving school she had done a business studies degree course at a polytechnic and, after failing in her ambition to get into television, went to work at the sweet factory that she had worked in as a child, this time in the offices. She laughed as she related the experience of getting her first 'proper' job, saying: 'I ended up going for an interview at an electrical engineering firm as a systems analyst trainee, and getting the job. I cried when I got it, because I really didn't want to do that, but we had no money and I needed a job. I stayed there for 11 years'. Later in our acquaintance she became much more reflective, talking about how a promotion to her first management role had coincided with the breakdown of her long-term relationship, and she was tearful when describing how a new relationship had ended in tragic circumstances when her partner had died suddenly, 'I was really quite ill as a result of all that. I struggled on in that job for two years, tried to get redundancy, couldn't get it, so ended up going on secondment to the Youth Business Trust. When I came to go back, they'd forgotten they'd got me, and they'd made me redundant!' At this point Charity had no career plans, applying for whatever jobs were advertized locally and eventually finding a position as a fund-raiser for the community activities of the county police.

(Cont'd)

She spent three years in this post and, as part of her job, came into contact with *Credit Line* 'to ask for some money for the community project'. The Head of Corporate Communications in the bank seemed impressed by Charity's energy and expertise and suggested that she might like to apply for a job in community relations. She was laughing again when she said, 'I got it and, as they say, the rest is history'.

She felt different to many of her fellow employees who she saw as 'middle class and cosseted'. Proud of her own working class background she saw her family as a source of inner strength, telling me that 'I was brought up working class, without money ... Mum found a fiver in the street once, and phoned the police and handed it in, you know ... I come from a very different place, I think, than a lot of our marketing department, who are graduates from top universities, who've probably been to public school'.

Although it was clear that she was passionate about the responsibilities that organizations have for their staff, the environment and the local community, Charity seemed quite cynical about her own job saying, 'My problem is that, in this organization, corporate social responsibility is a sham – it's just rhetoric – I mean how can we call ourselves responsible when we give credit cards to poor people and charge them 30 per cent APR just because they are a high risk?'. She was quite emotional when she described her own ambivalence, saying, 'I find it really difficult to square my conscience when I am representing the bank at some community event such as the launch of the clean needle exchange for heroin addicts and I know that we are also putting huge pressure on anyone who makes a late payment on their card'. However, she also acknowledged that she had been changed by her experience of working for a very high profile financial organization, telling me with a little glee that:

> My expectations have gone up. I mean, we went to America, Sadie and I, last month, and we got upgraded on the way out. And we then got to the hotel, and we didn't like it, so we upgraded ourselves. We checked out of that hotel and into the Ritz Carlton ... It was fantastic! We had, you know, the chauffeured car to take us everywhere, and we had the bellboys to take the stuff up to our room. I think, probably, I feel now that I deserve more. You know, being brought up with Catholic guilt and stuff ... I started here with a Ford Fiesta. I've now got a BMW 325i coupe with leather seats and CD player.

In this account I have merged the personalities of several of my research subjects and used interview transcripts, field notes, and my own impressionistic ideas about the organization and its employees to construct versions of what the fictional 'Charity' might have said. Although Charity is a construct she represents those individuals who felt marginalized and somewhat at odds with most of the mainstream financial, marketing and IT specialists who were the core staff of the organization. Charity's life history and voice are thus amalgamations of the stories and utterances of several resistant individuals located in pockets throughout the organization, in, for example, the call centre, public relations, projects, and debt recovery. The ethical precondition here was my duty to protect individuals in particularly vulnerable positions in the organization. In this situation, as Ellen (1984) has noted, anonymity can prove difficult where there are only a few organizations which match the case description and consequently where readers might try to work out the identity of particular research subjects. Emerson, Fretz and Shaw support the use of such semi-fictional accounts in ethnographic writing, arguing that 'members' meanings … are not pristine objects that are simply "discovered". Rather, these meanings are interpretive constructions assembled and conveyed by the researcher' (1995: 108). And, in the pragmatist terms discussed above, such semi-fictionalized writing can be characterized as 'true'.

fictionalized ethnographic writing: Tony's 'Scrimshaw scrimshanks'

I think that the 'semi-fictionalized' type of account which Michael has illustrated necessarily plays a role in most ethnographies where there is a need to protect individual or corporate confidentialities. When I wrote about my research on the role of strategy-makers themselves on the strategies of their businesses (Watson, 2003), for example, I was faced not just with the responsibility of protecting certain business confidentialities, but also of protecting both a marriage and a relationship between a pair of siblings. A considerable amount of 'disguising' therefore had to be done. And the same was necessary in a study of HRM strategy in a food-processing business (Watson, 2004b). In that case there was what might be termed 'absolute dynamite' in terms of 'insider information'. Fictionalizing was vital to avoid the risk of that dynamite blowing up in the faces of the people who were good enough to trust me with highly sensitive information both about the businesses and the personal lives of senior managers.

Some of the sensitivities that I was dealing with in these semi-fictionalized accounts are relevant to my ventures into more fully fictionalized writing. I have found that the more I get into strategy-level issues in ethnographic-style investigations – and especially when I pursue my key concern with the way strategists' personal lives connect to their 'business lives' – the more I find I have to engage in serious 'fictionalizing'. I have been very wary about bringing into formal 'academic' research writing the sort of intimate, emotional, and indeed sexual aspects of business life that my ethnographic experiences, across various organizations and over the years, have convinced me to be of great importance. I have pondered long and hard on how I could explore them. And I came to the conclusion that a fictionalized form of writing is the only way I could really get to grips with some of the more 'personal' and emotional aspects of emotion and behaviour that are, for very good reasons, kept beneath the surface in academic work.

Important as this factor of touching on the more 'personal' aspects of human lives is in the 'fiction-science' writing (Watson, 2000) I have done (all of it drawing on experiences and insights from field-work experiences), there is something even more important. This is something that distinguishes this work from mainstream 'creative writing': the informing of the writing by my knowledge of and fascination with social science theory. *The Gaberlunzie Girl* (Watson, 2004a) piece, which was rooted in some of the things I had seen and heard about when looking at family relationships within business, wears its theory component relatively lightly, but my story *In search of McManus: Mystery, myth and modernity* (Watson, 2008b) has a very explicit theoretical dimension with my fictional figures mixing the debate about how to theorize 'myth' with tales of sexual intrigue in 1930s Milan.

The example of fictionalized ethnography provided here (Watson 2008c: 304) has been chosen in order to highlight the theoretical dimension. The words are spoken by a fictional warehouse worker.

Scrimshaw scrimshanks

I had not heard the word 'scrimshank' until I went to work in the grocery warehouse. And I naively thought that the blokes had made up the word to name the sort of thing that Dave Scrimshaw got up to. It turned out that it was all a coincidence. But there's one thing I can tell you, Dave Scrimshaw was a real scrimshanker. Let me tell you the sort of thing I mean. When the warehouse boss used to come down to tell us that, say, a new delivery of breakfast cereals would soon be arriving, Dave would look really pleased and ask questions like, 'And which cereal is it arriving today, Mr Cooper?' He would follow this with 'Oh yes, Mr Cooper, I think that one has to be handled with special care, so we'll go very gently'. But when the boss had gone and the lorry arrived, Dave would conspic-uously throw or kick the boxes all over the warehouse.

When he'd had enough of this, he would engage in some other wheeze to impress the lads. One thing he liked to do was to construct for himself a little sleeping 'den' between the piled-up boxes. He'd then make a display of climbing into this space 'for a nice rest'. We'd then hear this snoring coming from his hiding place – whether he was sleeping or pretending to sleep, we never knew. But you can be damn sure of one thing – the boss never caught him being anything but the hardest working and most conscientious worker of us all.

The theoretical purpose of this piece is to illustrate one of the variants of a particular kind of organizational mischief that Fleming and Sewell (2002) call Svejkism (using the name of the hero of the novel *The good soldier, Svejk* by Jaroslav Hasek 1973). And where are the origins of the story? I did once work in a grocery warehouse (while on vacation from studying, among other things, 'deviance' and industrial sociology) and, when writing this story years later, I combined two different characters I knew there into this fictional scrimshanker (and, yes, there was a D. Scrimshaw in another setting where I worked and I've always wanted to use his name in one piece of writing or another).

In his autobiography, Duke Ellington (1973: 451) vividly expressed the layering of authorship and narrative:

> We suddenly realize that just below our mirror, there is another reflection that is not quite so clear, and not quite what we expected ... We examine this uncertain portrait and just as we feel inclined to accept it we realize that, down below this there is still another mirror reflecting another one of our selves, and more. For this third mirror is transparent ...

In this chapter we have explored the issue of representation in ethnographic writing by addressing what Jeffcutt (1994: 232) refers to as 'strategies of authorial voice and narrative form'. We have tried to illustrate our joint view that no research account can ever be totally 'true' but that some accounts are truer than others. The truer ones are those that would better prepare someone entering the area of life being studied to cope (or 'fulfil projects') in that sphere than would another account. These ideas and debates impinge on us as business school academics both when writing about organizations and when teaching students. Of course, there is a direct relationship between research and teaching, exemplified in the huge number of available case studies which range from the ostensibly 'true' to the completely 'fictional'. It seems to us that the more authentic the experiences depicted in our work are the more effective they are pedagogically. In this chapter we have tried to create a case study in academic authorship, by providing a flavour of ethnographic writing in examples of our own work across a 'spectrum of truth' and, in effect, allowing you 'the audience to see the puppet strings as they watch the puppet show' (Watson, 1994: 78). How effective this has been is a judgement we can only leave to you to make.

notes

[1] I learnt later that because of this expensive fence the running joke amongst the staff was that the current head of Hero University was known as 'the fence (e)rector'. This is doubly significant in that not only is it subversive humour, it is in English.

[2] We found out that the Dean had his own toilet which was locked with the key kept in a leather box on his secretary's desk. The Dean is a man in a predominantly female faculty, and the Vice-Deans are women as are all the Heads of Department, who use the same toilets as the students.

references

Atkinson, P. and Hammersley, M. (1998) 'Ethnography and participant observation', in N.K. Denzin and Y.S. Lincoln (eds), *Strategies of qualitative inquiry*. London: Sage. pp. 110–36.

Atkinson, P., Coffey, A., Delamont, S., Lofland, J. and Lofland, L. (eds) (2001) *Handbook of ethnography*. London: Sage.

Barter, C. and Renold, E. (2000) 'I wanna tell you a story: The use of vignettes in qualitative research', *International Journal of Social Research Methodology*, 3(4): 307–23.

Baszanger, I. and Dodier, N. (2004) 'Ethnography: relating the part to the whole', in D. Silverman (ed.), *Qualitative research theory, method and practice* (2nd edn). London: Sage. pp. 9–34.

Bate, S.P. (1997) 'Whatever happened to organizational ethnography? A review of the field of organizational ethnography and anthropological studies', *Human Relations*, 50: 1147–75.

Bryman, A. and Bell, E. (2003) *Business research methods*. London: Sage.

Casey, C. (1995) *Work, self and society: after industrialism*. London: Routledge.

Clifford, J. and Marcus, G.E. (1986) *Writing culture: The politics and poetics of ethnography*. Berkeley, CA: University of California Press.

Delbridge, R. (1998) *Life on the line in contemporary manufacturing: The workplace experience of lean production and the 'Japanese' model*. Oxford: Oxford University Press.

Denzin, N.K. (2001) 'The seventh moment: Qualitative inquiry and the practices of a more radical consumer research', *Journal of Consumer Research*, 28: 324–30.

Denzin, N.K. and Lincoln, Y.S. (eds) (1992) *Handbook of qualitative research*. Thousand Oaks, CA: Sage.

Denzin, N.K. and Lincoln, Y.S. (1998) 'Introduction: Entering the field of qualitative research', in N.K. Denzin and Y.S. Lincoln (eds), *The landscape of qualitative research: Theories and issues*. London: Sage. pp. 1–34.

Ellen, R. (ed.) (1984) *Ethnographic research: A guide to general conduct*. London: Academic Press.

Ellington, E.K. (Duke) (1973) *Music is my mistress*. New York: Da Capo Press.

Ellis, C. (1998) 'What counts as scholarship in communication? An autoethnographic response', paper presented at the National Communication Association Convention, Chicago. (Reprinted in *American Communication Journal*, 1(2), 1998, www.acjournal.org/holdings/vol1/Iss2/special/ ellis.htm.)

Emerson, R., Fretz, R. and Shaw, L. (1995) *Writing ethnographic fieldnotes*. London: University of Chicago Press.

Erickson, F. (1986) 'Qualitative methods in research on teaching', in M.C. Witrock (ed.), *Handbook of research on teaching* (3rd edn). New York: Macmillan. pp. 119–61.

Fetterman, D.M. (1989) *Ethnography step by step*. London: Sage.

Fleming, P. and Sewell, G. (2002) 'Looking for the good soldier, Svejk: Alternative modalities of resistance in the contemporary workplace', *Work, Employment & Society*, 36(4): 857–73.

Golden-Biddle, K. and Locke, K. (1993) 'Appealing work: an investigation of how ethnographic texts convince', *Organization Science* 4(4): 595–616.

Hammersley, M. (1992) *What's wrong with ethnography?* London: Routledge.

Heinlein, R. (1961) *Stranger in a strange land*. New York: Putnam.

Humphreys, M. (1999) *An ethnographic study of the work cultures of two higher education faculties: Reminiscing in tempo*. Unpublished PhD Thesis, Nottingham University.

Humphreys, M. and Brown, A.D. (2002a) 'Dress and identity: A Turkish case study', *Journal of Management Studies*, 39: 929–54.

Humphreys, M. and Brown, A.D. (2002b) 'Narratives of organizational identity and identification: a case study of hegemony and resistance', *Organization Studies*, 23: 421–47.

Humphreys, M. and Brown, A.D. (2008) 'Narratives of corporate social responsibility: Theorising identity at a bank', *Journal of Business Ethics*, 80: 403–18.

Humphreys, M., Brown, A.D. and Hatch, M.J. (2003) 'Is ethnography jazz?', *Organization*, 10(1): 5–31.

Jeffcut, P. (1994) 'From interpretation to representation in organizational analysis: Postmodernism, ethnography and organisational symbolism', *Organization Studies*, 15(2): 241–74.

Joas, H. (1993) *Pragmatism and social theory*. Chicago: The University of Chicago Press.

Manning, P. (2001) 'Semiotics, semantics and ethnography', in P. Atkinson, A. Coffey, S. Delamont, J. Lofland and L. Lofland (eds), *Handbook of ethnography*. London: Sage. pp. 145–59.

Mills, C.W. (1959) *The sociological imagination*. London: Oxford University Press.

Rose, D. (1990) *Living the ethnographic life*. Newbury Park, CA: Sage.

Smith, V. (2001) 'Ethnographies of work and the work of ethnographers', in P. Atkinson, A. Coffey, S. Delamont, J. Lofland and L. Lofland (eds), *Handbook of ethnography*. London: Sage. pp. 220–33.

Tedlock, B. (2000) 'Ethnography and ethnographic representation', *Handbook of qualitative research* (2nd edn). Thousand Oaks, CA: Sage Publications.

Van Maanen, J. (1988) *Tales of the field*. Chicago: Chicago University Press.

Van Maanen, J. (1995) 'An end to innocence', in J. Van Maanen (ed.), *Representation in Ethnography*. Thousand Oaks, CA: Sage.

Watson, T.J. (1994) 'Managing, crafting and researching: Words, skill and imagination in shaping management research', *British Journal of Management*, 5 (special issue): 77–87.

Watson, T.J. (1995) 'Shaping the story: Rhetoric, persuasion and creative writing in organisational ethnography', *Studies in Cultures, Organisations & Society*, 1(2): 301–11.

Watson, T.J. (2000) 'Ethnographic fiction science: Making sense of managerial work and organisational research processes with Caroline and Terry', *Organization*, 7(3): 513–34.

Watson, T.J. (2001) *In search of management* (revised edn). London: South-Western Cengage Learning (originally, Routledge 1994).

Watson, T.J. (2003) 'Strategists and strategy-making: Strategic exchange and the shaping of individual lives and organisational futures', *Journal of Management Studies*, 40(5): 1305–23.

Watson, T.J. (2004a) 'Shy William and the Gaberlunzie Girl', in Y. Gabriel (ed.), *Myths, stories and organizations: Premodern narratives for our times*. Oxford: Oxford University Press. pp. 223–35.

Watson, T.J. (2004b) 'Human resource management and critical social science analysis', *Journal of Management Studies*, 41(3): 447–67.

Watson, T.J. (2008a) 'Participant observation and ethnography', in R. Thorpe and R. Holt (eds), *Dictionary of qualitative management research*. London: Sage.

Watson, T.J. (2008b) 'In search of McManus: Mystery, myth and modernity', in M. Kostera (ed.), *Organization Olympians: Heroes, heroines and villains of organizational myths*. Basingstoke: Palgrave-Macmillan. pp. 142–54.

Watson, T.J. (2008c) *Sociology, work and industry*. London: Routledge.

3

Reading and writing as method: In search of trustworthy texts

Peregrine Schwartz-Shea and Dvora Yanow

'The research presented here is based on an ethnography of …': a researcher who situates a manuscript with this phrase signals to the reader that the research being presented is part of a particular tradition of scholarship. The statement stimulates in a reader, including one acting as a reviewer, *expectations* about the logic that the research has followed – expectations developed and honed through disciplinary practices and the reader-reviewer's own research, writing, and reading experiences.

The specifics of these expectations have been discussed, analysed and, to some extent, formalized in the burgeoning methods literature dealing with the criteria and standards best suited to evaluating ethnographic and other qualitative and interpretive research (e.g., Brower et al., 2000; Erlandson et al., 1993; Golden-Biddle and Locke, 1997; Lather, 1993; Lincoln, 1995; Lincoln and Guba, 1985; Miles and Huberman, 1994). Meeting a reader-reviewer's expectations requires the researcher to be familiar with the standards and evaluative criteria that are accepted within the epistemic community of which both are members and to enact them in the research narrative in a persuasive and compelling manner. It is to this writing and reading duality that we attend, first laying out our review of what that methods literature suggests are the most widely used standards informing reader-reviewers' expectations, and then explicating, with organizational ethnography as an illustrative case, the specific textual elements that researchers can use to meet these standards and expectations.

In practice, evaluative criteria and standards commonly figure in the context of research design, anticipating most immediately the fieldwork stage of research and, to some degree as well, the 'deskwork' stage (analysis after the completion of fieldwork). Less attention has been paid to the role these criteria play in the 'textwork' phase – the crafting of a persuasive manuscript (Van Maanen, 1996; Yanow, 2000) and its dissemination to reader-reviewers of various sorts[1] – because to the extent that writing is considered at all as a method, it is often conflated with the analytic stage of research. Although parsing research into stages in some ways oversimplifies – analysis, after all, begins with the development of a research proposal long before one enters the field, and it continues as one writes – it is useful to distinguish between deskwork and textwork in order to focus attention on this latter, neglected aspect. Of course, achieving persuasiveness in a research manuscript depends not only on the character of the writing itself, but also, importantly, on the quality of the prior execution of methods in the field. The proverbial 'silk purse' of a compelling narrative cannot easily be wrought out of a 'sow's ear' of field research: reading, writing, and research are, in other words, at this evaluative point, intertwined.[2]

Our own approach to ethnography falls within the community of scholarly practice that takes a constructivist-interpretive approach. Methodologists are increasingly distinguishing between 'qualitative' methods that are informed by positivist ontological and epistemological presuppositions and 'interpretive' methods that are informed by constructivist-interpretive ones. As the former increasingly encompass such things as focus groups, Chicago School-style field research is increasingly being referred to by the latter term (see the discussion in Yanow and Schwartz-Shea, 2006: xv–xix). In some disciplines or topic areas, e.g., anthropology, 'qualitative' and 'interpretive' may be used interchangeably, because 'qualitative methods' still, in practice, includes interpretive ontological and epistemological presuppositions. In others, such as organizational studies, 'qualitative methods' at times still refers to both constructivist-interpretive and objectivist-realist presuppositions. For the sake of clarity, we use the terminology of 'interpretive' rather than 'qualitative'. With the possible exception of reflexivity (see note 5), all of the evaluative criteria reviewed in the next section of the chapter are currently being applied to realist ethnographies as well as to interpretive ones, and the writing strategies discussed later (again, with the possible exception of reflexivity) similarly hold for realist ethnographers.

Interpretive methodologies provide conceptual grounds for understanding why research, writing, and reading should be intertwined. It is today fairly common to think about a double hermeneutic (Giddens, 1984; Jackson, 2006): that researchers interpret actors' interpretations (see also Geertz, 1973: ch. 1), a tenet of both phenomenology and hermeneutics. Drawing on literary studies, we wish to elucidate a third interpretive moment. Reader-response theory (e.g., Iser, 1989) emphasizes that textual meaning is conveyed not only through the writer's intent or the elements of writing (e.g., metaphor, word choice, rhythm), but that it also rests on the prior knowledge, from experience and situatedness in the world, that readers bring to their readings of texts. In this way, the interpretive *act of reading* links phenomenology to hermeneutics. Recognizing the existence of a 'triple hermeneutic' (Yanow, 2009) could lead ethnographers (and other interpretive researchers) to consider how to incorporate into their written accounts the various textual elements that address and engage the criteria by which their research will be evaluated and through which they will persuade readers of the trustworthiness of their 'truth claims'.

Trust is commonly treated as part of the researcher–researched relationship: it is implicated in the much-touted rapport that researchers work to build as part of their entrée into the field setting. Here, we engage it as essential to the researcher-reader relationship, the latter established through texts rather than face to face. Such trust is central to the conduct of science. We begin our discussion of establishing researcher-reader trust from the perspective of the reader, turning afterward to the writer. One of the questions this discussion raises concerns the responsibilities of each party to this writing-reading enterprise, which we engage in the concluding section.

This chapter assumes a research community and, particularly, reader-reviewers who, at minimum, are not so hostile to qualitative or interpretive research that they reject its scientific status out of hand. Ideally, the reader-reviewer also endorses, if not practises, such research. In reality, openness to qualitative-interpretive approaches such as ethnography varies considerably by discipline and even by epistemic community within disciplines. For example, some organizational studies subfields or journals are clearly demarcated by positivist-oriented editorial positions, including in the selection of reviewers, and there, ethnographic work is likely to be held up to criteria more appropriate for positivist science and its presuppositions. We hope that our discussion of evaluative criteria, in addition to being useful to those writing up ethnographic research, also helps inform editors and reviewers of such journals as to the standards accepted within interpretive science.

reading strategies: emergent standards for interpretive research

Historically, ethnographic and other field researchers have not always been explicit about the *sine qua non* for such research, relying instead on the tacit knowledge and common practices shared within what were comparatively bounded (and perhaps even insular) research communities. As the borders of disciplinary and epistemic communities have become more porous and both qualitative and interpretive scholars have increasingly found their work being assessed by researchers outside their own community boundaries, the need to articulate forms of evaluative standards that fit the presuppositions informing those methods has developed, with the consequent growth of that literature.

It is important to note that researcher-writers and reader-reviewers are differently situated with respect to evaluative criteria. Researchers, especially novices, are instructed by both methods texts and supervisors that these criteria matter, and several of them are typically incorporated into research designs. To state the obvious, researchers must attend to these criteria from the beginning stages of planning the research, through its execution in the field, to the final stages of analysis and writing, although the prominence or relevance of particular criteria may vary across the life of a research project. By contrast, a reader-reviewer is in the position of assessing a purportedly finished manuscript, an evaluation of the evidence it presents and the research processes that produced it as manifested in the writing.

We argue that researchers writing for readers across epistemic boundaries might write more scientifically persuasive manuscripts if they recognized that reader-reviewers are likely to be asking, implicitly if not explicitly, 'What makes this ethnographic account trustworthy?' This sort of question (see also Clifford, 1988) lies at the heart of the attitude of doubt (or, in the language of the philosophy of science, 'testability') that characterizes the scientific endeavour. At the very minimum, understanding the textual mechanisms that foster a reader's judgements of the text's trustworthiness might lead to better initial manuscripts and fewer rejections (assuming journals and reviewers who are in the same ethnographic or interpretive epistemic community as the author, or who are sympathetic to it). Greater transparency with respect to methods and methodologies might also serve to educate reviewers beyond that epistemic community. But more than that, trustworthy research is important for acts that build on that research, as is common in action research (see for example, Greenwood and Levin, 1998, and Chapter 11 by Sykes and Treleaven, this volume) and central to the more engaged research increasingly called for by sociologists, anthropologists, political scientists, and others (see Burawoy, 2004; Lamphere, 2003; Monroe, 2005).

But how can such trustworthiness be achieved? What do reader-reviewers expect? Situating ethnographic research within interpretive methods more broadly and summarizing across two decades of thinking with respect to evaluative criteria that are methodologically appropriate to interpretive ontological and epistemological presuppositions, Schwartz-Shea (2006) finds that six criteria seem to be most used and referenced within interpretive epistemic and methodological communities.[3] These common criteria lead reader-reviewers in those communities to expect a *thickly descriptive* manuscript that demonstrates *reflexivity* about the researcher's roles in the field. They expect to see in the manuscript, both in its methods section and, as important, woven into its substance, the results of decisions and actions taken in each research stage: the planning and fieldwork execution of the *triangulation* of evidentiary sources; the detailed *audit* recording research steps taken during fieldwork that divert from initial research design; the use of *negative case analysis* or some similar sense-making technique during analysis; and the use of *member checking* with respect to textwork drafts.[4] Based on the relative presence or absence of these six elements in a manuscript, reader-reviewers make judgements about the overall trustworthiness of the research narrative. In the more detailed discussion of these that follows, we have numbered these expectations for clarity; but reader-reviewers likely assess research manuscripts in a more holistic, rather than 'check-list,' fashion.

1 **Thick description** refers to the detailed descriptions of settings, events, activities, interactions, persons, language, and so forth, in such a way as to explicate the contexts of the 'lived experiences' of the people studied. The wealth of detail conveys a subtext: that the researcher was actually present

on site as an eyewitness – in the originating case of ethnography, the 'being there' that is distinctive of such research. (Historical and archival-textual 'ethnographic' research produces similar descriptive texture; see, e.g., Darnton, 1984; 2003; Jackson, 2006.)

Detail alone does not satisfy this criterion because its purpose is not the goal of complete description – an impossibility – but, rather, a nuanced portrait of the cultural layers that inform the researcher's interpretation of interactions and events. Readers look for *sufficient* detail, as relevant to the research question: to support the claim, for instance, that what the researcher saw was a 'wink' and not a 'blink', in Geertz' famous example, borrowed from Ryle (Geertz, 1973: 6–7); or, in an example of its use in document-based analysis, the claim that 'Western Civilization' (*Abendland*) had particular, strategic meanings in post-World War II German politicians' debates over reconstruction (Jackson, 2006). Sufficiency is not an absolute quality. Meaning depends on social, political, and organizational context, and thick description imparts the specificity of that context to the reader. Readers, like writers, make situation-specific judgements as to what constitutes relevant detail in 'sufficiently' thick texts. Unlike researcher-writers, readers are commonly less familiar with the research setting being described, something that researchers should bear in mind.

2   Researcher *reflexivity* shows that the researcher understands herself as the means, the instrument, through which the research (as well as its reporting) is produced. Researchers' demographic identities (gender, race, sexuality, social class, nationality, and other components), manifested in dress, accent, physiognomy, and other elements of nonverbal communication, and other aspects of their phenomenological backgrounds (education, training, upbringing, and other elements of lived experience carried internally), the contribute to a 'positionality' that can affect not only the character of the interactions and research questions posed, but also access to research sites and persons in them and the kinds of data co-generated with research participants.

Shehata (2006) and Pachirat (2009) show that the effects of researcher identities and organizational locations cannot be understood *a priori* because identities are negotiated in context: participants 'read' researcher identity and power in complex and, at times, unanticipated and even contradictory ways. This is why readers increasingly expect ethnographers (and other interpretive researchers) to document the role of the self in the research process and analyse aspects of their presence, persona, and location for the ways they might have affected the co-generation of data (and their analysis as well). Reflexivity, in other words, is conducted both in the field and in the text. It is increasingly acceptable, if not expected outright, that researchers do not hide behind a 'third person', omniscient exposition in their accounts – the so-called 'view from nowhere' or 'God's-eye view' (Haraway, 1988; Harding, 1993) – but, instead, weave their analyses of their positionality into their textual representations.[5]

3   *Triangulation* can be understood most broadly as drawing on different kinds of sources or analytic tools in trying to understand a phenomenon.[6]

Qualitative methods texts sometimes distinguish among several types of triangulation, including multiple methods of accessing data (observation, interviews, documents – this is the most commonly understood meaning), multiple data sources (e.g., persons observed and/or interviewed, locations within the research site, times of day, week or year), and multiple researchers (such as teams of ethnographers studying a single site).[7] Multi-sited ethnography (e.g., Hannerz, 2003; Marcus, 1995) might also be seen as a form of triangulation. Methodological discussions of triangulation emphasize the complexity of understanding social settings by noting not only the extent to which data from multiple methods, sources, researchers, and/or sites present possibilities for corroboration and refutation (that is, subjecting provisional inferences to testing), but also that such multiple approaches to data are likely to bring to light inconsistent and even conflicting findings (Hammersley and Atkinson, 1983; Mathison, 1988). Readers expect to find accounts of how researchers grappled with inconsistent or conflicting findings emerging from triangulation of whatever sort. As Becker (1998: 44) argues, simplicity should be 'an empirical finding rather than a theoretical commitment' (see also Law, 2004, on not eliminating the complexity of everyday life).

4   An *audit* (or 'audit trail'; Lincoln and Guba, 1985) documents, as completely as possible, while in the midst of research, changes in processes and steps used in the conduct of the research, as if those processes might be 'audited' at its conclusion – which is what reviewers are, in a sense, doing. The researcher identifies and describes any changes to the original research design made in response to situational realities – a commonplace of ethnographic (and other interpretive) research, by contrast with the normative ideal common in survey and statistical research of a fixed/*a priori* research design. The audit's purpose is to make the linkages among researcher decisions, evidence generated, and inferences drawn as transparent as they can be, serving to remind the researcher in the midst of analysing data and field notes and writing research texts of what transpired in the field from a methods perspective. Audits themselves are private records, much as fieldnotes are; readers look for statements or other indications that an audit has been kept and for the general attitude of transparency that auditing enacts.

5   *Negative case analysis* (or some similar process[8]) challenges researchers' own meaning-making processes. As an ethnographer immerses himself in data – sifting repeatedly through, say, field notes, reflexive diaries, interview transcripts, documents, and whatever other sources of data are at hand – negative case analysis is a technique of reflective inquiry designed to prevent him from settling too quickly on a pattern, answer or interpretation. Asking himself, 'How do I know what I think I know?' and 'How would I know if my analysis missed some angle?' he consciously searches for evidence that challenges or negates his initial impressions, pet theories or favoured explanations – the 'negative' case that would require their re-examination. It both improves analysis and demonstrates to reader-reviewers

that during data analysis, the researcher actively inquired into his own meaning-making processes, not looking for confirmatory evidence alone. Interrogating members' dissenting views, acquired through member checking (discussed next), is an example of negative case analysis.

6   Whatever the character of field relationships (that is, negative *or* positive), *member-checking* means going back in some fashion to the people in the setting studied for an assessment of whether the researcher did a good job of capturing *their* understandings of their own situations. This is not just the journalistic practice of 'fact-' or 'quote-checking' (which implies that there is a singular social reality that the reporter can capture). It is, instead, a fuller recognition that lived experience – for example, insider vocabularies, positioned understandings of an event, organization or policy, tacit knowledge of these – is quite complex and the researcher may or may not have fully grasped its meanings *from members' perspectives*. Member-checking focuses researchers' explicit attention on possible differences between their own and members' interpretations and calls upon them also to theorize those differences.

The charge is not necessarily to take members' critical responses at face value. The researcher may have access to information not available to (some) members that contextualizes their views in ways that they may not recognize; or she may have academic insights from research literature that will lead her to frame experiential data in a theoretical context unfamiliar to situational members (discussed further below). What member-checking highlights is researchers' engagement with their own and others' sense-making. As Atkinson et al. (2003: 194) advise, 'informants' accounts should neither be endorsed nor disregarded: they need to be analyzed'.

Moreover, neither the 'getting-it-right' from members' points of view nor reflective inquiry about the 'goodness' of one's analysis posits the existence of an external, objective reality that the researcher needs to capture with precision. Instead, both turn the analytical spotlight on the potential gulf in understanding and interpretation between researcher and research participants.

From a reader-reviewer's perspective, the degree to which a manuscript engages these six elements provides grounds for assessing its *trustworthiness*. Trustworthiness has become a widely invoked and accepted umbrella term or 'meta-goal' in qualitative and interpretive research communities. It is what such methodologists posit as a more appropriate criterion than 'validity', 'reliability', and the like, as these are rooted firmly in a positivist scientific methodology that rests on the presumption of a real social world that can be mirrored in social scientific studies. That presumption renders those criteria logically inappropriate for the evaluation of research rooted in phenomenological, hermeneutic, and other interpretive methodologies (Schwartz-Shea, 2006).[9] 'Trustworthiness' addresses the broadest question asked about any research project – whether the study is deserving of readers' trust in its representations, analysis, and findings. It is a comprehensive standard for assessing the overall quality of a research study, a summary judgement on the care taken by a researcher to document and justify the many steps in the research process that produced the research report. A study judged trustworthy may not be perfect, but its findings are worthy of being taken seriously as science. What is most notable about trustworthiness as a standard for assessment is that it places scientific research squarely in a social context, recognizing the interdependence of researcher and readers as contextually embedded, sense-making actors.

These six methodological expectations discussed in the standards literature are present in various ways in research manuscripts. Writing is thickly descriptive (#1) and reflexive (#2), or not; but the primary way a reader knows if the other four have been engaged during the research process is if the researcher says so in or through the text (thereby demonstrating analytic-textual reflexivity, beyond field-site positional reflexivity). Methods statements can explicitly indicate whether triangulation (#3, planned in research design and carried out during fieldwork), an audit (#4, implemented during fieldwork and drawn on during deskwork and textwork), negative case analysis (#5, a deskwork-based analytic process), and member-checking (#6, part of textwork) were used; and those uses are manifested elsewhere in the manuscript as field data are presented and discussed. Attention to an epistemic community's expectations for procedural and manuscript characteristics throughout research, analysis, and writing processes will likely enhance the overall trustworthiness of a research text (and, hence, of the research itself) because the presence of these elements in the manuscript demonstrates the researcher's methodological awareness.

It is not our intent to suggest that these standards be used by readers evaluating a manuscript (or by writers producing one) in a checklist fashion. Aside from being too constricting, such usage would be inconsistent with interpretive presuppositions which privilege context; and so we emphasize that their readerly use for evaluative purposes needs to be appropriate to study purpose and content (as does their use in the research and writing). They provide research communities with a starting point for thought and dialogue about the quality of a particular study, where judgements themselves need to be historically contextualized and contingent.[10] Thinking about reviewer-readers' expectations may help researchers improve their writing by reminding them that these various dimensions contribute to readers' assessments of textual *and, hence, research* trustworthiness.

But whereas they inform the (trustworthy) character of a text, the six elements do not instruct on the specifics of what needs to be written to make a good ethnographic case. We turn now to that level of writing. Although we focus on organizational ethnography, the strategies we discuss are relevant to other forms of interpretive writing, as well.

writing strategies: enhancing textual trustworthiness

Knowing and understanding the expectations that reader-reviewers will likely bring to a manuscript is important to textwork, but such knowledge is insufficient: an ethnographer cannot simply declare, 'Trust my research!' Readers' trust must be earned over the course of the narrative: it is built up in myriad ways, as noted above, following the norms particular to epistemic communities. The writer's craft consists in knowing those norms and signalling that they have been met, sometimes in rather direct ways, as in the methods section of a research report, but, also, indirectly, by manifesting them in the narrative itself. In this section we deconstruct trustworthiness by reviewing the specific sorts of textual elements that contribute to its creation. The planning for several of these is commonly discussed in a research proposal, but they need to be re-engaged in the research narrative, and their presentation there is typically not treated in methods textbooks. Here, too, our intention is not to constrict the creativity of textwork by listing these items in a recipebook fashion, but instead to heighten authors' (and reviewers') awareness of what goes into producing trustworthy texts.

The presence or discussion of eight elements conveys clearly the ethnographic character of a text and contributes to persuading a reader not only of the trustworthiness of the text, but of the research itself and its truth claims: *access, place/space, time, exposure, researcher role, silences, data details*, and *data representation* (Yanow, 2009). The first six elements enact a key characteristic and strength of ethnography: that it is built on and acknowledges the material dimensions of life – the ways in which human experience is situated, time bound, embodied, and partial. The researcher moves through, in, and about the organization (or other setting) for a limited period of time, interacting with organizational members who themselves have bounded views and understandings of their own worlds. The final two elements engage the materiality of the research text, reflecting the central role of symbols and meaning-making in ethnographic writing. How (and whether) organizational members talk to each other, how they conceive of organizational identity, membership, and activities, and how all this is (re)presented by the ethnographer are at issue in an ethnographic study. Together, these eight elements demonstrate the ways in which an ethnographic study consists of more than a set of interviews, although 'interviewing' – often described more commonly as 'talk' than as formal interviewing[11] – can be a central method in organizational ethnography, along with participant-observation and document analysis. They also demonstrate the systematicity required of ethnographic research and writing, as well as the ways in which single setting studies constitute more than a single 'n' observation.

A. the material dimensions of organizational life: research design in the text

1   Organizations can be studied from the outside, but organizational ethnography rests on **access** to their 'insides', to the meaning-making of organizational members in particular settings and contexts, as these are manifested in relationships both 'outside' and 'inside' the organization: the formal organization of

hierarchies and position descriptions and relationships with the environment, as well as the water cooler conversations, corner offices, informal memos, and internal rituals that shape organizational identities and membership (see also Chapters 1, 7 and 8 in this volume). Readers want to know the details of initial access – permissions granted, limitations, personal contacts. A feature of organizational (and other forms of) ethnography is the extent to which initial access is sometimes built on the researcher's prior experience and knowledge. Researchers often select and enter their settings because they spent time there in years past or have family ties, linguistic or some other personal connection to the place or activity they are studying.

However, the proverbial 'foot in the door' is only part of what access entails, because entrée can vary within organizational spaces (for example, from one department or office to the next) and across its occupational specialties and hierarchies (see for example, Pachirat, 2009), as well as over time. There is a 'relational turn' in ethnographic methodology that recognizes that access is about establishing relationships (see Feldman, Bell, and Berger (2003) and Chapters 10 (Beech et al.) and 4 (Down and Hughes), this volume). But access also involves developing and maintaining these relationships. Readers want to know not only what measures were taken to gain access but also those that were taken to sustain it – those participatory efforts such as volunteering for assignments, treating others to coffee or beer, or even babysitting the kids – as well as when access was not obtained or was truncated, and why.

In research conducted from an interpretive methodological perspective, one of whose ontological and epistemological presuppositions is that 'objectivity' – the ability of the researcher to stand outside of the subject of study – is not conceptually possible (see Bernstein, 1983; Hawkesworth, 2006; Yanow, 2006), there is no reason to hide any of the details of gaining and maintaining access. Aside from that, efforts to hide the fact that a setting was chosen because the researcher had prior knowledge of organizational activities or knew people who could facilitate an entrée often leave narratives feeling 'thin' or 'inauthentic', thereby weakening the trustworthiness of the analysis. The more explicit and transparent the explication of initial and ongoing access, the more trustworthy the research is likely to be – or at least, the less it will appear as if the researcher is trying to deceive the reader. Keeping a daily record of methods choices – an audit – from the very beginning of the research project, in addition to substantive field notes, can provide detail indispensable to the textual demonstration produced later of the ethnographer's commitment to transparency.

2   Ethnographers' research settings are distinctive; and, thus, a central feature of ethnographic writing is its extensive description of the **place** or **space** in which the research was conducted, as well as its context – that is, not only what the inside of the organization looked like, but also how it is situated in its historical, national, 'industry', and/or neighbourhood 'space'. Ethnographers make choices concerning place or space: what kind of industry or organization, or which department within an organization, or what set of

organizations within an organizational field, is likely to provide the best setting for exploring the theoretical matter under investigation? What is the best kind of neighbourhood or community, region or state within which to address the research question? Which level of government, which agency, which section, which department? Sometimes choice of place is constrained by difficulties in obtaining access, and serendipity and coincidence may also enter the picture; but the presence in the written report of deliberations concerning the selection of settings, the rationales behind the choices made, and the circumstances of the serendipities can help to situate the analysis and, in some cases, demonstrate reflexivity about the tacit assumptions of the researcher's epistemic community (see notes 5, 10). Detailing how various organizational members enact boundaries ('inside' versus 'outside'), contents, and contexts can contribute to a thickly written text.

This thinking extends to the choice of persons for formal interviews and other talk. Here, 'space' may metaphorically mean the organizational level or the departmental location within the organization's structure or the political or communal role of the person being interviewed, although it can also refer to choices of interview settings. For example, is this person likely to be more comfortable talking with me if we meet away from her workplace or his regular 'hang-out'? Will I get different information if we meet in a club setting where I might also be eligible for membership (see for example, Wilkinson, 2008)? For documentary aspects of an ethnographic project, space would refer more to the location and choice of archives, newspaper morgues, and the like in terms of the availability of certain materials, access to particular files, and the lack of access to others. Detailing the rationale for the choices made can help a reader evaluate the trustworthiness of the subsequent analysis and can also demonstrate the researcher's efforts to triangulate the phenomenon of concern (whether by organizational location in the hierarchy and/or types of evidentiary sources).

3   Organizational ethnographers engage *time* in at least two aspects. First, length of time in the field is the most basic information expected by readers. Too often, however, researchers neglect to make clear what constitutes 'a day' in the field – was this 9 to 5, and then the researcher went home? Or did research continue after that at the corner bar, at dinner, at an evening party? Another neglected facet of time in the field is the 'periodicity' of observation – how often and with what regularity did the researcher interact with research participants? Knowledge claims based on ten days' immersion in the research field – say, one 8-hour day a week for 10 weeks (8 hours $\times$ 1 day $\times$ 10 weeks; i.e., 80 hours; 10 days) – is likely to be seen as less persuasive than claims based on daily encounters for the same time period (that is, 8 hours $\times$ 7 days $\times$ 10 weeks; i.e., 560 hours; 70 days), let alone for six months or a year (with whatever periodicity), but perhaps more persuasive than ten 4-hour days over the same period (4 hours $\times$ 1 day $\times$ 10 weeks; i.e., 40 hours; 10 'days').

Second, time needs also to be considered in terms of possible organizational rhythms. The 'DDT' of observation can be essential to such an understanding of organizational life: over what *Dates* (seasons) of year was the project conducted, which *Days* of the week, what *Times* of day? To see why these might be significant, imagine a field research project assessing decision-making processes in an organization whose normal work takes place during business hours on weekdays from September through July. Spending time on location in August, on weekends, or before or after customary work hours would likely produce different understandings than research conducted at other dates, other days, other times. Prior knowledge may make this point obvious to a researcher; yet what is obvious to 'insiders' may not be so to 'outsiders', so that recording DDT details (for example in an audit) can help the later crafting of a convincing methods narrative.

4   Attending to organizational rhythms can help a researcher tune into the timings of observations. Similarly, bringing time and space together – ***exposure*** – can reveal other aspects of organizational activity. Think of exposure to the sun: maximizing it depends not only on the time of day, but also on where one is standing (vis-à-vis shade) and located (vis-à-vis the equator). In research this can be achieved, metaphorically, by 'mapping' the organization or part of one: maximizing the coverage of research-relevant managerial, professional or other occupational bases; of perspectives within a single department; of departments in an organization or a horizontal slice or regional arm of one; or of both vertical and horizontal swathes through it. In these ways, exposure to the different 'territories' of an organization or its constituent parts can reveal their varying rhythms and lived experiences: CEOs whose daily actions are affected by stock market fluctuations, whereas front-line workers' acts reflect clients' changing, perhaps seasonal, demands; state university presidents marking time by legislative schedules, whereas professors and staff mark time by the comings and goings of students and grading deadlines over the course of the academic calendar; middle managers struggling to meet the expectations and needs of both superiors and subor-dinates. Exposure to various organizational spaces, literally and figuratively, and across time, typically leads to greater, and deeper, insights and under-standings than what can be achieved by 'parachute' ethnography.[12]

'Purposive exposure' or 'snowball exposure', or a combination of the two,[13] in designing interviews and conversations can lead to 'saturation' as one begins to hear the same information in response to substantive questions or the same names in response to the question, 'With whom else should I be speaking?' (but see the discussion of silences, below). Influenced by a phenomenological position that interpretation and ensuing action reflect situated, lived experi-ence and/or a hermeneutic position that interpretation and action reflect the unspoken, common sense, tacitly known 'rules' at work in various communities of meaning, ethnographic interviewing (Rubin and Rubin, 2005; Spradley, 1979) is commonly undertaken in ways that attempt to map the full terrain of the topic of research, as noted above, seeking to garner exposure to viewpoints around the spectrum of opinion, experience, expertise, and so forth. This exposure approach enacts the criterion of triangulation, a point that can be noted in the methods section of a research narrative.

5   As ethnographers move through their organizational sites, they should also consider various aspects of their *researcher role* – how they present who they are and what they are doing and, importantly, the extent to which they emphasize or downplay their role as researcher. Some of this may be determined by the conditions under which they gained access – that is, as a welcomed partial insider or as a reluctantly admitted stranger. Ethnography entails participant-observation, with researchers choosing to position themselves at one or another point along a continuum. At one end, the researcher participates and observes in the role of researcher alone. At the other end, the researcher participates out of a situation-specific role crafted for the research, all the while still observing others, as well as herself, in her researcher role. In organizational ethnography, a researcher may combine various points on this continuum over the life of the research project, sometimes becoming the complete researcher-observer when interviewing, e.g., the CEO, at other times turning to a more situational participant-researcher role.

In the latter case, the ethnographer observes himself, as well as others, in a constant awareness of his researcher role and research purposes (Gans, 1976). Van Maanen's work on the making of policemen (1978) is a case in point. Having trained in the police academy with new recruits, he then rode along with 'real' police officers. In a classic example of reflexivity, he writes of one occasion in which he was faced with having to choose whether to act out a police officer role (which, as a non-sworn, he could not legally do). In his researcher role, he reflects on his own responses in that situation, incorporating them into his interpretations of how a new officer constructs his police role.

This dual role is central to participation-focused ethnographic research.[14] The more readers know about a researcher's situational and research roles, the circumstances under which she chose or acquired or developed them, and any advantages or problems presented by a situational role (e.g., role conflict), the better able readers are to evaluate evidence and truth claims. Discussion of the researcher role is also a logical textual place to display the sort of positional reflexivity that is increasingly expected, e.g., the ways in which one's personal characteristics affected the extent to which organizational members marked one as suspicious or as a person to be trusted. For example, Lin (2000) describes how being a young, Asian-American woman affected the ways she was received by the men she sought to interview in prisons; Shehata (2006) relates how shop floor workers thought him a spy working for managers at the top of the hierarchy until other workers vouched for him.

6   The systematic process of mapping the materiality of the organization often attends most strongly to *presence* – that which more active or vocal research participants have accomplished or think. But organizational ethnographers need also to attend to *absence*, to *silences*, those positions and views that may have been silenced by others or are, perhaps, silent by choice. Snowball exposure, for example, builds on relational networks, and networks, by definition, are selective in whom they include. Furthermore, the active, vocal opposition may be more easily discoverable than the voice of those who have chosen a metaphoric 'exit'

(Hirschman, 1970) or who have been pressured or outright forced to be silent. 'Saturation' could be an opportunity to begin inquiry, focusing attention on what one might *not* be hearing. Researchers may have to exert effort to identify oppositional voices outside of such networks, and readers want to know that the researcher has thought about whether there might be silent, and silenced, voices and, if so, what efforts have been made to identify, include, and analyse them.[15]

Drawing attention to silences is a significant way to enact in the narrative a number of readers' evaluative criteria. It can reveal the reflexivity of the ethnographer, for reflection calls into play an introspective contemplation of whether one has been caught up, exclusively, in the voices of active organizational members.[16] It can be part of negative case analysis, demonstrating an awareness of the connections between observed patterns and the tenor, tone, and strength of particular voices, opening the door to reflective inquiry concerning other organizational actors who might be articulating views that 'negate' what one has been predominantly hearing. It can be part of triangulation across methods, when, for example, a particular voice is absent in observed or reported conversations, but revealed to be powerfully present in a public relations document.

Demonstrating in the text the ethnographer's attention to *place* and *space, access, time, exposure, researcher role*, and *silences* provides grounding for a number of the evaluative criteria discussed in the previous section: *thick descriptions* of settings, persons, events, and interactions; the awareness of where evidence came from that is useful for both *triangulation* and *negative case analysis*; a sensitivity to the complexity of the researcher role that is essential to *reflexivity*; the hierarchical or other location of organizational members for *member checking*; and the changes in research design – from initial access to the moment of exit from the field – that comprise an *audit*. Some of these – especially place/space and data details, as discussed below – contribute to thickly described texts; others – time and exposure – contribute to thickly done field research. Taken together in an overall gestalt, clear statements about whatever of these elements is relevant to the study provide essential context that readers need to assess a project's truth claims. The completeness and detail provided – its evident systematicity as well as the transparency with which this is done – will increase readers' confidence in the narrative and, hence, in the research reported. These elements are interactive and study-specific: a researcher reporting having based research on three years in the field, for instance, may not need to provide details on daily engagement – an example of the limitations of using these elements in a checklist fashion, rather than making research-specific judgements.

_____ *B. the materiality of the research narrative: the text itself* _____

These first six aspects of ethnographic research – entering a collective entity, moving through organizational space and organizational time aiming for exposure, and presenting the self to others whose lives are entwined with activities located specifically *there* – emphasize the materiality of ethnographic research into organizational life. Coexistent with this material experiential space is the material space of the research text – the words and symbols that are used, or not used, to make and (re)present meaning about organizational activities, identities, and values (on this, see also Van Maanen, 1995). The narrative crafted in textwork constitutes these sorts of organizational aspects for readers.

7   The **data details** provided in the narrative construct the thick description that has become one of the most discussed aspects of ethnographic writing. The textwork challenge here is to engage readers with the details *that matter*, and to do so in a way that presents complexity, ambiguity, and nuance without losing readers or trying their patience! (On detail run amok, see Wolcott, 1990.) The six elements discussed above contribute to 'thickly done' field research; recording them builds 'thickly written' field notes; and both of these can result in thickly described texts that help readers trust that the analyst was there and understands the organization under study. As noted in the earlier discussion, the point is to detail the context(s) of event, action, person, and so on such that a reader can follow the inferences drawn.

8   Presenting in two-dimensional narrative the variety of the 'stream of experience' that is everyday organizational life is challenging. Moreover, critics have recently argued that thick description is not well understood, implying that it is naively used (see Atkinson et al., 2003, 114). For these reasons and also to stimulate authorial and readerly imagination, organizational ethnographers would do well to consider the full range of forms of **presentation** of their descriptions and analyses – from the basic graphic layout of the manuscript page (margins, font sizes and enhancements, set-offs, 'negative' [blank] spaces, numbered or bulleted lists, etc.) to various kinds of visual presentations of data, such as charts, diagrams, maps, photographs and, with internet publishing, videos (as applicable; e.g., organizational charts depicting the hierarchical relationships of authority and responsibility; flow charts diagramming Standard Operating Procedures).[17] Researchers can reflect, in writing, on the limits presented by textual media for communicating understandings of their organizational tales. They might even ponder how triangulation in publishing could open new vistas for communication as the inter-textuality of global conversations (Weldes, 2006) increases with the spread of the internet. And, finally, further complicating the task of representation and meriting space in the research text are considerations of privacy, ethics and, increasingly, policy demands made by various national human subjects protection regimes in both the private and public sectors (Yanow and Schwartz-Shea, 2008).

member-checking redux: from a writer's perspective

Because member checking is a complex endeavour (as noted by, e.g., Emerson and Pollner, 2002; Miles and Huberman, 1994: 275–7) and because so little has been written about how a writer might contend with members' feedback, we return for a moment to that topic and engage it from a textual perspective. Doing so requires, first, a brief analysis of members' possible reactions to a draft text, as well as researchers' possible responses to those reactions.

The relational character of field research lies at the heart of these mutual reactions. The way(s) in which members react and the way(s) those reactions are engaged in the final text will depend, at least in part, on researchers' relationships with members in the field (including whether continued access is a significant issue), as well as on researchers' purposes for engaging in the research project. As Beech et al. (Chapter 10 in this volume) observe, the character of these relationships can change over the life cycle of a research project, and these changes themselves may lead to one sort of response or another, on either side of the relationship.

The intricacies of 'research friendships' can lead to participants accusing the researcher of a range of (mis)interpretations and intentions, from 'just' 'getting it wrong' to betrayal of trust, or worse. We wish to highlight, however, how epistemological and power differences might also contribute to members' reactions. Members' reactions to an ethnographic study might vary by their understandings of what 'research', in general, is about and/or their expectations for the particular research project or researcher (ranging, for instance, from anticipations concerning who might read the report to the degree of trust placed in the researcher). Their reactions might also vary according to members' own situational or societal power. For example, members of vulnerable groups might be less likely to protest, vocally, researcher representations, fearing reprisals, for instance, whereas more socially or organizationally powerful group members might use their resources to press for changes in the text (see for instance Mosse, 2005).

The research purposes that can potentially inform researchers' responses to member reactions can vary, from a commitment to 'giving voice' to a marginalized group (e.g., the homeless), as in some action research (see, for instance, Wang et al., 2000, and Sykes and Treleaven, Chapter 11, this volume), to presenting a group's distinctive worldview for policymaking purposes (e.g., medical students, as in Becker et al. 1977 [1961], or addicts, as in Burns, 1980), common in policy-analytic ethnographic research, to providing a critical, even potentially emancipatory, perspective on group meanings and practices, as in some feminist research (see Pierce, 1995, on litigation lawyers, and Kaufman, 1989, on religiously orthodox women). Each of these purposes can affect the ways in which researchers choose to treat members' reactions in the final text.

Whatever the mix of researcher purpose and the power and expectations of members of the organization under study, one possible result is seamless agreement: all members agree that the researcher adequately expressed their perspectives. Alternatively, and more likely, one or more members may protest some aspects of the researcher's representations. What should a researcher do with comments or protests he or she receives? At the most basic level, the researcher can consult her field notes and review her data, and if she discovers that she has, in point of fact, made a mistake, she can make the correction, acknowledging the member's assistance. But if, upon rechecking her notes, the researcher feels that her interpretation is still appropriate, how can this difference be engaged?

Researcher judgement about the credibility and significance of the replies can lead to quite different responses. While we are mindful that a considered judgement concerning the character and/or source of the objection might make ignoring a member's critical comments the most appropriate response in some circumstances, we do not recommend this as an automatic or constant course of action, at the very least because it implies a dismissal of members' interpretations that is inconsistent with the spirit of member checking. If not ignored, the member's comment might be placed in a footnote, discussed in an endnote, or treated in the main text. Engagements with the comment in these three instances can vary in length, according to the seriousness with which the researcher regards the critical view. Those comments judged significant by the researcher might be included in the research report and assessed against other quotations and other thickly descriptive elements. The differences in view between the researcher and the member could both be presented (much as differences among member views themselves might), along with reasons why the researcher's analysis should take precedence over that of the member (if that is, indeed, the case). In these ways, the researcher demonstrates to reviewers and other readers that she has taken members' interpretations seriously.

We note, however, that the discussion of member-checking on the whole presumes that those members are themselves honest, trustworthy, and well-intentioned and that their comments are offered in a void of politics and power (perhaps because the methodologists who developed this concept were, for the most part, studying people of equal or lesser power to themselves, rather than people in more powerful positions). Researchers need to exercise judgement about what they need to send back, and to whom.

writing and reading responsibilities

What are the responsibilities of each party to the writing–reading enterprise? On the surface the answer is simple. Writers owe readers their best efforts, and that implies, importantly, truthfulness about what they have done so that readers can assess the strengths and weaknesses of the evidence, methodology, and arguments presented without worrying about authorial deception. This holds for reviewer-readers as well: a reviewer owes a writer, at a minimum, serious assessments using criteria and standards appropriate to the manuscript's epistemic presuppositions. In our discussion here, we have assumed researcher honesty and integrity because we think the conduct of science rests, in the end, on trust; and that rests on truthfulness (with public support and funding for science resting on both). But we are not naive about the power dimensions of scientific practices. When writers and readers share the same epistemic community, communication in the review process and, with publication, among a wider public may be *relatively* smooth. Even in this scenario, however, deception is always a possibility. The career-related pressures on researchers to publish in A-list journals[18] are increasing, and this might lead some (whatever their research approach) to consider trying to mask what they have actually done – to craft a text that implies the use of a different method, for instance, or a greater immersion in and exposure to the field than was actually the case. But the thick character of ethnographic writing cannot easily be manufactured, and practiced reviewer-researchers will develop a sixth sense concerning the truthfulness of an account, based on their own experiences of conducting and writing up field research and the extensive reading of others' accounts. Indeed, a not-so-hidden agenda of thick description, as noted above, is to persuade a reader that one has truly been where one claims to have been, has talked to those one claims to have spoken with, done the things, seen the events, had the interactions one claims to have engaged, and so on – and such is not easy to fake.

Outright deception in the sciences at large, however, appears to be relatively rare. The widespread public attention garnered by violators of accepted scientific procedures – those accused, e.g., of falsifying lab notes or manipulating experiments[19] – can be contrasted with the vast majority of researchers who conduct their studies in good faith. (A perhaps more insidious problem, the potentially deceptive nature of state-sponsored or -generated data, has received much less attention; see, for instance, Sadiq, 2005.) The presumption of researcher honesty can be seen in a number of arenas. Professional ethics statements, such as that of the American Anthropological Association, and research regulation policies, such as Institutional Review Board (IRB) policies in the USA, are written primarily to regulate the acts of researchers who would intentionally abuse *participants*, not those who would intentionally deceive *colleagues*. Likewise, IRBs presume that researchers will submit to their procedures – there are (as yet) no penalties at the postgraduate level for a failure to do so – and they also presume that in the field or in the laboratory, researchers will conduct themselves in the ways described in their approved proposals.[20] Without a general presumption of researcher honesty and ethics, the research endeavour could become mired in a monitoring system that would likely stifle its vitality.

The more difficult cases of writer–reader misunderstanding occur because of the diversity of epistemic communities and the consequent variety of understandings of the purposes of research and researchers' relation to society. One of the most pointed areas of disagreement involves understandings of objectivity. Methodologically positivist, variables-oriented researchers are much more likely to assume that scholars can and should be 'objective' – a claim that positions science outside the fray of political concerns. In contrast, interpretive researchers are often more politically involved, observing that 'neutral' scientists may play the role of experts who serve the state or the corporation in value-laden ways (e.g., seamlessly producing 'better' products to serve society or 'better' policy to 'control' it; see, e.g., Salemink's (2003) discussion of the role of ethnographers in supporting the US military and federal policymakers with respect to the war in Vietnam, or the general 2007 discussion of anthropologists embedded in the US military in Afghanistan and Iraq). Rather than 'objectivity', researcher 'reflexivity' becomes the significant marker of scientific research.

It is not only researchers who should reflect on their positionality in the research process (in the field, at their desk, during the dissemination of reports). Reader-reviewers should be more aware of how the interpretive act of reading shapes judgements on the trustworthiness of a manuscript. It is not simply ontological, epistemological, and/or methodological differences *in the manuscript* that are at play (although the importance of these should not be underestimated, as the discussion above highlights), but also what readers bring with them to their readings in the form of prior knowledge and expectations, of whatever sort. The positionality of *the reader-reviewer* may contribute to the assessment of the research. In assessing the trustworthiness of a particular account, reader-reviewers are often exploring whether they can base subsequent actions on those representations – whether those actions are practice-related (Can I translate this account into improving, e.g., organizational practices?) or research-related (Can I build further research on this project?). This highlights the political character of research: if its truth claims are judged credible, the research may have implications for maintaining or changing the status quo, with all the life- and other resource-affecting implications of either path. Attention to the third hermeneutic brings reader positionality into focus, thereby bringing 'reading as method' into the methodological picture. Just as reflexivity about the role of the self in research and writing has increasingly become de rigueur in interpretive and some qualitative work, greater reflexivity about the role of the self in reading and reviewing could also be salutary for research communities.

The complexity of the third hermeneutic moment should be apparent. Social science communities are far from fully cognizant, explicitly, of this moment, although science studies and feminist theory scholars are making a dent in those silences. We are disheartened, however, by two recent turns that could stymie further developments. First, researchers in many fields conducting qualitative research of an interpretive presuppositional character are being increasingly pressured by those who have embraced narrow understandings of science to conform to the characteristics of and criteria for positivist-informed quantitative research (e.g., King, Keohane and Verba, 1994; Pfeffer, 1993). In some disciplines and/or countries in which interpretive research has been a longstanding tradition, researchers have found themselves 'under siege' (e.g., Freeman et al., 2007: 25) from those who would mandate a unitary conception of natural and social science along the lines of positivist presuppositions, a position which threatens the existence of ethnographic research.

Second, some scholars (for example, Sutton, 1997) would advise qualitative researchers to hide what they are doing or downplay the role of their qualitative evidence in producing research findings. We hope that Sutton's advice, as another form of conformity, is outdated; we find it to be unenlightened, at best, and seriously misguided, at worst. It is unenlightened in that qualitative methods of an interpretive sort have long been a part of the organizational studies world and methodologists have worked to articulate and promote the standards and criteria that are appropriate for evaluating such manuscripts and the research they present. This work supports an argument that 'validity' and 'reliability' are no longer universally applicable for such research. The advice is misguided because interpretive researchers have moved far beyond defensive modes to exploring new methodological terrain that re-positions that research firmly within the canons of science (see, e.g., Prasad, 2005; Yanow and Schwartz-Shea, 2006). By granting legitimacy only to positivist-informed research, those who would follow such advice would deny the historical standing and significance of the contributions of qualitative-interpretive science. Moreover, a qualitative-interpretive science that tries to conceal the character of its evidence can only be a weak version of quantitative-positivist work (and vice versa): the presuppositions informing the conduct of each are simply too different for such a masquerade to be successful. From this perspective we might just as well give up the interpretive and ethnographic projects altogether.

Given this complex writer–reader terrain, the old adage directed at writers – 'Know your audience!' – is still relevant, but insufficient, advice. Because organizational studies and other cross-disciplinary fields mix epistemic communities, and communication across sub-field boundaries is often necessary and desirable, such 'knowing' is neither easy nor simple. Rather than conforming to outside pressures to adopt positivist criteria or disguising what they do, interpretive researchers should join in a proactive effort to educate members of other epistemic communities – journal editors and reviewers, as well as colleagues – in the methodological requirements, including evaluative criteria, of qualitative-interpretive research. That is one goal of this chapter – to articulate the once tacit criteria of these research communities so that the standards may be more effectively written into ethnographic texts, thereby supporting the standing of ethnography as science.

acknowledgements

We thank Lee Ann Fujii, Merlijn van Hulst, Frans Kamsteeg, Lorraine Nencel, Tim Pachirat, and Harry Wels for thoughtful comments on earlier versions of this chapter.

[1] Researchers – especially those just starting out – are often advised to share their draft manuscripts with a handful of colleagues to get feedback before submitting them to journals. Here, we have these 'informal' reviewers in mind as much as journal reviewers.

[2] Although this discussion raises issues concerning the power of rhetoric to persuade, including, at times, the possibility of producing a convincing, yet counterfeit, account (see note 19), for reasons of space, we cannot give this the full attention it deserves. On writing as method, see Richardson, 1994. On writing in ethnography, see Clifford and Marcus, 1986; Geertz, 1988; Golden-Biddle and Locke, 1993; Hammersley, 1990; Marcus and Fisher, 1999; Van Maanen, 1988.

[3] In contrast to most of the criteria literature, Schwartz-Shea (2006) proceeded inductively, starting with methods texts and the textual practices of interpretive researchers, to yield this historically contingent set of standards for evaluating the quality of particular research projects at this point in time. Turning from an *a priori*, theoretical, top-down enumeration of criteria to an inductive approach based in researcher practices has two advantages. It demonstrates a common methodological – presuppositional – grounding across all those research undertakings that share a constructivist ontology and interpretive epistemology, a commonality masked by the cacophony that characterizes the criteria literature. More importantly, a temporally-contingent set of standards allows for their evolution as research questions and approaches change in response to changing societal conditions. As Smith and Deemer (2003) argue, a definitive list of criteria – a universal, unchanging taxonomy – is inconsistent with interpretive presuppositions that all research efforts are historically contingent. This contextualized, historical flexibility is what an inductive, practice-based approach to standards affords.

[4] A sharp reader may find the ghosts of realism haunting some of these terms. That is not surprising given the hegemony of variables-based research against which the discussion of 'alternative' criteria has developed. For the purposes of this discussion, we have chosen to retain the categories from that literature, rather than to include a critique of their lingering realism by offering new terms, in order to capture aspects of the debate as it is presently constituted and unfolding and also because those terms help us better to theorize the research process and suggest replies to common criticisms of both qualitative and interpretive research.

[5] Counter to some common misperceptions, such accounts need not be 'navel-gazing', tell-all revelations. Moreover, reflexivity seems to be increasingly expected even of those ethnographic projects that are realist, rather than interpretive, in their ontological and epistemological presuppositions. This contributes to different understandings of what reflexivity entails, potentially introducing a tension between realist researchers' methodological positions and readers' more interpretive evaluative criteria. The point warrants further discussion that we are unable to take up here for reasons of space.

At another level of analysis, reflexivity asks researchers to reflect on the ways in which their research communities are historically constituted such that particular socio-political contexts shape, in unarticulated ways, the research questions asked or the very concepts used to investigate phenomenon (for trenchant examples, see Oren, 2006 and Lynch, 2006, as well as Chapters 11 (Sykes and Treleaven) and 12 (Ghorashi and Wels) in this volume). Such assumptions might fruitfully be brought to light in research narratives (see note 10).

[6] The term has its origins in the use of trigonometry for the purpose of surveying, whether on land or at sea. In this usage, it is a method for locating an unknown point by using two known points at the vertices of a triangle. It is notable as one of the few techniques endorsed by both positivist and interpretive social science methodologists. Within variables-oriented methods, it has the status of a supplementary technique, commonly referring to the use of multiple indicators in operationalizing a complex concept (Neuman, 1997), although it also increasingly refers simply to the use of different methods for accessing and generating data in the same study (Jones and Olson, 1996).

[7] Triangulation may remind some of 'multi-method research', referring commonly to the combination of quantitative and qualitative research methods (see for example the new *Journal of Mixed Methods Research*, Volume 1, 2007). Our own take on this is that using multiple methods is fine, and, indeed, interpretive research has long drawn on multiple types and sources of evidence. But multiple methodologies or paradigms in a single research project (for an example, see Papa et al., 1995), with their contradictory ontological and/or epistemological premises, re-cast the research such that it is no longer engaging the same research question, even when the various approaches may be poking at a similar topic or concern (see also Jackson, 2008, on this). For this reason we do not include here multiple theories as a kind of triangulation.

[8] Methodologists have used various terms for techniques intended to accomplish the same goal. For example, Miles and Huberman (1994: 262) refer to this idea as 'checking the meaning of outliers', 'using extreme cases', 'following up surprises', 'ruling out spurious relations', and 'checking out rival explanations'. Becker (1998: 192–4) discusses 'deviant cases'. Erlandson et al. (1993) and others use 'member checking' to mean much the same thing, whereas Lincoln and Guba (1985) also add 'peer debriefing' – having a colleague in the same research field critique one's preliminary analysis. Brower et al. (2000: 391) include 'weighing competing interpretations' and 'recognizing and examining competing views or voices' as ways of meeting the criterion they call 'criticality' (different from what Golden-Biddle and Locke (1993) meant by the same term).

[9] Looking at organizational ethnography, Golden-Biddle and Locke (1993) argued for three evaluative criteria: *authenticity*, *plausibility*, and *criticality*, the first two of which are requisite, in their view, for convincing readers of ethnographic texts. We suggest that those three are, in a sense, 'meta-goals', similar in status to *trustworthiness*.

[10] Such a 'dialogical' conception of social science is important for understanding how some research may be disregarded by its contemporaries and then seem particularly prescient to readers of a later era. For an example, see Brandwein's (2006) discussion of the reception of Crosskey's legal analysis of the history of the Fourteenth Amendment to the US Constitution. Similarly, Keller (1983) discusses how cytogeneticist Barbara McClintock's work, later deemed path-breaking, was ignored by her male contemporaries. As feminist philosophers of science have shown, who is part of the dialogue is critical to what 'counts' as knowledge.

[11] Anthropologists have always talked at length to people in the field – about kinship, tools, language, etc. – rarely, if ever, calling it 'interviewing'. The need to designate such talk with that word seems to have been driven by other social scientists working at the survey end of the 'talk' continuum who needed, or felt they needed, to locate what they were doing more firmly in 'scientific' space. In organizational ethnography, the decision-makers we sometimes want to talk to are often sitting in their offices rather than hanging out on street corners or in pool halls, which means we have to set up appointments to meet them. Hence, these talks become designated 'interviews'. Thanks to Merlijn van Hulst for helping to clarify this formulation of the point. Organizational anthropologist Malcolm Chapman (2001: 23) includes a humorous, but nonetheless illustrative, story about the distinction, drawing on his experience conducting a field research project jointly with a survey researcher: 'I think my colleague at the time viewed [the unstructured interview that characterized their research] as a subset of "interviews"; I regarded it as a subset of "talking to people"'.

[12] Paul Bate (1997) writes, critically, about business ethnographers who 'fly in' and 'fly out' of their research sites. We share this critique of a recent development in the world of 'applied' ethnography – the so-called 'quick ethnography' argued as suitable for studying organizational settings (businesses, schools, government agencies), public policy processes, and the like (see, for example, Handwerker, 2001). In our view, such analyses can miss the kinds of insights that are key to grasping from their perspectives why organizations and their members do what they do – insights that can often be developed only through dwelling in a place more intensively and 'deeply', over a longer period of time.

[13] Despite the ubiquity of the terms purposive and snowball 'sampling' in qualitative-interpretive research, we prefer the concept of 'exposure' to 'sampling'. The argument that ethnographic methods do not constitute 'sampling' is based on the term's close association with statistical science, where it is used to approximate the characteristics of the population under study. What interpretive research does is not sampling, in the sense that researchers make no claim for statistically scientific approximation, and the term's usage in an interpretive context glosses this distinction, as well as the ways in which 'representativeness' means different things in these different contexts. Moreover, the notion of 'sampling' implies a research design in which the researcher is 'outside' of the context and thus able to control the selection of information to be studied. Aside from the initial choice of location, ethnographic researchers' ability to 'sample' in this way is limited. The concept of exposure better reflects the epistemological assumptions of openness that are part of ethnographic research design.

[14] Humphreys (2005) and other auto-ethnographers position themselves at the end of the continuum where the researcher is the situational participant, raising other sorts of concerns that we cannot engage with here.

[15] Which is not to say that this is always possible, but at least one ought to put some thought and effort into it.

[16] This is part, at least, of what ethnographic methodologists intended by the phrase 'going native'. We think there is more to it, and we also think that the phrase itself is erroneous and misleading, predicated on some earlier, colonial-era understandings of the relationship between researcher and researched; but we do not have the space here to expound on this further.

[17] Within anthropology, visual ethnography has a longstanding history, dating back to the work of Margaret Mead and, later, Timothy Ash. Within organizational studies, its range has been much more limited (see for example Dougherty and Kunda (1992) on the use of photographs as data). On the visual (re)presentation of data, see Tufte (1997).

[18] We think these pressures are more pronounced in the UK and Europe these days, where departmental funding and even existence are more tied to quantified publication output measures, than they ever have been in the USA. We are also mindful of Sokal's (1996) hoax, in which he carefully adopted a 'post-modern' writing style and successfully achieved publication – in a hoax that allowed him to make a point about that kind of writing; but hoaxes are only successful when the deception is, in the end, unmasked.

[19] Researcher dishonesty typically draws widespread public attention in both print and audio-visual news media and even in fictionalized novels (see, e.g., the coverage of the accusations of data falsification in Whitehead Institute Director David Baltimore's lab, discussed, e.g., in Kevles, 1998; see also Goodman, 2006; LaFollette, 1992). We know of no such violations in organizational studies research.

[20] We thank Michael Musheno (seminar comment, 10 September 2007) for drawing our attention to this point. Whether this presumption will continue is uncertain. One of us heard an IRB administrator discuss the possibility of post hoc random sampling of completed projects to assess their compliance with IRB-approved research designs. We should also note that US graduate students may be denied their degrees if it is discovered that they have failed to submit their proposals for research involving human participants to their university IRB. For further discussion see Yanow and Schwartz-Shea (2007).

references

Atkinson, P., Coffey, A. and Delamont, S. (2003) *Key themes in qualitative research: Continuities and change.* Walnut Creek, CA: AltaMira Press.

Bate, S.P. (1997) 'Whatever happened to organizational anthropology? A review of the field of organizational ethnography and anthropological studies', *Human Relations*, 50: 1147–75.

Becker, H.S. (1998) *Tricks of the trade: How to think about your research while you're doing it*. Chicago: University of Chicago Press.

Becker, H.S., Geer, B., Hughes, E.C. and Strauss, A.L. (1977) [1961] *Boys in white: Student culture in medical school*. New Brunswick, NJ: Transaction Publishers.

Bernstein, R.J. (1983) *Beyond objectivism and relativism*. Philadelphia: University of Pennsylvania Press.

Brandwein, P. (2006) 'Studying the careers of knowledge claims: Applying science studies to legal studies', in D. Yanow and P. Schwartz-Shea (eds), *Interpretation and method: Empirical research methods and the interpretive turn*. Armonk, NY: M.E. Sharpe. pp. 228–43.

Brower, R.S., Abolafia, M.Y. and Carr, J.B. (2000) 'On improving qualitative methods in public administration research', *Administration and Society*, 32: 363–97.

Burawoy, M. (2004) For public sociology. Presidential address, American Sociological Association, San Francisco (15 August). Available at https://webfiles.berkeley.edu/~burawoy/PS.htm (accessed 27 December 2007).

Burns, T.F. (1980) 'Getting rowdy with the boys', *Journal of Drug Issues*, 80: 273–86.

Chapman, M. (2001) 'Social anthropology and business studies: Some considerations of method', in D.N. Gellner and E. Hirsch (eds), *Inside organizations: Anthropologists at work*. Oxford: Berg. pp. 19–33.

Clifford, J. (1988) *The predicament of culture*. Cambridge, MA: Harvard University Press.

Clifford, J. and Marcus, G.E. (eds) (1986) *Writing culture: The poetics and politics of ethnography*. Berkeley: University of California Press.

Darnton, R. (1984) *The great cat massacre and other episodes in French cultural history*. New York: Basic Books.

Darnton, R. (2003) *George Washington's false teeth: An unconventional guide to the eighteenth century*. New York: W.W. Norton.

Dougherty, D. and Kunda, G. (1992) 'Photograph analysis: A method to capture organizational belief systems', in P. Gagliardi (ed.), *Symbols and artifacts: Views of the corporate landscape*. New York: Aldine de Gruyter. pp. 185–206.

Emerson, R.M. and Pollner, M. (2002) 'Difference and dialogue: Members' readings of ethnographic texts', in D. Weinberg (ed.), *Qualitative research methods*. Malden, MA: Blackwell Readers in Sociology. pp. 154–70.

Erlandson, D.A., Harris, E.L., Skipper, B.L. and Allen, S.D. (1993) 'Quality criteria for a naturalistic study', in *Doing naturalistic inquiry*. Newbury Park, CA: Sage. pp.131–62.

Feldman, M.S., Bell, J. and Berger, M.T. (2003) *Gaining access*. Walnut Creek, CA: Altamira.

Freeman, M., deMarrais, K., Preissle, J., Roulston, K. and St. Pierre, E.A. (2007) 'Standards of evidence in qualitative research: An incitement to discourse', *Educational Researcher*, 35(1): 25–32.

Gans, H. (1976) 'Personal journal: B. On the methods used in this study', in M. Patricia Golden (ed.), *The research experience*. Itasca, IL: F.E. Peacock. pp. 49–59.

Geertz, C. (1973) *The interpretation of cultures*. New York: Basic Books.

Geertz, C. (1988) *Works and lives: The anthropologist as author*. Stanford: Stanford University Press.

Giddens, A. (1984) *The constitution of society*. Berkeley: University of California Press.

Golden-Biddle, K. and Locke, K. (1993) 'Appealing work: An investigation in how ethnographic texts convince', *Organization Science*, 4: 595–616.

Golden-Biddle, K. and Locke, K. (1997) *Composing qualitative research*. Thousand Oaks, CA: Sage.

Goodman, A. (2006) *Intuition*. New York: Dial Press.

Greenwood, D. and Levin, M. (1998) *Introduction to action research: Social research for social change*. Thousand Oaks, CA: Sage.

Hammersley, M. (1990) *Reading ethnographic research*. London: Longman.

Hammersley, M. and Atkinson, P. (1993) *Ethnography: Principles in practice*. London: Tavistock.

Handwerker, W.P. (2001) *Quick ethnography: A guide to rapid multi-method research*. Walnut Creek, CA: AltaMira Press.

Hannerz, U. (2003) 'Being there ... and there ... and there! Reflections on multi-site ethnography', *Ethnography*, 4: 201–16.

Haraway, D. (1988) 'Situated knowledges: The science question in feminism and the privilege of the partial perspective', *Feminist Studies*, 14: 575–99.

Harding, S. (1993) 'Rethinking standpoint epistemology: What is "strong objectivity"?', in L. Alcoff and E. Potter (eds), *Feminist Epistemologies*. New York: Routledge. pp. 49–82.

Hawkesworth, Mary E. (2006) *Feminist inquiry: From political conviction to methodological innovation*. New Brunswick: Rutgers University Press.

Hirschman, A.O. (1970) *Exit, voice, and loyalty*. Cambridge, MA: Harvard University Press.

Humphreys, M. (2005) 'Getting personal: Reflexivity and autoethnographic vignettes', *Qualitative Inquiry*, 11: 840–60.

Iser, W. (1989) *Prospecting: From reader response to literary anthropology*. Baltimore: Johns Hopkins University Press.

Jackson, P.T. (2006) 'Making sense of making sense: Configurational analysis and the double hermeneutic', in D. Yanow and P. Schwartz-Shea (eds), *Interpretation and method: Empirical research methods and the interpretive turn*. Armonk, NY: M.E. Sharpe. pp. 264–80.

Jackson, P.T. (2008) 'Foregrounding ontology: Dualism, monism, and IR theory', *Review of International Studies*, 34: 129–53.

Jones, L.F. and Olson, E.C. (1996) *Political science research: A handbook of scope and method*. New York: Addison Wesley Longman.

Kaufman, D.R. (1989) 'Patriarchal women: A case study of newly orthodox Jewish women', *Symbolic Interaction*, 12: 299–314.

Keller, E.F. (1983) *A feeling for the organism: The life and work of Barbara McClintock*. San Francisco, CA: Freeman.

Kevles, D.J. (1998) *The Baltimore case: A trial of politics, science, and character*. New York: W.W. Norton.

King, G., Keohane, R.O. and Verba, S. (1994) *Designing social inquiry: Scientific inference in qualitative research*. Princeton: Princeton University Press.

LaFollette, M.C. (1992) *Stealing into print: Fraud, plagiarism, and misconduct in scientific publishing*. Berkeley: University of California Press.

Lamphere, L. (2003) 'Perils and prospects for an engaged anthropology: A view from the U.S. Plenary address at the meetings of the 2002 European Association of Social Anthropology (Copenhagen)', *Social Anthropology*, 11(2): 143–51.

Lather, P. (1993) 'Fertile obsession: Validity after poststructuralism', *Sociological Quarterly*, 34: 673–93.

Law, J. (2004) *After method: Mess in social science research*. London: Routledge.

Lin, A.C. (2000) *Reform in the making: The implementation of social policy in prison*. Princeton: Princeton University Press.

Lincoln, Y.S. (1995) 'Emerging criteria for quality in qualitative and interpretive research', *Qualitative Inquiry*, 1: 275–89.

Lincoln, Y.S. and Guba, E.G. (1985) 'Establishing trustworthiness', in *Naturalistic inquiry*. Thousand Oaks, CA: Sage. pp. 289–331.

Lynch, C. (2006) 'Critical interpretation and interwar peace movements: Challenging dominant narratives', in D. Yanow and P. Schwartz-Shea (eds), *Interpretation and method: Empirical research methods and the interpretive turn*. Armonk, NY: M.E. Sharpe. pp. 291–99.

Marcus, G. (1995) 'Ethnography in/of the world system: The emergence of multi-sited ethnography', *Annual Review of Anthropology*, 24: 95–117.

Marcus, G.E. and Fischer, M.M.J. (1999) *Anthropology as cultural critique: An experimental moment in the human sciences.* Chicago: University of Chicago Press.

Mathison, S. (1988) 'Why triangulate?', *Educational Researcher*, 17: 13–17.

Miles, M.B. and Huberman, A.M. (1994) *Qualitative data analysis: An expanded sourcebook.* Beverly Hills, CA: Sage.

Monroe, K.R. (ed.) (2005) *Perestroika! The raucous rebellion in political science.* New Haven: Yale University Press.

Mosse, D. (2005) *Cultivating development: An ethnography of aid policy and practice.* London: Pluto Press.

Neuman, W.L. (1997) *Social research methods: Qualitative and quantitative approaches* (2nd edn). Needham Heights, MA: Allyn and Bacon.

Oren, I. (2006) 'Political science as history: A reflexive approach', in D. Yanow and P. Schwartz-Shea (eds), *Interpretation and method: Empirical research methods and the interpretive turn.* Armonk, NY: M.E. Sharpe. pp. 215–27.

Pachirat, T. (2009, forthcoming) 'The *political* in political ethnography: Reflections from an industrialized slaughterhouse on perspective, power, and sight', in E. Schatz (ed.), *Political ethnography: What immersion contributes to the study of politics.* Chicago: University of Chicago Press.

Papa, M.J., Auwal, M.A. and Singhal, A. (1995) 'Dialectic of control and emancipation in organizing for social change: A multi-theoretical study of the Grameen Bank in Bangladesh', *Communication Theory*, 5: 189–223.

Pierce, J. (1995) 'Appendix', in J. Pierce (ed.) *Gender trials: Emotional lives in contemporary law firms.* Berkeley: University of California Press.

Pfeffer, J. (1993) 'Barriers to the advance of organizational science: Paradigm development as a dependent variable', *Academy of Management Review*, 18: 599–620.

Prasad, P. (2005) *Crafting qualitative research: Working in the postpositivist traditions.* Armonk, NY: M.E. Sharpe.

Richardson, L. (1994) 'Writing: A method of inquiry', in N.K. Denzin and Y.S. Lincoln (eds), *Handbook of Qualitative Research.* Thousand Oaks, CA: Sage. pp. 516–29.

Rubin, I.S. and Rubin, H.J. (2005) *Qualitative interviewing: The art of hearing data.* Thousand Oaks, CA: Sage.

Sadiq, K. (2005) 'Lost in translation: The challenges of state-generated data in developing countries', in K.R. Monroe (ed.), *Perestroika! The raucous rebellion in political science.* New Haven: Yale University Press. pp. 181–99.

Salemink, O. (2003) 'Ethnography, anthropology and colonial discourse', in O. Salemink (ed.) *The ethnography of Vietnam's Central Highlanders: A historical contextualization, 1850–1990.* London: RoutledgeCurzon/Honolulu: University of Hawai'i Press.

Schwartz-Shea, P. (2006) 'Judging quality: Evaluative criteria and epistemic communities', in D. Yanow and P. Schwartz-Shea (eds), *Interpretation and method: Empirical research methods and the interpretive turn.* Armonk, NY: M.E. Sharpe. pp. 89–113.

Shehata, S. (2006) 'Ethnography, identity, and the production of knowledge', in D. Yanow and P. Schwartz-Shea (eds), *Interpretation and method: Empirical research methods and the interpretive turn.* Armonk, New York: M.E. Sharpe. pp. 244–63.

Smith, J.K. and Deemer, D.K. (2003) 'The problem of criteria in the age of relativism', in N.K. Denzin and Y.S. Lincoln (eds), *Collecting and interpreting qualitative materials* (2nd edn). Thousand Oaks, CA: Sage. pp. 427–57.

Sokal, A. (1996) 'A physicist experiments with cultural studies', *Lingua Franca*: 62–4.

Spradley, J.P. (1979) *The ethnographic interview.* New York: Holt, Rinehart and Winston.

Sutton, R.I. (1997) 'The virtues of closet qualitative research', *Organization Science*, 8: 97–106.

Tufte, E.R. (1997) *Visual explanations: Images and quantities, evidence and narrative.* Cheshire, CT: Graphics Press.

Van Maanen, J. (1978) 'Observations on the making of a policeman', *Human Organization*, 32: 407–18.

Van Maanen, J. (1988) *Tales of the field*. Chicago: University of Chicago Press.

Van Maanen, J. (1995) 'Style as theory', *Organization Science*, 6: 133–43.

Van Maanen, J. (1996) 'Commentary: On the matter of voice', *Journal of Management Inquiry*, 5: 375–81.

Wang, C.C., Cash, J.L. and Power, L.S. (2000) 'Who knows the streets as well as the homeless? Promoting personal and community action through photovoice', *Health Promotion Practice*, 1: 81–9.

Weldes, J. (2006) 'High politics and low data: Globalization discourses and popular culture', in D. Yanow and P. Schwartz-Shea (eds), *Interpretation and method: Empirical research methods and the interpretive turn*. Armonk, NY: M.E. Sharpe. pp. 176–86.

Wilkinson, C. (2008) 'Positioning "security" and securing one's position: The researcher's role in investigating "security" in Kyrgyzstan', in C.R.L. Wall and P.P. Mollinga (eds), *Fieldwork in difficult environments: Methodology as boundary work in development research*. Berlin: Lit Verlag. pp. 43–67.

Wolcott, H.F. (1990) 'Making a study "more ethnographic"', *Journal of Contemporary Ethnography*, 19(1): 44–72.

Yanow, D. (2000) *Conducting interpretive policy analysis*. Newbury Park, CA: Sage.

Yanow, D. (2006) 'Neither rigorous nor objective? Interrogating criteria for knowledge claims in interpretive science', in D. Yanow and P. Schwartz-Shea (eds), *Interpretation and method: Empirical research methods and the interpretive turn*. Armonk, NY: M.E. Sharpe. pp. 67–88.

Yanow, D. (2009) 'Dear author, dear reader: The third hermeneutic in writing and reviewing ethnography', in E. Schatz (ed.), *Political ethnography: What immersion brings to the study of power*. Chicago: University of Chicago Press.

Yanow, D. and Schwartz-Shea, P. (eds) (2006) *Interpretation and method: Empirical research methods and the interpretive turn*. Armonk, NY: M.E. Sharpe.

Yanow, D. and Schwartz-Shea, P. (2008) 'Reforming institutional review board policy: Issues in implementation and field research', *PS: Political Science & Politics*, 41: 483–94.

4

When the 'subject' and the 'researcher' speak together: Co-producing organizational ethnography

Simon Down and Michael Hughes

Some people who write books, I've read their stories where they build things up that's not there. (Ralph Kotay, a 'Kiowa elder and singer', quoted in Lassiter, 2001: 137)

A good many backs are no doubt patted at ethnography conferences congratulating researchers for giving voice to invisible constituencies – the marginal, unknown, suppressed, and ignored – or to the familiar made strange. We are keen to write for others who can't or won't tell their own stories, or whose stories we wish to tell differently. Generally, however, the formats in which we tell our stories allow for or demand a strong authorial voice: our own as researchers and the meta-voice of scientific analysis and scientific publishing conventions. The purpose of this chapter is to explore what difference it makes when ethnographic 'subjects' speak for themselves. The point is to suggest that our current analytical and theoretical preoccupations and presentational formats are not doing justice to how it feels to live and work in organizations: To agree that we need to engage in more co-production of knowledge alongside our respondents, where our scientific translation devices do not lead us to devalue the moral ideal and power of authentic experience.

What follows is an account of a manager coming to terms with organizational change. It's unusual in that this is an account by what academic ethnographers normally term a 'subject' that has been 'co-produced' by him and myself. The second author, Michael Hughes, works at a coke-making plant in a large steel works located near Sydney, Australia. Michael, as he himself will soon tell you, is becoming a manager. As a lecturer at a nearby university, the first author, Simon Down, was at the plant conducting research into organizational cultural change and self-identity. In this co-produced chapter, I, Simon, am functioning as the 'author in charge', and so, with the exception of 'Michael's story' below, I appear in the first person while speaking of Michael, my co-author, in the third person. Michael's story has been 'fully' co-produced; he has also had editorial inputs into the chapter as a whole. Any piece of jointly authored academic writing will have a mixture of co-produced and singly authored content; this chapter is no different: co-production does not require or specify equality or the proportionality of inputs. Moreover, the chapter is intended to illustrate the potential benefits of researcher/respondent co-production, not necessarily to act as an exemplar or prescribe a detailed recipe for how it might be done.

We (the two authors) jointly produced a piece of writing to convey something of the experience of going through a corporate cultural change programme from the perspective of a 'member' of the organization, in a particular position within it, and not just from the perspective of the ethnographic researcher. That paper, 'Michael's story', was originally co-presented at an academic conference in 2003 (Down and Hughes, 2003). Here, I wish to reflect on that piece, included below, and explore the implications of ethnographers' 'letting' the people we research speak for themselves: to explore the dynamic of engaging as a researcher with a member of the organization being researched, when that person is given voice on the printed page and 'allowed' to claim his or her own space. The effect is not an especially analytical or even a polemical one. The reader will not find much theorizing or romantic championing of the workers' (or managers') 'voice'. Rather, I am interested in provoking a contemplation of the effect that this giving space over has on the ethnographic researcher and the sorts of tales academics tell on the printed page. The result is predominantly focused on exploring what we understand by the 'authenticity' of accounts and how co-authorship and co-production of texts force ethnographers to scrutinize their own understandings and representations of lived experience.

Michael's reflections on his becoming a manager speak of how the steel works deepened the use of self-managing teams via a process of subcontracting-out certain operational activities. He tells of how he helped change existing work arrangements, worker designations and the authority relationship. Unlike most academic narratives Michael gives voice to emotional and moral value statements, which he attaches to his descriptions of these events. His story is not examined for hidden meanings. He has helped make the organizational changes at the plant, and they have had a profound impact on his life: they matter to him personally. In my role as a researcher, I got to know Michael well, as he was a key respondent in the project. Well enough for us to attend an academic conference together with other project colleagues, for him and his partner to visit my home in the UK, and for us to continue to be in regular contact.

The project upon which our collaboration is based derives from a year-long research involvement with the Utilities department of the plant, in 2002–2003. The coke-making plant is a separate business unit of a large corporate steel producer. My involvement in Utilities comprised on average one day per week over that year, interviewing, observing meetings and work, attending training events, playing cards in meal breaks, attending social events, and generally hanging around talking and getting to know the people and their work. The project was part of a series of studies at the coke-making plant which have taken place over a six year period and were funded by the Australian Research Council (see Badham et al., 2003; Badham, McLoughlin and Garrety, 2003; Badham and Garrety, 2004; Garrety et al., 2003). The Utilities project was funded via a separate grant from the University of Wollongong and sought to investigate self-identity, normative control and organizational change. I wore the same blue industrial clothes and the same silver plastic protection helmet as Utilities staff did. Though I was substantively focused on organizational change and self-identity, the most significant aspect of the project for me as a writer has centred on the methodological: specifically the emergence of collaborative relationships with respondents, which I explore here and, as I have discussed elsewhere, the emotionally challenging nature of the research (Down et al., 2006).

There are two interrelated dimensions to my research engagement with Michael's story that I discuss in this chapter. The first and most important relates to authenticity; the second, to the co-produced autobiographical format as a form of academic representation. Our collaboration – between subject and researcher – raises questions about how best to present the experiences of subjects. What or whose purpose might a collaborative representation of organizational change serve? What is an authentic account? Does authenticity matter and, if so, why? Can someone else's experience be translated onto the academic page? Is Michael's narrative really his, mine, ours, or yours? Who decides? Who has authority and power in the relationship? Of course, not all these rhetorical questions are resolved, let alone answered, but they variously point to a questioning of the authority and certitude with which academic accounts generally claim to represent research subjects. Being authentic is situated, and it is partly a product of one's ability to convince others, as is the production of good ethnography (Golden-Biddle and Locke, 1993). Being the 'author in charge', I, Simon Down, have more opportunity to do this than Michael does, in the normal run of events. Michael's narrative implicitly challenges the authority of researchers to speak for subjects. This problem of what to do 'when the ethnographic subject speaks back' (Behar, 1993; Prasad, 1998) forces organizational researchers to think about why they write what they write. As Prasad writes of Behar's book about Esperanza (the Mexican woman of her ethnographic tale), 'she speaks back by thwarting and resisting Behar's intellectual attempts at placing her within a preconceived theoretical space' (1998: 33). The co-production of Michael's account has had a similar impact on me and my own sense of authority as an academic.

The second dimension raised by these writings is the autobiographical format itself. Both Michael's story, but also my own personal reflections about the research are, to an extent, a form of autoethnography. In one sense the chapter empathizes particularly with an older tradition of oral documentation (Terkel, 1974). More specifically the chapter attempts to join in debate with those such as Wolcott (2004) and Humphreys (2005) who have explored the nuances of ethnographic autobiography and autoethnography. Though originally an anthropological innovation (Hayano, 1979) initially intended as 'conducting research as a true insider', studying 'those that share a common activity in which one is himself or herself engaged' (Wolcott, 2004: 98), this distinction was soon overlaid by studies where the researcher themselves, regardless of the social activity, became the object of study (Ellis and Bochner, 2000; Reed-Danahay, 2001). Since then, it seems, researchers have been falling over themselves to get into the action on the 'seemingly limitless topics' to which autoethnography has been applied (Humphreys, 2005). Having supervised a former colleague's PhD which saw him successfully explore the meaning of his academic career, I know that this form of analysis has added to knowledge about careers (Blenkinsopp, 2006; 2007). The suggestion here is that we might also think more about co-producing accounts, so as to produce hybrid 'true' narratives of both the researcher and the researched, where under-standing might be mutually arrived at.

Michael's story and my own reflections on research practice blend together the life story elements of ethnographic autobiography and the reflexivity of autoethnography. Michael's narrative shows how a 'research subject' articulates the emotional challenges and the identity work that organizational changes demand of the individual. This blending provides an alternative interpretation from the other analytical accounts drawing on Michael's data that I have been involved with – and discuss below – in that it is Michael's cosmology – his inter-ests in furthering his career and the success of his organization – that drives the account. We have to take each other's interests and world views seriously because we are co-producing the account. 'Michael's story' is not simply data to be fixed into a 'preconceived theoretical space' (Prasad, 1998: 33), but a co-produced – and hence formed through mutual consent and cooperation, not the diktat of the researcher – narrative worthy of direct attention. It may be more parochial in that it is particular to one person and setting, but it is closer to the experience that Michael and I lived. More authentic? Maybe, but certainly less ridden with the authority of the researcher, and perhaps more honest. In the final section, after 'Michael's story', I explore a little more of what happens to a researcher when at least some parts of the protective barrier between them and the researched are lowered in this manner.

Implicit in my presentation of Michael's story is criticism of the over-patterned, philosophically sophisticated and theoretically generalized nature of many organizational accounts. Organization studies in particular seems to under-value rich empirical tales and certainly finds little room for moral engagement, favouring muscular theoreticality over particular experience and emotional response. As I discuss later, social science generally shuts out the moral ideal of authenticity and eschews morally-engaged reason in favour of either a relativistic moral free-for-all where nothing and everything is authen-tic, or the knowing but dead moral hand of instrumental reason (Taylor, 1991). The organizational ethnographies described and referred to in this book go some way to providing thick description and do occasionally deal with moral and ethical issues. If the researcher is engaging with the respondent emotionally and morally, then co-production forces the moral engagement issues and pushes the researcher into a degree of mutuality. This might not always be possible or appropriate. Organizational ethnographers may sometimes have to do the opposite and detach themselves – when studying exploitative practices, for instance – in order to pursue that ethical and moral dimension and protect themselves emotionally. In the main, however, more co-production and engagement with subjects can help to highlight these often ignored aspects of organizational analysis. Michael's personal reflections on his becoming a manager demonstrate the complexity and emotional engagement required of those who work in modern organizations. Michael's struggles with and enthusiasms for his changing life have provoked much reflection for me about the natures of change, management, and the crafting of self-identity and academic representation, some small examples of which I explore further in the final section.

The contrast between the emotional and moral vitality of Michael's struggles and my own experiences, and the intentional emotional and moral emptiness of many academic representations of organizational life, is one example of how this engagement with Michael has provoked my research practice. As mentioned above, Michael's story and interview data are also being used with co-authors in two articles currently under revision for prestigious organization studies journals. In both cases there has been an uneasiness on my part over the place Michael should have in the article, with me wishing to foreground his (and my) experience and my co-authors stressing the theoretical contribution. On occasion these tensions have erupted into disagreements, which are normally resolved by some compromise or my ceding to my co-authors' claims to the primacy of theoretical knowledge when it comes to getting articles published. When this happens, reality as I see it, as I experience it, becomes too ordered, somehow artificial.

A concern over smoothing-over the propensities of academic analyses has troubled me even when the tensions were just my own, and there were no co-authors. Of my ethnographic study of a small firm and the self-identities of two owner-managers I wrote:

> As I read through this book I ask the question: is this really the Paul and John I know? I am struck by what has been left out of my story: the emotional attachment I have to Paul, the laughs I had with all of them. My joy, anger: my life. If my self-narrative only plays a cameo part in this story, then Paul and John's stories are similarly partial, though more elaborate. (Down, 2006: 116)

Michael is also becoming a stranger in the journal articles. And it leaves a bad taste in my mouth because what my co-authors and I write doesn't feel much like a story about Michael anymore. Michael has simply become a vehicle for something cleaner, more ordered and distant. Perhaps in these articles my co-authors and I are succeeding in creating a greater generalized truth about organizations, but I doubt this. For me a greater truth is not being attended to. This has something to do with living and doing things together. As Philip Roth has written:

The fact remains that getting people right is not what living is about anyway. It's getting them wrong that is living, getting them wrong and wrong and wrong and then, on careful reconsideration, getting them wrong again. That's how we know we're alive: we're wrong. Maybe the best thing would be to forget being right or wrong about people and just go along for the ride. But if you can do that – well, lucky you. (1998: 35)

I'm not totally sure what this means for doing research, but I remain uneasy as to the degree by which we consider and adopt emotional detachment as an automatic and unthinking guarantor of good social science. I want stories of real everyday heroes and enchantment; more emotional and moral engagement. Not the flim-flam of hagiography where heroic and apparently all-powerful leaders single-handedly turn companies around without the need of others or a regard for the changeable winds of economic conditions, but the truth of everyday experience where real people deal with organizational life. Would it do us any harm to inject some humanity into our accounts? Co-produced accounts might help achieve this.

Before we hear from Michael, you'll want to understand how the 'Michael's story' narrative was produced. As the co-authorship suggested, it was a joint product. The text was crafted from unstructured interviews and field notes that I generated from my research perspective and Michael's own writing which was produced in response to requests from me. The starting point was my asking Michael towards the end of the field research to write down how he felt about becoming a manager. I felt it might provide a novel insight into how Michael perceived his sense of self: a bit of identity (home) work if you like. As is customary between academic colleagues, after the fieldwork had finished he and I then passed the story back and forth via email for a while, and while I prompted him for the inclusion of certain points that he had brought up elsewhere in conversation, Michael had the editorial veto.

The idea of Michael attending the conference in Mexico came to me after he explained that he was going to be on an extended holiday in the USA at the same time. We thought that turning his story into a paper would be interesting. Michael has an interest in photography and we were both enthusiastic about juxtaposing his story about his emerging self-identity as a manager with pictures of the plant. These images of orange-hot cooked coke, monumental machines, slabs of white steam and motley groups of sweating workers became a poster presentation at the International Industrial Relations Association World Congress in Berlin, September 2003. In December Michael and I presented a Powerpoint version of this in Oaxaca, Mexico. It seemed appropriate afterwards to add some of Michael's impressions of the conference. Thereafter I worked on the story, refining some of the writing and working up an academic argument about organizational change for its submission as a journal article. Michael continued to read and comment on the article, but it was ultimately rejected. The manuscript then languished somewhat, simply a colourful A1-sized poster providing some small splash of colour in my office space, until a last minute reprieve provided by the editors of this book created an opportunity to reformulate a different methodological argument wrapped around 'Michael's story'.

While Michael has also read and commented on this chapter, I will not pretend here that I am not in control. Michael's interests lay in building a career in the steel works, not in publishing articles and influencing academic debates. And while I do conclude this chapter, I have not analysed his 'discourse'. There is no attempt at deconstructing the text via some objectifying scientific method. To an extent then the story remains untamed, raw. But this is in reality an illusion, as any authenticity claims need to be seen in the light of the crafting and shaping work of two people with differing agendas. Thus, although the story lacks an explicit theoretical analysis – that is, an interpretation and translation of the subject by the researcher – there is, by its absence, clearly an implied anti-theoretical point. This, as will become apparent, is not to suggest any 'authentic' superiority. Rather, it is an experiment to see what moral sense can be made for a researcher in 'letting' a subject speak, what the impacts are of finding some room for more direct feral conversations with those that we often claim to represent: to 'let' the ethnographic subject speak back. After Michael's story I return and develop a little further the ideas about authenticity, autobiography and presentation and how this engagement with Michael affected my own academic story.

Michael's story

I work in the arse-end of the steel works. The coke-making plant cooks coal dust in huge batteries of ovens [these are rows of tall narrow ovens, in which ground coal is cooked], and produces coke that is used for making steel. The section of coke-making I work in is called Utilities and we look after the doors on either side of the batteries: people call us the 'door people'. It is the arse-end of the works: dirty, hot and hazardous. Or at least it was when I was on the batteries. For the last year I have been mostly working in an office off the batteries in my new Technician's role. I've become a manager!

Last year coke-making started with Phase 1 of a corporate change initiative. Some of us from Utilities had been attending a Change Working Party to work out the best way to make the changes that management felt was necessary. I was keen to get involved. For one, you get off the batteries, and I've always wanted to get on and ahead; can't be busting your balls and getting caked in dirt your whole life. Working on the batteries takes it out of you physically; you should see some of the old guys.

We need to change. The old ways are no good. The steel works has this real antiquated culture of 'us and them'. I think that people should be treated as individuals, not as workers, managers, unions and all that. The Change Working Party seemed like a good idea to meet with people and do something different. Nobody was going to stop change. The company has to change or die in the face of competition from the Chinese. We had to compete with a totally different workforce.

Anyway, two years ago the big shake-up came along and the Door Adjusters (which was what we used to be called) split into two groups: Battery Specialists and Battery Technicians. The Specialists do the manual work on the batteries and the Technicians do the technical and administrative support. Our pay structure was changed too. We don't get any paid overtime now. Both Specialists and Technicians are salaried workers with an overtime component built into the salary. But we all get more money, less days at work because of the longer shifts, and we get paid four hours a week overtime whether we do it or not.

As part of these changes we subcontracted-out some of our non-core business: repairing the heat-refracting ceramic bricks in the ovens. Our manager was keen to ensure Utilities' survival and that we wouldn't get mucked about by the bigger corporate changes that we all knew were coming. We had all these meetings and there were different views about what we should do. One lot felt that we shouldn't give it away because it's the beginning of the end; it's the first job we give away, then we'll give away everything else and we'll have nothing left. There were some people who thought it was a shit job and let's get rid of it, and then of course, there were some that just sit on the fence and just go with the flow. I thought it made sense: we need to focus on what we do well. Everyone was keen to make sure that nobody got shafted. We knew that there would be people displaced, but we wanted to ensure that everyone got what they wanted.

We approached the subcontracting company which already did most of the ceramic work and made a verbal agreement that ensured that Utilities' employees would get first go at the new ceramic jobs if that's what they wanted. We workers took it upon ourselves to get agreement on these issues without management's knowledge. This subcontractor firm that was likely to get the contract (and eventually did) was simply one of a group of nominal contractors that would tender for the contract. Management couldn't collude with a specific contractor in advance of a commercial tendering process. We weren't really supposed to make any deals about jobs either, because of the Union and HR implications. The process was a subterranean one.

I guess there were some losers in the process, but most people were happy with what happened, even if some of them moaned later about how boring the Specialists jobs had become. The whole thing was quite interesting really; the way we had created our own futures and structured the details of the change process to our own ends.

Once the subcontracting thing has been sorted out, we split into Technicians and Specialists. Our manager, Albert, is pretty forward-looking and a real change enthusiast. He needed the Technicians to work on planning, projects and coaching. I was confident that I would get one of these positions – my manager had always encouraged me to get on and had said to us all that there was going to be a lot of opportunities in the 'new world'. All those that were interested in the six Technicians' jobs could apply, and the process was open and fair. Quite proper, but some that didn't make the cut were really pissed off. Some of the guys still think it was a big stitch-up.

So last year I metaphorically hung up my blue overalls and shifted over to 'staff'. I left the union. I wasn't a protected species anymore. I was management. The company could retrench me whenever they wanted, unlike the Specialists who were still protected by the enterprise agreement and the union. It is a bit scary really. But you have to take risks to get on in life.

We Technicians all started at the same time, and none of us really knew what we were doing. Really! Not then. It took a while to get confident. It wasn't clear at the beginning exactly what my purpose was. We had all these meetings and my manager would often say there's more change coming and we had to be flexible about our roles. I had a few projects to be getting on with, and we had all this training to go to all the time; a lot of it was pretty boring. I am one of the 'supervisors', but I don't supervise really. We don't have that type of autocratic system, and Albert is the only person with any proper authority. I ask the Specialists how they're doing, let them know what's needed operationally, and make sure they are doing things right. But they are supposed to manage themselves.

Some of the Specialists really don't believe it, but Albert really does care and look after his people. He wants us to do well too. I got a feel for all this earlier in the year when I did the manager's job while he was away on holiday for a month. I didn't do any of the serious senior stuff. I did the day-to-day stuff of managing Utilities and going to all the management meetings with other sections of the plant. It was a great opportunity and I learnt a lot. There is also a lot more to learn. I was pleased when he came back.

The place is constantly undergoing change. Everyone – well, the managers – is always talking about the 'new world', or going on a 'journey', or about how we have no choice but to change with the times. Simon thinks that it's strange that in a plant where the industrial process is continuous and fairly static, that it's really weird how the way that it's managed is always shifting and turning.

Except for the true believers (those with an irony bypass) – and we have a few of those – most people are fairly cynical about all the cultural change stuff, especially on the batteries. They realize that a lot of the cultural change stuff is really a political game that managers play. Managers compete with each other at different levels over the nuts and bolts of actually managing the plant (you know, the technical stuff), and it is dressed up in the guise of this or that particular management philosophy: whatever the flavour of the year or month is. But I don't agree that it's *all* a management game, the philosophies have real, if ambiguous and oftentimes unintended consequences.

And it is not the only game. All of us, despite or maybe because of the seriousness and potential danger of what we do, have a good laugh at work. Considering the shit we've all been through this year in particular, we still manage to enjoy ourselves. There are so many different types of blokes, and some pretty strange ones. But I think that we all enjoy the gossip, the stories, the camaraderie and the joking. I think it's important that there is warmth between most of us. We'd all go crazy without it.

There are things that need to change though. The industrial process may be fairly static, but the plant is like Gulliver, and we are all those little Lilliputians, trying to contain and channel it, hoping that the whole thing doesn't blow up. It's a dangerous and volatile process. It's all about men, fire, and large moving objects: it's bloody primeval! It all looks pretty quiet, but that's because we all manage it well. A few weeks ago there was a huge gas explosion that would have killed some of our guys if they hadn't had been on a break. We have to adapt to the conditions of the batteries. They change, we change. We have to change to survive. I really believe that.

But the change stuff doesn't make much difference to people's attitudes. Take my commitment to the place for instance. My own personal philosophy is that I will try my best no matter what, and that I should be grateful for my employment, no matter what the level. It is this attitude that has gotten me to this point: 'if it ain't broke why fix it'.

So I've become a manager. Do I feel different? When I think about this year, it's certainly been strange. I am a different person, but also the same. Simon asks me about how my sense of who I am – my identity – has changed as a result of becoming a manager. I know a fair bit about this self-identification business from my psych degree at uni[versity]. You know, Goffman and all that. Sure, I've changed, but it's not that simple. I'm still the same person, aren't I? I don't get as dirty as I used to and I have to do different things with different people. But I feel and think the same about things.

Simon reckons that he has noticed a change over the year in the way the other Technicians and I talk about the Battery Specialists: the 'shit-kickers'. He thinks that we have all got more aggressive and disparaging as the year has gone on. I guess he's got a point, but that's part of the new job. When we were Specialists (or Door Adjusters as it was then) we weren't going to slag ourselves off [meaning to denigrate, insult, criticize, talk down], were we? Now we know when they are shirking and pissing around, and it's getting in the way of our new work. So we are more frustrated about it than before. I don't think my basic attitudes and approach to life have changed.

I also think about work more than I used to do. There wasn't a great deal to think about at work to be honest, just doing the doors. I still manage to switch off totally at weekends, and I don't actually have to bring work home, but yeah, I think about work more. I have to.

Being a manager is different though. The words that convey how I feel about it are isolation and vulnerability; sounds great doesn't it! Before, I was part of a larger group of similar people. You know, part of that protected species mentioned earlier, part of a collective. Now I'm the link between workers and management, directly responsible for my own work and performance. Whereas I used to have a structured work life and training plan that governed my progression, now I have to structure my own work and learn things ad hoc. I also have responsibilities for others now under various laws (OHS, Industrial Relations, Anti-discrimination etc.); that can be pretty scary if you think about it. Having these responsibilities and not knowing the stuff real well also makes me feel vulnerable.

It's like when I did my line manager's job for a while. Going to his meetings, I realized that most people have only the broadest clue about what they're supposed to be doing, and those that pretend that they are in total control are normally deluded, bluffing or bullshitting; or all three. I realized that managers are just people and not some special breed. With experience and knowledge I can be one too. Hey, I am one! All this changed the way I looked at the plant: why things took so long to do, and why there were so many mess-ups.

But life's too short to worry. I love life and like my work. I like learning about people. I get to make a real difference and this job and all the change gives me a lot of opportunity. The company doesn't control who I am. The change process is just a normal part of work; we seem to be changing all the time. At the end of the day I get a real sense of freedom through my new work as a manager. I would like to do my boss's job. I'd like to steer and direct a like-minded group of people to a common goal. This would satisfy my need for freedom, space and working to my full potential.

I see writing this article with Simon and presenting at the APROS conference in Mexico (2003) as part of this development process. The presentations went really well. People seemed interested in what I had to say. I don't think that many low-level managers go to these types of conferences. I got the feeling that some of the academics were quite confronted by having a 'worker' in their midst. Simon joked that maybe I should study them!

I was surprised at the way many of the academics presented their research. Most of the change papers I saw and read seemed to deal with the high level management stuff: strategy and all that. The way they talked about change and organizations seemed very distant and generalized. I suppose there has to be a way of talking about *all* organizations, as if they all do and are run the same. It didn't seem all that interesting though. It's probably aimed at helping more senior managers manage change processes better. There didn't seem to be much about people; about how all these big decisions actually get implemented and how easy it is to damage people if it's done wrong.

I suppose this is what this chapter is about. I know that what happened at my plant is probably not that special or representative, but the employees had a real part to play in our changes, it's been a really important and positive thing for me. Some of the academics I listened to seemed stuck in the past, where managers and workers are like two opposing armies. For me at least, it's really not like this anymore. Maybe I've just been drawn in by management ideology. I'll let you decide.

conclusion

What are we to make of Michael's account? More to the point, what can we as ethnographers and other sorts of researchers make of it? Can co-produced accounts better convey what it means or how it feels to live and work in organizations? Do our current analytical and theoretical preoccupations and presentational formats fail us in this regard? Do our scientific translation devices lead us to devalue the moral ideal and power of authentic experience? Answers to these questions about the value and purpose of letting subjects speak more directly can be seen by elaborating a little on Michael's and my experience at the APROS conference in 2003.

Michael took part in two presentations. The first had Michael and I talking about his story, showing pictures of the plant and his colleagues. The second was more interesting as a presentation, thanks to inspired late night ideas from my colleague Richard Badham and a frenzied Powerpoint revision. Michael played the role of 'worker' in presenting the second paper, looking at the clichés of resistance at the steel plant (Down and Garrety, 2003). The purpose was in a limited way to debunk the often over-serious, over-important position of resistance in academic representations of contemporary work cultures. I started the presentation by explaining that Michael would speak about his experiences a little later. I tried my best to play the role of the over-serious, cartoon radical, left-wing academic – I had tried unsuccessfully to track down a Che Guevara t-shirt at a local market – and couched Michael and his work-mates in the role of poor, deluded, downtrodden workers who were subject to false-consciousness. At a pre-rehearsed point Michael forcefully interrupted me in a full peacock-feathered theoretical flow, explaining that it wasn't like this at all and that this was not how we had discussed things earlier. He pretended to be very angry. I pretended to be nonchalant and tried to continue to wear my scientist's white coat. At that point the role playing broke down and we revealed that we had deceived the audience. I was shaking. Michael loved it: he likes to show off and does amateur dramatics from time to time. We explained then the point of our ruse – to highlight the unrealism of debates about resistance in recent years – and went on to talk through the examples of what resistance seemed to mean in the steel works, with Michael elaborating on the specifics.

This role-playing incident is a case in point. Resistance all too often is a politico-theoretical football kicked hither and thither on the fields of academic debate, where the decline or transmogrification of 'resistance' points to some fundamental shift in capitalist organization. Gabriel has noted 'the pursuit of contemporary organizational controls and the attendant forms of resistance and subjectivity can be experienced at times as a safe haven within academic discourses where all is turbulence and chaos' (1999: 182–3). His point is that academic discourses and theories of control and resistance themselves remain resistant to the empirical knowledge we produce, particularly as it relates to more emotional and moral domains. Michael's story itself does not develop any fundamentally new insights into the nature of resistance. But this co-produced account has stopped me from over-theorizing the empirical material. Michael's account is ambiguous, contradictory and ambivalent. Regarding the nature of his relationships with subordinates, at times he stresses a duty of care and equality, but at other times he exudes a gung-ho paternalism: he always remains a prisoner of his structural role in the organization. Academic discourses tend to want to resolve the contradictory plurality of lived and storied experience. Fully co-produced accounts like 'Michael's story' have an unresolved quality that is resistant to the rationalizing intent of 'preconceived theoretical space' (Prasad, 1998: 33). Co-production can deflate the bombast of the scientistic pose. Ultimately, it can strengthen those theories.

Similarly, if 'treated' with identity construction theories, Michael's confusion about who he is could be rendered as a difficult identity-threatening struggle to find a functioning storied self. Reality is happily more mundane. His indeterminate becoming self should be put into the context of a co-produced relational narrative with me where trust, play and mutual exploration are prominent. Michael is very much a fully-storied person, sure of whom he is becoming. There is no crisis. However, before working together with Michael in producing his story, I was not really sure about what his identity work in becoming a manager really meant in practice. The back and forth between us while crafting his story, clarifying the points Michael wanted to stress and highlighting the person he wanted to present, was a form of identity work, a 'form of narrative incitement' (Holstein and Gubrium, 2000: 129). Of course, co-producing his story is no more Michael's true self than any other version. That's not the point. But it did show me something about the identity construction process and its inherently dialogical nature (Sennett, 1981: 117–18; Taylor, 1991: 35).

Michael's story is not especially emotionally or morally exciting or revelatory, but it is real and particular. It has weight. For Michael the academic work he saw at the conference 'didn't seem all that interesting'. This is because the things that the academic community currently finds authentic and interesting are different from what Michael thinks is important and authentic. Authenticity is situated. Co-produced autobiographically-based ethnography can provide a platform for co-joining notions of authenticity and producing morally-engaged knowledge about our organizational world that does not show a hubristic disregard for the individuals that we talk with and study. It has the potential not to be more authentic, but perhaps to be plurally authentic.

Then there are maybe some practical implications. We can expect the environment that supports research activity to change and to become more demanding in the next few decades. Should we be complacent and expect the representational world of journals and the institutions that support them to be unaffected by the broad technological challenges and changing socio-economic and political expectations of university education and research? Relevance in research is a complex issue, but can't we expect that fewer and fewer of our students will empathize with our finding philosophically-infused theoretical knowledge authentic and relevant? We need a more popular and engaged social science (Down, 2001). We need more vignettes about organizational life as it is lived (Humphreys, 2005). We need more co-production of ethnographic and other research texts. Arguably we also need more moralising and emotionalism. If nothing else, there needs to be more space for more plural, multi-vocal outputs in the journals that publish our work.

Michael may not realize it, but in his criticism of academic presentations he is getting to the heart of quite a weighty matter. If we suspend our relativistic reservations and assume that there is something more authentic about personal accounts of organizational happenings, that Michael's account does render the events more personally, emotionally and morally vital, then we are saying something quite profound about authenticity as a moral ideal. Charles Taylor (1991) has written that social science has tended to obscure moral ideals with its reliance on cosmologies and ontologies based on instrumental rationality. Can co-produced ethnography make a difference? What it clearly does is avoid the moral and emotional neutrality that social science so confidently claims, so often. It doesn't do this by a polemic. Rather, in however small a way, it establishes a community of interest between the researcher and the researched: a mutuality of accounts. Research practice in some areas such as those that study indigenous peoples already demands this type of mutuality as a matter of course (Smith, 1999). Perhaps a few more co-produced accounts might enhance our discipline too.

This also relates to Taylor's call for a less individualized notion of achieving authentic self-fulfilment. We need more accounts of people in organizations that recognize and value others. Those accounts need to worm their way into serious research that the powerful will read. The denial of a dialogue with our 'respondents' denies them a full identity, and without this we will fail to build any commitment to a community or political society (Taylor, 1991: 43). The researcher who co-produces research accounts ceases to be a powerful arbiter of knowledge but in a small way starts to become a community. We need to democratize at least some of our professional practice and give up the tools that separate us from our fellows. In a small way, as this book (and other work like it) is shared, borrowed and used in the classroom, that community grows, and what is seen as legitimate knowledge changes ever so slightly.

Clearly, any call to introduce more of this second dimension of my argument, the co-produced autobiographical format, will not be the first time such a call to collaborative arms has been made. Sykes and Treleaven (Chapter 11 in this volume) discuss action research, which could also take the form of a co-produced organizational ethnography. And, of course, anthropology (Lassiter, 2001; Reed-Danahay, 2001) and other related fields such as Indigenous studies (Morgan, 1989) have been experimenting for some time with co-production. Lassiter has put the benefits succinctly: 'While collaborative practice clearly has the potential to sharpen more complex understandings of culture, text, and dialogue in the ethnographies we produce, it may also address the problems of class and privilege' (2001: 145). If co-production can help remove the distance between researcher and researched in anthropology, it should be able to do it for the study of organizations, too. Since the numbers of people working in contemporary organizations unable to speak and write for themselves are relatively few, it would seem obvious that different forms of co-production and collaborative dissemination – the co-authoring of papers, vignettes, case-studies, co-presentation at conferences, etc. – should be far more normal than they are at present. The auto-biographical format used here is just one form which this co-production could take.

The benefits should not be exaggerated, though. No matter how research is done, there will always remain the anthropological irony that Clifford Geertz noted all those years ago: 'the imbalance between the ability to uncover problems and the power to solve them, and the inherent moral tension between the investigator and his subject' (1968: 155). Saying truth to power through research isn't nothing, but we shouldn't kid ourselves. Even when we co-produce accounts, Michael doesn't much care who's listening if it doesn't change something in Michael's work life. His contribution is a gift to me and you. This kind of gift can help us reclaim the moral authenticity to say something definite about organizational life, to emphasize the moral content and substance of our organizational tales rather than obsess about the manner in which we tell them. Maybe later in Michael's career, and in other organizational careers affected by chapters in this book, when he is tasked with further changes in his organization, maybe this type of knowledge will help shape that change. And that's not nothing.

references

Badham, R. and Garrety, K. (2004) 'Living in the blender of change: The carnival of control in a culture of culture', *Tamara*, 2(4): 22–38.

Badham, R., Dawson, P., Garrety, K., Griffiths, A., Morrigan, V. and Zanko, M. (2003) 'Designer deviance: Enterprise and deviance in organizational change', *Organization*, 10(4): 651–73.

Badham, R., McLoughlin, I., and Garrety, K. (2003) 'Push people's balls and push people's balls and push people's balls until something comes out', in D. Preece and J. Laurila (eds), *Technological change and organizational action*. Routledge: London. pp. 77–102.

Behar, R. (1993) *Translated woman: Crossing the border with Esperanza's story*. Boston, MA: Beacon.

Blenkinsopp, J. (2006) 'Narrative as an emotion-focused coping strategy in career'. Unpublished PhD thesis, University of Newcastle upon Tyne.

Blenkinsopp, J. (2007) 'The ties that double bind us: Career, emotion and narrative coping in difficult working relationships', *Culture and Organization*, 13(3): 251–66.

Down, S. (2001) 'The return of popular social science?', *Human Relations*, 54(12): 1639–62.

Down, S. (2006) *Narratives of enterprise: Crafting entrepreneurial self-identity in a small firm*. Cheltenham: Edward Elgar.

Down, S. and Garrety, K. (2003) 'The clichés of "resistance": Competing narratives of self-identification'. Presented at APROS in Oaxaca, Mexico, December.

Down, S. and Hughes, M. (2003) 'Images of change: Becoming a manager in a Corporate Culture Change Program'. Presented as a communication (poster) paper at the International Industrial Relations Association World Congress in Berlin, September, and at APROS, in Oaxaca, Mexico, December.

Down, S., Garrety, K. and Badham, R. (2006) 'Fear and loathing in the field: Emotional dissonance and identity work in ethnographic research', *M@n@gement*, 9(3): 87–107.

Ellis, C. and Bochner, A.P. (2000) 'Autoethnography, personal narratve, reflexivity: Researcher as subject', in N.K. Denzin and Y.S. Lincoln (eds), *Handbook of Qualitative Research*. 2nd edn. Thousand Oaks, CA: Sage. pp. 733–68.

Gabriel, Y. (1999) 'Beyond happy families: A critical re-evaluation of the control–resistance–identity triangle', *Human Relations*, 52(2): 179–203.

Garrety, K.R., Badham, R., Morrigan, V., Rifkin, W. and Zanko, M. (2003) 'The use of personality typing in organizational change: Discourse, emotions and the reflexive subject', *Human Relations*, 56(2): 211–35.

Geertz, C. (1968) 'Thinking as a moral act: Ethical dimensions of anthropological field-work in the new states', *Antioch Review*, 28(2): 139–58.

Golden-Biddle, K. and Locke, K. (1993) 'Appealing work: An investigation of how ethnographic texts convince', *Organization Science*, 4(4): 595–616.

Hayano, D. (1979) 'Auto-ethnography: paradigms, problems, and prospects', *Human Organization*, 38(1): 99–104.

Holstein, J.A. and Gubrium, J.F. (2000) *The self we live by: Narrative identity in a postmodern world*. Oxford: Oxford University Press.

Humphreys, M. (2005) 'Getting personal: Reflexivity and autoethnographic vignettes', *Qualitative Inquiry*, 11(6): 840–60.

Lassiter, L.E. (2001) 'From "Reading over the shoulders of natives" to "Reading along-side natives", literally: Toward a collaborative and reciprocal ethnography', *Journal of Anthropological Research*, 57(2): 137–49.

Morgan, S. (1989) *Wanamurraganya: The story of Jack McPhee*. Freemantle, WA: Freemantle Arts Center Press.

Prasad, P. (1998) 'When the ethnographic subject speaks back: Reviewing Ruth Behar's Translated Woman', *Journal of Management Inquiry*, 7(1): 31–6.

Reed-Danahay, D.E. (2001) 'Autobiography, intimacy and ethnography', in P. Atkinson, A. Coffey, S. Delamot, J. Lofland and L. Lofland (eds), *The handbook of ethnography*. London: Sage. pp. 405–25.

Roth, P. (1998) *American Pastoral*. London: Vintage.

Sennett, R. (1981) *Authority*. New York: Vintage.

Smith, L.T. (1999) *Decolonizing methodologies: Research and indigenous peoples*. London and New York: Zed Books.

Taylor, C. (1991) *The ethics of authenticity*. Cambridge, MA: Harvard University Press.

Terkel, S. (1974) *Working*. New York: The Free Press.

Wolcott, H.F. (2004) 'The ethnographic autobiography', *Auto/Biography*, 12: 93–106.

Part II

Familiarity and 'Stranger-ness'

5

Making the familiar strange: A case for disengaged organizational ethnography

Sierk Ybema and Frans Kamsteeg

I never saw the east coast
until I moved to the west …

I never saw the morning
until I stayed up all night

I never saw your sunshine
until you turned out your lovelight babe

I never saw my hometown
until I stayed away too long

Tom Waits[1]

Ethnographic fieldwork typically involves the development of close connections between the ethnographer and the subjects and situations being studied (Hammersley and Atkinson, 2007; Lofland, 1995; Prasad, 2005); that is, 'living with and living like those who are studied' in order to understand what the anthropologist Malinowski first called the 'native's point of view' (Van Maanen, 1988: 2, 49–50). In order to understand 'what goes without saying' (Bloch, 1997: 22 ff.), intimate knowledge of other people's lifeworlds is indispensable. However, while 'immersing' is generally acknowledged as a central feature of good ethnographic field research, its logical counterpart – 'distancing' – is a neglected topic in methodological textbooks, notwithstanding the obligatory warning 'not to go native'. It can be argued, however, that 'distance' is equally as important as 'closeness' for an adequate understanding of the 'natives' and, indeed, becomes crucial exactly when a researcher gets immersed in the field. Fieldworkers run the risk of becoming socially bound up with their field sites and thus becoming increasingly 'templated' by that field (Parkin quoted in Mosse, 2006: 936), particularly when they delve into contexts that are somewhat familiar to them, as is often the case in organizational ethnographic research. Researchers who do their fieldwork not in some isolated tribe but in their own global village are much closer to their 'natives' than anthropologists traditionally used to be, if only because the researched are often physically or virtually 'within reach'. So, for organizational ethnography, 'the real voyage of discovery begins not with visiting new places but in seeing familiar landscapes with new eyes' (Marcel Proust, quoted by Bate, 1997: 1148). Consequently, the fieldworker's strategy must be 'making the familiar strange rather than the strange familiar' (Van Maanen, 1995: 20).

In classic studies in anthropology, the fieldworker was initially an outsider to the social setting, unfamiliar with the culture studied. Strangeness was considered to be crucial for understanding:

> Anthropologists went to study foreign societies on the assumption that an outsider would be able to understand and analyse the culture of a group more keenly than those who carry it. 'It would hardly be fish who discovered the existence of water', Kluckhohn has remarked (in Wolcott, 1975: 115). Or as Agar (1980) phrases it, the ethnographer purposefully assumes the position of a 'professional stranger', for an outsider is presumably free of the same blinkers the carriers of a culture wear – albeit dressed in a different set – and is therefore more able holistically to interpret it. The intent of this position is that the ethnographer has a heightened sense of awareness when in a context not her or his own, and is therefore more sensitive to the nuance of things. (Rosen, 1991: 15)

Whereas traditionally, its strangeness made an unknown culture attractive, a desire to bridge that strangeness through familiarization created the attractiveness of ethnographic writings. In these, strangeness was the given, and immersion in the field countered it. When 'ethnographying' within one's own culture (Chock, 1986; Tota, 2004) – and that is where organizational ethnography is often done – we *are* much more like fish trying to discover the water that surrounds us. For organizational ethnographers, the very 'un-strangeness' of the surroundings in their research prevents them from seeing it. So, when doing fieldwork in situations or settings that are or have become strongly familiar to us, strangeness is not a given but an achievement.

Organizational ethnographers (and their readers) are often relatively close to the field being studied, both socially and culturally. They often solve the problems of accessing closed organizational circuits through drawing on connections in their personal networks, entering sites that are familiar to them, and/or becoming professional insiders or even full members of the organization (see Beech et al., Chapter 10, this volume). In doing so, they substitute the boundaries that kept them out with those that keep them in, thus facing the problem, as Mosse put it, 'not of *entering a different world* so as to be able to imagine or infer the taken-for-granted ... but of *exiting a known world* for the same purpose' (Mosse, 2006: 936, our emphasis). Being close to the 'natives' – or even being natives themselves, as in the case of at-home ethnography (Alvesson, Chapter 8, this volume) – organizational ethnographers may have an easier access to culture members' own perspectives, while simultaneously experiencing more difficulties in divesting themselves of taken-for-granted understandings (see, for example, the special issue edited by Brannan et al., 2007; e.g., Hamilton, 2007).

Ethnographic research can be viewed as a recurrent process of 'zooming in' on local practices, and 'zooming out' through contextualization and theorizing (Nicolini, Chapter 6, this volume). Rather than focusing on the potential of this iterative movement between theory and data to solve the problem of immersion, we problematize and reflect on the process of zooming in and out. Studying organizational settings 'in-depth' and 'up-close' confronts researchers with the question of how to 'resurface': how to contrive to return to engaging the scientific practices of distanced observation and analysis. If ethnographic research today entails studying those 'close by' rather than some distant 'other', how do we avoid getting bogged down in a myopic gaze or becoming blinded by the overly familiar? How do we pull ourselves out of the morass of the mundaneity of everyday organizational life and render 'strange' for ethnographic practice what is perceived to be 'normal' to the insider (Brannan et al., 2007)? And, if 'there is nothing as seductive for the fieldworker as being made to feel like an insider' (Kunda, 1992: 236), how do we step back and make sense of the situation from an outsider's perspective (Fetterman, 1998: 11)?

To answer these questions we will first argue that ethnographic understanding develops through getting close to the organizational field, while simultaneously preserving the distance that will foster a capacity for the ongoing experience of surprise. This approach calls for a dual stance on the part of the researcher: being both immersed and estranged, thereby holding on to a basic wonder about the unexpected, the noteworthy, and the counterintuitive of everyday 'normality' and its governing rules (Pickering, 2001: 174 ff). Subsequently, we describe various strategies through which organizational fieldworkers have tried to stimulate the interplay between distanced interpretation and immersed observation, exploring, among other things, the roles of surprise, paradox, play, and irony.

involvement and detachment

A proclaimed strength of ethnographic research is its capacity to tap into ordinary life, describe it in depth and in detail, and develop an understanding 'from within'. Organizational ethnography can in this way be seen as the art of exploring the complexities of everyday organizational life through immersion (as noted in the Introduction to this volume; see also Koot, 1995). Yet, at the same time, 'complexity' and 'everydayness' also pose problems for the 'immersed' researcher. The variety of field observations and the intensity of experiences when studying organizations 'up close and personal' are often confusing to such an extent that fieldworkers get 'lost' in the field, overwhelmed by the 'complexity' rather than capturing it. Likewise, when researchers get caught up in 'everydayness', organizational life may become as normal and 'infra-ordinary' (Perec, 1989) to them – and thus unworthy of observation – as water is to fish. If the mundane, taken-for-granted nature of everyday social life prevents culture members from seeing the *emic* rules and routines 'running the show', why would researchers not also run the risk of blocking their observational and interpretive capacities when immersing themselves in a culture, rather than unlocking them? Everyday organizational life is often hardly exhilarating and tends to become ever more unremarkable as the researcher becomes more and more deeply engaged and embedded in the field. The confusing complexity and blinding normality of everyday life constitute the strength of the in-depth study of everyday ethnography as well as its inherent weakness: immersion in the field opens up, as well as constrains, new understanding.

Often, however, researchers accept immersion in the field uncritically as an inherent quality and unproblematic asset of in-depth organizational research, while underplaying the importance of distancing. John Shotter (2006), for instance, critiques the dominance of what he calls 'aboutness-thinking' in theorizing social processes. This kind of theorizing, Shotter (2006: 585) claims, is 'mostly oriented toward helping us think about process "from the outside", about processes that we merely observe as happening "over there"'. Invoking a good/bad contrast, Shotter argues for 'understanding process from within', through 'thinking-from-within' or 'withness-thinking':

> Instead of turning away from events occurring around us, and burying ourselves in thought in an attempt to *explain* them within an appropriate theoretical scheme (thus to respond to them in our terms), we can turn ourselves more responsively toward them to respond to (aspects of) them *in their own* terms. In other words, seeing *with another's words in mind* can itself be a thoughtful, feelingful, way of seeing, while thinking *with another's words in mind* can also be a feelingful, seeingful, way of thinking – a way of seeing and thinking that brings one into a close and personal, living contact with one's surroundings, with their subtle but mattering details. (Shotter, 2006: 600, emphases in the original)

This 'thinking-from-within' is commonly what is understood as ethnography's main purpose and strength. Following a similarly sympathetic as well as one-sided line of argument, ethnographers claim to offer the perspectives of the members of a culture, as well as their practices (Prasad, 2005; Van Maanen, 1988). Such scholars prioritize the context-specific experiences of those involved over pre-specified, universal or generalized categories and/or concepts developed *a priori* by the researcher. This is what is captured in talking about *emic* understanding as distinct from *etic* understanding (Headland, Pike and Harris, 1990). The former – which Geertz (1983) called 'experience-near' – refers to the situated knowledge held by members of the setting under study, whereas the latter – 'experience-distant' – is a set of rules or generalized principles abstracted from situation-specific lived experience.

A long-term engagement with those studied and understanding cultures 'from within' are among the central canons of all ethnographic research, and rightly so. Yet, assuming that insights can be derived solely 'from within', from holding another's words in mind and leaving behind 'our own terms', is, as advice for social research, equally as unwise, one-sided and, therefore, inadvisable as it is sympathetic. The organizational ethnographer, like any other ethnographer, needs to approach the field of study not only with a basic openness and empathic understanding, but also with 'a constant urge to problematize, to turn what seems familiar and understandable upside down and inside out' (Czarniawska-Joerges, 1992: 73). For practitioners of organizational ethnography, 'utilizing familiarity' is as important as 'working on strangeness' (Neyland, 2008: 101–02). This means that alongside thinking-from-within, ethnographic analyses should also entail preserving and developing 'thinking-from-without' in order to overcome blind spots for what to us is – or has become – usual, ordinary, routine, or familiar. This is far from easy, as Becker (quoted in Hammersley and Atkinson, 1995: 103) reminded us: 'It takes a tremendous effort of will and imagination to stop seeing only the things that are conventionally "there" to be seen'.

Ethnographic fieldwork, we believe, thus calls for a dual stance on the part of the field worker: an intimate familiarity with the situation that is simultaneous with the distance and detachment from it. This combination of proximity and distance is key to the ethnographer's main research method, participant observation, a term that captures both aspects. It tells us to combine the role of 'insider' with the role of 'outsider', a thought also captured in depictions of the ethnographer as a 'marginal native' (Freilich, 1970), 'professional stranger' (Agar, 1980), 'innocent ethnographer' (Barley, 1983), 'self-reliant loner' (Lofland, 1974), and 'simultaneous insider-outsider' (Hammersley and Atkinson, 1995; see also Bartunek, 2002; Bartunek and Louis, 1992). The ethnographer's role in the field comes close to being both stranger and friend, according to Powdermaker (1966; see also Beech et al., Chapter 10, this volume):

> Involvement is necessary to understand the psychological realities of a culture, that is, its meanings for the indigenous members. Detachment is necessary to construct the abstract reality: a network of social relations including the rules and how they function – not necessarily real to the people studied. (Powdermaker, 1966: 9)

Being 'intellectually poised between familiarity and strangeness' (Hammersley and Atkinson, 1995: 112), ethnographers may variously take up the role of insider and outsider (Duijnhoven and Roessingh, 2006), oscillating between the 'external' view of the observer to the 'internal' view of the participant, mediating 'experience-near' and 'experience-far' concepts when analysing findings (Geertz, 1973; Marcus and Fischer, 1986). In the interplay between emic and etic understandings (Lett, 1990) or, rather, between the emic models of both observer and observed, the ethnographer switches between 'withness-thinking' and 'aboutness-thinking'.

Acknowledging the importance of our role as a 'relative outsider' to the field includes allowing ourselves to experience feelings of unease and accepting a 'painful sense of separation between the observer and the observed' (Lofland and Lofland, 1995: 52). The discomforting experience of being 'not one of them' or of feeling conflicting loyalties – 'a sense of schizophrenia' – does not necessarily need to be avoided or replaced by a more comfortable sense of feeling 'at ease' or being 'one of them' (Hammersley and Atkinson, 1995: 114–17). Quite the contrary. Without wanting to romanticize the frustrations that come with doing fieldwork, we believe that confusion, estrangement, loneliness, wonder, annoyance, and any other distancing emotion experienced during field-work, while hardly joyful, can be vital sources of inspiration for a researcher. These emotions may put the researcher at a reflexive distance from the field, a marginal position from where s/he may see things differently. If the research setting does take on the appearance of routine familiarity, inquisitiveness may be drained, and one constantly needs, therefore, to be 'on the alert, with more than half an eye on the research possibilities that can be seen or engineered from any and every social situation' (Hammersley and Atkinson, 1995: 116). To make reflection and analysis sufficiently distanced, one should avoid feeling 'at home' and should never surrender oneself entirely to the setting or the moment: 'There must always remain some part held back, some social and intellectual "distance". For it is in the space created by this distance that the analytic work of the ethno-grapher gets done' (Hammersley and Atkinson, 1995: 115). For these reasons, the sense of alienation and 'strangeness' experienced by the fieldworker can be seen as an intrinsic and important component of good ethnography, a critical companion or counterpart to the widely acclaimed and well-described ethno-graphic tenet of establishing a 'deep' or intimate familiarity with the field of study (Lofland, 1995; Lofland and Lofland, 1995).

unremarkable yet unexpected

Our plea for a disengaged engaged organizational ethnographer is as much a warning (against over-familiarization) as it is encouragement, because not becoming a 'full-fledged member' allows fieldworkers to preserve the benefits of being a stranger 'on the margins' of the organization. Fieldworkers can see the extraordinary-in-the-ordinary and generate new, creative insights out of the marginal position of not being fully immersed in the field of study (Lofland and Lofland, 1995: 22–3).

Assuming that it is the unexpected that makes us 'eye the unremarkable', as Silverman (2006) put it in a conference presentation, we may put our own surprise to use in our observations and interpretations. If ethnography's objec-tive is 'to reveal things we did not know already, that surprise, even stun us', as Paul Bate (1997: 1165) suggests, then doing and writing ethnography are essen-tially about fostering, preserving, cultivating, and conveying the surprises that the ethnographer experienced in the field. The road to revelatory findings and 'stunning' interpretations begins with naive questions, confusion, and curiosity; that is, with starting to realize what is new and surprising to us as strangers to the field. Empirical and theoretical findings often stem from puzzlement about what does not make immediate sense and, therefore, a basic wonder about contradictions and 'counter-intuitions' may be useful throughout the research process – in generating data, developing interpretations, enlivening the empirical narrative, and clarifying the relevance of the findings.

It is in this sense that we may view ethnographic fieldwork as a process of puzzling over and struggling to solve paradoxes. Rather than adopting a narrow definition of paradox, we follow Wittgenstein (1978: para 410) in defining a paradox broadly as 'something surprising'. Surprise is the essence of a paradox, because something is paradoxical when it is at odds with what we expected; that is, when experience runs counter (*para* = against) to expectation (*doxos* = opinion, expectation). It has frequently been pointed out that organizational researchers may gain new insights, create reflexive distance, or arrive at more sophisticated interpretations through a focus on paradox (see, for instance, Cameron and Quinn, 1988; Koot et al., 1996; Lewis, 1999; Poole and Van de Ven, 1989). A paradox provokes our presumptions, challenges our logic of things, and – if we keep an open mind – elicits our curiosity.

The close connections between ethnographic fieldwork and puzzling over paradoxes can be illustrated by invoking Wittgenstein's approach to the latter. Wittgenstein contended that 'something surprising, a paradox, is a paradox only in a particular, as it were defective, surrounding. One needs to complete this surrounding in such a way that what looks like a paradox no longer seems one' (1978: para 410). Wittgenstein tries to free the discussion of paradox from a strictly philosophical treatment, because, he argued, it hardly makes sense to reason in the abstract when trying to understand the brain-twisting logic of a paradox. We should rather try to understand the meaning of 'something surprising' in the everyday, resolving the paradox by placing it back into the original context in which it occurred. In this way, Wittgenstein takes on the attitude of an ethnographer, trying to understand what surprises him by picturing the 'complete surroundings'.

Two elements are crucial both to Wittgenstein's understanding of paradox and, we contend, to ethnographic (or, more broadly, all interpretive) research: (i) a basic wonder about the unexpected, the note-worthy, the counterintuitive of everyday realities ('something surprising'); and (ii) a recognition of the importance of context for a full understanding of something surprising ('completing the surrounding'). Ethnographers tend to prioritize immersing in the field (the second element) over distancing (the first element), while an approach through paradox takes 'something surprising' as its starting point for analysis, and then, as a second step, builds on an intimate knowledge of the 'surroundings'. Rather than solely or primarily seeking an insider's familiarity with the field, a focus on paradox takes advantage of that outsider's lack of familiarity with it. As researchers we are able to appreciate the idiosyncrasies and illogicality of everyday organizational life if we succeed in somehow preserving a newcomer's capacity for wonderment and in developing a habitus of surprise. Paradoxically, we are able to understand and describe the field *from the inside out* only if we approach it, in some way or another, *from the outside in*.

If things that run counter to first impressions or firm expectations are essential to organizational ethnography, what 'tools' do we have or what strategies can we pursue to preserve our initial wonder about seeming contradictions and irrationalities, and how do we convey our sense of surprise to our readers? We need to develop a distanced, reflexive stance that enables us to defamiliarize ourselves from an overly familiar field, to denaturalize the field's taken-for-granted understandings, and to solve mysteries and foster our readers' surprise. To explicate and illustrate how surprise may produce unexpected insights and interpretations in organizational ethnographic research, we draw on others' organizational ethnographic monographs and our own research experiences. We outline various instances of distancing and yielding surprise: *strategies of theoretically informed interpretation* (sections one, two, and three below) that show some of the ways in which theory and distanced analysis may play a role in disengaging the immersed researcher, and *strategies of observation* (sections four, five, and six) that suggest various ways in which researchers may take advantage of an insider/outsider role. We read all six examples as taking a 'disengaged engaged approach' that tries to make the familiar look strange and stunning, helping the organizational ethnographer to maintain, develop, and convey surprise.

1   *Holding on to the mystery* 'Mystery ... is a good place to begin field research' (Schwartzman, 1993: 68). We can derive reflexive distance from building on our own surprise or that of the researched. By asking participants about their introduction and initiation into the organization being studied and reviving their surprises by re-imagining them, and relating them to their experiences in different organizational fields, the researcher may tap into surprises experienced by the researched. The researcher, on the other hand, may preserve or stimulate her or his own surprise through an active engagement with theory and analysis during the empirical phase of research. A focus on 'the unanticipated and unexpected – things that puzzle the researcher' (Alvesson and Kärreman, 2006: 1266) may inspire critical dialogues between theoretical assumptions and empirical impressions.

Surprise and attention to the unexpected – or what Agar (1986: 20) calls 'breakdowns' in understanding – are particularly important when ethnographying in a familiar culture. Agar (1986) advises ethnographers to set out to create such breakdowns by way of an 'anti-coherent attitude' in which 'understanding is suspect; you self-consciously try to show that "what I think is going on probably isn't"' (Agar, 1986: 50): 'Even when they [ethnographers] think they understand ... they work to bring about a problem in understanding' (Agar, 1986: 49). Following Agar, Alvesson and Kärreman (2006) speak of discovering and/or creating a mystery, suggesting that a researcher constructs a mystery, follows it through in research and, ultimately, theoretically grounds it as a new and remarkable finding.

To illustrate this, we draw on an example from the field research of the first author which shows that, in order to be able to hold on to our own naive wonder and develop our not-understanding into novel insights, we may have to accept a less than heroic role for ourselves. Rather than a triumphal march, fieldwork may then resemble more 'the position of the Mr Bean rather than John Wayne side of the ethnographer' (Jemielniak and Kostera, 2007).

The first person voice in this research narrative belongs to Sierk Ybema: in my first weeks of fieldwork within the editorial staff of a Dutch national newspaper, it puzzled me to find that the identity question for the editors – 'Who are we and what do we stand for as a newspaper?' – seemed to be a question to which they had no answer. Having read some of the literature that narrates stories of organizational members' firm positioning of a shared and stable collective self vis-à-vis competitors or clients, and which theorizes social identities, ethnic identities, and organizational identities in terms of continuity, distinctiveness and cohesion, it seemed strange to me that the paper's identity – the key symbol of their collective identity – seemed to present itself to or to force itself upon the editors as a problem. While I naively expected them to clarify the paper's central, distinctive and enduring characteristics (on the basis of, for example, ideas on organizational identity, see, e.g., Albert and Whetten 1985), the editors claimed that neither the ideological content of the newspaper nor the symbolic boundaries between different newspapers could define their collective identity in a clear, unifying, historically consistent way. Rather than impress an outside world of competitors, readers or the general public by making self-praising comparisons with 'others' (as is usually described in the identity literature), the editors emphasized the increasing *in*distinctiveness of the newspaper vis-à-vis its competitors or made self-disparaging comparisons with 'others'. The long time it took me to understand the implications of this observation was frustrating and confusing, but it was only through taking seriously my own confusion and refusing to accept a pre-given interpretation – that is, through bringing about a problem in understanding, creating and holding on to the mystery – that new insights emerged.

2 *Looking for the 'irrational'* Making the familiar strange through juxtaposing theoretical propositions and empirical findings has proven to be an exceptionally fruitful strategy in organizational ethnography. Some first instances of, at the time, groundbreaking and surprising findings in ethnographic work can be found in classic studies of bureaucracies and bureaucratic underlife. Authors such as Blau (1955), Dalton (1959), Gouldner (1954), Selznick (1949) and, in an earlier period, Mayo (1933), and Roethlisberger and Dickson (1939) made the everyday look surprising by revealing some of the then-unexpected characteristics found in the organizational underlife of rational-bureaucratic institutions and corporations, such as 'informal relations', dysfunctional behaviour, and everyday politicking. Ironically, these irrationalities often appeared to be the unintended, paradoxical consequences of so-called 'rational' management models

prescribed by Taylor or described by Weber, thus showing a disjuncture between the formal rules of a bureaucracy and informal organizational practices. By looking for the irrational aspects of rational organizing, these researchers gave us basic insights into management and its consequences: 'Whenever people act towards some purpose, the outcomes will be a mixture of what was hoped for by the action and what was unforeseen and possibly undesired' (Grey, 2005: 29).

A more recent example of looking for the irrational behind the rational can be found in Robert Jackall's (1988) *Moral mazes*. Presenting an ethnographic account of how corporate managers think and act and how large corporations shape managers' moral consciousness, Jackall describes the decisive role of patron–client relations, self-promotion, and sharp talk for climbing the corporate ladder. He shows how contemporary organizations are much closer to a 'patri-monial bureaucracy' than to a Weberian rational ideal type. In a similar vein, ethnographic studies of non-bureaucratic forms of organizing look for the irrational in non-standardized working methods, democratic ideologies, partici-patory leadership and forms of culture management, like bureaucratic dysfunc-tionalism. Such studies show how these create their own unintended conse-quences, such as dreadfully slow decision-making processes, indecisiveness, and inertia (see, for example, Schein, 1991) or organizational members wholeheartedly embracing the member role prescribed for them by the culture (up to the point of burnout), as well as distancing themselves from their member roles (for example, Kunda, 1992). These descriptions of the unexpected, dysfunctional outcomes of rational and normative control show that an ethnographic focus on the often-unacknowledged 'irrationalities' of organizing can lead to important insights, thereby illuminating the surprising consequences of managerial control.

3 *Making it look strange* Another way an ethnographic researcher who is (or has become) too close to the 'natives' can 'distance' or 'defamiliarize' from the field is by using figures of speech in theorizing and writing in order to make the ordinary sufficiently 'strange' to be presented (Hammersley and Atkinson, 2007: 191 ff.). This can be done, for instance, by applying anthropological concepts or ideas acquired from studies of foreign societies to our own society (Marcus and Fischer, 1986: 137ff). This is a common strategy in studies of organizational culture and symbolism, to 'defamiliarize' pre-given assumptions about the rationality or normality of management and organizing (Linstead, 1996: 18). Scholars may see formal structures as 'rationalized myths', portray organizations as 'savage tribes', describe new organization members' socializa-tion processes as an 'initiation ritual', or illustrate how managerial discourse concerns the heeding of totems and taboos, resembling the ritualistic behaviour that helps to enhance managerial authority (for example, see Ingersoll and Adams, 1986; Linstead et al., 1996; Meyer and Rowan, 1977). Concepts and insights from field studies of other settings – or any other unusual area of inter-est – may serve as inspiration for developing new understandings of processes of organizing. This strategy suggests that, when we are *not* studying 'strange' cultures, we might approach the field *as if* we were studying a strange culture.

We now turn our attention away from these three theory-informed interpretive strategies to make-the-familiar-strange, to several different observational roles organizational ethnographers may adopt in the field that will help to disengage and distance themselves from it.

4 *Breaking the friendship bond* One strategy for regaining reflexive distance is through literally moving out of the field and creating a breach in intimate relations with those researched. In successive immersions and retreats, a fieldworker may move in and out of the field, creating distance through visiting different sites, studying new situations, and talking to the other parties involved. In *Men who manage*, Melville Dalton (1959) reminds us that organizational ethnographic research requires a constant switching between careful and intimate contact and distance:

> Studying [situations] at a distance the investigator may be so 'objective' that he misses his subject matter and cannot say just what he is objective about. Better, he alternately immerses himself in the areas he must know, steps out in the role of critic, reorients himself and re-enters. (Dalton, 1959: 283)

By zooming in on different practices (Nicolini, Chapter 6, this volume), doing multi-site ethnography (Marcus, 1998), following objects or shadowing subjects (Czarniawska, 2007), and investigating new subjects and settings, we may come across different readings of reality that can help us deconstruct taken-for-granted understandings. To illustrate what this 'side-stepping' might look like, we draw on a fieldwork example of the second author (see also Kamsteeg, 1998). Here, the first person voice is his.

Development agencies, like any other organization, produce smooth policy documents, which are at best only approximations of reality. When I started research under the umbrella of a Chilean non-governmental organization (NGO) in 1990, I was soon showered with testimonies of the efforts and reported results on the organization's struggle against Pinochet. I was welcomed as a member of the NGO-family and I developed a certain pride for working with people who had so bravely endured the regime's rule. My research on the effects of the NGO's religious (Pentecostal) change programme was heading towards a favourable outcome and, apparently, the effort and money spent (including large sums of Dutch donor money) had been worth it. But – with hindsight – something must have continued itching inside. Could this really be the complete story? Had I finally discovered the *rara avis* in the development world – a successful change programme? I certainly had noticed that the Pentecostal churches making all these development efforts had remained relatively small, whereas those churches that supported the Pinochet regime had grown rapidly. When I asked them to explain this, my hosts contended that the positive effects of all consciousness-raising efforts were doomed to produce church decline: true believers depended less on church leadership than those in the churches next door, who were still under the spell of their paternalistic and authoritarian pastors.

The self-congratulatory tone of this last remark made me cross the street and speak to members of these neighbouring congregations. I was surprised by the religious fervour displayed by their members, given what I had been led to expect. It was a confusing experience to see: so many church people following their leaders on a highly individual path to salvation instead of preaching political liberation. My friends were right that, here, religion was really keeping people socially and politically backward. Or was it? These 'brothers and sisters', seemingly happy in their politics-free but overcrowded community, warned me that the NGO I frequented was in fact run by only three families and had constituted a job machine (now in decline) for its church members. They urged me to talk to ex-members and ask how this 'nepotism' worked. 'What had this church accomplished except spending foreign money on well-paid jobs and well-furnished offices?', was the rhetorical question they asked.

Back in my Dutch university room, I realized that the image I had developed after 'talking to the enemy' was not necessarily more accurate than the beautiful dream I had been living in during the first part of my fieldwork. Yet crossing the boundary and seeing 'the enemy' of my friends had opened my eyes to some alternative views. For my friends, the fact that I went to their neighbours and took their views seriously was like betraying a trust relationship and spoiling the image of an organization that was so 'evidently' beyond all doubt. I paid the price of losing some friends by showing that they were no saints either (cf. Beech et al., Chapter 10, this volume). But I learned that immersion and (over) identification can inadvertently produce myopia.

5   *Distancing by immersion* Reflexive distance can be derived from literally distancing oneself as a researcher from the researched in order to refresh one's sense of surprise, but the opposite strategy might also be pursued. An example of ethnographic work creating and conveying surprise through immersion rather than distancing can be found in studies describing tensions between front-stage appearances and back-stage processes (see, for example, Goffman, 1983; Whyte, 1948). Fieldworkers investigate discrepancies between, for example, official organizational discourses and gossip and rumours, formal organizational design and informal politics, or what people say they do and what they can be seen to be doing (see the introductory chapter to this volume). Some studies describe, for instance, the marked contrast between amicability in public situations and animosities expressed in confidential conversations or, in a mirror image of this 'frontstage harmony/backstage conflict' pattern, how conflicts are fought out in meetings, after which the gamecocks reaffirm their collegiality in the bar (see, for example, Ybema, 1996).

David Collinson (1999) provides an example of the kind of surprise one can come across in behind-the-scenes research. Asked as a researcher to contribute to enhanced safety in an offshore organization after a huge disaster, Collinson conducted fieldwork on two oil platforms belonging to a North Sea operator as well as its head offices. In sharp contrast to official readings that reported the company's excellent safety record and contradicted managers' statements in which they maintained that 99.9 per cent of all accidents were reported, Collinson's study revealed that the platform's employees strongly under-reported the actual number of accidents. Workers on the platform displayed a high degree of impression management, making it look as though a 'safety culture' existed while in fact concealing a 'blame culture'.

It would, then, be a mistake to interpret our argument for reflexive distance as an argument against deep familiarity. In fact, findings from behind-the-scenes research all illustrate how distancing from and immersing in the field may be interrelated. Paradoxically, enmeshing oneself in the field and becoming an insider who can come in 'through the backdoor' might well be a necessary precondition for distancing oneself from frontstage appearances. Ethnographic research, such as Latour and Woolgar's (1979) study of the everyday scientific work involved in establishing a 'fact' in a laboratory, may thus reveal, for instance, that 'hard data' and 'objectivity' in scientific work are largely myths that are constructed from talk. One has to get really close to people in order to discover and know for sure that they are 'bullshitting'.

6 **'This fellow is wise enough to play the fool'** (William Shakespeare, *Twelfth Night*, Act 3, Scene 1) Finally, an ethnographer might play a role in the field that combines familiarity and strangeness by being oneself somewhat strange or out of the ordinary. As noted above, Hammersley and Atkinson (1995) pointed out that preserving distance starts with sticking to the 'discomforting' experience of *not* being 'one of them' and remaining, at best, a strange insider. But is it necessarily discomforting to be a stranger? Surely, remaining strange runs counter to inner drives to socially 'belong' and become 'one of the guys'. Yet, rather than focusing only on negative emotions, a more fruitful strategy might be to explore the 'maverick-researcher' role as a positive experience.

Adopting a view of ethnography and 'ethnographying' as a form of 'fieldplay' (rather than 'fieldwork'), we contend that taking comfort in holding on to the initial surprise, and thus cherishing and creating estrangement rather than trying to overcome it, can be worthwhile. Maintaining and developing an outsider's perspective can, in some circumstances, be refreshing or even redeeming, even though playing the maverick might not always be the most appropriate role for an organizational ethnographer. Each of the five strategies described above are serious suggestions for serious scientists, but they derive from and presuppose playfulness in gathering and interpreting research findings. Rather than discovering 'truths' or reporting the natives' point of view, they invite researchers to develop new and creative, thought-provoking insights and interpretations that put things in a different, 'strange-making' light.

We contend that making-the-familiar-strange is a serious effort that can benefit from the sense of irony and playfulness typical of fools, clowns or comedians who subvert normality by offering an 'upside-down perspective' on social life. Perhaps organizational ethnographers are, or should be, much closer to playing the role of the 'organizational fool' (Kets de Vries, 1990) than they are willing to admit or accept for themselves. The 'organizational fool', as described by Kets de Vries (1990), is inspired by the figure of the royal court jester we know from Shakespeare. Historically speaking, the medieval and Renaissance fools gradually became more or less servile extensions of the king (Zijderveld, 1982) – petty clowns within the king's inner circle who re-confirmed rather than upset normality. However, with Kets de Vries we prefer to draw instead on the mythologized version of the jester at the king's court that depicts him as the king's critical sparring partner, a person who subtly corrects his master by playing a disclosing, disarming, bridging and reconciling role, thus 'balancing a leader's hubris' (Kets de Vries, 1990: 751).

Yet, we also strongly believe that the modern jester is more than the manager's alter ego. Although he (or she) hardly qualifies for serving as a role model (and, indeed, we do not want to push her forward as the ultimate organizational ethno-grapher), we do think organizational ethnographers could draw serious inspira-tion in the field from his playful role, helping them to improve their 'playful commitment to increasing mutual understanding of the messy, contradictory and all too human nature of the experience' (Badham et al., 2007: 332). Humphreys et al. (2003) do something similar, albeit for different purposes, when taking the playful improvisations of a jazz musician as a metaphor for ethnographying. Those doing field research in organizational settings adopt a role in the field that may already resemble that of the mythical jester in a number of ways. Like jesters, they are 'professional strangers' (Agar, 1980), 'self-reliant loners' (Lofland, 1974), insiders and outsiders at the same time, who approach the field with a somewhat naive wonder about the way people think and act. And, as participant observers, organizational ethnographers (again, like jesters) need to use particular social skills to maintain relationships with all members of the royal household. Yet, unlike the jester, ethnographers tend to take themselves and their work rather seriously (Douglas, 1975; Driessen, 1996). If we are to believe Driessen (1996), fieldworkers even seldom laugh.

Researching serious organizational problems and processes is, however, not necessarily or always best done in a serious manner. We do not propose trans-forming the organizational ethnographer into a simple joker, nor do we want to turn fieldwork into cabaret entertainment or change organizational ethnogra-phies into comic books. Yet, we believe that adopting some of the jester's use of humour and sense of irony would not only lighten up over-serious ethnog-raphers (see, for similar views, Douglas, 1975; Driessen, 1996; Johansson and Woodilla, 2005), but the subversive and confronting effects of a jester-like positioning might also help the organizational ethnographer to maintain his/her professional strangeness. The thin line between seriousness and humour/irony, as elaborated in Huizinga's (1999) *Homo ludens*, underscores the potential benefits of the jester role model. We mention a few:

- Developing the jester's ability to divert and downplay tensions and address serious problems in a seemingly casual and less confronting manner may be fruitful from a researcher's perspective (Barsoux, 1993a; 1993b), because it encourages people to discuss sensitive topics more openly.

- Adopting the role of the innocent ethnographer (Barley, 1983) or the acceptable incompetent (Lofland and Lofland, 1995) and emphasizing one's ignorance and incompetence may give one a licence, psychologically, to ask more, seemingly sillier, or more provocative questions than organizational members themselves would (Neyland, 2008).

- Breaking the routine rules of everyday life with 'strange' behaviour may help to reveal the taken-for-granted assumptions embedded in mundane, ordinary action (Garfinkel, 1967).

- Assuming the jester's position in between seriousness and lightheartedness and in between proximity and distance, organizational ethnographers may enhance their empathic understanding as an insider while preserving the outsider's capacity for ironic distance and wonderment, thus enabling them to offer a specific, surreal and upside-down perspective that is typical of the jester (Berger, 1997: 73).

- Finally, taking and presenting themselves a little less seriously, ethnographers-cum-jesters could have the effect of producing, paradoxically, some redeeming laughter, leading themselves, thereby, to be taken more seriously (cf. Berger, 1997).

While acknowledging the advantages of taking on aspects of the jester role, we realize that the organizational ethnographer cannot always take the role of court jester too literally, because some circumstances may not call for jesters. The ethnographer-cum-jester who is getting caught up in organizational power games, showing too ironic a demeanour, or breaking too many politically sensitive taboos might await a similarly tragic fate as some of the jesters of yesteryear. Yet, we seriously believe that humourless seriousness is also a rather tragic fate for organizational ethnographers, and assuming the jester role may help to bring a light to the ethnographer's eye and spirits.

conclusion

Ethnography tries to give an in-depth account of the riches of everyday experience and, therefore, fieldworkers develop long-term engagements with those studied and prioritize the latter's experiences and perspectives in their writing. But, by embracing the member role, the ethnographer also runs the risk of adopting the member's poor awareness of his or her own culture. There is no reason to think that ethnographers who immerse themselves in the field are somehow free from the natives' blind spots. Precisely in order to understand 'the natives' point of view', they must try and preserve reflexive distance. We have therefore suggested that organizational ethnographers cherish their place on the margins of organizations and stay somewhat marginal, entering the field with an almost naive wonder about the way people think and act in organizations, and maintaining their engaged, yet simultaneously distanced, playful, and ironic stance. For generating data, developing interpretations, and representing findings, ironies and mysteries that come up in the interplay between data and theory and between the researcher and the researched can be rich sources of inspiration. Seeing the extraordinary-in-the-ordinary may help to elicit curiosity about people's 'strangeness', as well as challenge the taken-for-granted logic of things, both theirs and ours.

In the various sections of this chapter, we discussed ways in which fieldworkers may support the playfulness, ironic stance or 'wondering distance' while being immersed in the field. The various 'strategies' are not meant to be an exhaustive list, nor are the various approaches clearly demarcated. We could have discussed strategies adopted in the field, such as the ethnomethodologist's deliberate 'rule-breaking' described by Garfinkel, whose concern was also to expose 'the strangeness of an obstinately familiar world' (1967: 38); Neyland's (2008: 101) suggestion to return to previously made field notes to compare activities or situations observed later; Burawoy's (2003) staggered approach of taking time-outs and making focused revisits to the field; strategies developed by more analytically focused ethnographers (for example, Agar, 1986; Lofland, 1995; Snow, Morrill and Anderson, 2003); Bartunek and Louis's (1992) suggestion to bring insiders and outsiders together in joint research teams; Bourdieu's (1990) insistence on reflexivity as a necessary aspect of the research process, not only towards the practices of the researched (as we suggested in this chapter), but also to one's own practices as a researcher; or the detachment of writing itself as a mode of exit. All these strategies boil down to the question of how to maintain or regain the surprise of a newcomer. T.S. Eliot (quoted in Yanow, 1996: v) sounded this theme in his poem 'Little Gidding', when he wrote that the end of our never-ceasing exploration will be to return to the starting point and see it as if for the first time. In order to make the familiar strange, it may thus be fruitful – and fun, for that matter – to assume a sense of irony, thinking of our experiences in the field as if something strange is or has been happening, and adopting an attitude that closely resembles that of the French comic hero Obélix (see for example, Goscinny and Uderzo, 1978) visiting the Romans, the Belgians, or the Brits, tapping his forehead and muttering: 'These [Romans/Belgians/Brits] are crazy!'

notes

[1] 'San Diego Serenade'. Used with friendly permission from Fifth Floor Music.

references

Agar, M.H. (1980) *The professional stranger*. New York: Academic Press.
Agar, M.H. (1986) *Speaking of ethnography*. Beverly Hills CA: Sage.
Albert. S. and Whetten, D. (1985) 'Organizational identity', in L.L. Cummings and B.M. Staw (eds), *Research in organizational behavior*, 84: 485–503. Greenwich, CT: JAI Press.
Alvesson, M. and Kärreman, D. (2006) 'Constructing mystery: Empirical matters in theory development', *Academy of Management Review* 32(4): 1265–81.
Badham, R., Garrety, K. and Zanko, M. (2007) 'Rebels without applause: Time, politics and irony in action research', *Management Research News* 30(5): 324–34.

Barley, N. (1983) *The innocent anthropologist: Notes from a mud hut*. London: Colonnade.

Barsoux, J.-L. (1993a) *Funny business: Humour management and business culture*. London: Continuum.

Barsoux, J.-L. (1993b) 'The laugh that dare not speak its name', *Journal of General Management* 19(3): 43–7.

Bartunek, J.M. (2002) *Political and other dynamics in academic–practitioner collaboration*. Key note lecture at the EGOS Conference on Organizational Politics in Barcelona, July 2002.

Bartunek, J.M. and Reis Luis, M. (1992) 'Insider/outsider research teams: Collaboration across diverse perspectives', *Journal of Management Inquiry* 1(2): 101–10.

Bate, P. (1997) 'Whatever happened to organizational anthropology? A review of the field of organizational ethnography and anthropological studies', *Human Relations* 50(9): 1147–71.

Berger, P. (1997) *Redeeming laughter: The comic dimension of human experience*. Berlin: Walter de Gruyter.

Blau, P. (1955) *The dynamics of bureaucracy: A study of interpersonal relations in two government agencies*. Chicago: University of Chicago Press.

Bloch, M.E.F. (1997) *How we think they think: Anthropological approaches to cognition, memory, and literacy*. Boulder, CO: Westview Press.

Bourdieu, P. (1990) *Homo academicus*. Cambridge: Polity.

Brannan, M., Pearson, G. and Worthington, F. (2007) 'Ethnographies of work and the work of ethnography', *Ethnography* 8(4): 395–402.

Burawoy, M. (2003) 'Revisits: An outline of a theory of reflexive ethnography', *American Sociological Review* 68(5): 645–79.

Cameron, K.S. and Quinn, R.E. (1988) 'Organizational paradox and transformation', in R.E. Quinn and K.S. Cameron (eds), *Paradox and transformation: Toward a theory of change in organization and management*. Cambridge, MA: Ballinger. pp. 12–18.

Chock, P.P. (1986) 'Irony and ethnography: On cultural analysis of one's own culture', *Anthropological Quarterly* 59(2): 87–96.

Collinson, D.L. (1999) 'Surviving the rigs': Safety and surveillance on north sea oil installations', *Organization Studies* 20(4): 579–600.

Czarniawska, B. (2007) *Shadowing, and other techniques for doing fieldwork in modern societies*. Malmö/Copenhagen: Liber/CBS Press.

Czarniawska-Joerges, B. (1992) *Exploring complex organizations: A cultural perspective*. London: Sage.

Dalton, M. (1959) *Men who manage*. New York: Whiley.

Douglas, M. (1975) *Implicit meanings*. London: Routledge and Kegan Paul.

Driessen, H. (1996) 'Do fieldworkers laugh? Notities over humor in en over het etnografische veld', *Focaal* 28: 17–27.

Duijnhoven, H. and Roessingh, C.H. (2006) 'The tourist with a hidden agenda? Shifting roles in the field of tourism research', *International Journal of Tourism Research,* 8: 115–26.

Fetterman, D. (1998) *Ethnography* (2nd edn). London: Sage.

Freilich, M. (1970) *Marginal natives: Anthropologists at work*. New York: Harper & Row.

Garfinkel, H. (1967) *Studies in ethnomethodology*. Englewood Cliffs, NJ: Prentice-Hall.

Geertz, C. (1973) *The interpretation of cultures*. New York: Basic Books.

Geertz, C. (1983) *Local knowledge: Further essays in interpretive anthropology*. New York: Basic Books.

Goffman, E. (1983) [1959] *De dramaturgie van het dagelijks leven [The presentation of self in everyday life]*. Utrecht: Bijleveld.

Goscinny, R. and Uderzo, A. (1978) [1960] *Asterix en de Britten [Asterix and the Brits]*. Brussels: Dargaud.

Gouldner, A.W. (1954) *Patterns of industrial bureaucracy*. New York: Free Press.

Grey, C. (2005) *Studying organizations*. London: Sage.

Hamilton, L. (2007) 'Muck and magic: Cultural transformations in the world of farm animal veterinary surgeons', *Ethnography* 8(4): 485–501.

Hammersley, M. and Atkinson, P. (1995) *Ethnography: Principles in practice* (2nd edn). London: Routledge.

Hammersley, M. and Atkinson, P. (2007) *Ethnography: Principles in practice* (3rd edn). London: Routledge.

Headland, T.N., Pike, K.L. and Harris, M. (1990) *Emics and etics: The insider/outsider debate*. London: Sage.

Huizinga, J. (1999 [1938]) *Homo ludens: A study of the play-element in culture*. London: Routledge.

Humphreys, M., Brown, A.D. and Hatch, M.J. (2003) Is ethnography jazz? *Organization* 10(1): 5–31.

Ingersoll, V.H. and Adams, G.B. (1986) 'Beyond organizational boundaries', *Administration & Society* 18(3): 360–81.

Jackall, R. (1988) *Moral mazes: The world of corporate managers*. Oxford: Oxford University Press.

Jemielniak, D. and Kostera, M. (2007) *And now for something completely different: Tales of ethnographic failure and fiasco*. Available online: http://www.hull.ac.uk/hubs/downloads/qrm_abstracts.pdf

Johansson, U. and Woodilla, J. (2005) 'Irony – its use and potential in organization theory', in U. Johansson and J. Woodilla (eds), *Irony and organizations: Epistemological claims and supporting field stories*. Copenhagen: Liber, Copenhagen Business School Press. pp. 25–50.

Kamsteeg, F.H. (1998) *Prophetic pentecostalism in Chile: A case study on religion and development policy*. London: The Scarecrow Press.

Kets de Vries, M. (1990) 'The organizational fool: Balancing a leader's hubris', *Human Relations* 43(8): 751–70.

Koot, W. (1995) *De complexiteit van het alledaagse. Een antropologisch per-spectief op organisaties [The complexity of the everyday: An anthropological perspective on organizations]*. Bussum: Coutinho.

Koot, W., Sabelis, I. and Ybema, S. (1996) *Contradictions in context: Puzzling over paradoxes in contemporary organizations*. Amsterdam: VU University Press.

Kunda, G. (1992) *Engineering culture: Control and commitment in a high-tech corporation*. Philadelphia: Temple University Press.

Latour, B. and Woolgar, S. (1979) *Laboratory life: The construction of scientific facts*. Beverley Hills, CA: Sage Publications.

Lett, J. (1990) 'Emics and etics: Notes on the epistemology of anthropology', in T.N. Headland, K., L. Pike and M. Harris (eds), *Emics and etics: The insider/outsider debate*. Newbury Park, CA: Sage Publications. pp. 127–42.

Lewis, M.W. (1999) 'Exploring paradox: Toward a more comprehensive guide', *Academy of Management Review* 25(4): 760–76.

Linstead, S. (1996) 'Understanding management: Culture, critique and change', in S. Linstead, R. Grafton Small and P. Jeffcutt (eds), *Understanding management*. London: Sage. pp. 11–33.

Linstead, S., Grafton Small, R. and Jeffcutt, P. (eds) (1996) *Understanding management*. London: Sage.

Lofland, J. (1974) 'Styles of reporting qualitative field research', *American Sociologist* 9: 101–11.

Lofland, J. (1995) 'Analytical ethnography: Features, failures, futures', *Journal of Contemporary Ethnography* 24(1): 25–40.

Lofland, J. and Lofland, L. (1995) *Analyzing social settings: A guide to qualitative observation and analysis*. Belmont, CA: Wadsworth.

Marcus, G.E. (1998) *Ethnography through thick & thin*. Princeton: Princeton UP.

Marcus, G.E. and Fischer, M.M.J. (1986) *Anthropology as cultural critique*. Chicago: University of Chicago Press.

Mayo, E. (1933) *The human problems of an industrial civilization*. New York: Macmillan.

Meyer, J.W. and Rowan, B. (1977) 'Institutionalized organizations: Formal structures as myth and ceremony', *American Journal of Sociology* 83(2): 340–63.

Mosse, D. (2006) 'Anti-social anthropology? Objectivity, objection and the ethnography of public policy and professional communities', *Journal of the Royal Anthropological Institute* 12(4): 935–56.

Neyland, D. (2008) *Organizational ethnography*. London: Sage.

Perec, G. (1989) *L'infra-ordinaire*. Paris: Editions du Seuil.

Pickering, M. (2001) *Stereotyping: The politics of representation*. New York: Palgrave.

Poole, M.S. and Van de Ven, A.H. (1989) 'Using paradox to build management and organization theories', *Academy of Management Review* 14: 562–78.

Powdermaker, H. (1966) *Stranger and friend: The way of an anthropologist*. New York: Norton.

Prasad, P. (2005) *Crafting qualitative research: Working in the postpositivist traditions*. Armonk, NY: M.E. Sharpe.

Roethlisberger, F.J. and Dickson, W.J. (1939) *Management and the worker*. Cambridge: Harvard University Press.

Rosen, M. (1991) 'Coming to terms with the field: Understanding and doing organizational ethnography', *Journal of Management Studies* 28(1): 1–24.

Schein, E. (1991) 'The role of the founder in the creation of organizational culture', in P.J. Frost, L. F. Moore, M. R. Louis, C. C. Lundberg and J. Martin (eds), *Reframing organizational culture*. London: Sage. pp. 14–25.

Schwartzman, H.B. (1993) Ethnography in organizations. *Qualitative Research Methods*, Volume 27. Newbury Park: Sage.

Selznick, P. (1949) *TVA and the grass roots: A study in the sociology of formal organization*. Berkeley: University of California Press.

Shotter, J. (2006) 'Understanding process from within: An argument for 'withness-thinking'. *Organization Studies* 27(4): 585–604.

Silverman, D. (2003) *Interpreting qualitative data: Methods for analyzing talk, text and interaction* (3rd edn). Thousand Oaks, CA: Sage.

Snow, D.A., Morrill, C. and Anderson, L. (2003) 'Elaborating analytic ethnography: Linking fieldwork and theory', *Ethnography* 4(2): 181–200.

Tota, A.L. (2004) 'Ethnographying public memory: The commemorative genre for the victims of terrorism in Italy', *Qualitative Research* 4: 131–59.

Van Maanen, J. (1988) *Tales of the field: On writing ethnography*. Chicago: University of Chicago Press.

Van Maanen, J. (1995) 'An end to innocence: The ethnography of ethnography', in J. Van Maanen (ed.), *Representation in ethnography*. Thousand Oaks, CA: Sage. pp. 1–35.

Whyte, W.F. (1948) *Human relations in the restaurant industry*. New York: McGraw-Hill.

Wittgenstein, L. (1978 [1956]). *Remarks on the foundations of mathematics*. Oxford: Basil Blackwell.

Yanow, D. (1996) *How does a policy mean? Interpreting policy and organizational actions*. Washington, DC: Georgetown University Press.

Ybema, S. (1996) 'A duck-billed platypus in the theory and analysis of organizations: Combinations of consensus and dissensus', in W.C.J. Koot, I. Sabelis and S. Ybema (eds), *Contradictions in context: Puzzling over paradoxes in contemporary organizations*. Amsterdam: VU University Press. pp. 39–61.

Zijderveld, A. (1982) *Reality in a looking glass: Rationality through an analysis of traditional folly*. London: Routledge & Kegan.

6

Zooming in and zooming out: A package of method and theory to study work practices

Davide Nicolini[1]

A common theme running through contemporary organization studies is the shift towards appreciating organization as an accomplishment rather than a state and a quasi object. Cooper and Law (1995) have named this processual way of studying organizational phenomena 'proximal'. This approach leads to organization being viewed as the result of social practices of organizing, so that organization and organizations emerge from the practical ordering of heterogeneous human, material, and symbolic elements, and from how these ways of ordering are actively interconnected and worked together.

One of the implications of this performative understanding of organization is a renewed focus on work practices in organizational research. Explaining how organizations are socially and materially constructed through activity and effort requires bringing 'work back in' and focusing on 'the concrete activities that constitute the routines of organizing' (Barley and Kunda, 2001: 84). This in turn requires studying work practices and their relationships in situ – that is, ethnographically. Only through immersing oneself and being there is one capable of appreciating, understanding, and translating the situated, creative, interpretive and moral nature of the actual practices of organizing. At the same time, the ethnographic approach helps us appreciate that work practices do not take place in a vacuum and that people's organizational lives are shaped both through individual agency and historical conditions. The work of ethnographers promises to bring into focus not only actors and processes but also context and history (Bate, 1997).

The aim of this chapter is to propose a package of theory and method for studying the organizing of work through the ethnographic appreciation of practice. I shall characterize this package as the recursive movement of zooming in and zooming out on the data and between data and theory.

The package of theory and method requires first that we zoom in on the details of the accomplishment of a practice in a specific place to make sense of the local accomplishment of the practice and the other more or less distant activities. This is followed by and alternated with a zooming out movement through which we expand the scope of the observation following the trails of connections between practices and their products. The iterative zooming in and out stops when we can provide a convincing and defensible account of both the practice and its effects on the dynamics of organizing, showing how that which is local (for example, the doctors' and nurses' conducts on one site) contributes to the generation of broader effects (for example, sustaining or upsetting the historical hierarchical relationship between the medical and nursing professions).

I call this a 'package' to emphasize that for studying practices one needs to employ an internally coherent approach where ontological assumptions (the basic assumption about how the world is) and methodological choices (how to study things so that a particular ontology materializes) work together. For example, studying practices through survey, or through interviews alone, is not acceptable for researchers. These methods are in fact unsuitable for studying work practices as they are not faithful to the processual ontology that underpins an ethnography of practice approach.

I call it recursive because to investigate the material connections and mutual dependencies between practices, the researcher inevitably ends up carrying out several successive local investigations led by the connections which emerge in the field. Zooming in on an activity inevitably reveals the connections that link it with many others. Think, for instance, of how your current practice of reading this text is linked to the practices of those who are working to provide the illumination of your room or the work of those who edited and published this book. These other activities can take place nearby or far away in space and time. By following connections among activities, what I call here zooming out, the research is led to new sites where a fresh effort of zooming out is required and new interesting aspects come to life (for example, by studying how this book was conceived, negotiated, and edited you would find out that this chapter could have been very different). At each step the researcher must patiently study the practice at hand, engage with his or her data, trace connections and re-interpret the findings in the light of the insight provided by the new positioning in the field. The research continues until a coherent picture emerges.

The approach advocated here partially coincides with multi-sited ethnography and can thus tap into the methodological toolkit and expertise developed around this particular way of interpreting the ethnographic project (Marcus, 1995; Hannerz, 2003). What the proposed package adds to the idea and methodology of multi-sited ethnography is the specific focus on practice as the object to be followed. Central to the argument developed in this chapter is in fact the assumption that much is to be gained if we take practices as our central epistemic object and focus of attention. Although a detailed attempt at defining practices goes beyond the scope of this chapter, in this text I shall refer to practices as the actual, constantly evolving accomplishment of an object-oriented activity which obtains some durability and diffusion by virtue of being sustained by a social grouping and inscribed in some material or symbolic intermediaries. When I speak of practice I thus always refer to 'practising', real time doing and saying something in a specific place and time which in turn: (i) entails some form of agency, materiality, and history, (ii) depends on other practices to happen, and (iii) produces some form of effect in the world. Practices, in other words, are not objects, they are not in the heads of people, and they are not stored in routines or programmes. Practices only exist to the extent that they are enacted and re-enacted. Focusing on practices is thus taking the social and material doing of something as the main focus of the inquiry.

One of the consequences which stems from such a processual understanding of practices is that its study necessarily entails a preliminary focus on the mundane activity at hand. To put it differently, the study of practices always starts in the middle of action. In the practice of the ethnographer, this means choosing a specific practice (for example, baking, designing jet engines, carrying out open heart surgery, running a building site, directing a play) and observing, appreciating, and often being sensorially assaulted by the richness of its real time accomplishing, putting to work many of the tools and techniques described in other chapters of this volume. I suggest, however, that practice sensitivity accrues the traditional toolkit of the ethnographer by attracting attention to certain specific aspects, among them:

- the actual doing and its temporal flow

- the interactional patterns performed by the practice

- the horizon of sense, intelligibility, and concern within which the practice unfolds

- the active contribution of artefacts and other practices in the accomplishment of the activity at hand.

This set of sensitizing concepts and themes helps orient the interests of the ethnographer towards practices by guiding the collection of data and the process of writing up the results of the inquiry. As such, they do not constitute a rigid framework and should rather be considered as a palette of ethnographic sensitivities and sensibilities which ethnographers have at their disposal.

The result of adopting the above set of sensitizing concepts and the practical and recursive movement of zooming in and zooming out is, or should be, a convincing and meaningful description of what a practice is, why it is the way it is and why it is not carried out differently. Most of the time, in fact, practices could be otherwise – doctors and nurses could be working on a more equal footing, hospital patients could be less passive. The fact that practices are as they are is usually related to a precise pattern of interests with recognizable historical antecedents. This, in turn, requires understanding the circuits, associations and regimes of mutual dependency which keep practices in place even though they are carried out at different times and in different spaces.

The rest of this chapter is aimed at clarifying and articulating in more detail the proposed approach. In order to illustrate my argument, I will use examples drawn from an extensive, four year-long ethnographic research project on telemonitoring serious chronic heart failure patients at home. Telemonitoring is an innovative practice, usually carried out by expert nurses, mainly aimed at preventing hospitalization. The activity implies monitoring patient status, making dietary and lifestyle recommendations, correcting and adjusting the therapeutic regime, and providing information and instructions to patients and their families. Details on the research project that took place at G., the telemedicine centre of a specialist cardiac hospital in northern Italy, are provided elsewhere and are omitted here for reason of space (see Nicolini, 2006; 2007; 2009b for further discussion).

zooming in on practice: starting in the middle of the action

In this section I will discuss in detail the proposed palette of sensitizing concepts for zooming in on practice. I will argue that focusing on sayings and doings, their temporal flow, the interactional patterns performed by the practice, the horizon of sense, intelligibility, and concern within which the practice unfolds, and the active contribution of artefacts constitutes a useful and practical starting point to orient the ethnographic gaze towards practices. A short example from my study of the new practice of telemedicine (Nicolini, 2006; 2007) can illustrate my argument.

One of the things that struck me while observing how the nurses did telemonitoring was that they could tell in advance whether a call was routine or a possible emergency just by knowing who was calling. When responding to messages on the answering machine, they seemed to have a special method for granting precedence to some phone calls over others. In non-practice-oriented ethnographies, this fact might have been addressed, for example, by reporting that 'the nurse felt that the call was important' and hence accorded priority to some calls. This type of description, however, still focuses on the nurse and her supposed mental powers. It highlights a trait of the local 'culture' (an ability to produce reassurance by responding in good time to the request for assistance), but it fails to unpack the practical skill of how nurses recognize which are the calls that require urgent attention and which are not. A more practice-based way of addressing the issue would be by asking: how did the nurse reportably find out that certain calls were so important?

By digging deeper and zooming in on the practice of calling the patients, one could, for example, observe that nurses routinely distinguished 'check-up' and 'assistance' calls from all the others. This first type of call was carefully planned. These constituted a sort of local ritual: their schedule was fairly precise, they followed a very standard pattern, and they were made at precise times during the day, usually mid morning or in the early afternoon, when the nurses expected they would have had enough time to prepare for the calls, to talk with the patients without interruptions and to end the conversations appropriately. The second type included those calls when the patients reported anomalies or a crisis requiring urgent intervention. The number of these calls varied according to the type of patient, because people in a more critical condition are generally more anxious than those in the other group.

Calls of both types generated issues that needed a number of calls for them to be resolved – they produced a 'coda' so to speak. In other words, a single call may not be able to close a whole conversation, and patients or the nurse must make arrangements for follow-up calls: 'See how you do and we can talk on Monday …' or 'Call me and let me know if you feel better'.

The nurses used the situated temporal unfolding of the calls as a practical clue to their possible meanings. When they received calls that could not be immediately linked to any previous conversation, nurses knew that something might be happening. By noting who was calling and when, they could somewhat anticipate why the call was made. Unless they originated from patients who customarily called the centre in search of psychological support or other reasons, 'unexpected' calls almost always took precedence over all the others. Of course nurses always responded, even to those calls that originated from patients who had a history of 'false' alarms. The nurses, however, approached these calls with much less apprehension than on other occasions. The rhythm and how the calls and related activities unfolded in time became in themselves the context by which the nurses could distinguish between urgent and not-so-urgent calls.

_____ *a palette for zooming in* _____

A first and critical way of zooming in on work practices is approaching them as a knowledgeable accomplishment. Making practice the object of ethnographic observation thus requires that we turn our attention towards issues such as: What are people doing and saying? What are they trying to do when they speak? What is said and done? How do the patterns of doing and saying flow in time? What temporal sequences do they conjure? With what effects? Through which moves, strategies, methods, and discursive practical devices do practitioners accomplish their work? What practical concerns move practitioners? How are the constant micro changes of the practice coped with? How are the different elements realigned?

The endeavour of zooming in on the actual accomplishment of work practices can be pursued by drawing, for example, on the wisdom, toolkit, and writing style of ethnomethodologically inspired approaches. Authors such as Garfinkel (1969) and Sudnow (1967) developed a way of appreciating practice which puts an emphasis on routines and practical activities; unlike other types of ethnography, these authors do not try to penetrate or expose the actors' value systems, relying instead mainly on the observation and description of their conduct. In this way the focus shifts from individuals performing actions to the capacities or competencies necessary to perform membership in that practice, bringing activity to the centre stage. Attention to the accomplishment of the practice also highlights its constantly evolving nature. Zooming in on practice also requires thinking about how practitioners address the small and big conflicts and breakdowns that they encounter in their daily practising. In this sense, zooming in on practice as a context of continuous learning constitutes another rich source of information and understanding.

A second way to zoom in on practice is by paying attention to the specific interactional order between human (and at times non-human) participants. The specific guiding themes for the ethnographer are, in this case: What sort of interactional order is performed by this specific practice? How do they differ from similar practices performed elsewhere? What positions does this specific practice make available? How are these positions negotiated or resisted? What type of collective interests are sustained and perpetuated by the specific practice? How is the practice transmitted? How are asymmetries and inequalities produced or reproduced in the process?

Focusing on how a particular way of doing sustains specific patterns of sociality and empowerment is a way of zooming in on the inherently political nature of practices. For example, this approach allows the researcher to conclude that a specific way of doing medicine empowers people differently. While traditional medicine distributes roles in such a way that often family doctors will control the access to specialists, telemedicine empowers hospital doctors vis-à-vis their community colleagues. The latter end up, in fact, being marginalized by the direct contact between patients and specialized centres. By drawing attention to the fact that practice is a critical passage for the reproduction or subversion of existing conditions of action, studying practice allows human activity to be viewed from a political angle, bringing forward the 'cui prodest' ('who is benefiting from it') dimension of all activities (Ortner, 1984).

In order to shed light on the sociality which revolves around practices, valuable insights can be reached if one manages to zoom in on the activity of novices, apprentices, and learners, using for instance the ethnographic method of shadowing (McDonald, 2005; Czarniawska, 2008). Senior members will often feel a moral duty to explain, illustrate, and teach features of the current practice to novices. In so doing, they will pry open the logic of the practice, something that a researcher can appreciate. At the same time, in observing the unfolding of the socialization process, investigators can learn the specific ways of seeing, talking, and feeling that make a person a member of that specific practice. By the same token, researchers can also identify who occupies the different positions made available by the activity and appreciate the expectations and privileges that come with them. The researcher can thus attain an insider's view of the patterns of relationship, the different perspectives among co-participants – who is who and who knows what, the interests at stake, and how these different perspectives, usually sustained by specific discourses are worked together, aligned, or played against each other, creating differential power positions in the field.

A third focus of attention for zooming in is the horizon of sense, intelligibility, and concern associated with a specific practice. While all work and organizational practices are carried out in view of a set of rules, norms, and specific local institutional conditions, these aspects are experienced by practitioners in terms of lived concerns, expectations, and a sense of what is appropriate to do next. It is in this form that the normative texture of organizational life is perceived by the members, and that should be studied. In order to zoom in on this aspect one can focus on questions such as: How do norms and goals manifest themselves in practice? What local forms of intelligibility are available to the practitioners? How do they become normatively binding? How are they acquired and sustained? What is the role of discourse in all this? It is in this way that zooming in provides a view of the sense, intelligibility, and concern that are visibly experienced by the practitioners and govern the practising. Among the many ways of capturing and exploring this specific dimension of the practising, I found the technique of the *instruction to the double* particularly interesting (Oddone et al., 1977; Gherardi, 1995; Nicolini, 2009a). This is a projective technique which requires interviewees to imagine that they have a double who will replace them in their job the next day. The informant is then asked to provide the double with the necessary detailed instructions which will ensure that the plot is not unveiled and the double is not unmasked. The interview is usually triggered by a short example and the researcher usually remains silent during the process, so that organizational members can freely use local language, codes and expressions. By eliciting descriptions with a very pronounced normative overtone, the *instruction to the double* provides precious insights into both the doing itself and the ways in which practitioners try to make themselves accountable, i.e., the main practical concerns that govern their attention (see Nicolini, 2009a, for a discussion).

Finally, one should zoom in on the heterogeneous and material multiple 'entities' which will play an active part in the accomplishment of the practice. Zooming in on this critical aspect implies investigating both the active contribution of artefacts in the practice as well as the ways in which these artefacts establish relationships between practices. One way to do this is to take note of the fact that practice always has to do with the lived-in body. Zooming in should therefore be oriented toward observing and recording the corporal choreography that goes into accomplishing any practice. How is practice accomplished through the body? What is the material and symbolic landscape in which the practice is carried out? How is the body shaped by the practice? We can also examine the scene of the practising by asking what active effects are produced by different artefacts. Attention is, in this case, on the material (a desk) and the symbolic tools (a document) which are used to accomplish the practice: How do these artefacts contribute to accomplishment? How are the artefacts used in practice? In which way do they contribute to giving sense to the practice itself? What visible and invisible work do the artefacts perform? What connection do they establish with other practices? What type of practical concerns or sense do artefacts convey to the actual practicing? What is the intermediation work they perform? Are the tools and the practice aligned or are there conflicts and tensions between them?

using the palette as a toolkit for moving between data and theory

The palette described above is useful not only for directing the researcher's attention toward solving the practical issue of what to observe once in the field, it is also a conceptual resource and toolkit for moving towards theorizing. The approach I am advocating here is in fact alien to the naturalistic orientation of some ethnographers and is based on the assumption that representing practice is already a theoretically laden effort (Gubrium and Holstein, 1997; Silverman, 2000). Theorizing begins with the choice of what to represent when moving from observation to re-presentation; for example, the choice of articulating practice as an occasioned, connected, and contextually dependent phenomenon instead of, say, the production of conduct deriving from a set of rules. The palette described above provides tools for working through the data and allowing the emergence of theoretical considerations of the local 'whats' and 'hows' of the production of organizational effects. It is, in effect, a tool for zooming in on details and a device for taking stock, so that patterns, regularities, and provisional 'phenomena' can come to light.

The example above regarding the ways in which tele-nurses 'sense' the urgency of calls, for instance, goes some way to illustrating that the palette which orients observation can also be used to move between observation and theory. By orienting attention towards the actual doings and the temporal unfolding of the calls, the palette helped advance our critical understanding of the phenomenon in at least three ways. First, it helped provide a better understanding of how telemedicine is carried out and what some of the tricks of the trade are that make a difference in its accomplishment. The description turned the observation into a learnable skill that others in similar situations could find instructive and useful. Second, it generated some conceptual resources for studying the temporal unfolding of the practising which could be used for appreciating similar phenomena in other contexts. I would expect to find the same mechanism for classifying phone calls in many other places where people deal with similar issues. Finally, the palette helped to contribute to the academic debate on temporality in work studies and on what constitutes 'a context'. The description above supports the idea that context describes the conditions created by an activity which make that activity meaningful. The relationship between context and activity is one of mutual emergence – a view that differs substantially from the traditional idea of context and the immutable background against which phenomena take place. In all three instances the palette and the zooming in approach were a way both to focus on the data and to move between data and theory.

from zooming in to zooming out: proceeding rhizomatically

One of the critical characteristics of the zooming in movement and the corresponding palette of sensitizing concepts is its capacity to displace attention from the human actor as a primordial and unitary source of agency. In its stead, zooming in brings into focus the act of practising, exposing and articulating its inherent complexity and multiplicity. The zooming in, however, also brings to light a second important aspect of practice: that activities never happen in isolation and that practices are always immersed in a thick texture of interconnections. For example, zooming in on the practice of telemedicine as it happens reveals that its accomplishment depends on the work of a variety of people and on other practices. These include not only the nurse and the patients but also other people at the telemedicine centre: the makers of the artefacts that are used in the practice (e.g., the manufacturers of the electronic device for transmitting the ECG or the computer used by the nurses), the people in the lab who conduct the tests the patients have to carry out before calling the centre, and so on. All practices thus depend on other practices. The zooming in shows, however, that the converse is also true. One practice often constitutes the resource for the accomplishment of others. Telemedicine contributes to the production (and, in our case, to the change) of phenomena such as the telemedicine centre at G., the discipline of cardiology, and the Italian health care system. In a sense, then, all practices are involved in a variety of relationships and associations that extend both in space and time and form a texture of dependencies and references.

For this reason, the study of practices cannot be limited to focusing on the details of their accomplishment. There is a need to integrate and alternate the zooming in movement with one which is a horizon-widening zooming out. As such, understanding practice requires moving between practice-in-the-making and the texture of practices that causally connect one particular instance to many others.

The practical and theoretical movement that I am suggesting is rhizomatic in nature. A rhizome is a form of 'bulb' that extends its roots in different directions. Every root extension forms a new small plant that, when matured, extends new roots and continues the spread (see Figure 6.1). In a similar fashion, I propose that studying practices starts in one place with an in-depth study of that specific location and then spreads following emerging connections. These connections lead to other practices, which in turn become the target of a new round of zooming in. The study of practice thus starts with the zooming in movement to understand how the activity is accomplished in one site, proceeds with a zooming out movement which exposes the relationships between practices, and continues with a new effort of zooming in on the new site, and so on. The goal of this recursive and alternating movement is to build an appreciation of both why the practice is practised in the way it is, and how it came to be this way, why it is not

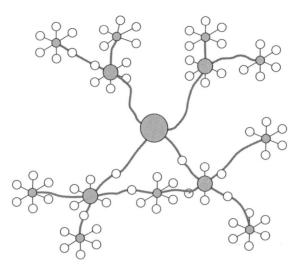

Figure 6.1 A rhizome

different, what the consequences and effects are that this state of affairs produces in the world at large, what is different and who is empowered or disempowered in the process.

When understood in this sense, the alternate movement of zooming in and out conjures a multi-study design composed of several connected instances of focused ethnography (Knoblauch, 2005). The basic principle is similar to Hughes's (1971) precept of following the actor, except that in our case the effort is trailing the practices wherever they lead, appear and/or produce notable effects. Following the practice implies doing ethnography in several places, often at the same time, carrying out studies of different durations, some longer, some shorter, and thematizing both the local variations of practice and the connections among these. As previously mentioned, while this design partially coincides with multi-sited ethnography, it is characterized by its focus on a specific practice and by its reliance on a typical strategy for following the practice (as well as specifying some preferential places where multi-sited search should be started). The next section is devoted to examining such strategies and its tools.

a palette for zooming out

Zooming out on the texture of practice requires patiently following the trails of connections between practices; observing how these connections come to form entrenched nexuses or nets; how such nets of action produce effects; how such overarching or global practice-nets manifest themselves in the local practising; and how 'local' performances are in part constituted through distant flows and motilities.

This in turn can be achieved if we focus our attention on three areas:

1 the intermediaries of the practice, that is, the people, things, and discourses that make the practice appear in different places;

2 the relationships through which practices are weaved together and the effects that their connections produce in the world. These effects can be both material (how the results of the practice are used in other contexts) and social (in what ways the practice reproduces existing social arrangements or generates conflicts);

3 how different practices are performed in different places and under different conditions and how local variations of similar practices emerge from specific historical trajectories and local power dynamics.

Some of the actual research tools to be used for zooming out will be very similar to those used for zooming in. Shadowing, for example, is a critical resource both for zooming in on an activity and for following a practice and its connections (Czarniawska, 2008). In zooming out, however, the focus is different. Let's examine these three areas of concern in some detail.

Zooming out by following intermediaries   First, one way to instigate zooming out is by trailing the intermediaries that enter a specific practice, to locate what makes the practice the way it is. This implies, for example, asking what resources are required for the practice to be performed, or what material and social antecedents preceded the practice in space and time. This often leads to other practices carried out elsewhere. In a hospital, the diagnostic work of, say, a radiologist, depends on a large number of other practices carried out by more or less distant people. These include the nurses and technicians who assist the doctor during a visit, the administrators who admitted the patient and prepared the necessary paperwork, the company that invented and built the radiology machine, all the way to the people at the power station who provide the electricity which allows the machine to function. In the specific case of telemedicine, shadowing patients through their enrolment in the service (an aspect that emerged from zooming in) showed that the practice of telemonitoring was built upon a number of educational activities which were carried out at G. These practices started well *before* patients were enrolled in the telemedicine programme. Through these activities patients learned about their disease and became accustomed to self-managing their condition. Observing these practices, which became the object of a separate activity of zooming in, helped me to realize that such pre-socialization was critical for the success of telemonitoring in the same way that an active collaboration by patients was essential for telemedicine to work. It brought into focus that the principles and practices of encouraging patients to become active managers of their disease pre-dated the emergence of telemedicine and partly explained why this new practice had taken root in this hospital faster than in others (as telemedicine here could build upon pre-existing practices).

Following artefacts and their trajectories provides another useful starting point for zooming out on practice. Artefacts, both material and symbolic, quickly lead to the places where practices are stabilized and work together to produce wider effects, often revealing the political processes behind what appears as a given or taken for granted way of doing things. In the study of telemedicine, for example, while zooming in foregrounded the medical protocols to which nurses continually referred during their work, zooming out brought to the fore the political process through which the practice of telemonitoring had been assembled at G. It also revealed that different interests and expectations of a variety of groups had been embodied in this new way of caring for patients (Nicolini, 2009b). The attempt at further zooming out following the protocol also pointed farther away, to the process through which the practice of telemedicine was being turned into a legitimate and accepted way of treating serious chronic heart failure in northern Italy (the process took place during my observation). Trailing the protocol thus – literally – led me to the regional offices of the health care service. Here I was able to appreciate the practical ways in which different practices developed locally in places like the Centre of G. are stabilized, and how they worked together (or against each other) through conflict and negotiation and turned into standardized and prescriptive rules. This new round of observation allowed me to document, in particular, the specific activity through which a local practice is turned into a health policy and how such policy, once embodied in intermediaries of laws and protocols, becomes a resource and a constraint in the existing practice of other health care establishments (Fasol and Nicolini, 2004; Nicolini, 2009b). In a sense, the zooming out allowed me to make sense of the conditions which made the practice of telemedicine the way it is and see how the practice of G. participated in larger events and phenomena. It revealed the conflict and negotiation process among different ways of practising telemedicine, as well as the vast network of interests that each way of doing represented. It also shed light on the fact that what others would call 'the Italian health care service' is in fact the collective name for a vast assemblage of doings, sayings, and artefacts. That is to say, it illustrated that what we call macro socio-economical structures and processes are work and practice 'all the way down'.

Zooming out by following the relationships among practices While the first strategy required trailing intermediaries, the second way to zoom out on practice requires investigating the social and material relationships sustained by the practice and the effects that the practice at hand has on other related practices. While in the previous case we were asked to follow the practice in search of its resources and antecedents, this time we need to follow it in the opposite direction (downstream, so to speak) by asking how the effects of the doings and sayings will enter the daily lives of people, how the practice sustains other activities, and in which ways its results as carried by material, human, or symbolic intermediaries produce a difference in the world.

For example, in G. telemedicine produced several effects, which ranged from promoting the organizational legitimacy of its proponents (they had acted as institutional entrepreneurs and were now cashing in on their return in social capital), to modifying the relationships between nurses and doctors (nurses, as I shall discuss later, became much more proactive and autonomous), to reconfiguring the proviso of care (cardiology assistance could now be delivered from a distance to patients who were not physically present).

Trailing the effects of the practice also brought to light other, less obvious effects. Through shadowing the personnel of the telemedicine service and discussions with family doctors, it emerged that the nature of the tele-care process not only rendered the patients more active and autonomous, it also tended to marginalize family doctors and other community health care practitioners. Because telemedicine establishes a direct relationship between patients and specialized providers who might be far away from their communities, there is a risk that the telemonitoring service becomes a 'closed environment', cutting the general practice out of the loop first in terms of decisions and later (possibly) in terms of the flow of resources. This in turn could generate all sorts of ripple effects in the broader arrangement of an Italian health care system that, currently, is clearly divided into primary and secondary care.

Zooming out as comparing sites   A third way of zooming out consists in identifying different sites where the same practice is carried out and comparing them. This is often quite easy as practitioners will tend to know about other people doing similar things and they will then congregate into networks of practice (Brown and Duguid, 2000). Comparing practices provides important data as it shows how very different meanings can be attributed to the same practice in different places, thus producing different effects and consequences.

A good way to follow a practice in this fashion is to systematically pursue the social relationships that take place through and because of the practising (the key question here is: whom else should I speak to?). A practice is in fact always an activity sustained and legitimized by a specific group or 'community' into which newcomers need to be socialized. This pattern of relationships often extends beyond a single workplace, and by following the practitioners, for example at meetings, parties, congresses, and events, one very soon finds new instances of the practising. By zooming in again on each of these sites, it is possible to use comparing and contrasting as a powerful tool for furthering understanding of the practice at hand.

In my telemedicine study, for instance, I identified two medical centres that were using variants of the telemonitoring developed at G. By moving among these three sites, I was able to document the capacity of different telemonitoring practices to perform quite different professional identities and power effects. An ethnographic observation of these other two centres quickly revealed that the local practice of telemonitoring was producing a 'nurse' who was much less autonomous and empowered than at G. (so that most of the traditional hierarchical relationships between doctors and nurses were maintained). The critical difference was that instead of relying on direct, scheduled contacts between patients and nurses, doctors in this new site had pursued a stronger technological option and had delegated a large part of the nurses' work to an interactive voice recording system which allowed the centre to detect variations in the conditions of the patients. Whereas at G. nurses managed medicines and made life-saving decisions, the work in the other telemedicine site I observed was largely of a secretarial nature. The two practices produced 'nurses' who were significantly different, at least with respect to their level of competence and autonomy. Following and comparing these different ways of carrying out the same activity helped to document that far from being neutral, all practices, even the more minute ones, constituted identities and sustained hierarchical power relationships. The research illustrated how the unequal landscape of power that one can observe, e.g. in hospitals, can be conceived and described in terms of the effects of the texture of local practising that takes place daily in the specific site and in all the other sites connected with it.

when to stop zooming out

Relevant at this point is how to start the processes of zooming in and out, and when to stop.

Concerning the first issue, my discussion above suggests that, for investigating practice, one must always start by zooming in through immersion in the action. It is only when the actual local accomplishment of a real time practice is appreciated 'from within', so to speak, that one can proceed to zoom out by making sense of the data collected, identifying connections and trailing them. I would like to add that while the image of zooming in and out conjures the image of an orderly reiterative sequence, the reality of rhizomatic research is quite different. Very soon, in fact, instead of alternating between zooming in and out, the ethnographer will find herself handling multiple studies at the same time, each at different stages of the research (access, preliminary observation, in-depth observation) and each focusing on phenomena characterized by different temporalities (that is, events can take minutes or even months to unfold, such as a phone call as opposed to the approval of new legislation). In the telemedicine research, for example, once I started to follow the practice I found myself carrying out observations in three different places (the telemedicine centre, the emergency room where all the nurses had worked before, and a second telemedicine centre), alternating more or less extensive periods of observation in each site. As these observation were aimed at different purposes and were hence carried out with a different intensity and duration, I soon found myself summarizing the results of one while continuing to work on others (observation in the telemedicine centre continued sporadically for three years) and negotiating access to yet another one.

While the rhizomatic nature of the approach and the necessity to carry out several parallel mini-projects make each project unique and idiosyncratic, one aspect that stands out is that the process is not linear. Contrary to descriptions of research which suggest an orderly progression from observation to the interpretation of data and writing up, the rhizomatic character of the study design requires that the ethnographer goes through multiple cycles of observation, analysis, and reflection.

This leads us nicely to the second aspect – when to stop the zooming out effort. As with all other types of ethnography, the answer here is mainly practical and requires a balance being struck between two types of considerations. On the one hand, the aim of zooming out is to document and re-present the texture of the connections between practices. In this sense the more we extend the zooming out in time and space the better. On the other hand, the 'more is better' principle, which is often fed by the well known anxiety of ethnographers in not having collected enough field data, is moderated by the constraints posed by the circumstances of the research, which can quickly spiral out of control in terms of the number of sites and the focus of attention. A sensible lower limit for zooming out is the capacity for providing a convincing explanation of why the practising is the way it is and not otherwise, and to document how the local practice connects with non-local effects. In my examples above, the connection is that which links the local practising at G. with the policymaking process: the effects included the emergence of a new type of direct and the protracted relationship between patients and a secondary acute care establishment (which potentially subverts the very distinction between primary, secondary and acute care) and the possible sidelining of the family doctor. My claim, then, is that the minimal amount of analysis and description required for the ethnographic study of practice is not only the performance of a real-time activity in one specific time and place, nor the ethno-methods that are used to accomplish it: studying practice also requires an appreciation of the texture of material relationships and other practices on which the practice depends and which it sustains. Put another ways, the combined package of method and theory needed to study work practices is a practice net – a bundle of practices and their causal and historical connections.

_____ **concluding remarks** _____

In this chapter I outlined a package of theory and method for turning the ethnographic gaze on work and organizational practices. My suggestion has been that focusing on the lived practices of work, zooming in on their accomplishments and zooming out on their relationships, can contribute to 'closing the chasm between practice-driven theorising of what people do in their workplace and academic theory-driven theorising about it' (Yanow, 2006: 1745).

The first assumption in my discussion has been that studying the process of organizing, as emerging from how practices interweave, requires the adoption of an ethnographic stance. If the aim of the ethnographer is re-presenting what is actually done in the doing of work together with how those doing the work make sense of it (Orr, 1996), the study of practice requires immersing oneself and being there. Only in this way is one capable of appreciating, understanding, and translating the situated, temporal, creative, interpretive and, above all, moral and committed nature of the actual work. Practising is, in fact, by definition improvizing, risking, and taking chances, as 'what to do next' is fraught with consequences for the practitioners. These moral and emotional aspects of practising can only be apprehended by being involved in the hurly burly of the practising itself. At the same time, practice cannot be studied through verbal reports only. When describing their own professional activities practitioners will systematically disregard what they take for granted in such a way that real time work disappears (Suchman, 1995). Closeness to the practice is thus the only alternative, and the cognitive, emotional and aesthetic experience of being thrown into a new situation is hence the first and most powerful epistemic tool available to both the new and the experienced fieldworker interested in studying practices.

It must be added that the ethnographic approach to the study of work practices not only grants us access to the critical features of the process of organizing, it also enhances what Cicourel (1982) calls the ecological validity of the inquiry. Ecological validity describes the capacity of social science to capture the daily conditions, opinions and values, attitudes and knowledge base of those we study as expressed in their natural habitat (1982: 15). When ecological validity is low, as in survey based research (but also in extreme formal ways of analysing human conduct, such as Conversation Analysis conducted within the tradition set out by Emanuel Schegloff), there is always the possibility that the wording and content of the questions are comprehended differently by different people within the sample and by the researcher.[2] Because natives take their knowledge for granted and as nothing remarkable, the problem of understanding can be solved only through some form of *in situ* direct observation of the linguistic games from which words and language get their meaning. Getting close to work as it happens not only gives us access to critical aspects (the 'data') of organizational practising, it also enhances the robustness and validity of these data.

While getting close to the reality of the organizing process is central to my argument, my approach cautions against the idea that an increased granularity – pushing the zooming in to an ever greater level of detail – guarantees a deeper understanding of work and organizational practices. In fact, I have suggested that the opposite is true: when zooming in is pushed to an extreme, the ecological validity and interpretive capacity of the description diminish, so that we are left with an analysis which can be very rigorous and very detailed but which may well fail to make sense and render the practising present. For this reason, the package that I outlined here includes both a zooming in and a zooming out movement. Zooming in and observing work in situ enables identifying connections. Following these connections leads to other places where more zooming in is in order. To summarize what happens if one combines the movement of zooming in on practice, zooming out by following relationships, and then zooming in again, I have suggested the idea of a rhizome. Research conducted using the package presented here is likely to develop in a rhizomatic way, spreading out from the original object of investigation in different and often unexpected directions. The idea of following the practice – instead of, say, attempting to describe the entire hospital's cultural system or reconstructing all the work practices of nurses in a particular location – is, of course, not new. Focused ethnographies have been carried out for at least half a century, starting with the work of Goffman and the early ethnomethodologists (see Lofland, 1984, and Flynt, 1991, for a discussion) and continuing with the work of the practice-oriented sociologists of science (see, for example, Pickering, 1992). What the proposed package adds here is the necessity to investigate not only different sites but also the causal and historical relationships among them. As I suggested above, the underlying idea is that what appears as a local practice is inevitably only a node of a wider practice net or action net (Czarniawska, 2008), which in effect constitutes the object under study.

In this sense, zooming in and out and thematizing the relationships between practices becomes more than a simple exercise of contextualization, when the latter is understood traditionally as an attempt to integrate the analysis of global processes with ethnographic details (Stocking, 1993). According to authors such as Morsy (1990), contextualization is achieved through the contribution of other academic fields from which the ethnographer draws categories for explaining the data. In her case, political economy concepts and the Wallersteinian world-system theory serve as a framework for her ethnographic study of health inequalities (Morsy, 1990). This position is significantly different from the one outlined here. Because the theories drawn from other academic fields are used as a static background and are not thematized as part of the study, the risk is that they become over-determining reference points for the analysis. In other words, the risk is that these theories and their objects (the world order, the categories of political economy) will be used to explain the ethnographic data instead of becoming what needs to be explained. The local is explained in reference to global theories, which is exactly the opposite of what I am advocating here. The method package outlined in this chapter adheres to the principle that the basic study domain of the social sciences is 'neither the experience of the individual actor, nor the existence of any form of social totality, but social practices ordered across space and time' (Giddens, 1984: 2). It makes a case for explaining what we perceive as local and what is perceived as global using the same methods and categories.

In sum, taken as a package of methods and theory, the approach proposed here depicts the ethnography of practice as the patient, craft-like, and necessarily time-consuming work of identifying connections and exploring relationships that generate images of organizational life and organizations as a contingent and ever-changing texture of human practices. In so doing, it promises to increase our understanding of the fragmented, distributed, and fast moving reality of late modernity post-bureaucratic organizations, enabling the ethnographic project to come to grip with phenomena such as distant work, virtual organization, multiple memberships, and other fluid ways of organizing that more traditional theoretical and methodological toolkits are increasingly incapable of capturing.

notes

[1] I am in debt to Sarah Evans, Dawn Coton, Katrin Gilbert and the book editors for their precious comments and assistance on previous drafts of this chapter. As customary, all the responsibility for ignoring some of their valuable advice rests firmly with the author. The picture in Figure 6.1 was created by Jeff Vail and is used here with permission.

[2] As Moerman (1988) put it, 'how could the conversation analyst recognise an utterance as a pre-invitation, for example, without trading on covert native knowledge of dating practices and the special significance for them of Saturday night?'(p. 4).

references

Barley, S. and Kunda, G. (2001) 'Bringing work back in', *Organization Science*, 12(1): 76–95.

Bate, S.P. (1997) 'Whatever happened to organizational anthropology? A review of the field of organizational ethnography and anthropological studies', *Human Relations*, 50(9): 1147–75.

Brown, J.S. and Duguid, P. (2000) *The social life of information*. Cambridge, MA: Harvard Business School.

Cicourel, A.V. (1982) 'Interviews, surveys, and the problem of ecological validity', *American Sociologist*, 17: 11–20.

Cooper, R. and Law, J. (1995) 'Organization: Distal and proximal view', in S. Bacharach, P. Gagliardi and B. Mundell (eds), *Research in the sociology of organizations: Studies of organizations in the European tradition*, 13. Greenwich, CT: JAI Press. pp. 237–74.

Czarniawska, B. (2008) *Shadowing and other techniques for doing fieldwork in modern societies*. Copenhagen: Liber and Copenhagen Business School Press.

Fasol, R. and Nicolini, D. (2004) 'Imprenditorialità nel campo della telemedicina', in S. Gherardi and A. Strati (eds), *La telemedicina: Tra tecnologia e organizzazione*. Rome: Carocci. pp. 120–32.

Flynn, P.J. (1991) *The ethnomethodological movement: Sociosemiotic interpretations*. New York: Mouton de Gruyter.

Garfinkel, H. (1967) *Studies in ethnomethodology*. Englewood Cliffs, NJ: Prentice-Hall.

Gherardi, S. (1995) 'When will he say: "Today the plates are soft"? The management of ambiguity and situated decision-making', *Studies in Cultures, Organizations and Societies*, 1(1): 9–27.

Giddens, A. (1984) *The constitution of society*. Cambridge: Polity Press.

Gubrium, J.F. and Holstein, J.A. (1997) *The new language of qualitative method*. Oxford: OUP.

Hannerz, U. (2003) 'Being there ... and there ... and there! Reflections on multi-site ethnography', *Ethnography*, 4(2): 201–16.

Hughes, E. (1971) *The sociological eye*. Chicago, IL: Aldine.

Knoblauch, H. (2005) 'Focused ethnography', *Forum Qualitative Sozialforschung* ('Forum: Qualitative Social Research', online Journal), 6(3), Art. 44. Available at: http://www. qualitative-research.net/fqs-texte/3-05/05-3-44-e.htm (accessed 11 December 2007).

Latour, B. (2005) *Reassembling the social*. Oxford: Oxford University Press.

Lofland, J. (1984) 'Erving Goffman's sociological legacies', *Journal of Contemporary Ethnography*, 13(1): 7–34.

Marcus, G. (1995) 'Ethnography in/of the world system: The emergence of multi-sited ethnography', *Annual Review of Anthropology*, 24: 95–117.

Marcus, G. and Cushman, D. (1982) 'Ethnographies as texts', *Annual Review of Sociology*, 11: 25–89.

McDonald, S. (2005) 'Studying actions in context: A qualitative shadowing method for organizational research', *Qualitative Research*, 5(4): 455–73.

Moerman, M. (1988) *Talking culture: Ethnography and conversation analysis*. Philadelphia: University of Pennsylvania.

Morsy, S. (1990) 'Political economy and medical anthropology', in T.M. Johnson and C.F. Sargent (eds), *Medical anthropology: Contemporary theory and method*. New York: Praeger. pp. 26–46.

Nicolini, D. (2006) 'The work to make telemedicine work: A social and articulative view', *Social Science & Medicine*, 62: 2754–67.

Nicolini, D. (2007) 'Stretching out and expanding medical practices: The case of telemedicine', *Human Relations*, 60(6): 889–920.

Nicolini, D. (2009a) 'Articulating practice through the interview to the double', *Management Learning*, 40(2): 195–212.

Nicolini, D. (2009b) 'Medical innovation as a process of translation: A case from the field of telemedicine', *British Journal of Management*, (in press).

Oddone, I., Re, A. and Briante, G. (1977) *Esperienza Operaia, Coscienza di Classe e Psicologia del Lavoro*. [Workers' Experience, Class Consciousness and Work Psychology]. Turin: Einaudi.

Orr, J. (1996) *Talking about machines: An ethnography of a modern job*. Ithaca: Cornell University Press.

Ortner, S. (1984) 'Theory in anthropology since the 60s', *Comparative Studies in Society and History*, 26(1): 126–66.

Pickering, A. (ed.) (1992) *Science as practice and culture*. Chicago: University of Chicago Press.

Schatzki, T. (2002) *The site of the social: A philosophical exploration of the constitution of social life and change*. University Park, PA: The Pennsylvania State University Press.

Silverman, D. (2000), *Doing qualitative research: A practical handbook*. London: Sage.

Stocking, G.W. Jr. (ed.) (1993) *Colonial situations: Essays on the contextualization of ethnographic knowledge* (History of Anthropology Series., Vol. 7). Madison: University of Winsconsin Press.

Suchman, L. (1995) 'Making work visible', *Communications of the ACM*, 38(9): 56–64.

Sudnow, D. (1967) *Passing on: The social organization of dying*. Englewood Cliffs, NJ: Prentice-Hall.

Yanow, D. (2006) 'Talking about practices: On Julian Orr's talking about machines', *Organization Studies*, 27(12): 1743–56.

7

From participant observation to observant participation

Brian Moeran

Nowadays, managers and marketers make much of the word 'organizational ethnography'. But ethnography has long been the defining methodology of the discipline of anthropology in which I myself specialize. How do traditional understandings of ethnographic fieldwork as practised by anthropologists fit in with what is termed 'organizational ethnography'? Is fieldwork in organizations (by which I am referring primarily to corporations and other group forms associated with contemporary capitalism, but also to agencies, associations, institutions, hospitals, schools, city halls, and so on) any different from fieldwork among slash and burn cultivators in highland Burma, miners in rural South America, or pastoral cattle herders in the Upper Nile? Does each involve the same sense of 'being there'?

The answer is both 'yes' and 'no'. For both traditional anthropology and organizational ethnography, fieldwork is still in some sense a *rite de passage* defining a community of researchers whose ambition is the same: to map 'a continuously changing human diversity' (Hannerz, 2006: 24). Most organizational settings also tend to have a structured locale, which – whether it be a remote rural craft community or global publishing conglomerate – consists of a set of tensions and therefore tends to erect barriers that are difficult to break down. Some such communities (like a village, for example) combine work, common-interest and residential functions that make it extremely difficult for the fieldworker to penetrate at first, but which – once penetrated – make life much easier for him or her precisely because of their interlocking structure. However, other communities – and here I am thinking of some business organizations – do not embrace their members' lives so comprehensively. Employees spend only their working hours in such organizational settings before dispersing to their homes. This makes the fieldworker's task of a holistic study – in an anthropologist's sense – virtually impossible and limits the extent to which he or she can be incorporated as a full community member.

Based on long-term fieldwork in a Japanese advertising agency, this chapter describes typical fieldwork challenges: access; how to go about the first stages of research; the methodology of participant observation; and ways to overcome the difficulty of how to distinguish between what people say they do and what they actually do. All of these challenges are also faced by a fieldworker studying the customs of certain Western Pacific islanders; race relations in a Mississippi township; or the influence of the organization and practices of a Hollywood studio on the content of the films it produces (Powdermaker, 1967). The ideals of intensive participant observation, holism, context sensitivity, long-term duration and total social immersion put forward here, as well as in many anthropological discussions of fieldwork, should also be adhered to by organizational ethnographers (see, for example, Kunda, 1992).

These ideals, however, present their own difficulties, whatever discipline the fieldworker owes allegiance to, so that even the 'purest' ethnographer may find him- or herself unable to adhere to all methodological and analytical ideals in equal measure. So much depends on other people. Just how much will a fieldworker be allowed to participate in, as well as observe, what is going on around him in an organization? How immersed can she ever be in practice – especially if she wishes to retain some semblance of sanity and/or family life? Is it realistic to suggest that the fieldworker can somehow 'bond' with informants? Are all fieldworkers equally context sensitive? What happens when an organization refuses to allow fieldwork to continue beyond, say, three months? Does long-term fieldwork automatically lead to a fieldworker being able to link up credibly in her analysis socio-cultural features that are apparently unconnected?

These are important questions, and this chapter seeks to unravel some of the difficulties surrounding answering them, for there are immediate, pragmatic issues that someone wishing to conduct fieldwork in an organization needs to consider. The particular point that I wish to drive home here is, first, that the fieldworker needs to immerse him or herself in the everyday lives and practices of informants in whatever setting he or she has chosen for research. This is what is called participant observation. But, second, at some stage in this total social immersion, a fieldworker should aim to make a subtle shift from participant observer to observant participation; in other words, to shift from an essentially passive to a much more active role. In my opinion, this transition brings about a qualitative leap in understanding on the fieldworker's part (because he or she learns things with their whole body and not just with their mind), and thereby leads to a far more nuanced analysis of the organization being studied.

The study of business and, indeed, other kinds of organizations is fraught with difficulties, not least of which is the fact that managers (that is, potential informants) are often themselves already disaffected from the practices of business research (Chapman, 2001: 2). For a start it is often very difficult to get initial *access* to an organization. Even when this has been achieved, and as a researcher you have gotten one foot in the corporate door, the *kind* of access you are permitted may well prove problematic. Will you be able to watch people in their working environment – at their computers, in meetings, having lunch together, visiting customers, and so on? Or will you be confined to interviews with selected managers and/or employees of the organization? What will be the character of those interviews? Will you be obliged to submit questions in advance and structure them accordingly? Or will you be able to roam more freely from one topic to another in an unstructured manner that allows those you are interviewing to talk about what is closest to their hearts?

Clearly, answers to these questions will vary. As such, they will determine the kind of data an organizational ethnographer will be able to gather, as well as define whether in fact he does or does not carry out fieldwork in the anthropological sense. My own experiences in Japan (and, to a lesser extent, in France, Hong Kong, the UK and USA) suggest that there are a number of common features faced by most fieldworkers when undertaking research in a particular organization or community of people. Briefly, a fieldworker has to: make use of various connections to target the right person in the group being studied; be able to make a succinct presentation (or, in advertising jargon, pitch) of what the intended research is all about; display an appropriate attitude towards those with whom she is liaising in the organization concerned; accept whatever is offered but always aim for more; and somehow engineer a lucky break and turn it into a golden opportunity.

getting in

These principles apply to a greater or lesser degree whenever a fieldworker goes about trying to get access to a research site of any kind. People always want to know why you are there, what you are doing, where you have come from, and who let you in in the first place (see Moeran, 2005, for examples). So probably *the* most difficult – certainly the most tense – part of the fieldwork experience is gaining access to a particular community of people. Generally speaking, all fieldworkers have to effect an introduction to their would-be informants before being allowed to start on their research. But *how* can they get an introduction to people whom they have never met, who cannot immediately understand why they should be 'studied', and who may well have never heard of 'fieldwork' or 'ethnography'? Should would-be fieldworkers write a letter or email message to someone whose name they have (perhaps fortuitously) discovered? Should they turn up at the fieldwork site unannounced and hope for the best? The latter option may (at times, but by no means always) work on a South Pacific island or an African jungle settlement, but it is not likely to work in most modern organizations.

The problem of access is a double one. In the first place, the fieldworker needs to be able to make, and take advantage of, *connections*. Whom you know may count initially for far more than your nationality, status, university affiliation, and so on (see, for example, Powdermaker, 1967: 138–43). Second, you will have to know – or be able to guess – whom to *target* in the organization which you intend to study. This is where using the 'right' connection can be vital.

For example, when I first decided to conduct a study of an advertising agency, I used to mention the idea to Japanese friends and colleagues during my comparatively frequent visits to Japan in the late 1980s. One of these was a Mr. Suzuki, the foreign correspondent of a Japanese regional newspaper in London.[1] Suzuki and I had first met when he contacted me as Chair Professor of Japanese Studies at London University to ask whether I would contribute the occasional column to the *Hokkaidō Shimbun*. This I did three or four times a year and continued to do so after Suzuki was recalled to Japan in 1987. I used to call on him when visiting Tokyo – both because of past relations and because I was at the time involved in setting up a student exchange programme between London University and the Hokkaido University of Education. The *Hokkaidō Shimbun* proved to be an active supporter of the initiative. In late 1988, I mentioned my advertising agency project and, during my next visit early in 1989, Suzuki introduced me to the advertising manager of the newspaper.

The first aspect of targeting, then, is that the person who introduces you to the fieldwork group or community must be the 'right' connection and not just anyone who happens to know somebody in the targeted group. I could have tried to gain access to the agency by way of Suzuki, but the latter was smart (and diffident) enough to realize that – since I was trying to do fieldwork in an advertising agency – it should be his newspaper's advertising manager, Honda, rather than an international news journalist, who should act as the go-between. The former asked me a few questions about what I wanted to do and why, before suggesting that I study an agency of which I had never heard: ADK (or, as it was then called, Asatsu). 'It's very Japanese', he said proudly. 'I'll try to arrange a meeting with the CEO while you're here. Asatsu is a very good customer of our newspaper'.

This marked the second aspect of targeting. A fieldworker must be introduced to the *decision-maker* in the group to be studied (and, as advertising agency account managers know – often to their cost – those in official positions in an organizational hierarchy are not necessarily the ones who make the decisions [cf. Moeran, 1996: 71–98]). In the case of an earlier study of folk potters, for example, I was introduced to a younger potter working in the community and not to the elected leader of the potters' cooperative. Although the community was so small that I was able to address them all together and explain my aims and objectives before going to ask official permission to do my research from the cooperative leader, there were later occasions when some of the elder potters expressed their resentment that I had not come through 'official channels'.

In the case of the agency, there was no confusion between the organization's hierarchical structure and actual decision-making power. So the *Hokkaidō Shimbun*'s advertising manager took me straight to the top. Two days later, at 9 a.m. on a Saturday morning, I found myself with Honda visiting ADK's CEO, Inagaki Masao. He was joined by the chief of his 'President's Office', a Mr. Takano, and his Personal Assistant, Ms Iwao. It was at this point that the presentation principle came into effect. Honda effected a masterly introduction (see Moeran, 2005: 86–7) that, among other things, carefully positioned me and my university vis-à-vis his own newspaper and the ad agency that I wished to study, before inviting me to take over.

As I looked across the Board of Directors' table at the enquiring face of Inagaki CEO, I learned a third basic lesson in fieldwork access: how to make a pitch (that most crucial of all advertising practices). Instinctively realizing that this was a make or break situation, I mustered as much self-confidence as I could and embarked upon a two to three minute presentation (in fluent Japanese) of myself and my research plans. I kept things fairly simple and as much to the point as I could. As an anthropologist, I said, I was interested in how people related to things and in how things themselves tended to organize people. Although advertisements were remarkable examples of contemporary popular culture, I wanted to study how people went about making ad campaigns. What were the social processes underlying these products and their images? What kinds of people were involved in which stages of an advertisement's production? How were they organized so that they could carry out their work effectively? What kind of problems and challenges did they face, and why? This could only be learned by carrying out fieldwork in an advertising agency, which – I added, with the necessary hint of flattery – was a unique kind of organization that nobody had hitherto studied, either in Japan or in the rest of the world. I would therefore be extremely grateful if Inagaki CEO would allow me to study *his* agency.

Inagaki watched and listened to me carefully throughout, and I was conscious of being judged, of having every phrase carefully weighed by a shrewd businessman who had established his own agency 40 years earlier and taken it to the Number 6 spot in Japan's advertising industry. When I had finished, he picked on something that I had not said (indeed, something that I was keen to avoid, if at all possible), but that he himself inferred from my discussion of social processes. 'Yes, we Japanese are always being misunderstood', he said quickly. 'Just look at the way in which the Americans are complaining about unfair trade practices. Somebody has to explain to them what we Japanese really are about'.

I was not all that keen to get involved in this kind of discussion in my research, unless there was some obvious connection between international trade friction and domestic Japanese advertising practices. However, what I later realized was that a question that most decision-makers surely ask themselves, when approached by an academic's request to do research is, 'What's in it for us?' Inagaki was looking for a way to justify my presence in his company, should he decide to accept me as a researcher. This he was doing primarily for his two subordinates present at the table (and possibly for himself), rather than for me. Although it took me some time to understand this, I did at the time instinctively make use of another basic lesson in both fieldwork and advertising. This was one of attitude: I made sure to agree (or, at least, not to disagree) with the client. So, I made various sympathetic comments about the plight of Japanese trade negotiators and criticisms of American cultural practices before steering the discussion back to my project.

Inagaki asked various questions – presumably to get more factual information, as well as to give himself more time to judge if I was acceptable (that is to say, trustworthy) as a person, or not. How was I going to survive financially in Tokyo? It was an expensive city to live in. Did I know that? Was I sure I could manage on my own salary? Hopefully, I replied, especially if I was awarded a research grant. And how long did I wish to stay in the agency doing fieldwork? At this point I took a deep breath. 'One year', I replied.

Inagaki was silent for a few seconds, weighing all that I had said. Well, he concluded, I could stay for three months perhaps. One year was a very long time to be there. He suggested that I start out by doing three months and then he could see how things were going before committing himself further. That was the best offer I could get, but it taught me another lesson in the advertising business (or in Japanese advertising, at least): accept the little that a client first offers you and make sure (or hope) you get more later.

I learned yet another advertising professional's lesson a few months later when I was awarded a Japan Foundation fellowship. This not only reassured Inagaki that I would not be a financial burden on his agency in any way, it also convinced him that I was a recognized bona fide scholar who could add (just a little) prestige to his organization by my presence there. In short, I learned the lesson of the contagious magic of status. It was this status and the fact that I did not make any major faux pas during the first weeks of my stay in the Agency that enabled me to stay the full year. During the entire period of my fieldwork, people in the Agency would refer to me as a 'Professor of London University' and 'Japan Foundation scholar' when introducing me to clients (at formal presentations or informal meetings). That was what was in it for ADK. I could be classified in such a way that brought credit upon the agency, since the 'symbolic capital' (to use Bourdieu's term [1984]) of my own academic institution and financial guarantor could be used to enhance that of ADK and thereby, perhaps, its economic capital.

fieldwork practice

One of the tenets of fieldwork is that you should collect as much concrete data as possible over a wide range of research-related issues. But one difficulty facing fieldworkers has been how best to embark upon the research process. It can be difficult – if not impossible – to start out by collecting data on magical beliefs and practices, for example, if, as a foreign researcher, you are not fully conversant with the language of those you are studying. Under such circumstances, theoretical issues need to be put aside until a later date. At the same time, as I learned to my own cost in a pottery village (Moeran, 2005: 23–34), it may not be advisable to start off your participant observation by enquiring into your informants' financial affairs but rather by gathering data on something less threatening, like household genealogies.

In general, then, fieldwork might proceed initially along somewhat haphazard lines, as the ethnographer instinctively keeps to subjects deemed 'safe' by his informants. Only later will she begin to bring up topics that *she* wants to pursue, rather than discuss those that her informants wish her to pursue. But what about fieldwork conducted in organizations? Is it less haphazard, more organized? After all, the fieldworker in an organization is not always situated at the higher end of the kind of power relationship characterizing anthropologists working in colonial environments in the 1950s and 1960s. Rather, she is 'studying up' (Nader, 1969), as well as 'down', 'sideways' and 'through' (Hannerz, 2006).

It was agreed that I should start my fieldwork in ADK on the first working day after the New Year in 1990. A few weeks before I left England, however, I received a letter from Takano, chief of the President's Office, outlining the agency's proposals regarding how my fieldwork should proceed. I was to spend the first two weeks in his office, familiarizing myself with the Japanese advertising industry, before spending a month in the Media Buying division where I would learn about magazine, newspaper, television and radio advertising. I was to move from there to the Marketing division, and thence to Market Development. After that, I should join Account Services, before studying in the Creative, Promotions, International, Personnel, Finance and Computer divisions. All in all, I was to spend approximately one month in each division. By the end of my year of fieldwork, I should have gained a thorough, rounded comprehension of Japan's advertising industry.

This prepared programme both surprised and worried me, although at the time I merely wrote back to confirm Takano's plan and thank him for his time and trouble in arranging everything on my behalf. I was pleasantly surprised because, for the first time in my fieldwork experience, I did not have to work out for myself where to start my fieldwork enquiries. Whereas, on previous occasions, I had had to learn by trial and error how to go about studying a particular community of people, this time my collective inform- ant, the advertising agency, was itself telling me where to begin. My immedi- ate worry was that the agency's management might be guiding me to examine what it wanted me to examine, rather than what I myself might wish to follow up. After all, as someone 'studying up', I was dealing here with a collective organization that was in an infinitely stronger power position than my own and with people therein who might well manage the terms of my research engagement (Marcus, 1998: 121–2). I began to envis- age arguments about academic freedom, on the one hand, and an ethical deadlock of some kind, resulting in my leaving the agency on less than the best of terms, on the other. In fact, this worry proved to be totally unfounded, since – once fieldwork had started – I found myself more or less free to study what and where I wanted, provided that I liaised with Takano and the others concerned to make sure that everybody knew what I was doing and where I was located at any one time. (This was, in fact, standard practice for *all* employees in the agency.)

A second remarkable feature of my agency fieldwork was that I found myself frequently being given lectures on the 'theory' of advertising, before being immersed in its actual practices (cf. Hine, 2001: 65). The advantage of this type of fieldwork was that for the first time I was able to practise a form of 'grounded theory' that allowed me to pursue formal lines of enquiry by the informal means of participant observation. Previously, when in the field in rural areas, I would not have access to books or materials enabling me to apply theories to data gathered during research and to let this combination of theory and data inform my fieldwork investigations as part of an ongoing project. In ADK, however, there was a wealth of statistical detail and case study material to support the stories that I was told during my everyday inter-views and conversations. I was thus able to practise a grounded fieldwork that made use of these data and materials continuously to inform my further research enquiries. Such grounded fieldwork – and the emphasis here is on its 'grounded' rather than its theoretical nature (cf. Stewart, 1998: 9) – was a crucial element in my ability to understand and grasp the complexities of the advertising industry that I was studying.

local knowledge

All of this in itself, however, was not sufficient means to ensure that field-work proceeded towards a successful conclusion. Here I come to what I earlier referred to as 'the lucky break'. Many ethnographers can recount particular moments in the participant observation process when they were afforded insights that they might not otherwise have had, or suddenly found themselves closer to informants than might otherwise have been the case (witness Clifford Geertz's [1973: 412–17] famous depiction of a Balinese cockfight). These moments are, in retrospect, used to justify or validate particular positions adopted or held by anthropologists. Certainly, they form a *rite de passage* in their quest for 'local knowledge' (Geertz, 1983). I myself am very aware of such moments in all three of my longer periods of field-work. While the first two depended in large part on a particular personal relationship that I had established with someone in the community being studied (in other words, on my personality and the interpersonal dynamics between myself and those I was studying [cf. Powdermaker, 1969]), the third came about as a result of a particular business problem to which I was able to make a – as it turned out – successful contribution. As every advertising account executive knows, one has to create circumstances that allow the lucky break to occur (so that the break is rationalized as being not as 'lucky' as it might at first glance appear); then one must take maximum advantage of the opportunity offered.

I do not intend to go into all the details that enabled me to come up with a tagline for an advertising campaign presentation which, in turn, helped the agency win a multi-million dollar account from a prestigious Japanese electronics firm called Frontier (for these details, see Moeran, 2006: 3–17). What is important about the lucky break is that it frequently enables a shift both in the fieldworker's status and in perceptions of the fieldworker on the part of those working in the organization being studied. In ADK, my success meant that I was no longer regarded exclusively as a visiting foreign researcher or 'professor', but that my informants came to realize that I might be able to contribute to the work that they were doing. Because I had demonstrated 'solidarity' (cf. Geertz, 1973: 416), I found myself invited to take part in and contribute to a number of other ongoing projects. These ranged from dreaming up a name and associated services for All Nippon Airways' business class (*Club ANA*) to devising a marketing and creative concept for a Nihon Lever fabric softener (*Happiness is a Soft Blanket*).

As a result of this participation in all kinds of projects in which I would not otherwise have been involved, I was able to begin to put together the numerous pieces of information that I had gathered during the Frontier presentation preparations and fit them into various theoretical jigsaw puzzles of the kind that I have written about over the years (e.g., Moeran, 1996; 2006). In a way, then, the Frontier case marked a subtle shift in my role as fieldwork researcher. Instead of being a participant observer in the classic anthropological manner, I became an *observant participant*. Although not too much is said about this sort of thing in the social science literature, observant participation should, I believe, be the ideal to which we all aspire during our research.

Now, it may seem to one or two of my readers that there is not that much of a distinction to be made between participant observation and observant participation and that I am merely splitting hairs by stressing the importance of the latter. But what I want to get across is the fact that this distinction – however crude or subtle it may seem – in fact marks an important *rite de passage* in fieldwork itself and affects the *quality* of any information given and later analysed. *The* problem facing any researcher – whether organizational studies scholar, anthropologist, sociologist, historian, political scientist, or some other – concerns the relevance, accuracy, and so forth of the data gathered. Does this survey ask the right kind of questions so far as the research hypothesis is concerned? Is this historical document – dug up in a castle attic – as authentic as it seems, or is it a fake, written deliberately to pull the wool over an unsuspecting reader's eyes? Is this informant telling me what he really does in a particular situation or what he should be doing but in fact does not do? In every field of study scholars have to wrestle with such problems regarding the validity of their data.

In fieldwork, one of the difficulties facing the ethnographer is trying to distinguish between what people *say* they do and what they *actually* do. Indeed, this is a problem facing all those in management and organizational studies who make use of interviews to gather primary research material. People are always trying to manage impressions and to put across an image that may in fact be rather different from their 'real' selves. This is fairly easy to do when their interviewer has just walked in off the street with a series of prepared questions to ask during the next hour. It becomes less easy when that same interviewer has been hanging around the office for the past three months, watching what is going on and asking questions of anyone who has the time or inclination to talk to her. For her own part, the fieldworker may be desperately trying to make sense of this new social world into which, for one reason or another, she has made her way. What those around her take for granted as 'the normal course of events' can often strike her as not just strange, but from another planet. In a slightly different sense from that originally intended by Oliver Sacks, this fieldworker may well feel as if she is an 'anthropologist on Mars'.

What marks the shift from participant observation to observant participation, I think, is precisely the ability to see beyond the social front that informants present to strangers in their everyday lives, to know that there is a difference between what Erving Goffman (1990) refers to as 'front stage' and 'back stage' behaviour, and to have ready access to that back stage. As I remarked earlier, fieldworkers at times can initially find themselves pursuing topics that their informants want them to pursue and can be severely restricted in their access to more sensitive themes. The problem facing fieldworkers, then, is how to move beyond surface appearances and study what they, rather than their informants, think is important. The ability to move back stage depends partly on your personality as fieldworker, partly on the intimacy that you forge with your informants through participant observation (see Chapter 10 [Beech et al.], in this volume), and partly on your ability to seize a fortuitous occasion and turn it to your advantage.

Once you have crossed the invisible line separating front stage from back stage, things are never again the same as they were before. You, too, like your informants, can play both front and back stage games according to context and social role. Moreover, your informants may come to realize that you have learned the rules and know the difference between front and back stage games, and, as a result, they may stop pretending when in your presence and allow themselves to be seen as they are. This is immensely helpful in terms of the quality of research that you, as a fieldworker, are able to conduct and, therefore, of the quality of analysis that follows – provided, of course, that you remain alert to potential conflicts of interest between your informants' practices and your own integrity as a researcher. But as you learn to play the game, you will be increasingly able, I think, to separate fact from fiction and gossip from information, while strategically using both to gain further data. The sheer wealth of information, criticism and commentary that can be made available by informants – who are now essentially colleagues – can lead to a further acceptance of the fieldworker as an insider who will then use his myriad data to create a holistic analysis. In short, observant participation leads to the kind of involved detachment that characterizes the very best of social scientific analysis.

Thus, in my own case, once I had done my bit in the Frontier presentation and had come to be seen as an 'ad man', I was – so to speak – accepted by agency employees as 'one of them', rather than continually treated as an outsider. This led to my being freely given access to informal, inside knowledge of agency–client and agency–media relations, as well as of the agency's own organizational features. Although, of course, there is no guarantee that the length of the fieldwork in itself will bring about the passage from participant observation to observant participation, this shift from front to back stage in my research would never have been possible without the long-term duration of my fieldwork.[2]

In spite of these 'successes', however, total social immersion and intimacy have depended very much on the type of fieldwork being conducted (cf. Moeran, 2005: 198–9). For example, in the rural community in southern Japan where I lived with my family for four years, our lives were entirely overtaken by community affairs. During these goings-on, all of us developed close friendships with local potters, farmers, foresters and their wives and children, and shared in their daily (mis-)fortunes (see Moeran, 1997; 1998). In the advertising agency, however, the situation was rather different. For a start, there is a limit to the amount of time anyone in any walk of life – even the most devoted banker, shop owner or academic – can spend in his place of work. Even though, from time to time, I would stay late at my desk on weekday evenings, and occasionally go into the agency on a Saturday to see who else was there, doing what with whom, while overtly catching up on my notes, I rarely put in the long hours of overtime that were customary for my Japanese informants. Nor did I ever meet them in their home environments. The nearest thing I got to an invitation to extramural activities was an occasional quick drink with a colleague in a neighbourhood bar or a slap-up meal with a managing director who would take me along as an 'interesting rarity' to help entertain a client.

If my fieldwork in the agency was not entirely true to the ideal of total social immersion – a feature that has come under some scrutiny in recent years (cf. Amit, 2000: 5–11) – in the sense that, as mentioned at the outset, an organization like a company is limited to work and does not usually extend to inclusive residential or other common-interest functions, it was marked by the development of quite close personal working relationships with individual personnel employed there (on this, see also Chapter 10 by Beech et al. in this volume). It is almost certainly the quality of such relationships that influences what kind of findings and insights a fieldworker gets. As mentioned earlier, the intimacy developed with informants is very important because it helps the ethnographer depict people not as one-dimensional research subjects, but as rounded individuals (Amit, 2000: 2–3). At the same time, it enables the researcher to see crucial connections between totally unexpected – and seemingly separate – things, events and practices (see Chapter 6 by Nicolini in this volume). This is where fieldwork has the measure of all other research methodologies.

problematics

So much for the euphoria. It is now time to recognize that the grass in the ethnographic field is not necessarily greener. Fieldwork brings with it certain problems that we need to face up to in the study of organizations and which make it a tricky methodology to market successfully to would-be research settings. Two of the most enduring of these problems are fieldwork duration and method.

Let us start with duration. For organizational ethnographers, fieldwork takes quite some time. In general, ethnographic fieldwork should last between six months and one year. For managers seeking to make use of the ethnographer, however, this is often an unacceptable proposition. Business moves too fast, they would say, for us to hang around and wait six months for an answer to our problems. We need answers tomorrow or – at the latest – next week, not next year!

At first glance, this seems like a reasonable enough objection, but a seasoned fieldworker might well present a counter-argument along the following lines. A lot of organizational problems (like Japanese company employees spending an undue amount of time away from their desks in cafés, for example) are in fact surface reactions to unchanging, fundamental issues (connected, in this case, with the tension arising from the demands of corporate identity, on the one hand, and the need as a manager to cultivate independent personal networks, on the other). In such cases – and here comes the ethnographic pitch – an organization would be well advised to employ a fieldworker to carry out a study of its practices, since good, extended fieldwork will undoubtedly reveal surprising links (like that between café frequentation and the inherent structural tensions in Japanese corporate organization) that ordinary questioning via short-term research might take years to disclose.

Nevertheless, there are certainly issues that might well be studied and resolved in a shorter period of time. One way for a fieldworker to go about this is to team up with fellow fieldworkers and conduct a group study of the issue in question. This saves time and enables a lot of information to be gleaned in a short time frame, as those concerned can pool their cumulative knowledge at regular intervals (e.g., daily or half-daily) and use that knowledge to further their enquiries. The only trouble is that a group study of this kind does not usually permit its participants to see through the distinction between what people say they do and what they actually do because of the limited time available for fieldwork. It hinders the move from front to back stage that, I have argued, is a vital step in fieldwork. This necessarily affects the quality of the analysis, so that organizations hosting fieldworkers need to balance this quality–time equation in order to meet their specific requirements. You might even wonder, then, why ethnographers research this way in the first place. For many in the advertising and consumer marketing professions, for instance, even the briefest fieldwork's results are often so superior to those produced by the various methods of market analysis (surveys, questionnaires, focus groups, and so on) practised hitherto that 'ethnography' is understandably preferred, although we should also note, along with Sunderland and Denny (2007: 14), that market researchers have 'often transformed themselves into "ethnographers" with few changes in practice beyond the name'.

This brings me neatly to the second main challenge of fieldwork: its method. The central problematic of organizational ethnography is that it promotes a method that cannot be carried out consistently. This is because, as a fieldworker, you will invariably find yourself in a series of processual social situations, in which all kinds of unexpected and unplanned events can occur. You will thus be obliged to make innumerable small decisions at every twist and turn of your daily routine – to choose between attending a media awards event or sitting in on a business guru's lecture, between having lunch with a group of employees or with a mid-rank manager, and so on and so forth. Each choice necessarily invites, and simultaneously excludes, certain kinds of potential information, which itself then guides, or partially obstructs, you as you blunder on in search of enlightenment about the social world into which you have plunged. Under these circumstances, you have no alternative but to be adaptable – both to the events and to the people that you come across there. This would be virtually impossible were you to stick to some idea of 'method'.

Thus, even though Takano had carefully drawn up a schedule for me prior to my starting fieldwork, by the fifth week, I was already going off on a research tangent as I followed the production of animated cartoons (as a follow-on to television programme buying). Within three months I found myself involved in preparations for a presentation put on by the International Division, even though I was not to begin my formal study there until the eighth month of my research. For four to five months in the middle of my fieldwork period, I was following the day-to-day development of a contact lens campaign, while also formally learning about market development, account services, creative work, and promotions, as originally planned.

So fieldwork demands an immense amount of flexibility that makes method a bit of a moveable feast and consistent methodology bad method-ology (Miller, 2003: 77). Perhaps this is why some scholars regard fieldwork as a 'messy, qualitative experience' (Marcus and Fisher, 1986: 22) and suggest that its 'methods' are in large part a 'myth' (Karp and Kendall, 1982: 251). However, we should not dismiss the idea of method entirely. After all, we are always talking to people, watching how they interact, and trying to put two and two together, as we make use of our disciplinary training to see how individuals manoeuvre within an organizational structure and how that structure itself constrains and yields to such manoeuvring. Prolonged field-work enables the regular cross-checking of facts and opportunities to confirm or disconfirm observations. Participant observation allows the recording of 'speech-in-action' (Sanjek, 1990: 211).

There are some 'tricks of the trade' (Becker, 1998), of course, to help you along. The best one I know is the 'Close the notebook' trick. When someone starts telling you some *really* interesting stuff that is definitely back and not front stage, and when that informant seems slightly self-conscious or hesitant about whether he is doing the right thing, you very deliberately close your notebook and put it away in your pocket so that he knows you are no longer taking notes (cf. Chapman, 2001: 28). And when somebody is *only* telling you front-stage stuff and seems embarrassed, for whatever reason, by your presence, you can do the same. In the first instance, your informant can carry on saying what she wants to say without fear of being recorded. In the second, there is a good chance that she will suddenly open up to reveal things that the notebook inhibited her from saying. All you have to do is try to remember the gems that then litter the conversation. If nothing else, it is a good way to train your memory.

But this trick of the trade itself invites another: what I like to call 'Case the joint'. Like a thief before a burglary, you check out the area around where you are going to conduct an interview. On the assumption that something might well happen to make you close your notebook (and you can see from these examples that, for better and for worse, I am one of those fieldworkers who prefer not to use tape recorders), you should make sure you know where to run to after it is over in order to get down everything you have not been able to record and write up in fuller detail what you *have* recorded while it is still fresh in your mind. So, the trick is to find a café or restaurant or a reasonably quiet bar – even a car (Powdermaker, 1967: 157–8, 215) – where you can sit, think through, recall and, these days, type up on a laptop computer the interview you have just completed.

But, as I said above, there are probably not *that* many useful and practical tips for the participant observer, for whom fieldwork is primarily a combination of understanding and causal explanation (Burawoyet, 1991: 3) and a movement from observation (where method helps) to participation (where it does not) and thence to interpretation (where it might). 'Fieldworkers are notorious analytic bricoleurs, sniffing out and sifting through current theory for leads as to how fieldwork materials might be conceptualized' (Van Maanen, 1988: 66).

concluding points

So what does this slightly confessional narrative about an anthropologist's experience of fieldwork in a Japanese advertising agency tell us about organizational ethnography?

In the first place, I have tried to show the strategic use to which randomly struck-up connections can be put by the fieldworker – in the same way that they are regularly used by people in the business world. One chance can lead to another, and it is the ability or inability of both fieldworker and businessman to make the most of an opportunity that leads to success or failure in the endeavour in hand. Thus, while access to an organization often depends to some extent on chance, despite what Buchanan et al. (1988: 56) say to the contrary, skill *is* needed to take advantage of an initial opportunity.

Second, I have highlighted how access is crucial to success or failure in ethnographic research. The fact that I had the blessing of the agency's CEO in conducting my research led to my having a whole fieldwork schedule prepared for me in advance. It also meant that I was properly introduced to all the agency's staff at its monthly early morning assembly (where I again had to introduce myself and state my research aims) and that I was then taken around every section and department in every division of the agency by a senior member of the President's Office. For better or for worse, everyone knew who I was and could therefore approach or avoid me, depending on how they felt.

But access in itself is not necessarily sufficient to ensure quality research, since it has to be renegotiated (Gellner and Hirsch, 2001: 5) every time the fieldworker moves about 'his' organization. I mentioned earlier the difficulty facing the organizational ethnographer, where people are very willing to talk about things that they want to talk about but are usually equally competent at not talking about what they do not want to talk about. This kind of impression management may not be noticed by the management studies-kind of researcher who confines herself to conducting one-off interviews with people (often just managerial staff) in an organization. But it usually hits the full-time participant observer a few months into his research, when he comes up against a brick wall designed to prevent any further understanding of how an organization really works. In other words, as a fieldworker you somehow have to move from front-stage impression management where people *tell* you what they do to back-stage reality where you can see what they *actually* do. It is only by so doing that you can work out the structure of the field in which 'your' organization is positioned *and* analyse the social mechanisms by which informants position themselves therein (cf. Bourdieu, 1993: 58). This is one of the essential commitments of fieldwork in general and of organizational ethnography in particular (cf. Miller, 1997: 16–17).

This is why I have my reservations about research based only on formal and informal interviews. The advantage of organizational ethnography is that it offers a broad approach whose 'open-ended flexibility' incorporates other research methods like informal and formal interviews, text analysis, question-naires, historical research, and so on (Macdonald, 2001: 78). Full-immersion fieldwork enables the ethnographer to structure the 'multiple voices' of his informants (Moeran, 2006: 37–58) and to become aware of unanticipated details, as well as of the relevance of apparently irrelevant things that are said and done (cf. Chapman, 2001: 24). It is by observing and participating in informants' interactions during both front- and back-stage performances, moreover, that you will be able to arrive at a holistic study with general theoretical implications (cf. Gellner and Hirsch, 2001: 9–10).

But are there not disadvantages to the kind of fieldworker integration that I have argued for here? Doesn't successful observant participation imply that the fieldworker has succumbed to anthropology's occupational hazard by 'going native' (Powdermaker, 1967: 115–19)? Clearly, the fact that, as a field-worker, I came to understand and participate in the back-stage behaviour of my informants precluded me from entering the back stage of other – media, entertainment and client – organizations that formed part of the field of Japanese advertising. It can be difficult, after all, to be an 'insider' in more than one competing organization. Yet I have argued that the very richness of the data that derived from observant participation overcame this disadvantage. I am convinced that this is *always* the case.

At the same time, there is probably something to be said for the argument that the strength of observant participation may also be its weakness. There is, after all, a fine line between 'going native' and remaining a committed fieldworker – a line between participation and observation that defies detection for much of the time. This is why it is extremely important to get away from the field and return to one's 'home base' at an academic institution or wherever, in order to gain distance from the ethnographic experience. Without such detachment, the organizational ethnographer will never be able to separate experience from analysis. This is not say that you should deny that experience; merely that you should keep it at bay in the ordering, understanding and writing up of fieldwork material. The strength of observant participation, I think, is that it enables fieldworkers to reconstruct 'the relationship between objectivity and subjectivity, scientist and native, Self and Other' as mutually constituent, rather than see it as 'an unbridgeable opposition' (Tedlock, 1991: 71). It is this ability that separates organizational ethnography from all other methods of business and management studies research, for it brings a much-needed humaneness to the study of business organizations.

notes

[1] I have changed the names of all individuals mentioned in this paper, with the sole exception of that of ADK's former CEO and now chairman, Inagaki Masao, since it would be a little ridiculous to try to conceal his name, given his prominence in the Japanese advertising industry.

[2] For the record, I should perhaps add that it usually takes me about three months of intensive participant observation before the facade that separates front from back stage begins to crack. I have no idea if there is a norm for this movement from tolerated outsider to accepted insider or, if so, what the norm might be.

references

Amit, V. (2000) 'Introduction: Constructing the field', in V. Amit (ed.), *Constructing the field: Ethnographic fieldwork in the contemporary world*. London: Routledge. pp. 1–18.

Becker, H. (1998) *Tricks of the trade*. Chicago: University of Chicago Press.

Bourdieu, P. (1984) *Distinction: A social critique of the judgement of taste*. London: Routledge & Kegan Paul.

Bourdieu, P. (1993) *Fields of cultural production*. Cambridge: Polity.

Buchanan, D., Boddy, D., and McCalman, J. (1988) 'Getting in, getting on, getting out and getting back', in A. Bryman (ed.), *Doing research in organizations*. London: Routledge. pp. 53–67.

Burawoy, M. (1991) 'Introduction', in M. Burawoy, A. Burton, A. Arnett Ferguson, K.J. Fox (eds), *Ethnography unbound: Power and resistance in the modern metropolis*. Berkeley: University of California Press. pp. 1–7.

Chapman, M. (2001) 'Social anthropology and business studies: Some considerations of method', in D. Gellner and E. Hirsch (eds), *Inside organizations*. Oxford: Berg. pp. 19–34.

Geertz, C. (1973) 'Deep play: Notes on the Balinese cockfight', in C. Geertz, *The interpretation of cultures*. New York: Basic Books. pp. 412–53.

Geertz, C. (1983) *Local knowledge: Further essays in interpretive anthropology*. New York: Basic Books.

Gellner, D. and Hirsch, E. (eds) (2001) *Inside organizations*. Oxford: Berg.

Goffman, E. (1990) [1959] *The presentation of self in everyday life*. Harmondsworth: Penguin.

Hannerz, U. (2006) 'Studying down, up, sideways, through, backwards, forwards, away and at home', in S. Coleman and P. Collins (eds), *Locating the field*. Oxford: Berg. pp. 23–42.

Hine, C. (2001) 'Ethnography in the laboratory', in D. Gellner and E. Hirsch (eds), *Inside organizations*. Oxford: Berg. pp. 61–76.

Karp, I. and Kendall, M. (1982) 'Reflexivity in fieldwork', in P. Secord (ed.), *Explaining human behavior, human action and social structure*. Beverly Hills, CA: Sage. pp. 249–73.

Kunda, G. (1992) *Engineering culture: Control and commitment in a high-tech corporation*. Philadelphia: Temple University Press.

Macdonald, S. (2001) 'Ethnography in the Science Museum, London', in D. Gellner and E. Hirsch (eds), *Inside organizations*. Oxford: Berg. pp. 77–96.

Marcus, G. (1998) *Ethnography through thick & thin*. Princeton: Princeton University Press.

Marcus, G. and Fisher, M. (1986) *Anthropology as cultural critique*. Chicago: University of Chicago Press.

Miller, D. (1997) *Capitalism: An ethnographic approach*. Oxford: Berg.

Miller, D. (2003) 'Advertising, production and consumption as cultural economy', in T. de Waal Malefyt and B. Moeran (eds), *Advertising cultures*. Oxford: Berg. pp. 75–90.

Moeran, B. (1996) *A Japanese advertising agency*. London: Curzon.

Moeran, B. (1997) *Folk art potters of Japan*. London: Curzon.

Moeran, B. (1998) *A far valley: Four years in a Japanese village*. Tokyo and New York: Kodansha International.

Moeran, B. (2005) *The business of ethnography*. Oxford: Berg.

Moeran, B. (2006) *Ethnography at work*. Oxford: Berg.

Nader, L. (1969) 'Up the anthropologist', in D. Hymes (ed.), *Reinventing anthropology*. New York: Pantheon. pp. 284–344.

Powdermaker, H. (1967) *Stranger and friend: The way of an anthropologist*. London: Secker & Warburg.

Powdermaker, H. (1969) 'Field work', in D. Sills (ed.), *The international encyclopedia of the social sciences*. New York: Macmillan and Free Press. pp. 418–24.

Sanjek, R. (ed.) (1990) *Fieldnotes: The makings of anthropology*. Ithaca: Cornell University Press.

Stewart, A. (1998) *The ethnographer's method*. Newbury Park, CA: Sage.

Sunderland, P.L. and Denny, R.M. (2007) *Doing anthropology in consumer research*. Walnut Creek, CA: Left Coast Press.

Tedlock, B. (1991) 'From participant observation to the observation of participation: The emergence of narrative ethnography', *Journal of Anthropological Research*, 47(1): 69–94.

Van Maanen, J. (1988) *Tales of the field*. Chicago: University of Chicago Press.

8

At-home ethnography: Struggling with closeness and closure[1]

Mats Alvesson

It is rare that academics study the 'lived realities' of their own organizations. There may be good reasons for this. It is difficult to study something one is heavily involved in. One may fear that those targeted for study might experience breaches of trust. Personal involvement should not necessarily rule out inquiry, however, as that is linked with intimate knowledge, which means involvement may be as much a resource as a liability. Feelings of organizational loyalty requiring that one not expose 'backstage' conditions may lead to, or be an excuse for, self-discipline and subordination to conventions of proper behaviour which otherwise are taken for granted.

Understanding organizations calls for the 'micro-anchoring' of more abstract phenomena. This is typically understood as implying a qualitative approach in which the researcher tries to get relatively 'close' to the meanings, ideas, and discursive and/or social practices of a group of people that the researcher is studying. Qualitative research is often seen in geographic terms: as a movement when a researcher, initially at a distance, comes closer to the lived realities of other people. The geographic terminology is not solely metaphoric. In anthropology the ethnographer may travel long distances in order to come into physical contact with those being studied, making observations at, perhaps, five to ten yards from the 'natives'. In qualitative social science fields that address less 'exotic objects of study,' the researcher perhaps travels a few miles and then carries out fieldwork at microphone-holding distance – say two yards – from the 'subjects'.

In this chapter I explore the possibilities of research that avoids the element of physical and metaphoric distance-reducing activity, that is, studying one's own setting – a domain in which one is normally present oneself for a part of the day – rather than the setting of a group of other people. I introduce and explore the idea of an at-home ethnography and elaborate on its possibilities and difficulties. I will start, however, with a brief review of some problems in qualitative research, particularly with interviewing, indicating why we need to go into more of an ethnographic direction, and then discuss why we may want to explore new ways of doing so. I will concentrate on these two methods (i) for reasons of space, (ii) as these are probably the most popular ones, and (iii) the points made about interviews also indicate some of the problems with methods such as focus groups and diaries, e.g. highly selective reports.

some problems with research interviews

The difficulties in doing research about one's own setting, by definition including (although not necessarily focusing on) the researcher-author her- or himself, are great (as will be addressed later): there are intellectual as well as political problems involved. Why make research life so complicated and risky? One answer to this question comes from problems with the alternatives.

Qualitative research often involves conducting and interpreting interviews. The rationale is that such an approach can produce and document a rich set of accounts of the interviewees' experiences, knowledge, ideas and impressions. Most of the literature on interviewing deals at length with how this practice may be utilized as effectively as possible. While recognizing some of the complexities involved, the literature assumes that skills may be developed and an approach taken in which errors are minimized and high-quality empirical material may be be produced.

Nevertheless, some methodologists find serious problems with the 'scientific' character of interviews. For example, as Silverman (1989; 2001) has stressed, the value of interview statements is in many cases limited in terms of their capacity to reflect reality 'out there' as well as the subjective world of the interviewee (beliefs, attitudes, psychological traits, etc). This is partly the case because the statements are liable to be determined by the situation, i.e., statements are related to the interview context rather than to any other specific 'experiential reality' beyond this context, and partly because they are affected by the available cultural scripts about how one should normally express oneself on particular topics (see also Dingwall, 1997; Potter and Wetherell, 1987; Shotter and Gergen, 1989; 1994).

However, these problems cannot really be avoided through the use of techniques aiming to make interview work as rational and reliable as possible. There are always sources of influence in an interview context that cannot be minimized or controlled (Alvesson, 2003). These sources of influence go far beyond what may be seen as pure 'errors' and are basic parts of human interaction, putting imprints on what is happening in interview situations, making them much more complicated than what most advocates of interviews – as an instrument for accessing practices or experiences – assume to be the case.

This is not to say that we can't learn from asking questions of people and – with some scepticism – listening to their answers. Still, there are good reasons to be more restrictive than is presently the case in our reliance on interviewing as the main technique for acquiring knowledge of what goes on in daily organizational life, outside interview situations. It is simply too difficult to sort out script-following, the social dynamics of the interview situation, impression management, and (other forms of) politically conscious language use from valid accounts about people's feelings, thoughts and ideas, respectively, and social practices 'out there'. It is seldom possible to separate the 'distortions' from 'authentic experiences' or 'correct information' (Alvesson, 2003; Silverman, 2001).

ethnography

An alternative to solely or mainly relying on a set of interviews is to carry out an ethnography. There are, of course, different opinions about what should be included in the concept of ethnography, meaning studies involving a prolonged period of fieldwork in which the researcher tries to get close to the organization or group being studied; relies on their accounts as well as on first-hand observations of a rich variety of naturally occurring events (as well as on other material, e.g., documents or material artifacts); and has at least some interest in cultural issues (meanings, symbols, ideas, assumptions) (for example, Wolcott, 1995). There seems to be increasing interest and talk about ethnography in social science but, paradoxically, observation-based studies may be increasingly less common in light of the trend to do more 'efficient' interview studies (Dingwall, 1997). Pressure to publish and an increased short-turn orientation and focus on journal publication may also discourage researchers from doing 'full-scale' ethnographies. The variation among those wanting to associate themselves with ethnography as a label means that it becomes diluted as a term, and perhaps even as a methodology.

Ethnographies have some clear advantages over other methods. Observations of naturally occurring events avoid – or, more usually, reduce – the researcher's dependence on the accounts of respondents. However, without the accounts of the people being studied, it is very difficult to say something about the meanings of and ideas guiding particular behaviours and practices. The use of multiple methods – sometimes referred to as triangulation, sometimes as mixed methods – is often to be preferred, not in order to zoom in on the 'truth' through different methods, but in order to create a richer picture (Denzin, 1994; Schwarz-Shea, 2006).

Of course, ethnographies can also have disadvantadges, such as being time-consuming, often personally tiring, and stressful to carry out. 'Hanging around' commonly involves a lot of dead time as not much of interest is happening on the surface level a large part of the time (in many offices, for example, most people may spend most of their time looking at screens). Ethnographies are thought too ineffective for many research purposes (Wolcott, 1995). A fundamental problem, which also characterizes other qualitative research, concerns the difficulties in handling all the empirical material that the researcher generates and in producing a text that does justice to it. Even if the ethnographer claims that his or her firsthand experiences of the object of study provide a strong basis of authority for his or her knowledge claims, the text produced is not just a document mirroring something 'out there' (Clifford and Marcus, 1986; Geertz, 1988; Marcus and Fischer, 1986; Van Maanen, 1988; 1995). Ethnography has gone from a relatively unreflective, closed and general description of 'a whole way of life' – not too difficult to depict/portray in a text – to an undertaking that, instead, emphasizes a more tentative, open and partial interpretation, drawing attention to matters of uncertainty and style in writing (Geertz, 1973, 1988). The text is seen as the central part of the research project. It tells a story, it uses a particular style, and includes much more than simply the reporting of data and a description of objective reality (Alvesson, 2002). Things going on in social reality 'out there' may inspire the author but put highly uncertain imprints on the text. The final academic text is an outcome of many other things: the choice of theory, political struggles and fashions within the academic community, the researcher's idiosyncrasies, established conventions for writing, the use of language, format, etc. Of course, these problems hold not only for ethnography, although they are possibly more pronounced and apparent there, but are also relevant for practically all qualitative research.

To sum up, there are many advantages with 'conventional' ideas about ethnography. However, ethnographies are time-consuming and often uneconomical, and they often mean that 'empirical material' (piles of interview and observation notes) receives (too) much attention, at the expense of other virtues in research, such as reflexivity at various levels of one's research, the creation of distance to empirical material, and (theoretical) analysis (cf. Lofland, 1985; Snow, Morrill, and Anderson, 2003).

at-home ethnography

As a response to some of the problems of interview-based qualitative research and ethnographies, I propose what I call at-home ethnography. At-home ethnography is a study and a text in which the researcher-author describes a cultural setting to which s/he has a 'natural access' and in which s/he is an active participant, more or less on equal terms with other participants. The researcher works and/or lives in the setting and uses the experiences and knowledge of and access to empirical material for research purposes. This research is, however, not the individual's major preoccupation, apart from the time when the empirical material is targeted for close scrutiny and writing. The person is thus *not* an ethnographer in the sense of being a 'professional stranger' (Agar, 1986) or a researcher primarily oriented to studying the specific setting. Participant observation is thus not a good label in this case; 'observing participant' is better at capturing the meaning I have in mind (see Chapter 7 by Moeran in this volume). Participation comes first and is only occasionally complemented with observation in a research-focused sense. One may also imagine versions of at-home ethnography, but perhaps there are certain moments that are more intense – the ethnographer is called to duty – when the monitoring of what goes on becomes a chief preoccupation. In this case, at-home ethnography borders on participant observation. A significant difference between the two is that the conventional ethnographer uses any kind of active participation for an instrumental purpose – the ethnographer working as a lumberjack does so in order to be able to produce research about lumberjacks, not because of an inner urge to cut down trees – whereas the idea of at-home ethnography is to utilize the position one is in for another, secondary purpose, that is, doing research on the setting of which one is a part. Alternative terms might be home-culture-ethnography or insider-ethnography. (Brannick and Coghlan, 2007, talk of insider research, but relate it primarily to action research. This term is also used by researchers from third world countries studying their own culture.)

The term at-home ethnography draws attention to one's own cultural context, what goes on around oneself rather than putting oneself and one's experiences in the centre. At-home ethnography, then, is a bit different from some recent work in which the deeply personal experiences of the researcher are in focus. This kind of work is often labelled autoethnography (Ellis and Bochner, 2000). 'Autoethnographies are highly personalized, revealing texts in which authors tell stories about their own lived experiences, relating the personal to the cultural' (Richardson, 2000: 931). There is a strong inward-looking element in this kind of work, even though the researcher goes back and forth between focusing outward on social and cultural aspects of their personal experience, and then, they look inward, exposing a vulnerable self that is moved by and may move through, refract, and resist cultural interpretations (Ellis and Bochner, 2000: 739).

A related stream, more common in Europe, is called memory work and is linked to feminism (see Widerberg, 1995). Memory work and (auto)ethnography share a focus on strongly personal experiences, e.g., as a patient in the hospital system (for example, Kolker, 1996) or as a woman in a male-dominated society (Widerberg, 1995). These texts tend to be more autobiographical than observational in a conventional social science sense. Often the outcome of the research (writing) appears so personal that its contribution to scientific study is, for many readers, not clear or convincing.

Unlike autoethnography and memory work, at-home ethnography emphasizes the careful documentation and interpretation of those social events that the researcher witnesses, and the analysis does not necessarily emphasize the personal meaning or strongly subjective aspects of the research/event/experience. The at-home ethnographer may be wise to address phenomena with which he/she is not deeply personally involved, e.g., when others in the environment are gendering each other or discussing strategy with which the researcher is not directly involved. This does not imply that the at-home ethnographer is necessarily detached, objective or neutral, but that a low or moderate degree of personal involvement is of benefit. Trying to take a step back from the flow of interaction and look at events from a researcher's, rather than an organizational member's, point of view is a key ambition.

In this kind of research the work situation provides the viewpoint, but the aim is to carry out cultural analysis more than introspection, although it is important not to overstress this division between these two, as one's own feelings, thoughts and experiences may offer valuable material for understanding the topic of the study (Jaggar, 1989). As Van Maanen (1988) suggests, ethnographies are sometimes written in a confessional style, that is, the researcher-author writes from a strong and explicit personal position and proceeds from personal experiences of the encounter with those being studied. At-home ethnography does not necessarily imply a confessional style; it can be written in a conventional (realist) or some other way. One possibility for 'realistic' writing is to provide detailed (and as neutral as possible) accounts of social events that the researcher observes but is not directly engaged in. A confessional style may be very appropriate in at-home ethnographies, but writing personally does not necessarily imply some strong personal involvement in the issues studied.

At-home ethnography is especially relevant to research on universities and higher education, as these are the settings in which many researchers work. Other sites in which researchers are engaged, for example neighbourhoods, consultancy work, political organizations, other associations, and commercial settings encountered as a customer, may also be targeted. Researchers use public transport, go to restaurants and shops, and visit hospitals and childcare institutions, all of which offer material for ethnographic organizational study. PhD students combining work and research in regular work organizations have excellent opportunities to do at-home ethnography. People wanting to start a PhD programme while working might well use the time before enrolling to do at-home ethnographic work – although without PhD training and supervision it may be difficult to produce sufficiently high-quality material that would be useful in dissertation research. There are a few research efforts within organizational studies that bear a resemblance to at-home ethnography. Watson (1996) studied his students and his interaction with them in class, Tierny (1993) wrote, using a fictional form, about policy changes regarding homosexuals in universities, and Fairclough (1993) used his own application for promotion as an example of the marketization of universities. I have myself used my university department as a case for illustrating 'multiple cultural configurations' in organizations (Alvesson, 1993). Van Maanen (1991) wrote about his experiences as a Disney employee. One person in a research team got data about a task force of which he was a member (Gioia et al., 1994), but this study is focused more on coding procedures and abstractions from the setting, at the expense of rich descriptions of events, talk and actions, and avoids any recognition of personal experiences. In most of these cases, one can hardly talk about a full at-home ethnography.

A major difference between at-home ethnography and more conventional ethnography is that the territory of the former is the setting being studied. When a conventional ethnographer takes a job or adopts some other situational role in order to learn the culture and get data as a (temporary) member of an organization or community, he or she undergoes a socialization process. When the ethnography is a PhD project, a double socialization process takes place: (i) the researcher is being socialized to the research community, ending with full membership and the internalization of appropriate orientations; and (ii) the researcher is at the same time being socialized within the community being studied, ending with a good understanding and mastery of cultural rules, but also (hopefully) retaining considerable distance in order to avoid 'going native' – and thus losing sight of interesting theoretical research contributions. While conventional ethnography is basically a matter of the stranger entering a setting and 'breaking in', trying to create knowledge through understanding the natives from their own points of view and their own readings of acts, words and materials used, at-home ethnography is more of a struggle to 'break out' from the taken-for-grantedness of a particular framework that is already quite familiar. It is a process of creating knowledge through trying to interpret the acts, words and materials used by oneself and one's fellow organizational members from a certain distance. In the first case, we have the researcher as burglar, in the second as fly on the wall. The burglar-researcher wants to overcome obstacles in order to get in contact with a target of interest; the 'invisible' researcher struggles in order to create sufficient distance in order to get a perspective on a very familiar lived reality. Ethnographers, in particular, struggle with the dilemma of closeness/distance, balancing the two and knowing where to draw the line (see Ybema and Kamsteeg, Chapter 5, this volume). While the conventional researcher (with an anthropological orientation) may ask, 'What in hell do *they* think they are up to?', the at-home ethnographer must ask, 'What in hell do *we* think we are up to?' I will address how this may be accomplished later on.

It is, of course, often difficult to decide on the precise territory of the at-home research project: in a university context, is it the department, a fraction of it, the school, faculty, university or the occupational community, or perhaps the system of higher education (in a particular country)? I would say that those parts of the social setting with which one directly interacts and thus may observe with some regularity form a productive terrain for ethnographic work. Universities – like most organizations – are not homogeneous, and the idea of exploring a university culture as a whole risks encouraging too superficial a work. But even though universities or even departments within them are better conceptualized as multiple cultural configurations (Alvesson, 1993; Trowler, 1998), there are blind spots and intellectual closures shared by people in universities that make the project of a researcher studying a department – different from his or her own in significant ways – also difficult. All research on familiar groups then must take the problem of 'breaking out' seriously.

The conventional ethnographer typically spends an enormous amount of time on note-taking. Scribbling down observations, informal interviews and, perhaps, one's thoughts and associations, can sometimes appear to be the cornerstone of an entire project, central also for the researcher's feelings (Jackson, 1995). An at-home ethnographer is more inclined to rely on their familiarity with the setting as an empirical starting point. The trick is more a matter of accomplishing a description and insightful, theoretically relevant ideas and comments out of the material. It is a matter of thinking through an understanding one may already have that is good, although perhaps non-articulated and partly taken for granted. Sometimes in research there is a trade-off between a good cultural description and an interesting theoretical idea being abstracted from (theory-impregnated) interpretive description.

Denzin (1997) writes that 'ethnography is that form of inquiry and writing that produces descriptions and accounts about the ways of life *of the writer* and those written about' (xi, emphasis added). This is a rather peculiar definition, at odds with almost all the other views on ethnography. Normally, ethnographies study a group that the writer is not a member of, which, of course, does not prevent the study from saying something of relevance for the self-understanding of the researcher's working environment, but the latter is not necessarily aimed for. Geertz's famous (1973) study of the Balinese cockfight is, for example, not about the ways of life of Princeton University professors. Denzin's definition has, however, an unintentional bearing on what I have in mind with the concept of at-home ethnography.

One rationale for at-home ethnography concerns its capacity to come up with novel and interesting empirical material in an 'economical' way. This is partly related to the amount of time the at-home researcher can devote to the scanning of his/her domains for the spotting of interesting events or phenomena. While the conventional ethnographer perhaps spends a few months full-time every fifth year or so doing research, the at-home ethnographer is doing the scanning most of the time on an on-going basis. The insider is, potentially, better positioned than the outsider to reveal 'the true story', although position alone is insufficient to realize that potential. The stranger-ethnographer will normally – undoubtedly – have some access problems, particularly on the level of depth access, i.e., stories on sensitive matters that may not readily be produced. Covert studies may score better on this point, but here we face ethical problems. Another possibility in at-home ethnography is that the deeper and more profound knowledge of the setting may lead to a theoretical development that is more well grounded in experiences and observations than is common. Compared to studying settings which the researcher, even after months of research work, still has a relatively limited knowledge of, the study of settings that the researcher really is familiar with may be even more productive.

In particular, the excellent access possibilities of the at-home ethnographer – although within a limited field – may lead to accounts that give a better feeling for what goes on than what 'conventional' ethnography allows . Many of the arguments for at-home ethnography are the same as for ethnographic work more generally. There is much dissatisfaction with social research for its inability to portray everyday life. Representations are often remote, artificial and clumsy. The reliance on procedures for data collection, categorizations, and attaining high evaluator interreliability steers research away from presenting valuable insights in an attractive text. This is especially the case with quantitative studies, but many qualitative research efforts do not score much better. They are, many people feel, boring to read (Richardson, 1994). Some researchers advocate 'fictional ethnographies' in order to be able to produce sensitive and insightful accounts (see Tierney, 1993; Watson, 2000).

Without underestimating the importance of writing skills and putting one's own lived experiences in perspective (i.e. maintaining a critical distance), proceeding from the rich empirical material at hand in one's own everyday organizational life could give ample opportunities to produce good accounts. With access to a large number of events, the study of selected parts of what is happening around you should make it possible to spot, document and interpret some sufficiently interesting and revealing examples, without even having to use fiction – in the sense of inventing or combining material to produce text that is interesting to read. This advantage allows the at-home ethnographer to stay 'faithful' to specific empirical material, that is, to stick to what one has seen and heard in a particular context and resist the temptation to invoke one's fantasy to portray and interpret social reality.

on the practice of at-home ethnography

The idea of at-home ethnography is consistent with a variety of different ways of creating and doing something with the empirical material: from a *planned-systematic* kind of 'data collection' to an *emergent-spontaneous* approach.

In the first case the researcher has a reasonably clear idea of what to study, how to plan the work (although in ethnographies never in a detailed sense) and deal with the pile of notes or interview statements that they must work with and from. This appears rational and scientific and looks good in methods sections in research texts. A planned-systematic study tends to be bound to the empirical material gathered as planned. To some extent the research interest must be decided upon in advance or at least at some point, perhaps after having noticed that there seemed to be an interesting theme calling for systematic documentation and investigation. One may, for example, be interested in such diverse topics as the consequences, interpretations or talk about policy issues at the local level, references to top management at the shopfloor level, or incidents involving gender, and one may then make observations and take notes every time one encounters such material. The material may be interesting or not. You can't know in advance, although with effort, creativity and writing skill – combined with some free interpretations – empirical material that appears none too promising may still lead to an interesting and rich text. Studies of 'trust' in top management may, for example, be based on all the references made to top management (actions, role, qualities, etc.) over a number of weeks within a specific department or group monitored by a researcher. Arguably, this says more – or at least something different – than asking people to fill in questionnaires or questioning them about their 'trust' in, or general views of, top management.

A less structured at-home ethnography uses an emergent-spontaneous study that begins when something revealing happens. In such a study the researcher waits for something interesting or generative to pop up. This may sound risky and not very ambitious. There are, however, some advantages. The most significant one is that it increases the likelihood of coming up with interesting material. The idea here is that the researcher does not find the empirical material; rather, it finds him or her. The researcher's energy, on a low level, is spent keeping their eyes and ears open and the laptop switched on, ready for their fingers to hammer on it, while still carrying out ordinary academic work or doing something else – visiting the doctor, the gym, the supermarket or talking with the neighbours, etc. What it is really about is developing a sensitivity for and preparedness to do something with the rich empirical material that one, at least occasionally, will be facing. The idea is that a consistent, long-term scan of what one is experiencing produces a more extended set of incidents or an especially rich and interesting event calling for analysis.

The reader may wonder here, what is interesting? This depends of course to some extent on one's personal taste and pre-understanding, but there is a relatively high level of intersubjectivity in the evaluation of what is interesting (Davis, 1971). An interesting account tells us something revealing about what goes on in a particular site. It explores something unexpected or allows us to see something familiar in a new light. One idea is to search for phenomena that can be seen as mysterious (see Ybema and Kamsteeg, Chapter 5, this volume), as difficult or impossible to understand given one's framework or other available theories. Establishing and solving a mystery then becomes the challenge, offering a route to new theory (Alvesson and Kärreman, 2007). A certain level of generality is typically called for in good empirical material. Highly idiosyncratic stuff may be entertaining but is not necessarily intellectually interesting. Typically, an interesting account touches upon a mix of familiarity/surprise. This mix assures some element of generalization (although of course not in any statistical sense) and some element of variation/uniqueness. All social situations contain both, but not all will trigger the right combination. One criterion is that the topic appeals to something in the experiences of readers (cf. the concept of 'naturalistic generalization', Stake, 1994).

In order to produce something interesting out of the mystery, but even more in order to avoid abstractions in which specific processes, acts and events are turned into unrecognizability, it is important to 'micro-anchor' the account. This means that specific acts, events, and situations are in focus. A good account then involves actors, acts (processes), and an organizational context. This may be referred to as a situational focus (Knorr-Cetina, 1981). Instead of finding something average or system-like through rigorous comparisons of a number of micro-situations, the study concentrates on exploring the richness of one or a few situations and then relies on one's general knowledge for evaluating what is fairly typical compared to what is outside the mainstream of the organization being explored (Alvesson, 1996). The researcher must support the choice of a focused situation or event through being able to refer to at least a few other instances in which the same theme or process is present, thereby indicating that the focused situation is of some relevance for illuminating broader chunks of the organizational context in which the focal situation is played out. This would increase the chances of being fair in the portrait painted of the setting.

Of perhaps greater interest than the empirical material is what the researcher-author may do with it. The material must then work in a productive and inspiring way and lead to interpretations of a more theoretical nature. One may, however, imagine different 'ratios' in terms of the intrinsic/instrumental value of an empirical account. It may in itself be informative and revealing – a thick description – or it may work as a lever for the production of a more abstract, conceptual contribution.

some problems in at-home ethnographic research

Doing at-home ethnography is difficult, and I don't think this a method for everybody to use, at least not at any key time in one's life and career. It is a risky business from an intellectual point of view as it is more difficult to draw upon – and hide behind – an apparatus of techniques and procedures for controlling 'subjectivity' and assuring the reader that Science has as much to say about the outcome as personal idiosyncrasies. Being personally involved in the object of study (the context in which one is studying) also means that one may be less able to liberate oneself from some taken-for-granted ideas or to view things in an open-minded way.

This kind of research situation is in certain ways also more politically complex than is common. Social research in general is never neutral and cannot avoid either supporting or questioning existing social institutions (Burrell and Morgan, 1979; Alvesson and Deetz, 2000). But one may easily be more politically sensitive and biased in working on one's home base. It is easy to express views that support one's owns interests and/or to be sensitive about the responses of people in the 'neighborhood' who might be reading the research text. Just anticipating what people will think and feel may lead to more careful and flatter descriptions than a freer and bolder approach would imply. Of course, diplomacy is a part of all (qualitative) research efforts, and this may contribute to the end products frequently being somewhat watered down, but it may be easier to cope with this aspect if those people who are less than happy about the research outcome are at some distance from the everyday life of the researcher. There is also an important ethical aspect to this – respect for the feelings and interests of those being studied must guide research, and their acceptance of the study must at some point be attained for it to be published or widely distributed.

This approach forces researchers to address 'subjectivity' and prior knowledge as a complex mix of resource and blinder. Arguably, social research (and perhaps many other forms of research) is profoundly affected, indeed driven by, the personal feelings and life histories, cultural frameworks, social belongings, etc. of researchers. This does not mean that idiosyncrasy, personal opinions and arbitrariness necessarily rule – or that they do so in a manner which means that the research text is of more interest to one's psychiatrist than somebody who wants to learn about a particular social or organizational phenomenon. What is strongly engaging, personally, for the researcher may well be of great interest to other persons also. As Jaggar (1989) claims, emotions are often shared between people and are an important element in research work. Still, ways of dealing with the problematic side of closeness and personal involvement must be considered. Careful reflections are crucial in doing at-home ethnography.

The major problem is not necessarily 'subjectivity', in the sense of highly individualistic biases. In general, such research is characterized by the inability of researchers to liberate themselves from socially shared frameworks (paradigms, cultures). That, evaluators would agree, may not be a sign of objectivity as much as culturally or paradigmatically shared biases (Alvesson and Deetz, 2000). The trick is to get away from frozen positions, irrespective of whether they are grounded in personal experiences or shared frameworks. A problem here is that staying within socially shared frames and biases may make research life easier – while what are seen as personal biases are sanctioned, and proceeding from and reproducing socially shared biases may be applauded. The general problem can be formulated as accomplishing openness in relationship to a prestructured, fixed line of focusing/interpretation.

struggling with closure: creating breakdowns

In ethnographic work, the difference between the expectations of the researcher and those of the object of study is sometimes reported to have produced a breakdown in understanding, 'a lack of fit between one's encounter with a tradition and the schema-guided expectations by which one organizes experience' (Agar, 1986: 21). The researcher – the professional stranger – deals with this by investigating the cultural elements encountered, triggering the breakdown and then adjusting her/his schema. Breakdowns will continue to appear until the researcher 'fully' – given what is to be investigated – understands the culture under study, and therefore ethnography can be described as 'a process of coherently resolving breakdowns' (Agar, 1986: 39). When studying relatively familiar phenomena such as the workplaces and educational institutions of one's own country, this problem is not so much about resolving breakdowns but *creating* them (Alvesson and Kärreman, 2007). In the study of foreign cultures breakdowns will occur automatically, but in one's own these are mostly marginal. The trick then is to locate one's framework (cultural understanding) away from the culture being studied, so that significant material to 'resolve' emerges. The problem – and rationale – for organizational culture studies is to turn the well known and self-evident into the exotic and explicit: to raise and answer the question 'What does it mean (apart from the obvious)?' (Asplund, 1970). This is, of course, to a large extent a matter of creativity, but it is also a matter of aspiring to accomplish 'ethnographic' rather than technical/pragmatic results. To some degree it is a matter of using the 'critical strategy of defamiliarization': 'Disruption of common sense, doing the unexpected, placing familiar subjects in unfamiliar, even shocking, context are the aims of this strategy to make the reader conscious of difference' (Marcus and Fischer, 1986: 137).

The art of producing breakdowns in settings only too familiar is not easy to master. The more familiar the setting, the fewer the breakdowns. The challenge to self-evident forms of understanding is taken up by gathering a rich and generative kind of empirical material, reserving plenty of time to consider what it means and securing access to a broad set of different resources – theories, vocabularies, experiences (Alvesson and Kärreman, 2007).

To discover or to emphasize the need for effort and construction, to *create* revealing situations, is one vital element. I prefer micro-anchoring and rich descriptions rather than covering broader areas in a thin way, although the challenge is to see how chunks of social reality are 'writ small' in specific events, these showing some similarity with a 'reasonable' number of other events in the myriad of micro-situations making up social reality. To work with a situation or a process that is bounded in time and space and thus possible to grasp gives the researcher an energy and mindpower to illuminate it from different angles (Alvesson, 1996). Considering a variety of perspectives, and regularly shifting these, is always important in research, but perhaps especially so in the type of research here suggested. As said previously, the trick is to try to get away from the inclination to see things only in a specific light – as this means that one's personal and paradigmatic-cultural blinders tend to shadow other aspects than those preferred. I will briefly indicate five ways in which one may improve the prospect that this will be accomplished.

One way of creating distance towards one's self and one's cultural inclinations is to try to embrace positions of irony and self-irony (see Brown, 1977; Woolgar, 1983; see also Ybema and Kamsteeg, Chapter 5, this volume). These must not necessarily dominate the final text but may be taken temporarily in order to create a certain distance to the more serious arguments put forward. Modern higher education, described by its advocates as a triumph for equality and as knowledge for everybody and/or a motor for economic development, has been called a McUniversity (Parker and Jary, 1995), where standardization, rationalization and managerialization take over, following McDonald-like principles. Instead of describing oneself or, more modestly, one's ideal as the scholarly champion of academic freedom and knowledge, one may sketch a self-portrait of the high-brow egocentric in their ivory tower. Such alien and ironic representations may be played with as thought experiments, or applied, more explicitly, in analysis.

A second way to create distance is in the use of theories which challenge common sense, not only for a direct application but also for encouraging a perspective on one's own lived reality and thus facilitating looking upon things in a more all-sided way than is spontaneously the case or if one tries to adopt a grounded theory approach.

A third way is to build up an interpretive repertoire sufficiently broad enough to read empirical material in a variety of ways, thereby considering and perhaps developing themes not too closely tied to one's personal-political tastes. This third way may overlap the two just mentioned.

A fourth may be to work systematically with a notion of reflexivity, in which one tries to change the level of interpretation so that one's favoured interpretations are called into question from a meta-level position inspired by another standpoint. This other standpoint then functions in a metatheoretical way, that is, it addresses one's interpretations and not directly 'reality out there' (Alvesson and Sköldberg, 2009). An effort to develop a particular point may be challenged by approaching it from, for example, a feminist perspective exploring the (false) gender-neutral nature of the prior interpretation, or from a poststructuralist position exploring the fragility behind the claims for the authority of a preferred interpretation. Through incorporating challenges from counter-perspectives framing the issue and line of interpretation in another way, the researcher is forced to work through the preferred wisdom and unfreeze the position associated with personal history and shared taken-for-granted meanings.

A fifth approach may be to explicitly work with the processual nature of the researcher's self, that is with different self-concepts. Weedon (1987) and Deetz (1992) talk about process subjectivity in order to indicate that we can – and actually do – move between different ways of conceiving ourselves and our orientations. As a researcher, one is not only a student of education, but also perhaps a woman, middle-aged, senior (to some), junior (to others), a teacher, a union member, an engaged critic, a detached and non-biased interpretivist, etc. Attitudes are not fixed or absolute, but context dependent. The same person who is in favour of accountability and performance evaluations might also like autonomy and freedom from dysfunctional measurements. Drawing upon different orientations – taking different positions, with different perspectives – may facilitate one's avoidance of getting caught in a certain set of blinders. This way, of course, to some extent overlaps with and is assisted by the other approaches suggested above.

Much more can be said about breaking out of constraining frameworks, and many versions are possible. The important thing is that at-home ethnography calls for some additional efforts, compared to 'conventional' modes of doing research, to escape the specific traps facing the insider position of the researcher.

the who and when of at-home ethnography

Doing at-home ethnography is probably not for everybody. However, certain social situations, experiences and periods in one's career may facilitate it. Having been in a certain job and organization for a long time and having limited access to other work organizational experiences would make the research difficult. Being a newcomer and thus having to learn the local culture makes the job in some ways intellectually easier, but politically more risky and, possibly, emotionally more stressful. Being active in other spheres of working and public life, e.g., consultancy and political work, may also be helpful. In connection to career changes and the adaptation to new situations, e.g., becoming a department chairperson, may also help to make at-home ethnographic work less tricky to carry out. A sabbatical leave may also offer not just time but may also produce the perspectivating experiences that could facilitate at-home ethnography. Doing such research may thus be partly a matter of timing. Some periods may be more suitable for it than others. Of course, apart from the personal side, periods of great transformation and/or specific organizational changes in which the ongoing production of social reality is disrupted can offer good occasions for at-home ethnographic work.

There are also variations among people, partly related to familiarity with other sites than universities, that are helpful in at-home ethnography. Multiple work-related social identities – university professor, consultant, affiliations with more than one academic discipline – can make it easier to avoid onesidedness in at-home descriptions. Being an outsider rather than a mainstream person (belonging to a minority in terms of gender, ethnicity or political values) may work in the same way. Co-authored work in which an insider and an outsider collaborate may be another option.

Apart from making wise choices if and when one is the right person and has the right kind of background and experiences in order to 'look through' one's own workplace culture, it is also a good idea to think about the politics involved. I believe that four issues matter here: one is the tolerance and openness of people in the workplace ('the victims'), a second is one's own position – a prestigious, tenured researcher has more leeway – and the third relates to the extent to which one constructs oneself in terms of integrity and inner-directness. At-home ethnography is not for the mainstream, organizational person eager to conform to workplace norms and be loyal. The fourth concerns the presence and enforcement of an explicit set of rules for ethics.

My idea in raising the issue of the when and who of at-home ethnography is only partly to aid people in terms of putting or omitting at-home ethnography research in their career planning calendars or to assist recruiters of at-home researchers to develop personality profiles for candidates. My point concerns the need for working through the problem with a constraining, taken-for-granted cultural framework on the subject matter. Cultural myopia means a high degree of closure to the rich variety of potential ways of interpreting one's organization. These problems can be coped with, but there may be a trade-off between the efforts called for and the output of the project. The advantage of at-home ethnography in terms of saving energy may not be available for everybody to exploit at any given moment.

conclusions

As a social scientist one is, of course, not obliged to leave one's home base in order to encounter productive empirical material. This chapter argues for at-home ethnography as an alternative or a complement to other ways of doing research. Arguably, there are some major *advantages* with the approach here suggested, of course conditioned upon an ability to deal with the – considerable – traps involved in this kind of work. At-home ethnography offers good research economy, in particular if we accept the rather basic and profound problems with interview material (and other methods assuming that the individual simply reports experiences, insights and meanings) as reflections of what goes on 'out there' and view conventional ethnography as time-consuming and uneconomical. Second, at-home ethnography is a sound base for the production of rich empirical accounts. Given that one is not deciding *a priori* – thereby constraining the options – that a particular time and space area is to be researched, but is modestly engaged in scanning one's lived reality for research options for some time, there is a good chance that one sooner or later runs into events that will make a good account possible, providing a feeling for what goes on as well as facilitating productive interpretations.

There are of course problems and difficulties of both an intellectual and a political character. In order to cope with the taken-for-granted assumptions and blind spots and to utilize the full potential of the researcher, s/he needs to engage in an ambitious struggle with her/his personal and cultural framework. The chapter has pointed at a number of possibilities in this respect. While a challenge for the ethnographer is to avoid 'going native', the at-home ethnographer must make strong efforts to avoid 'staying native'. It is, of course, hardly sufficient that the researcher-native avoids excessive idiosyncrasies and gets approval of other natives for a particular version of the world. The problem of a closed mind may be less a matter of personal bias than about subscribing to the tribe's cultural frame. People tend to share their inclinations to see things in a particular way and be closed in terms of alternative ways of seeing and thus producing interesting observations and descriptions. While the other natives are inclined to 'stay native' – they have no (research-motivated) reasons to escape cultural closure – some difference, or tension, between the researcher-runaway and the researchers-buddies-inmates may emerge regarding how a lived social reality is best made sense of. The at-home ethnographer's efforts may well involve demystifications and the questioning of basic ideas and assumptions. At-home ethnography makes the politics of research more complicated (if one avoids painting a rosy picture of those being studied) – it cannot be held at arms length as is perhaps common in studies of 'other kinds of people'. The ethical problems involved here call for careful attention.

The challenge of ethnography, and of most qualitative work, is to be close and avoid closure. The first element is not a problem in at-home ethnography; the second calls for struggle. Unlike 'conventional' ethnography the challenge of at-home ethnography is one of creating breakdowns, as one may not spontaneously experience them. Doing at-home ethnography at the right moment, when the mix of local familiarity and access to other frameworks is a good one, may reduce problems. Working with theories treating academic social practice in a somewhat radical – mindshaking – fashion may also be productive. Co-research with an outsider could also work well.

The idea of at-home ethnography pushes for an intellectual curiosity that is not only delimited by and well-packaged into specific projects focusing on specific objects of study at a safe distance from one's everyday life. At-home ethnography implies a mindset that is to some extent in opposition to a more technocratic-bureaucratic approach in which procedures, rules and techniques define and legitimize the scientific project. It calls for a more reflective approach in which data management matters less than a revealing, insightful account and interpretation. Self-reflection is thus crucial. At-home ethnography is indeed a risky project, but may offer an interesting alternative to other approaches.

note

[1] This chapter draws upon an article first printed in Alvesson, M. (2003) 'Methodology for close up studies. Struggling with closeness and closure', *Higher Education*, 46: 167–93, used with the kind permission of Springer Science and Business Media.

references

Agar, M.H. (1986) *Speaking of ethnography*. Beverly Hills, CA: Sage.

Alvesson, M. (1993) *Cultural perspectives on organizations*. Cambridge: Cambridge University Press.

Alvesson, M. (1996) *Communication, power and organization*. Berlin/New York: de Gruyter.

Alvesson, M. (2002) *Postmodernism and social research*. Buckingham: Open University Press.

Alvesson, M. (2003) 'Beyond neo-positivism, romanticism and localism. A reflexive approach to the research interview', *Academy of Management Review*, 28(1): 13–33.

Alvesson, M. and Deetz, S. (2000) *Doing critical management research*. London: Sage.

Alvesson, M. and Kärreman, D. (2007) 'Creating mystery: Empirical matters in theory development', *Academy of Management Review*, 32(4): 1265–81.

Alvesson, M. and Sköldberg, K. (2009) *Reflexive methodology* (2nd edn). London: Sage.

Asplund, J. (1970) *Om undran inför samhället* ('On reflecting on society'). Lund: Argos.

Atkinson, P. and Hammersley, M. (1994) 'Ethnography and participant observation', in N. Denzin and Y. Lincoln (eds), *Handbook of qualitative research*. Thousand Oaks, CA: Sage. pp. 248–61.

Baszanger, I. and Dodier, N. (1997) 'Ethnography: Relating the part to the whole', in D. Silverman (ed.) *Qualitative research*. London: Sage. pp. 8–23.

Brannick, T. and Coghlan, D. (2007) 'In defense of being "native": The case for insider research', *Organizational Research Methods*, 10(1): 59–74.

Brown, R.H. (1977) *A poetic for sociology*. Chicago: University of Chicago Press.

Burrell, G. and Morgan, G. (1979) *Sociological paradigms and organisational analysis*. Portsmouth, NH: Heinemann.

Clifford, J. and Marcus, G. (eds) (1986) *Writing culture: The poetics and politics of ethnography*. Los Angeles: University of California Press.

Davis, M.S. (1971) 'That's interesting! Towards a phenomenology of sociology and a sociology of phenomenology', *Philosophy of the Social Sciences*, 1: 309–44.

Deetz, S. (1992) *Democracy in an age of corporate colonization*. Albany: State University of New York Press.

Denzin, N. (1994) 'The art of interpretation', in N. Denzin and Y. Lincoln (eds), *Handbook of qualitative research*. Thousand Oaks, CA: Sage. pp. 500–15.

Denzin, N. (1997) *Interpretive ethnography*. Thousand Oaks, CA: Sage.

Dingwall, R. (1997) 'Accounts, interviews and observations', in G. Miller and R. Dingwall (eds), *Context and method in qualitative research*. London: Sage.

Ellis, C. and Bochner, A. (2000) 'Autoethnography, personal narrative, reflexivity', in N. Denzin and Y. Lincoln (eds), *Handbook of qualitative research* (2nd edn). Thousand Oaks, CA: Sage. pp. 733–68.

Fairclough, N. (1993) 'Critical discourse analysis and the marketization of public discourse: The universities', *Discourse & Society*, 4(2): 133–68.

Fontana, A. and Frey, J. (1994) 'Interviewing: The art of science', in N. Denzin and Y. Lincoln (eds), *Handbook of qualitative research*. Thousand Oaks, CA: Sage. pp. 361–76.

Geertz, C. (1973) *The interpretation of cultures*. New York: Basic Books.

Geertz, C. (1988) *Work and lives: The anthropologist as author*. Oxford: Polity Press.

Gioia, D., Thomas, J.B., Clark, S.M. and Chittipeddi, K. (1994) 'Symbolism and strategic change in academia: The dynamics of sensemaking and influence', *Organization Science*, 5(3): 363–83.

Jackall, R. (1988) *Moral mazes: The world of corporate managers*. New York: Oxford University Press.

Jackson, J. (1995) '"Déjà Entendu": The liminal qualities of anthropological fieldnotes', in J. van Maanen (ed.), *Representation in ethnograhy*. Thousand Oaks, CA: Sage. pp. 36–78.

Jaggar, A. (1989) 'Love and knowledge: Emotion in feminist epistemology', *Inquiry*, 32: 151–76.

Knorr-Cetina, K. (1981) 'Introduction. The micro-sociological challenge of macro-sociology: Towards a reconstruction of social theory and methodology', in K. Knorr-Cetina and A. Cicourel (eds), *Advances in social theory and methodology*. Boston, MA: Routledge and Kegan Paul.

Kolker, A. (1996) 'Thrown overboard: the human costs of health care rationing', in C. Ellis and A. Bochner (eds), *Composing ethnography*. Walnut Creek, CA: AltaMira Press. pp. 132–59.

Kunda, G. (1992) *Engineering culture: Control and commitment in a high-tech corporation*. Philadelphia: Temple University Press.

Lofland, J. (1985) 'Analytic ethnography', *Journal of Contemporary Ethnography*, 24: 30–67.

Marcus, G. and Fischer, M. (1986) *Anthropology as cultural critique*. Chicago: University of Chicago Press.

Meyer, J. and Rowan, B. (1977) 'Institutionalized organizations: Formal structure as myth and ceremony', *American Journal of Sociology*, 83: 340–63.

Miller, G. (1997) 'Towards ethnographies of institutional discourse: Proposal and suggestions', in G. Miller and R. Dingwall (eds), *Context and method in qualitative research*. London: Sage.

Mills, C.W. (1940) 'Situated actions and vocabularies of motives', *American Sociological Review*, 5: 904–13.

Parker, M. and Jary, D. (1995) 'The McUniversity: Organization, management and academic subjectivity', *Organization*, 2(2): 319–38.

Perrow, C. (1978) 'Demystifying organizations', in R. Sarri and Y. Hasenfeld (eds), *The management of human services*. New York: Columbia University Press.

Potter, J. and Wetherell, M. (1987) *Discourse and social psychology: Beyond attitudes and behaviour*. London: Sage.

Richardson, L. (1994) 'Writing: a method of inquiry', in N. Denzin and Y. Lincoln (eds), *Handbook of qualitative research*. Thousand Oaks, CA: Sage. pp. 516–29.

Richardson, L. (2000) 'Writing: a method of inquiry', in N. Denzin and Y. Lincoln (eds), *Handbook of qualitative research* (2nd edn). Thousand Oaks, CA: Sage. pp. 923–48.

Rosen, M. (1985) 'Breakfirst at Spiro's: Dramaturgy and dominance', *Journal of Management*, 11(2): 31–48.

Schwartz-Shea, P. (2006) 'Judging quality: Evaluative criteria and epistemic communities', in D. Yanow and P. Schwartz-Shea (eds), *Interpretation and method: Empirical research methods and the interpretive turn*. Armonk, NY: M.E. Sharpe. pp. 89–113.

Shotter, J. and Gergen, K. (eds) (1989) *Texts of identity*. London: Sage.

Shotter, J. and Gergen, K. (1994) 'Social construction: Knowledge, self, others, and continuing the conversation', in S. Deetz (ed.), *Communication Yearbook*, vol. 17. Newbury Park: Sage. pp. 3–33.

Silverman, D. (1985) *Qualitative methodology and sociology*. Aldershot: Gower.

Silverman, D. (1989) 'Six rules of qualitative research: A post-romantic argument', *Symbolic Interaction*, 12(2): 25–40.

Silverman, D. (2001) *Interpreting qualitative data* (2nd edn). London: Sage.

Snow, D.A., Morrill, C. and Anderson, L. (2003) 'Elaborating analytic ethnography', *Ethnography*, 4(2): 181–200.

Stake, R. (1984) 'Case studies', in N. Denzin and Y. Lincoln (eds), *Handbook of qualitative research*. Thousand Oaks, CA: Sage. pp. 236–47.

Tierney, W. (1993) 'The cedar closet', *Qualitative Studies in Education*, 6(4): 303–14.

Trowler, P. (1998) *Academics responding to change*. Milton Keynes: Open University Press.

Van Maanen, J. (1988) *Tales of the field: On writing ethnography*. Chicago: University of Chicago Press.

Van Maanen, J. (1991) 'The smile factory', in P.J. Frost et al. (eds), *Reframing organizational culture*. Newbury Park: Sage. pp. 58–76.

Van Maanen, J. (ed.) (1995) *Representation in ethnography*. Thousand Oaks, CA: Sage.

Watson, T. (1994) *In search of management*. London: Routledge.

Watson, T. (1996) 'Motivation: That's Maslow, isn't it?', *Management Learning*, 27(4): 447–64.

Watson, T. (2000) 'Ethnographic fiction science', *Organization*, 7: 493–510.

Weedon, C. (1987) *Feminist practice & poststructuralist theory*. Oxford: Basil Blackwell.

Widerberg, K. (1995) *Kunskapens kön* ('Gender of knowledge'). Stockholm: Norstedts.

Wolcott, H. (1995) 'Making a study "more ethnographic"', in J. Van Maanen (ed.), *Representation in ethnography*. Thousand Oaks, CA: Sage. pp. 79–111.

Woolgar, S. (1983) 'Irony in the social studies of science', in K. Knorr-Cetina and M. Mulkay (eds), *Science observed: Perspectives on the social study of science*. London: Sage.

Part III

Researcher – Researched Relationships

9

Lies from the field: Ethical issues in organizational ethnography

Gary Alan Fine and David Shulman

introduction

Idealized visions of how professionals should work are difficult to reconcile with ethical compromises that are made in practice. In an earlier paper, Fine identified ten moral dilemmas in ethnographic field methods that arise from an inability to comply with ideals (1993). The actions of organizational ethnographers and, as important, how they report those actions, are constrained by their complex working conditions, the demands of academic standards, and accepted textual practices. As a result, presentations of fieldwork in organizational ethnographies may be varnished, and will lead to incomplete accounts of the practical moral dilemmas that are involved in, and perhaps unique to, completing an organizational ethnography. This chapter depicts some of these covert ethical dilemmas and 'lies' of fieldwork, and offers examples of how they occur as predictable difficulties when conducting organizational ethnography.

Every job has techniques for doing things – standard operating procedures – that practitioners will avoid exposing to outsiders. Life in an operating room, in a kitchen, in a factory or in a police station is not always the stuff of heroic public images. As insiders know, the production of good things is not pretty. Workers are caught in a web of demands that compel them to deviate from formal and idealistic rules. Yet for public consumption, practitioners must present glossy versions of how they work. These illusions are essential for occupational survival. When the work is messy, workers have to clean up well.

Depictions of how organizational ethnographies are conducted are similarly varnished. They may omit the problematic details of how fieldworkers gathered their information. Such antiseptic accounts cost readers and practitioners, offering an incomplete account of the practical ethical dilemmas that are involved in completing an organizational ethnography. There are layers of gatekeepers, greater numbers of people to interact with and all sorts of conflicting responses from organizational stakeholders. Our goal is to expose the nuts and bolts of organizational ethnography.

We focus on how ethical dilemmas in organizational ethnographies can reveal fieldwork, *as practised*, in a less flattering but more realistic light. Organizational ethnographers make tough choices and confront moral dilemmas. The situations in which they work often veil those choices and dilemmas. More than many informal settings, organizations are explicitly hierarchical and political, and the ethnographer must confront the power gradients of organization life. Yet, as in other settings, much fieldwork is hidden and backstage. Analysis *in situ* is private, field notes are rarely available for secondary analysis, and much ethnographic writing is accepted on faith. We comfort ourselves that good and sufficient ethical rationales exist for this secrecy. Fieldworkers tell themselves that they must maintain confidences and their own autonomy. Yet this space also creates opportunities for deception.

In fashioning halos to preserve their professional reputations, practitioners also may deceive themselves. Illusions about work can grow, lay down roots, and become taken for granted. Organizational ethnographers would benefit from greater self-awareness. They should recognize explicitly that they are making choices that result in their behaving differently from how they would like the public to assume that they behave.

Idealism must be balanced against a reality that fieldworkers in organizational settings engage in exercises of unvarnished opportunism. To collect a thrilling story, we become manipulative suitors, seducing organizations and individuals into sharing information. We potentially harm our organizational hosts by taking time, focus and energy from their pursuits to suit our own purposes. We also flatter to develop a rapport to acquire secrets and whisper sweet nothings to ferret out the truth when we feel deceived. Despite this emotion work, our published tales of our fieldwork may account for our activities in a more clinical, orderly, and principled way than had actually occurred.

Although researchers are fundamentally honest, as lawyers, clergymen, politicians, and car dealers are fundamentally honest, everyone's goal is to permit life to run tolerably smoothly – to engage in impression management, preserving reputations in local domains. The actions of organizational ethnographers, and how they report their actions, are constrained by their working conditions, the demands of academic standards, and accepted discursive practices.

The moral dilemmas in ethnography that Fine (1993) labelled as the 'ten lies' of ethnography, constitute illusions about work that practitioners offer for public consumption, based on partial truths or self-deceptions. We revisit those ten lies: accounts of the kindly ethnographer, the friendly ethnographer, the honest ethnographer, the precise ethnographer, the observant ethnographer, the unobtrusive ethnographer, the candid ethnographer, the chaste ethnographer, the fair ethnographer, and the literary ethnographer, connecting them to organizational ethnography.

These ten lies represent the common images that ethical and competent field researchers would wish to embody through their reputations. Some represent challenges to the 'classic virtues' of ethnographers. These virtues – sympathy, openness, and honour – have been challenged by postmodern researchers, but they remain touchstones of how a 'true' ethnographer should treat informants. These 'classic virtues' represent the standards of observational morality, grounded in science and the Western ethical tradition.

A second set of issues lies in challenges to 'technical skills'. When we teach students to perform the mechanics of ethnography, we are adamant that they must be precise, observant, and passive. How could we claim that our work should not be precise and observant or that we should direct the scene? These challenges are grounded in the inevitable limits of competence. Other lies are tied to discursive practices, ways of preserving the 'ethnographic self', and refer to the conventions which ethnographers use to present themselves to their colleagues as morally upstanding and trustworthy.

a kindly trojan horse taking notes

The classic methodological issues of informed consent, avoiding harm, and even-handedness are pressing ethical concerns at the inception of all research. To address those issues, fieldworkers must provide assurances about their intentions to gain organizational access and meet standards of professional practice. Those promises can sometimes be easier to make than keep.

The fieldworker is supposed to access a research site without compromising editorial freedom (even while agreeing to the conditions for entry); disclose their research goals fully (even though doing so may lead to them being rejected); reassure readers that the site fits the project's aims (even though the site may not be ideal); and argue that the research will not harm the organization (even when the findings may be detrimental).

Ethnographers are more often beggars than choosers. Often we don't contact the perfect organization, set an appointment with a top executive who can provide access, and then commence a trouble-free ethnographic expedition. Instead, we may have to rely on a convenience sample because that chosen site is what is available. Sometimes we may rely on friends, family or acquaintances to secure access (Buchanan et al., 1988). Morrill (1995) gained initial entry to an organization depicted in *The Executive Way* by jogging with a manager. Ethnographers do not disqualify themselves from using their networks in establishing access; using connections can be valuable. Yet, as in other careers, admitting to relying on friends for one's professional success is slightly shameful.

We also may apply a misdirection in claiming one research goal while pursuing another. Consider the difficulty Robert Jackall had 'breaking in' when starting his research for *Moral Mazes*:

> Jackall ran into trouble starting his research because thirty-six corporations had flatly turned down his request to study ethics on their premises ... Eventually, he found his way into a chemical company that encouraged him to study the effect of chlorofluoro-carbon regulation on corporate practices. (Allen, 1997: 10)

After revealing some unsavoury examples of *in situ* ethics:

> Jackall received phone calls from managers deep within the company (and other companies) congratulating him for his acuity, but the top dogs demanded to know why he had

been allowed on the premises. 'All the managers had to do was pull my proposal out of the file and say, "We thought he was here to study chlorofluorocarbon regulation"', explains Jackall, adding that what looks like deception can sometimes be part of an elaborate linguistic code in which no one is really fooled and nearly everyone is satisfied – not least because there is always someone else to blame for the researcher's unflattering revelations. (Allen, 1997: 10–11)

Ethnographers are supposed to be fond of their respondents, but this is not inevitable. Sometimes we will research unpleasant groups and organizations – and we will choose to do so with malice aforethought, all the while camouflaging our disdain. Examining disparaged groups – groups that one begins the research expecting to dislike – occurs in the social sciences (e.g. Peshkin, 1986), although not frequently.[1] An illusion of sympathy can help the research process move forward but it is deceptive.

an ethnographic honest broker

When an ethnographer portrays more sympathy than he or she really has, such a stance presupposes limited informed consent in that what is being informed is less than what the subjects would wish to know in hindsight. It is also less than what the researcher recognizes that s/he should report.

In research on unsympathetic organizations, we sometimes neglect the standard ethnographic injunction to understand the world sympathetically through the informant's eyes (Wax, 1980: 278). We dehumanize our informants, placing them outside our moral community. The researcher appears to be a kindly soul, but turns out to be a 'fink' (Goffman, 1989: 125), an undercover agent operating against the interests of the observed group (Johnson, 1975). Even though this approach is justified in terms of its overall benefit, it is based on a lie – a lack of kindly intentions, a secret hidden from the start.

Most, if not all, ethnographers will appeal to their subjects by suggesting that they are intensely sympathetic and kind chroniclers. Carolyn Ellis (1986) presented herself deceptively in researching *Fisher Folk*, an ethnography of coastal fishing communities on the Chesapeake Bay. Ellis wrote disparagingly about this community, but never warned her respondents that she was conducting in-depth research, even while she befriended many members of the community. In the words of one embittered woman, 'I thought she was nice … but she turned out to be a liar' (Allen, 1997: 2). Coming across as kind, interested and sympathetic helps to gain access, but at a price when the masquerade ends. The inverse can also occur. When studying an organization to which social scientists are sympathetic, peers can apply pressure to be more kind than the data warrant.

The most aggressive strategy in organizational ethnography for gaining access is not to reveal that one is conducting research. Here the organization lacks informed consent. A long and contentious debate still exists over employing covert identities to access research sites. Critics believe that disguised observation makes the researcher an espionage agent, reflecting a lack of concern with the 'right' of informants not to be deceived, particularly when the beneficiary is the deceptive researcher. Supporters, such as Judith Rollins (1987; see Reynolds, 1982), would suggest that hidden research does little harm and may be important in studying elites. Although organizational ethnographers are not undercover journalists or ex-employees with axes to grind, one might wonder what organizational secrets would remain unknown had someone not been hidden in order to expose them. Sometimes only insiders will have a privileged enough position to learn valuable information about how an organization works, such as Melville Dalton (1959) had in *Men Who Manage*. That strategic positioning may be unavailable to fieldworkers who are honest about their true purpose.

Some ethnographers have called for an investigative model of conducting ethnography, in which deception is justified because informants in organizations will dissemble rather than reveal discrediting truths (Douglas, 1976; Shulman, 1994). Some organizational ethnographers are willing to contravene professionally pleasing ethnographic techniques to avoid being tricked. Informed consent, harmlessness, and empathy are ethical issues that are intertwined with the idealized virtues of a kindly ethnographer.

the 'friendly' ethnographer

Many organizations and groups operate in private spaces. If management grants access, workers in organizations may be directed to speak with or tolerate an observer. However, gaining access is necessary but insufficient. The organizational ethnographer must cultivate a rapport by appearing to be friendly and honest. Once organizational ethnographers join a group or organization, they then engage in impression management to sustain that rapport.

Successful emotional labour and play-acting help earn the confidences of informants. We must be friendly, patient and not too explicit about our intentions. We must act interested when bored and encourage informants to provide richer details. We must nod our heads with polite eyes but bored ears at verbose informants and wait for chances to redirect the conversation.

The friendly ethnographer hides their frustration. Who are these people to not allow us to observe them as we please? They may avoid returning phone calls or emails, say no to requests, renege on their promises, and in general be obstructive. Organizational ethnography does not happen on an even playing field. Subservience and deference may be necessary. The organizational ethnographer lacks control, held captive to bureaucracy, the rhythms of work and the fears of workers. Some informants, knowing they have the power to say no, can be especially irksome and require patronization. While in print most fieldworkers will acknowledge their gratitude and debt to all informants, they may silently curse some for having been hindrances.

Ethnographers feel driven to like everyone and are dismayed if some on the scene greet their friendly overtures with hostility. This spurning is not necessarily idiosyncratic, but can arise from the conditions of research, although it has been treated as an embarrassment to be hidden from the reader's prying eyes. We can confess to several instances in which bad feeling, developed between our subjects and ourselves. Fine described one instance in the methodological appendix to his study of Little League baseball, in *With the boys: Preadolescent culture and Little League baseball* (1987), but he did not reveal this dislike within the main text itself or in articles, seemingly suggesting that while such dislike was relevant methodologically, it was not relevant substantively.

One coach felt that Fine was collaborating with his rivals in the league, and refused to permit him to collect questionnaires from the boys on his team. During the season, he attempted acts of humiliation, for instance, not accepting a line-up card that another coach had asked Fine to deliver. Fine took pleasure in writing about this man and his son, although he was 'ethical' in never mentioning his name and excluding identifying features. Those with access to 'the media' have power that others cannot match. Our structural position as reporters makes us gatekeepers. Taunt us if you dare.

Of course researchers should not dislike anyone. Yet, most will discover that they are incompatible with some. We do not like everyone that we meet – certainly not everyone that we meet in workplaces, particularly when goals and motivations conflict. In reality, we will find individuals with whom we do not become close, but with whom we can maintain cordial, if distant, relationships when we do not have conflicting goals. Many relations are 'provisionally friendly', particularly in organizations where people may be required to interact with one another. Then there are some with whom we feel acutely uncomfortable and from whom we maintain a distance. Even in ethnographic research we can create elaborate rationales to keep our distance. Finally, we will honour those sacred few of whom we can say with confidence that we actively dislike.

Shulman (1994) abhorred the private detective who enjoyed explaining how he could use his martial arts training to kill people instantly. The other customers at a diner shot strange looks at the table when hearing this man describe how his martial arts skills taught him to use a toothpick 'like a fucking spear through your brain'. Many ethnographers uncover such persons – targets of distaste. Hopefully not too many or this style of research, which depends on pleasantries, would be impossible. Hated individuals are found within our ethnographic worlds, but in our narrative representation of those worlds, they will vanish. We will crop them from the picture. The illusion is that we have managed our affairs sweetly and well. We wish to present ourselves as likable, and also we know that most researchers outside of the 'confessional' mode (Johnson, 1975; Van Maanen, 1988) see any discussion of personal animosities as irrelevant or discrediting.

An ethnographer is not necessarily an official member of the team, but that does not mean that one forgoes an implicit agreement with or sympathy to local norms. An investigator told Shulman of trading sex for pay when an attractive female client lacked money but needed his help. Even if this claim were true, and not male braggadocio, Shulman felt such compensation schemes were rare and omitted this detective's account from publication. His informant described the kinds of female figures he preferred for the 'best screws'. If informants are willing to talk, ethnographers are ready to encourage them to learn more and build rapport. If informants talk about sexual activities, prowess and objects of desire, we listen. Organizational ethnography requires extending an exquisite tolerance towards informants. Casual interaction requires participating in topics and activities that are part of the organizational culture's norms, like gossiping and going for a drink. Though ethnographers are supposed to be flies on the wall, they will get dragged into the action. Social participation is a source of affiliation that sustains rapport.

Ethnographers are expected to be straightforward about their reasons for being present. The more directive ethnographers are in encouraging informants to talk, the more of a problem they will face in either leading an informant or being led. Many would claim that research subjects have a right to know the ethnographer's goals. This sentiment sounds proper and has been institutionalized through a maze of governmental and academic regulations. However, such advice is contrary to the writings of classic ethnographers (and other methodologists) who are concerned about 'reactivity'. Two valued goals therefore conflict.

Informed consent is complicated by an ethnographic commonplace, gleaned from Glaser and Strauss's (1967) *The discovery of grounded theory*, that good ethnographers do not know what they are looking for until they have found it: theory is grounded in empirical inspiration. This model suggests that there is a truth here that we must be careful not to pollute. Not only are we unsure of the effects of explaining our plans, but we may not know what we are searching for until well into the research project. Qualitative researchers are often asked to complete an Institutional Review Board form or a grant application that requests the study's hypotheses. Often the only honest response is that we are studying You.

The expanded version of explaining that we are studying you is to say, with vague truth, that we are interested in the problems faced by people in your organization and position, what you do, and how you think. In many research settings, this is satisfactory, particularly when groups feel underappreciated. This explanation proved admirably suited to Fine's (1996, 1998) research with professional cooks and amateur mycologists, both of whom felt that the public did not appreciate them: the descriptive ploy seduces many an informant.

How much and what kinds of explanations we provide during fieldwork in organizations are choices that we make from a position of power and information control. Borrowing a metaphor from the espionage community, Fine distinguishes three strategies of information control: Deep Cover, Shallow Cover, and Explicit Cover (Fine, 1980). In the first of these, Deep Cover, the researcher does not announce his/her research role. Rather, the researcher participates in the group as a full member. Operating under Explicit Cover, the researcher makes as complete an announcement of the goals and hypotheses of the research as possible, not worrying if this explanation will affect behaviour. The third technique, Shallow Cover, finds a middle ground. The ethnographer announces the research intent, but is vague about the goals. These divisions, and the grey areas between them, remind us forcefully that the line between being 'informed' and 'uninformed' is uncertain (Thorne, 1980: 287). All research is secret in *some* ways, since subjects can never know everything (Roth, 1962: 283).

By 'not being honest', we do not mean that ethnographers fib, although they might, but rather that ethnographers shade what they know to increase the likelihood of acceptance: placing our ease before that of our informants. Throughout life we will mislead others for goals that appear worthy – or at least convenient. Why should honesty in practice, as opposed to in theory, be seen as virtuous, particularly in the absence of harm?

the imperfectly observant ethnographer

We assume that in ethnographic texts there exists a firm correspondence between what is said to have occurred, and what 'actually' happened. We believe that little of importance was missed – at least when the ethnographer was present. But suppose that this comforting belief is inaccurate. The ethnographer may not have been sufficiently observant. The ethnographic picture will always lack detailed shading, and sometimes these absences are relevant in that other ethnographers might have reached sharply different conclusions by highlighting other material.

This criticism seemingly targets 'bad ethnography'. Science fiction writer Theodore Sturgeon allegedly noted in response to claims that most science fiction is of poor quality, '90 per cent of science fiction is crap, but then 90 per cent of everything is crap'. Following Sturgeon's Law, 90 per cent of all ethnography is crap. While we should dispute the numbers and be wary of transforming quality into a dichotomous variable of 'crap/not crap', the point remains. However, we must transcend this chill assertion of scholarly incompetence and recognize that we lack the ability to be totally aware. We mishear, we do not recognize what we see, and we may be poorly positioned to recognize happenings around us.

Everything is capable of multiple interpretations and *mis*understandings. Some things we do not see because we are not trained or knowledgeable. Paul Stoller's rich (1989) ethnography of the Songhay of Niger, *The taste of ethnographic things*, reminds us that we rely on our visual and auditory senses, to the neglect of touch, smell, and taste. We are not observant: the very skill on which competent participant observation is supposedly – and actually – based.

In researching organizations we may lack a wide-ranging familiarity and experience with local activities. In *From hire to liar*, Shulman (2007) had to learn the complex deceptions that are particular to specific lines of work. For instance, market researchers can deceive clients by fudging sampling procedures, and software programmers can deceive by writing bugs into their programs that they then are paid to fix. A naive observer must learn how to uncover examples of deception that are transparent only to those who know what to look for.

A further cause of being unobservant results from personal, temporal, and situational pressures. Ethnography can be stressful even in the best circumstances. Hours of observations are followed by hours of composing field notes. When Fine was conducting research with fantasy role-playing gamers – those who played *Dungeons & Dragons* – he would spend the lengthening hours from seven in the evening until four the following morning with these young men. It would have required a very dramatic event to capture his attention in the wee small hours of a long night. For much of the time he was simply present, barely monitoring what transpired among these gamers. When he drank alcohol or puffed marijuana with informants his powers of concentration were altered. When he had a vexing day at the university or a dispute with his wife, his concentration diminished. Researchers who bring their children into the field must also cope with multiple distractions (Cassell, 1987). How could it be otherwise? As we know from straining to decipher scribbled field notes, sometimes we simply do not type all of the things we have noted or, worse, cannot read our own handwriting. Some ethnographers, in fact, do not write field notes, instead trusting their memory. One claims, memorably, 'I am a fieldnote!' (Jackson, 1990: 21).

What is depicted in the ethnography is not the whole picture. The pace of watching multiple activities, and the limitations of physical endurance, concentration and experience, make missing information inevitable. Obviously for reasons of space some events are excluded, but much is excluded because it passed right under our nose and through our ears, and because our hands were too tired.

the precision of organizational ethnography

A dearly held claim is that field notes are data and reflect what 'really' happened. We trust that quotation marks reveal words that have been truly spoken. This is often an illusion, a lie, and a deception. We engage in the inverse of plagiarism, giving credit to those undeserving, at least not for those precise words. To recall the exact words of a conversation, especially if one is not trained in shorthand (and not even then, as stenographers and court reporters can attest), is impossible. This is particularly applicable with those who maintain the illusion of 'active' or 'complete membership' (Adler and Adler, 1987) by not taking notes within the limits of the public situation. We bolster an illusion of omniscience by recreating a scene with attendant bits of talk, skating on ever-thinner ice.

We become playwrights, reconstructing a scene for the pleasure of readers, depicting ongoing events in our minds and inscribing those scenes (Bartlett, 1932): turning near-fiction into near-fact. We claim that the scene really happened, but the scene didn't happen precisely in the form we proclaim.

We are like popular biographers who in order to make a scene compelling and 'real' create dialogue, and in the process we support our own arguments. The dialogue is not accurate in that an attestation that these 'precise' words were said is futile. One would need a gifted, encyclopedic ear: an ear never seen. When conscientiously compiled, the quotations are both true and false. They are true in that with conscientious researchers they represent something 'along the lines' of what was said – transformed into our own words that we place in a methodologically unsanitary way into the mouths of others. We make our informants sound like we think they should sound, given our interpretations of who they 'really' are (Atkinson, 1992: 26–7).

The illusion of verisimilitude is crucial for qualitative research. We embrace our method's rich precision. The belief that this is 'real life', and not fiction or guesswork, provides a charter for ethnography. This depiction of reality gives ethnography an advantage over survey research and experimentation, but it is a belief that is at best only approximately true. In organizational settings tumult makes ethnography complex.

the passive but intervening ethnographer

Most textbooks on qualitative research emphasize that an observer should avoid influencing the scene (Taylor and Bogdan, 1984). Underlying this attitude is the principle that the researcher should not become a 'participant' observer. After all, what would we learn if researchers burst into a social scene and took charge, pushing events in directions in which they would not otherwise have gone? While this would *still* be a social environment, it might not be the environment one had planned to examine. Too great an involvement in a social scene can transform ethnography into a field experiment.

Yet, recognizing that the researcher should not direct a scene, we might wonder whether active observers do not and should not have influence. Ultimately the methodological goal is to become a full member of a scene: to 'settle down and forget about being a sociologist' (Goffman, 1989: 129). How is this possible when one is just an observant piece of furniture? While we should avoid putting too great a spin on a setting, we will add ourselves to the mix, and attempt to understand how we feel as participants.

The degree to which one is an active member of an organization affects the extent to which this sympathetic understanding is possible, and this is a function of one's social location: Fine was more involved in being a fantasy role-play gamer and mushroom collector than as a Little League baseball player, high school debater, or a professional cook. Kleinman (1991), describing her research on a holistic health centre, bids us recognize that our emotions directly influence what we see, how we feel towards others, and the strategic choices that we make in our ethnographies. We can never be a cipher.

To do no harm is a prime injunction for all ethnographers. Yet we do leave tracks. Ethnographers are sometimes motivated to 'give voice' to groups and organizations as a form of social justice advocacy. They also may expose information that is harmful to an organization and that informants vociferously oppose exposing. John Braithwaite's study of corporate crime in the pharmaceutical industry was delayed for two years by lawyers who represented managers that Braithwaite had interviewed, arguing that Braithwaite lied about them. Braithwaite (1985) advocates that all interviewers studying corporate crime use two interviewers and/or a tape recorder to prevent managers from arguing that the ethnographer fabricated their comments.

In field notes published in *Kitchens: The culture of restaurant work*, Fine notes 'the workers trust that I will place myself on their side as a true, if limited, member of their group, embracing their underside' (Fine, 1996: 234). This is a mild example of role conflict, whereby ethnographers participate in light deviance with workers, helping to establish a rapport. Does the ethnographer have an obligation to management gatekeepers to report the deviance that management opposes? The ethnographer usually asserts that he or she will not be an undercover operative for management, but that does not necessarily mean that the ethnographer must participate in activities that management deems improper. Yet, it is doubtful that kitchen staff would have accepted Fine so warmly had he been unwilling to participate in and/or overlook this slight malfeasance, like taking food home or receiving free beer.

The ethnographer also has an undeclared relationship with those clients that the organization serves, who may be unaware that an ethnographer helped prepare the meal that they ate or that the advocate helping them is also studying them. The client is an unwitting participant in the research. Role-conflict occurs when ethnographers do not tell organizational clients that they are observing. When studying private detective agencies, Shulman was once mistaken for an investigator. He was with an investigator conducting surveillance on a person suspected of submitting a fraudulent worker's compensation claim. As they watched the suspect's home, the investigator decided to confront the suspect. The investigator requested that David say nothing. They approached this man's door to be greeted by a frail-looking man who looked to be in his late fifties and who walked with a limp. The investigator identified himself. The man asked why two investigators were there to hassle and intimidate him. Did the suspect have a right to know that Shulman was not an investigator?

A conflict exists between disclosing one's research identity to outsiders and being deceptive. How far does informed consent stretch? Does it only pertain to the researched group or to all those people who the organization and the observer affect? Shulman did not lie to his host organization, but deceived others, by omission, that the organization worked with, such as the organization's targets and, in other instances, clients. This deception is secondary, while lying to the organization itself is a primary deception.

writing organizational ethnography: how candid should one be?

Ethnographers differ little from Erving Goffman's social actors; they rely upon impression management. Although Goffman (1989: 128) proposes that a good ethnographer must willingly look like a 'horse's ass', this is easier said than done. No one wishes to look bad, and self-conscious ethnographers censor much information. Many researchers adopt a fly-on-the-wall model – ethnography without an ethnographer: the fully unobtrusive ethnographer, as described above. Indeed, much journalism operates on this claim, not just of objectivity, but also on the more radical belief that, in Edward R. Murrow's terms, *You are there*. This illusion can be recognized for what it is when the writer relies on the passive voice, indicating that someone 'was asked', eliding the reality that the asker was the writer.

The question ultimately becomes who is the 'who' in the text? How many imperfections will one report? The issue of what and how much to report does not have any eternal answers. Answers are always grounded in choices, wherein the cynic can claim, as we do here, that the researcher is either not being candid or, on the other hand, is over-glorifying the self in a report that none but one's relatives might voluntarily read.

The choice is not entirely theoretical. We cannot disentangle the personal demands of presentation of self – how one will appear to others – from the question of what one should do 'in the name of science'. Being candid is a situated choice, forever linked to how the candour might affect one's scholarly reputation. We have our careers to think of, and issues of honesty and ethics must be analysed within this personal nexus (Barnes, 1979: 179). Recent attempts to move oneself into the centre of ethnography can no more escape the dilemmas of candour than can attempts to pretend that one wasn't present. Every other technique of ethnographic description demands the same bracketing of candour as does the claim of the absent ethnographer. The sour reality is that the presentation of one's role is invariably an exercise in tact. The reader always looks over the writer's shoulder.

the chaste ethnographer

As an example of 'candour', one dirty little secret of ethnography, so secret and so dirty that it is hard to know how much credence to give it, surrounds saucy tales of lurid assignations, couplings, and trysts between ethnographers and those they 'observe'. The closest that we usually come to this in the published record is the inverse: cases in which male subjects harassed female ethnographers (for example, Conaway, 1986; Easterday, Papademas, Schorr, and Valentine, 1977; Hunt, 1984; Wax, 1979). These noxious and brazen attempts at sexual acquaintanceship are part of the territory in a sexist and sexual world. Why should the female ethnographer be treated differently from any other female? One wonders about male ethnographers and their female informants. Are academics more moral than other professions?

Erich Goode's (1999; 2002) disclosures about sleeping with several of his respondents during different research projects opened the door to a deeper consideration of the ethics and impact of sexual relations by fieldworkers. Goode's sexual activities caused a stir but also led to an exploration of this often omitted and sanitized subject. Katherine Irwin (2006) recently wrote about her experience in marrying a key informant whom she met while observing a tattoo parlour. The relationship crossed many of the boundaries of research relations. How the fieldwork is presented to readers becomes more salient because of the marital relationship. Irwin had to introduce her informant to colleagues as a 'husband', a startling departure from the typical compartmentalization of subject and researcher.

Just as long-term relationships arise, so too do brief encounters – equally passionate, if limited in time and space. Humans are attracted to each other in all domains. They look, leer, flirt, and fantasize. The written record inscribes little of this rough and hot humanity. Of course, ethnographers value and demand their privacy. This desire is surely understandable and from the ethnographer's perspective defensible. Sexual contact stigmatizes the writer – particularly female writers (Whitehead and Price, 1986: 302). We are to create social science, not porn. Malinowski's (1967) diaries were only published posthumously and one rare book about a female anthropologist and her relations with a male informant appears under a pseudonym (Cesara, 1982: 55–6). The taboo on including these data may mislead naive readers about the emotional and personal qualities of this methodology. The question is whether we can preserve our privacy while we reveal the impact and relevance of our private and public behaviour.

the fair ethnographer

Is fairness ever possible? The label 'fair' can consist of two alternative meanings: *objectivity* and *balance*. Each is problematic, and each is far from universal in qualitative research narratives. Some would urge that they should not even be goals.

Qualitative researchers need not be warned about the difficulty, if not the impossibility, of claiming objectivity. Objectivity is an illusion – an illusion snuggling in the comforting blanket of positivism – that the world is ultimately knowable and secure. Alas, the world is always known from a perspective, even though we might agree that frequently these perspectives do not vary dramatically. An ethnographic movement, enshrining subjectivity and originating in anthropology in the writings of James Clifford and his colleagues, has steadily spread into other arenas of ethnographic work – including education and sociology (Atkinson, 1992; Gubrium, 1988). Few ethnographers accept a single objective reality, but in realist ethnographies

(Van Maanen, 1988) such a doubt was not explicitly stated. The illusion was quite the reverse.

Fine's study of Little League baseball masquerades as informing the outsider about the 'real facts' of this hidden social world, without being self-conscious about his role (except in the appendix). He demands trust, even while his theories of child rearing and his own fitful and unsuccessful experiences as a young athlete are discretely ignored. Fine presented himself as an honest broker with nothing to hide and with everything to share, parsing the facts about this organizational form. This claim bolstered his professional reputation, while ignoring the romanticism of a sitcom suburban life that he never shared.

Ignoring the motives and themes of researchers in interpreting 'reality', accepting an image of fairness in the name of objectivity is misguided. However, excising such a claim does not solve the problem. The response, embracing subjectivity, is equally problematic. The reality of occupational backstages is that values inevitably conflict. By admitting one's perspective or by describing the world in terms of ideology and narrative, we wear a mask of openness without doing justice to all the ways in which a setting might be understood. We do not present the diversity of worldviews, because we are an interested party whose definitions of the scene are distorted by what we can see, and by our unwillingness to admit that our informants believe the world is objective. This cannot be avoided, but we should admit the paradox. As Margery Wolf (1992) demonstrates in *A thrice told tale*, the same set of events can be understood quite differently through separate discursive practices.

Charles Bosk (2003) recently made a startling admission in his revised methodological appendix for the second edition of *Forgive and remember*, his ethnographic study of medical errors in surgical training. Bosk admitted changing the gender of a surgical trainee from female to male to protect her identity. He offers a mea culpa that his omission of the gender of this inform-ant, though done to protect her identity, meant that he covered up gender discrimination and social control. To know that the medical resident was a woman would have clarified that his depiction of this person as irrational partly reflected an atmosphere of gender discrimination at the hospital. That interpretation is not available to readers of the first edition of *Forgive and remember*, because the irrational person appears to be a male being judged by other men, not a sole female, who was judged as irrational by male surgical attending physicians. Bosk embraced the ethic of anonymity but was not fair when he did not tell readers a critical detail that affected their ability to understand the gendered environment of surgical training.

This issue of fairness becomes particularly salient for ethnographers engaged in policy-relevant or applied research: a branch of qualitative public sociology that expanded in the 1980s (Estes and Edmonds, 1981; Loseke, 1989). The classic instance of 'motivated ethnography' is Kai Erikson's (1976; see Glazer, 1982: 62) *Everything in its path*, an ethnographic examination of the aftermath of a dam collapse in the Buffalo Creek area of West Virginia. Erikson was hired to collect data for a law firm that was suing the mining company for negligence. We do not suggest that Erikson was dishonest, but his perspective channelled the data that he collected (and couldn't collect) and shaped his interpretations.

However, policy issues need not be central to the research for the selection and self-censorship of data to be an issue. Data are never presented in full, and choices are inevitable. In protecting people, organizations, and scenes we shade some truths, ignore others, and create fictive personages to take the pressure off real ones (Adler and Adler, 1993; Warren, 1980). A colleague once informed Fine that he shaved data that might harm the public perception of the ethnic group with which he was in sympathy, feeling that they had enough trouble without having to confront his truths. Car salesmen, clergymen, politicos, and ethnographers massage the realities they share with their audiences.

Participant observation may become participant intervention. In finding a problem, we wish to fix it. Identifying with our informants we take their side (Barnes, 1979: 171): to protect them from harm and make everything right. As a result, qualitative evaluation research, like all evaluation research, is contaminated by the perspective of the researcher and by the emotions that arise in the field.

Ethnographers do not wish to be wrong. We develop an expertise in a particular organizational arena, hoping we are not misled or gullible. Objectivity is a strategy that defends against insecure fears of incompetence and carelessness. Naivety can be camouflaged. In consequence we may emphasize those claims of which we feel most confident and that appear most impregnable to criticism. We hope that objectivity shields us from being declared wrong and that balance hides that we depended more on some informants than others to buttress our claims.

writing the literary ethnography

Ethnography is nothing until inscribed: experience transformed into text. The idiosyncratic skills of the ethnographer are always evident, nowhere more so than in the literary production of ethnography. Each text attempts to fit a world into a genre (Atkinson, 1992: 29–37), and make the account seem a competent version of the kind of thing that this genre should entail. This is at the heart of the textual practices of the qualitative researcher.

Inscription is dangerous for all writers (Fine, 1988; Fine and Kleinman, 1986) – for those who are 'bad' and those who are 'good'. For the bad writers, the problem is in keeping the interest of readers, assuming that one can get published. These writers must ensure that the writing is not so muddled that their intention or the reader gets lost (Richardson, 1990). Bad writing, assuming we can define it, is a simple problem. Teaching social scientists to write, while not easy, is something that we know how to do.

But what about writers who are not burdened by literary incompetence? Many writers write well, but in a language that is not easily translatable by those outside of the community. Typically associated with postmodernists and some radical theorists, they may express themselves fluently, but not enough of their readers can acquire a ready sense of what words mean in context. These authors belong to a different universe of discourse from their audience.

Other writers may write so well in conventional terms that the reader is more entranced by the writing than by the substance. The writing can hide a lack of evidence, as sometimes happens in quasi-popular works (Becker, 1986). Ethnographers must be willing to share the messiness of their observations without tidying them up excessively. This is a methodology that depends on the presentation of the lives-in-full of an organization and its workers. Those who write too well and share too little do a disservice to readers.

In addition, ethnography can feature hidden co-authors that have helped to craft the literary quality of the work. Reviewers, editors and friendly peers can police problematic prose. Much of this editing is unannounced, separating the polished ethnographic product from its humble origin in fieldnotes. The finished product may appear to be a personal expression, but several sets of eyes and editors have made the words sparkle more than they would have done otherwise. Each ethnography tells a tale of multiple sites – the field site and the sites of the interventions of colleagues, mentors, reviewers and publishers.

the lies of organizational ethnography

All trades develop a body of conceits that they hope to hide from those outside the boundaries of their domain and so it is with ethnographers of organizations. We do not denigrate our common enterprise, but we must not be blind to our limits. Let us open our conceits to our readers and ourselves. Knowing oneself, one can improve but, more significantly, the limits of the art are part of the data. Some lies are more crucial than others in that one can hope to be reasonably observant and precise, whereas protecting one's self from harsh critique is central to one's professional standing.

Workers must learn to manage the informal and formal demands that confront them. Their initial naivety can be cured. Should it remain uncured, it will impede their professional progress. Similarly, an organizational ethnographer must conquer two planes: those demands inherent to studying an organization and the idealized professional expectations of ethnographic practice. Reconciling these produces practical moral dilemmas that sometimes mean that an organizational ethnographer will avoid full informed consent, engage in deceptive impression management, and exclude information in published material. Organizational ethnography may require a Faustian bargain, but hopefully a benevolent one. Yet the nature of ethnographic practice is that naivety often loses out to the benefits of being streetwise.

For the most part the lies of organizational ethnography are not lies that we can choose to avoid; the reality is that they are part of the methodology by which we prepare reality for presentation. Ethnography is ultimately about transformation. We take idiosyncratic behaviours, events with numerous causes, which may – God forbid! – be random (or at least inexplicable), and we package them as an understanding of an organization. We contextualize events in a social system, within a web of meaning, and then name a cause, excluding other patterns or causes. Transformation is about hiding, about magic, about change. This is the task that we face and the reality that we must embrace. Ethnographers cannot help but to lie, but through lying we also present truths about organizations that escape those who are not so bold.

---

note

[1] This has been a particularly salient issue in social movement research, in which there are 'good' and 'bad' social movements, often studied differently. Civil rights groups, gay rights movements, and pro-choice lobbies are treated quite differently and examined more often than groups that are identified as racist, homophobic, and anti-choice.

---

references

Adler, P.A. and Adler, P. (1987) *Membership roles in field research*. Newbury Park: Sage.

Adler, P.A. and Adler, P. (1993) 'Ethical issues in self-censorship', in C.M. Renzetti and R.M. Lee (eds) *Researching sensitive topics*. Newbury Park: Sage. pp. 249–66.

Allen, C. (1997) 'Spies like us: When sociologists deceive their subjects', *Lingua Franca*, November.

Atkinson, P. (1992) *Understanding ethnographic texts*. Newbury Park: Sage.

Barnes, J.A. (1979) *Who should know what?* Cambridge: Cambridge University Press.

Bartlett, F.C. (1932) *Remembering*. Cambridge: Cambridge University Press.

Becker, H.S. (1986) *Writing for social scientists*. Chicago: University of Chicago Press.

Bosk, C. (2003) *Forgive and remember: Managing medical failure* (2nd edn). Chicago: University of Chicago Press.

Braithwaite, J. (1985) 'Corporate crime research: Why two interviewers are needed', *Sociology*, 19: 136–8.

Buchanan, D., Boddy, D. and McCalman, J. (1988) 'Getting in, getting on, getting out and getting back', in A. Bryman (ed.), *Doing research in organizations*. London: Routledge. pp. 53–68.

Cassell, J. (1987) *Children in the field*. Philadelphia: Temple University Press.

Cesara, M. (1982) *Reflections of a woman anthropologist: No hiding place*. New York: Academic Press.

Conaway, M.E. (1986) 'The pretense of the neutral researcher', in T.L. Whitehead and M.E. Conaway (eds), *Self, sex, and gender in cross-cultural fieldwork*. Urbana: University of Illinois Press. pp. 52–63.

Dalton, M. (1959) *Men who manage*. New York: John Wiley & Sons.

Douglas, J. (1976) *Investigative social research*. Beverly Hills: Sage.

Easterday, L., Papademas, D., Schorr, L. and Valentine, C. (1977) 'The making of a female researcher: Role problems in field work', *Urban Life*, 6: 333–48.

Ellis, C. (1986) *Fisher folk: Two communities on the Chesapeake Bay*. Lexington: University Press of Kentucky.

Erikson, K. (1967) 'A comment on disguised observation in sociology', *Social Problems*, 14: 366–73.

Erikson, K. (1976) *Everything in its path*. New York: Simon and Schuster.

Estes, C. and Edmonds, B.C. (1981) 'Symbolic interaction and policy analysis', *Symbolic Interaction*, 4: 75–86.

Fine, G.A. (1980) 'Cracking diamonds: Observer role in Little League baseball settings and the acquisition of social competence', in W.B. Shaffir, R.A. Stebbins and A. Turowetz (eds), *Fieldwork experience*. New York: St. Martin's Press. pp. 117–32.

Fine, G.A. (1983) *Shared fantasy: Role-playing games as social worlds*. Chicago: University of Chicago Press.

Fine, G.A. (1987) *With the boys: Little League baseball and preadolescent culture*. Chicago: University of Chicago Press.

Fine, G.A. (1988) 'The ten commandments of writing', *The American Sociologist*, 19: 152–7.

Fine, G.A. (1993) 'Ten lies of ethnography: Moral dilemmas of field research', *Journal of Contemporary Ethnography*, 22: 267–94.

Fine, G.A. (1995) 'Public narration and group culture: Discerning discourse in social movements', in H. Johnston and B. Klandermans (eds), *Social movements and culture*. Minneapolis: University of Minnesota Press. pp. 127–43.

Fine, G.A. (1996) *Kitchens: The culture of restaurant work*. Berkeley: University of California Press.

Fine, G.A. (1998) *Morel tales: The culture of mushrooming*. Cambridge: Harvard University Press.

Fine, G.A. and Martin, D.D. (1990) 'A partisan view: Sarcasm, satire, and irony as voices in Erving Goffman's *Asylums*', *Journal of Contemporary Ethnography*, 19: 89–115.

Fine, G.A. and Kleinman, S. (1986) 'Interpreting the sociological classics: Can there be a "true" meaning of Mead', *Symbolic Interaction*, 9: 129–46.

Glaser, B. and Strauss, A. (1967) *The discovery of grounded theory*. Chicago: Aldine.

Glazer, M. (1982) 'The threat of the stranger', in J.E. Sieber (ed.), *The ethics of social research: Fieldwork, regulation, and publication*. New York: Springer-Verlag. pp. 49–70.

Goffman, E. (1989) 'On field work', *Journal of Contemporary Ethnography*, 18: 123–32.

Goode, E. (1999) 'Sex with informants as deviant behavior: An account and commentary', *Deviant Behavior*, 20: 301–24.

Goode, E. (2002) 'Sexual involvement and social research in a fat civil rights organization', *Qualitative Sociology*, 25: 501–34.

Gubrium, J. (1988) *Analyzing field reality*. Newbury Park: Sage.

Hunt, J. (1984) 'The development of rapport through the negotiation of gender in field work among police', *Human Organization*, 43: 283–96.

Irwin, K. (2006) 'Into the dark heart of ethnography: The lived ethics and inequality of intimate field relationships', *Qualitative Sociology*, 29: 155–75.

Jackall, R. (1988) *Moral mazes: The world of corporate managers*. Oxford: Oxford University Press.

Jackson, J. (1990) '"I am a fieldnote": Fieldnotes as a symbol of professional identity', in R. Sanjek (ed.), *Fieldnotes: The makings of anthropology*. Ithaca: Cornell University Press. pp. 3–33.

Johnson, J.M. (1975) *Doing field research*. New York: Free Press.

Kleinman, S. (1991) 'Field-workers' feelings: What we feel, who we are, how we analyze', in W.B. Shaffir and R.A. Stebbins (eds), *Experiencing fieldwork*. Newbury Park: Sage. pp. 184–95.

Loseke, D. (1989) 'Evaluation research and the practice of social services', *Journal of Contemporary Ethnography*, 18: 202–23.

Malinowski, B. (1967) *A diary in the strict sense of the term*. London: Routledge.

Morrill, C. (1995) *The executive way: Conflict management in corporations*. Chicago: University of Chicago Press.

Peshkin, A. (1986) *God's choice: The total world of a fundamentalist Christian school.* Chicago: University of Chicago Press.

Reynolds, P.D. (1982) *Ethics and social science research.* Englewood Cliffs: Prentice-Hall.

Richardson, L. (1990) *Writing strategies: Reaching diverse audiences.* Newbury Park: Sage.

Rollins, J. (1987) *Between women: Domestics and their employers.* Philadelphia: Temple University Press.

Roth, J. (1962) 'Comments on "secret observation"', *Social Problems,* 9: 283–4.

Shulman, D. (1994) 'Dirty data and investigative methods: Some lessons from private detective work', *Journal of Contemporary Ethnography,* 23: 214–53.

Shulman, D. (2007) *From hire to liar: The role of deception in the workplace.* Cornell University Press.

Stoller, P. (1989) *The taste of ethnographic things.* Philadelphia: University of Pennsylvania Press.

Taylor, S. and Bogdan, R. (1984) *Introduction to qualitative research methods* (2nd edn). New York: Wiley.

Thorne, B. (1980) '"You still takin' notes": Fieldwork and problems of informed consent', *Social Problems,* 27: 284–97.

Van Maanen, J. (1988) *Tales of the field.* Chicago: University of Chicago Press.

Wax, M.L. (1977) 'On fieldworkers and those exposed to fieldwork: Federal regulations and moral issues', *Human Organization,* 36: 321–9.

Wax, M.L. (1980) 'Paradoxes of "consent" to the practice of fieldwork', *Social Problems,* 27: 272–83.

Wax, M.L. (1982) 'Research reciprocity rather than informed consent in fieldwork', in J. Sieber (ed.), *The ethics of social research: Fieldwork, regulation and publication.* New York: Springer-Verlag. pp. 33–48.

Wax, R.H. (1979) 'Gender and age in fieldwork and fieldwork education: No good thing is done by any man alone', *Social Problems,* 26: 509–22.

Warren, C.A.B. (1980) 'Data presentation and audience: Responses, ethics, and effects', *Urban Life,* 9: 282–308.

Whitehead, T.L. and Price, L. (1986) 'Summary: Sex and the fieldwork experience,' in T.L Whitehead and M.E. Conaway (eds), *Self, sex, and gender in cross-cultural fieldwork.* Urbana: University of Illinois Press. pp. 289–304.

Wolf, M. (1992) *A thrice told tale: Feminism, postmodernism and ethnographic responsibility.* Stanford: Stanford University Press.

10

'But I thought we were friends?' Life cycles and research relationships

Nic Beech, Paul Hibbert, Robert MacIntosh and Peter McInnes

This chapter is concerned with a relatively under-explored aspect of 'engaged research'– the nature of friendship relations between researchers and practitioners, and the ethical dilemmas that arise in such relationships. Attention has been paid to the relational aspects of research in the methodology literature, but this chapter focuses more closely on friendship in particular. The chapter is framed around two guiding concerns: how do friendships, formed in and around research, change over time; and in view of friendship conceived in this dynamic fashion, what ethical questions and dilemmas arise for the 'friends'?

The chapter is structured as follows. Since the development of friendship might be expected to be more prominent in forms of research that presuppose a close engagement between researcher and research participant than those which are based on distance and an 'objective' separation between researcher and subject, we start by briefly exploring the nature of 'engaged' forms of research. Second, we explore the friendship literature as it relates to the identities people construct for themselves and others in research relationships. Third, a phased model of research engagement is presented, highlighting the way the relationship between researchers and research participants develops over time. Finally, we present two 'tales from the field', of contrasting examples of friendship in research relationships, and we highlight some of the ethical questions that arise in such situations.

engaged research

'Engaged research' is a somewhat ambivalent term, which carries several meanings. In essence, it is research that is close to practitioner concerns and aims. It incorporates ideas and practices from traditions such as Participant Observation (Spradley, 1980; Bernard, 2006), Action Research (Eden and Huxham, 1996; Reason and Bradbury, 2001), and 'Mode 2' research (Tranfield and Starkey, 1998; MacLean et al., 2002). Taking each of these in turn, Participant Observation is distinguished from hidden or remote observation by the acknowledgement that the observer's presence will inevitably have an impact on the activities, artefacts and discourse that are observed (Johnson et al., 2006). Rather than adopting an objective, detached stance, the researcher moves within organizational processes and interactions in an attempt to 'understand from the inside' (Alvesson and Deetz, 2000). In so doing, the researcher establishes a subjective connection to the participants in the research setting, through which mutual influence occurs (Spradley, 1980). Indeed, it could be argued that if there is no subjective connection (Johnson et al., 2006), then the desired 'understanding from the inside' has not been achieved. Participant Observation is able to offer rich insights when the process has brought about a change in the observer's perspective or a new understanding of the setting (Bernard, 2006). Transforming one's understanding entails some degree of personal change on the part of the researcher, and openness to such subjective changes is intrinsic to this method (Geertz, 1983; Jackson, 1998).

Action Research also makes participation and engagement explicit, as the researcher is present with the intention of having an impact on how the people and organization work (Greenwood and Levin, 1998; see also Sykes and Treleaven, Chapter 11, this volume). The very presence of the researcher connotes a desire to help improve the situation for 'clients' in the organization. This can entail the researcher becoming part of a team that is trying to achieve particular organizational or operational goals (Coughlan and Coghlan, 2002) or the researcher taking on aspects of a managerial role (Coghlan, 2001). In either case, for such research to be effective, it must both help members of the organization with matters that are important to them, as well as develop more general learning that stimulates the researcher's theory generation. Action researchers thus adopt hybrid roles – both inside the organizational setting and doing theoretical work outside – and are embedded in subjective connections to the communities of practice inside the organization and in the academic world. The resultant depth of knowledge, and the consequent ability to theorize from the experience, relies on being able to genuinely 'be part of the experience' rather than being detached from it.

Mode 2 research, a form of engaged research that has been promoted by the British Academy of Management (Tranfield and Starkey, 1998), stresses the co-production of knowledge. It is contrasted with Mode 1 research, in which concepts are developed through theorizing and subsequently applied, in a top-down fashion, to the workplace. Mode 2 is anti-hierarchical in that 'empirical settings' are conceived neither as places for 'transferring knowledge' to practitioners nor as sites for experimental data gathering (Van Aken, 2002). Rather, practitioners and researchers jointly define the problems and issues to be explored; both parties bring skills and knowledge to the process; and reflection and feedback on the work occur within the setting as well as being written up for academic consumption (MacLean et al., 2002). In this style of research, the role distinctions between practitioner and researcher are blurred, and both take on activities and purposes that would traditionally (that is, in Mode 1 research) be the preserve of the other. For example, researchers might take on the role of providing management expertise, and practitioners could become involved in developing theoretical concepts for publication.

There are subtle but significant differences between the specifics of Participant Observation and Action Research, with Mode 2 operating as an umbrella term that highlights similarities and common ground with respect to the nature of the engagement between the researcher and the practitioner. Engaged Research can therefore be conceived as an effort to co-produce knowledge in which both researchers and practitioners seek to improve things in the workplace while simultaneously marshalling and producing formal and informal knowledge. The engagement increases the possibility of subjective change, mutual influence and interpersonal relations that go beyond traditional Mode 1, objectivist and detached styles of research. Hence, this is particularly fertile ground in which to explore the idea and practice of friendship between researchers and research participants.

'Engagement' implies more than a cognitive framework for the production of knowledge. It is an emotional and risky business, sometimes ambivalent, sometimes exciting, but always crossing organizational and intellectual bound-aries. In subjectivitist research (Burrell and Morgan, 1979) the researcher is interested in understanding the subjective realities of the actors in the situation. But beyond this, we find that as researchers we become subjectively involved – wanting to help, having a view on what would be good and bad, and feeling a sense of shared objectives and 'togetherness' with other people who have similar views. It is unsurprising that under such circumstances, in-group ties and social group formation can take place (Tajfel and Turner, 1985). Friendships can develop; and when this happens the engagement between friends goes beyond shared views and perceptions of the issues at hand (Pesamaa et al., 2007) to incorporate an emotional attachment and even a degree of identification.

However, the concept of friendship plays a small role in the literature on Participant Observation, Action Research and Mode 2 research. We argue that this is an important omission because when friendship grows, ethical dilemmas also arise. With friendship may come improved access and openness, but to what extent should one initiate or foster friendship? When the researcher and practitioner are in friendship relations, how should one use privileged information? To what extent should political activity or advocacy become part of the researcher's purpose? When the research project finishes, what happens to the 'friendship'?

In this chapter, our aim is to elucidate engaged research from the perspective of the phases of friendship development, growth and decline – and to identify the ethical questions and dilemmas that the researcher encounters during such social processes. We will argue that in addition to altruistic intentions and the authenticity of self towards other, which would be expected in a friendship, in order to remain engaged the researcher may also need to act in arguably more negative ways, such as fudging, performing and silencing/self-silencing.

The common-sense understanding of friendship is that it is a sharing, a joining together and a mutual liking. In Marmaros and Sacerdote's (2006) study, factors such as proximity, frequency of interaction and similarity of background were correlated with friendship formation. Similarly, Markiewicz et al. (2000) found that patterns of friendship within organizations correlated with sex; same-sex ties were generally found to be stronger than different-sex ties. They also found that 'successful' friendships were associated with job satisfaction and career success, particularly for men. Whether or not the friendships were deliberately instrumental, there appears to be some functional utility to such friendships.

A sense of instrumentality is also evoked by Nietzsche (1977), who uses the metaphor of two boats when discussing friendship. For a time, the boats can have one destination, and while they are in harbour, they can celebrate and feast together. But inevitably their tasks take them in different directions, and a distance develops. Hence, for Nietzsche, friendships persist while they are helpful to both people either in assisting towards a shared task, or fulfilling the social function of joint celebration and fun, but once the friends develop different interests, or have divergent tasks, the friendship will decline.

Leach (1982) also draws attention to the temporal character of friendship, which he contrasts with the permanence of kinship relations. Friendship is regarded as impermanent and contingent. In addition, Leach highlights the role of exchange in friendship relations. Many things can be exchanged in friendship, including status, access to in-groups, political support, emotional support and personal closeness. While exchange-based relationships are not necessarily friendly (indeed, enmity can also be conceived as a form of social exchange), exchange in friendship, according to Leach, is typified by trust. The friends will not start out with a contract-like mindset or measurements of the relative value of exchanges that typify low-trust relations. However, that is not to say that friends do not make assessments of equity in what each puts into the relationship, and feelings of inequity can provoke a diminution of the friendship.

It is notable that the aspects of exchange raised here have resonances for research friendships, as well as other sorts. Status, access and support are all involved in developing research activities and insights, and these are not necessarily sought for altruistic reasons. It might be that there are genuinely shared interests as implied by the literature on engaged research cited above; however, it could also be that there are times when it is advantageous to the researcher to fudge or even fake the trust that Leach sees as differentiating friendly exchange from other forms of exchange. In what might be an extreme case, Kipnis et al. (1984) define friendship as a management tactic that, in their view, is an alternative to the use of power; it is proximal to coalition forming and bargaining in their conceptualization. This view of 'friendship' would barely conform to the understanding developed by Nietzsche and Leach, as it seems to advocate giving the appearance of friendship in order to get something from the other party without actually developing trust, emotional support and personal closeness. Although, Kipnis et al. regard this as distinct from power, it could be argued that such an approach is interwoven with power of both subtle and unsubtle types. It seems that friendship is complex and dynamic.

If friendship is regarded as dynamic, it will grow or deteriorate as interests, tasks and personal bonds change over time (Sias et al., 2004). Social Identity Theory (Tajfel and Turner, 1985) traces the mechanisms by which people enter and leave in-groups, such as friendship groups. Transition rites and practices often mark movement across boundaries as people develop stronger ties, maintain positions and subsequently loosen ties. These processes can include the adoption of identity markers or symbols of group membership such as shared dress, the espousal of socially approved values and the enactment of 'appropriate' behaviour (Berger, 1997). However, tension can still arise in relationships given their tendency to deterioration (Sias et al., 2004), and so there is a need for 'identity work' (Sveningsson and Alvesson, 2003) to maintain position and membership. Without maintenance, friendships can be expected to atrophy, such that the in-group ties become vulnerable to dramatic or gradual decay. Hence, the dynamics of friendship involve development or decline in relation to shifting exchange, trust, perceived utility or shared interests, and are also based on emotional bonds and support between people. Given the mix of trust and support with exchange-utility, ethical questions can arise as people ask why they are being friendly with this person rather than that, how far what they 'get out of the relationship' inspires action to connect or disconnect, and when (if ever) it is acceptable to fake friendship, producing a pretence in order to serve personal needs. In the next section we introduce a way of thinking about friendship in a series of temporal phases. This will then be applied to two examples of researcher–research participant friendships.

relationship phases in engaged research

When reflecting on our own experiences of engaged research and on the friendship literature, we identified four phases in research relationships: invitation; momentary auditions; engagement; separation. Of course, not all friendships go through all of these phases, and the flow through them is not always unidirectional (hence, we are not proposing a classic 'stage theory'). However, we suggest that the phases offer a potentially useful way of characterizing the nature and dynamics of 'friendly' research relationships.

invitation and relationship formation

During the initial phases, friendship formation entails the tentative 'offering and acceptance' of the idea of being friends. The offering and acceptance may not typically be explicit, but are implicit in tone of voice, non-verbal behaviours and verbal behaviours, such as repeated agreeing and the supply of words by one for the sentences of the other. These same verbal and non-verbal actions can also denote opposition. For example, one could feel constantly interrupted, but when there is a spark of friendship there is a recognition of the interplay as an invitation to join, rather than as someone overriding your words. This stage is often referred to as gaining entry or gaining access (Feldman et al., 2003). Feldman et al. place an emphasis on the relational character of gaining access, but even more than this, an invitation to friendship entails two-way access that is personal and possibly self-revealing. Hence, there is a need for gradual trust building between the parties.

The invitation to friendship may accompany an implied enquiry and negotiation that we would normally expect in the 'gaining access' phase. That is, what can each of us expect from this relationship? In engaged research relationships, attempting to negotiate an entry to the organization is an occasion when the careful balancing of research interests against the requirement for practical outcomes comes to the fore. For researchers, openness to surprises and the unexpected is part of what makes research interesting and empirically grounded (Vinten, 1994). However, this same characteristic can make it difficult to explain to potential research sponsors and participants exactly what the benefits of the research will be for them. Sponsors often look to the researcher as someone capable of providing insight, guidance and, depending on the character of the contract, interventions of a functional and managerial nature. This encourages researchers to construct themselves as external consultants, while being mindful of the issues of integrity this might raise later in the research process.

In summary, in this phase the researcher typically becomes involved in relationship-oriented activity on two fronts: with the research sponsor, who is likely to need some reassurance that things will proceed as agreed; and with a wider set of research participants, with whom trust and credibility must be established. The researcher can make new friends and develop research agreements, but the nature of the 'contracting' of the research and the initial invitations to friendship are different from each other, and neither necessitates the other.

momentary auditions and testing out the friendship

Acclimatization is a key period of familiarization for researchers coming to terms with a new organizational setting. Balancing the expectations of self and other is highlighted during this phase. The researcher's expectations and previous experience may shape his/her perceptions in trying to understand the organization; but organizational members also have expectations and previous experiences, which, reciprocally, may shape their perceptions of the researcher as they try to work out the researcher's agenda. Nevertheless, the researcher's prior experience can be significant in developing friendship relations beyond those with initial 'gatekeepers' who may have facilitated access (Chikudate, 1999).

As friendships develop, a process of normalization and boundary-establishment unfolds. Each party tries out language, behaviours, preferences and tastes to see what is acceptable in the relationship. Such momentary 'auditions' take place where organizational members form a judgement on the researcher as a potential 'friend', and passing such auditions is critical to the researcher's ability to achieve engagement on his or her own terms rather than in response to the 'gatekeeper's' requests or demands. During and immediately after an audition, researchers need a high degree of criticality in assessing the dialogue that develops (Alvesson, 2003; Wilson, 2004), as it is easily possible to misread how one has done in an audition, and indeed to misperceive the auditions themselves.

engagement

As friendships flourish, norms of behaviour, shared values and mutual reliance become more taken for granted. Breaches of these tacitly accepted boundaries can provoke urgent relationship-maintenance activities or can lead to a cooling of relations. If one continues to pass the ongoing series of momentary auditions, relationships between the researcher and the researched become more established. Trust can develop as each person builds up a story of the other that incorporates a match between promise and delivery, and perceptions of consistency develop.

In this phase the challenge is to continue *active* participation in the research situation by deliberately – but 'naturally' – provoking discussion and dialogue in order to test assumptions and generate new levels of insight. Friendship can provide a framework that allows critical engagement and provocative dialogue. On the other hand, there can be a danger that critical dialogue is not welcomed from a friend, and hence the strength of the friendship can be diminished, for example, where it is revealed that what had been taken as shared assumptions turn out not to be shared.

A further risk of active participation is that we develop emotionally committed positions or become embroiled in political manoeuvrings (Pettigrew, 2003; Kock, 2004), which make it difficult for researchers as friends to stand back from what is taken for granted. As Galibert (2004: 456) puts it, 'How can we be astonished by what is most familiar, and make familiar what is strange?' Answering this question involves a balance between engaging *enough* to be able to develop informed interpretations about observed practices, while also limiting that engagement in order to maintain some distance from the situation (Weeks, 2000). For the friendship this means that engagement is not always fully open and unconditional.

Within research friendships is the need for a balance between engagement and distance. This may also be true of friendships more generally, but in the case of research friendships, the closeness between friends can enhance mutual subjective understanding and the ability of the researcher to build theory based on an 'insider view'. However, if the researcher does not maintain sufficient distance, he or she runs the risk of accepting one version of events as the truth and of being unable to critically engage with alternative perspectives.

In a context in which friendship relations have developed, conceptualizing 'distance' is highly problematic, but the very recognition of this as a question may signal the final phase in the process.

separation

Ethnographers often speak of the warm relationships they have built up during engagement (Kondo, 1990; Watson, 2001), and it is not unknown for enduring friendships to be formed (Oakley, 1981). However, research projects do draw to a close. While in some cases it might seem that there is no need to develop an 'exit strategy', because the project has a fixed term that has been contractual, the best way of respectfully facilitating disengagement is by no means obvious in all circumstances. Leaving the organization can be a bittersweet experience of nostalgia tinged with regret, as all participants come to terms with a shift in their relationship.

In circumstances where a friendship has developed it can be hard for both parties when the time comes to leave. Research friends may develop an attachment to the research process and feel a certain dependence on it (or on the researcher) as part of their own sense-making. Similarly, researchers may themselves develop attachments to the research as part of their own identity and/or sense-making, allowing themselves to be drawn back again and again to search for yet more subtle and detailed nuances in the research story, without recognizing either the possibility of diminishing returns or accepting the end of the research operation. On the other hand, friendships can form which mean that both the researcher and the research participant seek out new opportunities to work together in the future.

phases of friendship and ethical questions

Each phase of establishing, developing, progressing and terminating the research engagement can give rise to ethical issues, including around such matters as: what each party presents to the other; the interests and purposes that are pursued; and how the relationship should be conducted as it approaches and crosses temporal, organizational and friendship boundaries. The need for an ethical focus in research (Kondo, 1990) and for reflexive engagement (Ellis and Bochner, 2000) has been established in general terms, but our concern here is how ethics and reflexivity play out when friendship develops in the research relationship.

Table 10.1   The phases of friendship and ethical questions that can arise

Invitation and relationship formation	• How helpful can we be to each other?
	• How should we engage with each other (e.g. how long might this relationship last)?
Momentary auditions and testing out	• How close should we get?
Engagement	• How far should I follow my friend's influence?
	• How far should I try to influence my friend?
	• Do we agree what friendship means in attitude and behaviour?
Separation	• Am I acting reasonably?
	• Is there an appropriate balance between us?

During the invitation to friendship phase there is a combination of self-interest and altruism. Both parties typically want to get something out of the relationship and, as researchers, we want good access and the ability to engage in a way that will enable theory building. However, in organizational ethnography we may also be interested in helping to make what we would see as improvements in the situation. We are not neutral about how we 'leave things behind' at the end of an engagement. This relates both to utilitarian aspects of the friendship in which the relationship serves mutual needs and to the aspiration that relationships should be more than merely self-serving. However, as was pointed out above, friendships have a temporal nature. In research settings this is usually explicit, as there will be an agreement (even if relatively informal) on the terms and conditions of the research engagement, and this will usually include an envisaged end-point. There is, therefore, an awareness and even an expectation that this sort of relationship may well be time-bound.

During the audition and testing-out phase, in addition to utilitarian questions of how useful each might be to the other are questions of the extent to which we share a view of the world and approach to work and research. How do we see our roles? What are the things we ought to do (and ought not to do)? In the case of engaged research, this includes a subjectivist perception of the roles of researcher and research participant (as opposed to the objectivist detached view in which the researcher ought not to get too close to the research subject).

During the engagement phase, the friendship is being lived. In addition to the highlighted questions in phases one and two, at this stage questions for the researcher can arise concerning: to what extent should I support my friend – am I also a political ally? How far should I go in questioning my friend's view of things? How far should I go in trying to influence and change my friend's behaviour? How much should I try to influence other people's perceptions of my friend? In short, there are a series of questions relating to power and influence – how far should I follow my friend's influence and how far should I try to influence my friend?

Finally, there is often a tacit question of whether or not we agree on what it means to be friends, as expressed in our attitudes and behaviours.

During the separation phase there is an overall question of whether or not I am acting reasonably. This incorporates the concern that my friend and I might not have the same view that the relationship has run its course: is one perceived as leaving before the other is ready? It also includes the question of whether the departure is effected appropriately. Is each party following the expected norms of friendship in this regard? Finally, there is the question of balance, in terms of residual social obligations: does either owe anything to the other?

Although the questions raised here are not exclusive to particular phases of the friendship, our experience is that they usually have particular relevance in particular phases as the relationship grows and declines. The Table summarizes the phases and some of the questions that might be expected to arise in each one.

tales from the field

The following two illustrative examples are derived from the research experiences of two of the authors and are narrated from the researcher's perspective. They trace contrasting experiences through the four relationship phases identified above, analysing some of the ethical questions that arise. The stories were initially told by the researcher who was directly involved, and subsequent analysis was conducted by the authoring team.

research setting one: science

Phase I. invitation and relationship formation

I began my relationship with a particular organization – the 'Lead Institution' – as a competitor: the 'Lead Institution' had lost an earlier competitive tender to the organization that employed me. However, even during that 'competitive' phase, I made an effort to modify the relationship with the Lead Institution from competitor to potential collaborator as the project we had won through the tender depended on key inputs from the Lead Institution. There was some complex stagecraft at that time. On my side, I sought to present myself not as the victorious competitor, but rather as a neutral contractor. On their side, the Lead Institution managers gave the appearance of public-spirited cooperation without delivering much in the way of actual information. Their occasional brusque rudeness about the (much smaller) company by which I was employed was perhaps characteristic of the coldness of relations at that time.

Nevertheless, I was interested in the Lead Institution's likely lead role in a programme to develop Science Networks – an area of management practice central to the doctorate I was pursuing on a part-time basis. It was at least partially for that reason that I took considerable pains to develop collaborative relationships with key managers in the Lead Institution. An example of the kind of actions undertaken to recast relationships was that I gave the senior manager from the Lead Institution the opportunity to comment on a report for the project. While this voluntary action made the completion of the competitive project a little more time consuming, it gave the Lead Institution the opportunity to forestall any major embarrassments or inconveniences in the report, which might have impacted on their reputation or strategic position in later projects.

This action of opening up the report therefore helped in two ways. First, it gave the impression that I was *not* trying to engage in developing competitive advantage at their expense. Second, it meant that the senior manager took an active interest in the report – and could see that it was of a good standard, since very few changes were suggested by him. The relationship investments seemed to pay off, as the Lead Institution engaged my firm as a sub-contractor when the Science Networks contract was awarded to them.

Analysis   At this phase of the relationship, friendship had not yet begun. The question of how helpful each party can be to the other arises. From the researcher's perspective, there is potential self-interest in developing a relationship with the Lead Institution, and so he is careful not to undertake actions which could alienate the managers in the Lead Institution. He makes an 'offering' to them by revealing the report, and this is stepping beyond what would normally be done in the circumstances. They respond in a reciprocal fashion; and hence, there is a degree of openness in addressing the question 'How should we engage with each other'.

Phase II. momentary auditions and testing out the friendship

Making myself at home in the research situation was partially deliberate, through sharing enough of my personal background to let my new collaborators see that we had a common history in the same niche area of the natural sciences, something that was not obvious to them from our earlier, competitive, business interactions. Our shared background as professionals in a particular area of science was something of a surprise for the manager in the Lead Institution, and my ability to join in technical conversations was a key moment of change in the relationship. Having passed a momentary audition by means of our shared professional training I was, from then on, treated as 'one of us'. Discussions about the project were framed to include much more scientific content and dialogue. It seemed that being able to identify myself as a scientist – like them – caused me to be regarded as an insider, and many barriers were lowered.

I also made the most of my position as the nominal expert within my firm on the processes of collaboration. This was important, as managing the collaboration would be central to the success of the Science Networks project. However, while I was the academic 'expert' in this field, it is fair to say others in the firm could probably have undertaken the same collaborative process work at an acceptable standard. My interest in maintaining an expert position was due to the legitimacy it provided for me in the networks I was research-ing. Emphasizing my personal expertise made the Lead Institution managers more likely to ask for my personal involvement, rather than looking for generic support from another member of the firm.

While I had done a lot of work to fit in with and appear useful to the Lead Institution, relationships were further deepened by the serendipitous realiza-tion that the manager and I had a longstanding mutual friend. Although I didn't *really* get on with this third party, the stories we swapped about him helped to make me a part of the social circle – not just the scientific community – within the Lead Institution. This, however, took conversations beyond a task-orientation into more personal areas that held forth the potential of shared connections.

Analysis During this phase of the research relationship, acclimatization entailed the taking and enacting of a role (being a scientist) along with others for whom being a scientist was an important part of their self-identity. Self-interest was still being pursued in the sense of making sure that there was good research access to gain data for a PhD.; however, the relationship went beyond the utilitarian. In answer to the question 'How close should we get?', there was a testing out of whether or not we liked mutual acquaintances. Often this is a risky moment, but agreement (or simulated agreement) regarding the acquaintance signalled the perseverance of relationship building and an increasing closeness (particularly when compared to the initial competitive stance between the researcher and the manager in the Lead Institution).

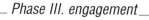

Phase III. engagement

Having seemingly been established as a member of the scientific community at the Lead Institution and luckily been able to develop deeper friendship relations, I seemed to be called upon to fulfil my duties as a 'good citizen'. For example, I was asked to join a national committee dealing with a niche area of science, at the request of the senior manager from the Lead Institution. This added some depth to my study of science networks, but it also made me fearful of exposing the limits of the currency of my scientific awareness. While this exposure never actually occurred, I was also conscious that I was getting embedded a little more than was comfortable, partly because the relationship had the potential to develop greater depth than I was seeking and partly because of the risk of an 'unmasking' as less expert than I appeared to be.

At the same time, I actually liked and respected the people from the Lead Institution whom I worked with and found myself not wanting to let them down in the committee work, despite it being rather a strain. There was some confusion developing in my mind as to whether my principal responsibilities should be concerned with the advancement of management research or with my new committee role supporting the natural sciences. I was beginning to 'go native' in the sense that I was increasingly engaged principally in participation and less in observation. For example, I was concerned with the *content* of decisions in the committee and less with the social processes that framed and enabled those decisions.

Analysis During this phase of the research relationship there are questions of how far the friends should influence each other and what constitutes friendship as expressed through attitude and behaviour. In this example, the researcher starts to feel a degree of discomfort as he is influenced to take on a position of responsibility, which in turn gives him some influence. The researcher feels that he ought to take on the committee work as the offer was made in friendship and it would be an unfriendly act to reject the opportunity. In addition, there was some self-interest operating as the position offered further useful research access. There was a degree of altruistic activity in which self-interest was very secondary to the concern for shared goals. The relationship had moved beyond the stage of regular auditions to each side coming to rely on, and act in the interests of, the other.

Phase IV. separation

The responsibility dilemma was eventually resolved in a rather dramatic fashion – I quit my consultancy job and took on a full-time academic research position – and explained the move to the managers at the Lead Institution, who were of course aware of the research interests I had been trying to advance on a part-time basis. On reflection, I think that I was becoming rather cynical about the impact of consultancy work, and I was also not convinced that it was appropriate for me to be working on standards committees in the natural sciences – neither my interests nor abilities really supported either of these endeavours. I sought to make the change easier for the Lead Institution and my consultancy employers by taking a colleague from the consultancy firm along to my final series of meetings. During this time I gradually withdrew and allowed my colleague to take the lead in interactions with the managers at the Lead Institution. My erstwhile colleague is still involved with the Lead Institution, but for me, as the work connections have stopped, the friendships have also faded and contact has reduced to almost nothing.

Analysis At this phase there was an effort to act reasonably. There was no real question that the researcher should remain in the situation, and the experience related to the notion of the declining friendship as Nietzsche's 'boats from the harbour' follow routes to different tasks. Both sides can regard this as legitimate because it is not simply choosing no longer to be friends, but rather perceiving an 'external' cause for separation – in a sense both parties could read the situation as if the new tasks had dictated the parting. This makes the separation much easier than attributing it to 'internal' causes (for example, 'I no longer like you').

The organization that provides the second illustration is in the Creative Industries sector. Its main 'products' are international music festivals, which take place each year, and running three large and complex concert venues in which classical and popular concerts are staged.

Phase I. invitation and relationship formation

One of the international festivals was, in general, perceived to be highly successful. It had a worldwide reputation and generated large audiences and a significant boost to tourism. Senior management, however, had some concerns about how the festival was being run and were worried that there was the potential for problems to arise. I was (and remain) friends with a senior manager who asked for some informal help. The plan was that I would provide him with an external perspective on the needs of the managers and the organization and see how things were 'really' going in order to understand what 'might' go wrong. I agreed to do some interviews and focus groups to help diagnose the problems. Part of the reason for my agreement to undertake this initial stage of what became a much bigger research project was our friendship, but I also had a research interest in the area. We agreed that although I would not be paid for the work, I would be able to use the data for research purposes. I was introduced to the Chief Executive and other members of the organization and felt quite an affinity with them.

Friendship was operating at two levels in this case. In part, there was an engagement between established friends, and there was also the introduction to new friendships. These introductions were mediated by the first friendship. Hence, people's reactions to me were relative to their opinions and alliances with my friend, the senior manager. In some cases this led to expectations of shared values and interests, and in others, to a degree of suspicion.

Analysis This first phase of research relationship was based on the idea that the parties could be helpful to each other. There was overt mutual interest, but even if there had not been much interest, the researcher would have helped out because of the friendship. However, he would have helped out to a lesser degree, hence self-interest was present along with an altruistic concern for his friend.

Phase II. momentary auditions and testing the friendship

The interviews and focus groups were fun to do. People were dedicated to the cultural mission of the company and they were interesting people. The problem I discovered related to complex constructions and the sense that various parties were making of each other. As a result of these ways of thinking, people had different priorities. Although they were aware of differences between them, it was difficult for them to see the overall picture or to see why some of the others appeared to be opposed to taking what, for them, seemed obvious steps forward. This was combined with, and amplified by, strong in-group communications and weak inter-group communication. Within the festivals' organizing team there were strong friendships that had lasted years and which had an impact on how people related professionally. However, their relationships with other parts of the organization, such as Finance, Staging and Box Office, were less close. This introduced certain dilemmas for me. To appear to be too close to one side could reduce the possibility of getting open views and information from the other.

The situation was fascinating from a theoretical perspective. From a practical perspective it was solvable. Many organizations manage to function with this sort of irritation, but it was worth trying to improve matters. At a personal level, I developed new friendships in the company, particularly with the CEO and with a middle manager. Momentary auditions were particularly important when my friend was absent. Being sufficiently knowledgeable about music was important. However, having a background in musical *performance* was crucial as it enabled me to ask questions about preparation and performance processes that made it clear that I knew what I was talking about and that I shared their understandings of these processes. I became increasingly interested in the type of music they were promoting, attending performances and becoming a consumer of this particular cultural product. This inevitably led to a deepening of the research relationships as well as the personal ones. I also became very interested in their mission and wanted to help. A short report was produced for the senior management.

Analysis   During this phase the parties were discovering similarities with each other and starting to develop closer relations. The researcher was not detached from the issues although a report was produced that sought to interpret the views of others. The closeness was developing across work boundaries as socialization outside work and shared musical interests were forming.

_____ *Phase III. engagement* _____
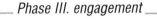

Following initial problem diagnosis, there was a lull in research activity. During this time a high profile problem arose, and this motivated the senior management to investigate more thoroughly. They gained a grant to fund the research work and embarked upon a deeper engagement. I spent a lot of time in the organization observing, being part of the management group processes and also interviewing various organization members. I was accepted in such settings partly because I had achieved the status of 'friend' in earlier interactions. It is also highly unlikely that a newcomer to the conversation would have been welcomed during this turbulent time.

The actions coming out of the investigation process involved me in running some workshops, which meant that I had to play a somewhat detached role. More significantly, I was involved in assisting managerial decision-making about organizational structure, people's roles and reporting relationships. This meant that some people felt that I acted in a managerial rather than a friendly way. Some people felt angry with me because of this, while for others, my standing up and taking these actions led to an increased level of trust and friendship as we had 'come through a difficult time together'. In falling out with some friends, I fell in with others. This intense period of engagement lasted for about four months. It became a dominant part of my life, but it was also significant for the organization as they had delayed various decisions and put things on hold while the investigation was underway. I was being paid for the work now, but I actually did far more than I was being paid for because of my friendship and personal connection with the people. At one level I felt that I had a personal responsibility for trying to make things work. The process was not one of writing a report and walking away. Rather, I became part of the management team, albeit as a semi-detached member.

Analysis   In this phase of the friendship the researcher was strongly influenced by research participant friends in carrying the investigation beyond the agreed bounds and in seeking to mediate to produce a constructive outcome. The research participants were also influenced by the researcher and in subsequent conversations discussed how the changes made at the time have had an impact on what they do and how they see themselves. Equally, the experience and relationships have had an impact on the researcher and led to a redirection of his research focus. Being friends meant going beyond the normal role boundaries of researcher/investigator and research participant in time/effort and emotion/attachment.

_____ *Phase IV. separation* _____

Eighteen months on from the start, major changes had been made, and I was no longer officially engaged in the organization. However, I couldn't just walk away. I remain friends with the CEO and the senior manager, and I am also in touch with the middle manager and give informal advice on how to take things forward in implementing the changes. I am still interested in them and their product. I am also fascinated by how the relationships are working out. We look out for opportunities to work together, and I have been back to the organization to do some 'How is it going now?' follow-up sessions. I do not really feel that I am disengaged from them.

Analysis   Although a stage came when the series of activities initially agreed to came to an end and there was a 'signing off' of activities, there was a deliberate effort to maintain contact and, subsequently, further opportunities were taken/created to work together. It is arguable that in this example there is not friendship separation. The question of whether either party owes something to the other does not arise, at least not in the mind of the researcher. Answering the question 'Am I acting reasonably?' instead focuses on maintaining the friendship beyond the work and the research relationship.

concluding discussion

In this chapter we aimed to elucidate an aspect of engaged research: friendship. We described four phases through which friendships could pass: coming into being; passing through a testing phase; development; and finally, decline. We have linked these phases to the extant literature on friendship and to a series of ethical questions that reflect both altruism and self-interest.

We then described two of our experiences of research, using the phase framework as a template for characterizing them. In our reading of the illustrations, both went through phases one to three, but it is arguable that only the first illustration went through all four phases. As the friendships moved through the phases it was notable that attributed status, shared interest and mutually oriented action occurred. The exertion of influence on and for each other also occurred. In our illustrations actors on both sides of the friendships carried out actions that went beyond a strict definition of their functional roles, and as Leach (1982) would expect, a degree of trust and emotional bonding developed. However, in illustration one, as Nietzsche (1977) would predict, there was a drifting apart as different tasks took those who had been in friendly relations in separate directions.

Along with mutuality and altruism, the relationships were useful for the friends, and there were utilitarian outcomes for all concerned. This does not detract from the friendships; in fact, we were glad that we could be of use to our friends. Therefore, we would argue that while the utilitarian aspect of friendship might become an irritation, this is probably more likely when there is a lack of balance between friends. However, there were times when there was an appearance of balance rather than genuine equity; in particular, there was a degree of faking and fudging in the build up of the relationships. For example, the impression that there was greater agreement on the character of a former colleague than was actually the case was used as a way of passing an audition in illustration one. For many this might be seen as a normal part of lubricating the wheels of friendship, and it is not necessarily problematic as long as it does not imply that disagreements are tacitly forbidden, particularly on important matters.

The intention in proposing the phased model of research friendships was not to argue that all such relationships would pass through all four phases, in order and with no reversals. Indeed, one of our own illustrations did not pass through all of the phases. Rather, the intention was to provide a way of reflecting on the experience of friendship in research such that both researchers and research friends can be more aware of what is going on and decide on how they want to answer the ethical questions associated with their experience of the relationship at any particular phase. We hope that this will be a useful reflective tool for those who are serious about pursuing engaged research.

references

Alvesson, M. (2003) 'Beyond neopositivists, romantics and localists: A reflexive approach to interviews in organizational research', *Academy of Management Review*, 28: 13–33.

Alvesson, M. and Deetz, S. (2000) *Doing critical management research*. London: Sage.

Ayas, K. (2003) 'Managing action and research for rigor and relevance: The case of Fokker Aircraft', *Human Resource Planning*, 26: 19–29.

Berger, A.A. (1997) *Narratives in popular culture, media and everyday life*. London: Sage.

Bernard, H. (2006) *Research methods in anthropology: Qualitative and quantitative approaches*. Lanham, MD: Altamira Press.

Boje, D.M., Luhman, J.T. and Baack, D.E. (1999) 'Hegemonic stories and encounters between storytelling organizations', *Journal of Management Inquiry*, 8: 340–60.

Burrell, G. and Morgan, G. (1979) *Sociological paradigms and organizational analysis*. London: Heinemann.

Chikudate, N. (1999) 'Generating reflexivity from partnership formation: A phenomenological reasoning on the partnership between a Japanese pharmaceutical corporation and Western laboratories', *Journal of Applied Behavioral Science*, 35(3): 287–305.

Coghlan, D. (2001) 'Insider action research projects: Implications for practising managers', *Management Learning* 32(1): 49–60.

Coughlan, P. and Coghlan, D. (2002) 'Action research for operations management', *International Journal of Operations and Production Management* 22(2): 220–40.

Cunliffe, A. (2003) 'Reflexive inquiry in organizational research: Questions and possibilities', *Human Relations*, 56: 983–1003.

Eden, C. and Huxham, C. (1996) 'Action research for management research', *British Journal of Management* 7(1): 75–86.

Ellis, C. and Bochner, A. (2000) 'Autoethnography, personal narrative, reflexivity', in N. Denzin and Y. Lincoln (eds), *Handbook of qualitative research*. London: Sage. pp. 733–68.

Feldman, M.S., Bell, J. and Berger, M.T. (2003) *Gaining access: A practical and theoretical guide for qualitative researchers*. Lanham, MD: Rowman Altamira Press.

Forte, A. (2004) 'Business ethics: A study of the moral reasoning of selected business managers and the influence of organizational ethical climate', *Journal of Business Ethics*, 51(2): 167–73.

Galibert, C. (2004) 'Some preliminary notes on actor-observer anthropology', *International Social Science Journal*, 56: 455–66.

Geertz, C. (1983) *Local knowledge*. New York: Basic Books.

Greenwood, D.J. and Levin, M. (1998) *Introduction to action research: social research for social change*. London: Sage.

Heracleous, C. (2001) 'An ethnographic study of culture in the context of organizational change', *Journal of Applied Behavioural Science*, 37: 426–46.

Humphreys, M., Brown, A. and Hatch, M. (2003) 'Is ethnography jazz?', *Organization*, 10: 5–31.

Jackson, M. (1998) *Minima ethnographica*. Chicago: University of Chicago Press.

Johnson, J.C., Avenarius, C. and Weatherford, J. (2006) 'The active participant observer: Applying social role analysis to participant observation', *Field Methods*, 18(2): 111–34.

Kipnis, D., Schmidt, S.M., Swaffin-Smith, C. and Wilkinson, I. (1984) 'Patterns of managerial influence: Shotgun managers, tacticians and bystanders', *Organizational Dynamics*, Winter: 58–67.

Kock, N. (2004) 'The three threats of action research: A discussion of methodological antidotes in the context of an information systems study', *Decision Support Systems*, 37: 265–86.

Kondo, D.K. (1990) *Crafting selves: Power, gender, and discourses of identity in a Japanese workplace*. Chicago: University of Chicago Press.

Kogler, H.H. (1999) *The power of dialogue: Critical hermeneutics after Gadamer and Foucault.* Cambridge, Massachusetts: MIT Press.

Leach, E. (1982) *Social anthropology.* London: Fontana.

MacIntosh, R., MacLean, D. and Burns, H. (2007) 'Health in organizations: Towards a process-based view', *Journal of Management Studies*, 44(2): 206–21.

MacLean, D.R. MacIntosh and S. Grant (2002) 'Mode 2 Management Research', *British Journal of Management* 13/3: 189–207.

Markiewicz, D., Devine, I. and Kausilas, D. (2000) 'Friendships of women and men at work: Job satisfaction and resource implications', *Journal of Managerial Psychology*, 15(2): 161–84.

Marmaros, D. and Sacerdote, B. (2006) 'How do friendships form?', *Quarterly Journal of Economics*, 121(1): 79–119.

Nietzsche, F. (1977) *A Nietzsche reader.* Edited by R.J. Hollingdale. London: Penguin.

Oakley, A. (1981) 'Interviewing women: A contradiction in terms', in H. Roberts (ed.), *Doing feminist research.* London: Routledge. pp. 30–61.

Pesamma, O., Ortqvist, D. and Hair, J.F. (2007) 'It is all about trust and loyalty: Partner selection mechanisms.' *World Journal of Tourism and Small Business Management* 1(2): 12–18.

Pettigrew, P. (2003) 'Power, conflicts and resolutions: A change agent's perspective on conducting action research within a multiorganizational partnership', *Systemic Practice and Action Research*, 16: 375–91.

Prasad, A. (2002) 'The contest over meaning: hermeneutics as an interpretive methodology for understanding texts', *Organizational Research Methods*, 5: 12–33.

Reason, P. and Bradbury, H. (2001) *Handbook of action research.* London: Sage.

Reimer, K. (2005) Revising moral attachment: Comment on identity and motivation. *Human Development*, 48(4): 262–6.

Sias, P.M., Heath. R.G., Perry. T., Silva, D. and Fix, B. (2004) 'Narratives of workplace friendship deterioration', *Journal of Social and Personal Relationships*, 21(3): 321–40.

Spradley, J.P. (1980) *Participant observation.* London: Holt, Rinehart and Wilson.

Sveningsson, S. and Alvesson, M. (2003) 'Managing managerial identities: Organizational fragmentation, discourse and identity struggle', *Human Relations*, 56(10): 1163–93.

Tajfel, H. and Turner, J.C. (1985) 'The social identity theory of intergroup behaviour', in S. Worchel and W.G. Austin (eds), *The psychology of intergroup relations.* Vol. 2. Chicago: Nelson-Hall. pp. 7–24.

Tranfield, D. and Starkey, K. (1998) 'The nature, social organisation and promotion of management research: Towards policy', *British Journal of Management* 9: 341–53.

Van Aken, J.E. (2002) Mode 2 Knowledge Production in the Field of Management. Eindhoven Centre for Innovation Studies, The Netherlands. Working paper 01.13.

Vinten, G. (1994) 'Participant observation: A model for organizational investigation', *Journal of Managerial Psychology*, 9: 30–8.

Warnke, G. (2004) 'Tradition, ethical knowledge and multicultural societies', in M.S. Phillips and G. Schochet (eds), *Questions of tradition.* Toronto, University of Toronto Press. pp. 258–73.

Watson, T. (2001) *In search of management: Culture, chaos and control in managerial work.* 2nd edn. London: Thomson Learning.

Weeks, J. (2000) 'What do ethnographers believe? A reply to Jones', *Human Relations*, 53: 153–71.

Wilson, H. (2004) 'Towards rigour in action research: A case study in marketing planning', *European Journal of Marketing*, 38: 378–400.

11

Critical action research and organizational ethnography

Chris Sykes and Lesley Treleaven

In studies of organizations, action research generates a wide range of data, principally through participation in group inquiry processes (Heron and Reason, 2001; Reason and Bradbury, 2001). However, action research is more than just a collection of methods or even a methodology. Its relation to the co-construction of knowledge places it firmly within the domain of episte-mology (Greenwood and Levin, 1998; Park, 2001). It is possible to draw some strong links between action research and ethnography from their common epistemologies and the methods each employs. Nonetheless, there are also clear distinctions that can be drawn in the ways that action researchers are positioned, how knowledge is co-constructed, and the power relations that can be investigated when a critical approach forms the basis of inquiry. This chapter highlights the potential of a form of critical action research for use by organizational ethnographers in doing research into the complexity of everyday organizational life.

The chapter is structured as follows. First, we present action research as a way of knowing. Second, we discuss the links between action research and ethnography. Third, we elaborate on third-person action research as the partic-ular form of critical action research that we use. We then discuss three important distinctions between this approach to critical action research and traditional ethnography. The chapter concludes with some thoughts on the contribution of this action research approach to ethnographic studies of organizations.

action research as a way of knowing

No general consensus exists within the research literature about the specific definition or methodology of action research (Cairns et al., 2003). That said, Reason and Bradbury's comments in the *Handbook of Action Research* (2001) delineate some principles that are widely accepted within the broad action research community: that it is '... a participatory, democratic process concerned with developing practical knowing ...' (2001: 1). The ideas of joint or participatory research processes oriented towards action are concepts gener-ally found in action research approaches in their many forms (Dick, 1991;

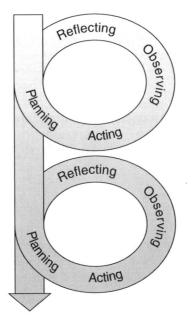

Figure 11.1   The action research spiral (adapted from Kemmis and McTaggart, 2005: 564)

Kindon, Pain and Kesby, 2007; McTaggart, 1991; Reason and Bradbury, 2001). These processes of inquiry have traditionally been represented as a spiral, illustrated in Figure 11.1, and include planning, acting, observing and reflecting (Kemmis and McTaggart, 2001).

Action research has a distinctive theoretical positioning in relation to the process of knowledge construction. Knowledge construction is not regarded as the work of researchers alone. Instead, it is understood to be co-constructed by researchers working with participants in shared webs of significance and action (Greenwood and Levin, 1998). The intention of such research is to produce practical knowledge that is useful, both for and in action. In this way, action research moves beyond observation and description by engaging in the 'turn to action'. Such a view flies in the face of other social science discourses informed by logical positivism – the view that the world exists in an already given or determined logical state, in which the work of the researcher is to apply a range of specific objective methods to reveal the truth (Greenwood and Levin, 1998).

In contrast, action research builds on a rich philosophical foundation beginning in the West within Greek philosophy. Aristotle distinguished between types of knowledge in which practical knowledge, or *phronesis*, was recognized and valued equally with *theoria*, or speculative knowledge. Aristotle, the son of a physician, recognized that the knowledge required by the sailor or the physician is of a different order from that concerned with the metaphysical notions of 'truth', 'god' or 'mind'. In this view, the use of knowledge is determined by situation and timeliness, and practical knowledge is not subsumed by prioritizing higher-order speculative knowledge, as in many modern rationalist approaches dominated by the philosophy of Descartes (Toulmin, 2001).

A range of theoretical and philosophical approaches is taken up in action research. As their point of departure, most are opposed to prioritizing Cartesian rationalism that privileges detached, analytic cognition over action. Greenwood and Levin highlight the importance of the work of the American pragmatist philosopher, John Dewey, who emphasized the 'connections between human inquiry and democracy' and 'his refusal to separate thought from action' (1998: 72–3). Instead, the various action research approaches consider knowledge and action to be mutually constitutive, not sequential and separate. Knowledge construction is not seen as the exclusive right of those who may prioritize scientific methods, philosophical rationality or ideological power over alternative forms of knowledge construction. Critical orientations to action research, in particular, contest dominant discourses and taken-for-granted power relations. For example, Marxist approaches, such as in the work of Freire (1970), and Foucauldian ideas of discourse have contributed to the development of emancipatory and critical action research that is associated with feminist praxis (Stanley, 1990), poststructural approaches (Lather, 1986; 1991) and liberation theology (Gutierrez, 1973).

Drawing upon diverse schools of thought, action research has developed multiple applications and approaches, such as action learning (Argyris and Schön, 1978); participatory action research (Kemmis and McTaggart, 2001); cooperative inquiry (Heron and Reason, 2001); and action science (Argyris, Putnam and Smith, 1985). Applications of action research have been employed by qualitative researchers intent upon producing action-oriented studies that generate new transformative knowledge (Gaventa and Cornwall, 2001; Park, 2001; Reason and Torbert, 2001). It has been widely used in many disciplines and contexts, such as education (Freeman, Clarkeburn and Treleaven, 2007; Grundy and Kemmis, 1982), community services (Braithwaite, Cockwill, O'Neill, and Rebane, 2007; Cairns et al., 2003; Wadsworth, 1991), adult education (Marshall and Reason, 1994) and organization and management (MacIntosh and Bonnet, 2007).

Within organizational studies, the work of Kurt Lewin in action science and Chris Argyris and Donald Schön on learning within organizations provided early important theoretical and methodological contributions toward dissolving the boundary between analysis and action. These scholars/researchers developed participative approaches involving 'learning laboratories' (Lewin, 1946), participatory groups within organizations employing 'learning loops' (Argyris and Schön, 1978), and reflection upon practices leading to action responses (Schön, 1983) that, in turn, created new processes structured into cycles of organizational learning (Argyris and Schön, 1978; Senge, 1990). In more recent times, action research is being used extensively in organizational studies (see, for example, MacIntosh and Bonnet, 2007).

We are not suggesting that action research and ethnography are essentially the same, nor are we saying that ethnographers ought to employ action research in all situations, for clearly this must be determined by the 'fit' of the research at theoretical and contextual and personal levels. We do suggest, however, that some strong epistemological and methodological parallels and commonalities exist that link the two approaches and that these links are worth closer examination.

links between action research and ethnography

Like participatory action research, ethnography has been defined both as a set of methods used (Hammersley and Atkinson, 1997), such as participant observation, interviews, and collection of artefacts, and as a methodology that may be located within interpretivist, hermeneutical or phenomenological traditions. In his landmark work, *Writing culture*, James Clifford (Clifford and Marcus, 1986) suggested that ethnography is not limited to the application of particular methods but is inseparable from writing or representing 'thick description' (Geertz, 1973). In a similar way, action research is a set of methods that engage co-researchers not just in action but also in a form of knowing that is inseparable from action, from doing. When doing action research or ethnography, researchers seek to position themselves alongside research participants and their everyday actions in order to engage both with and in the meaning-making of the participants and the particular phenomena under investigation.

From this perspective, ethnography, like action research, is a way of knowing, an epistemology, where the ethnographer's task is both semantic and semiotic – oriented toward both specific meanings and the 'signs' through which meaning is conveyed. Geertz, drawing upon Weber, suggests that 'man is an animal suspended in webs of significance he himself has spun' (Geertz, 1973: 5). He likens doing ethnography to reading a manuscript which is foreign and faded and re-constructing the story not of conventionalized symbols but of 'transient examples of shaped behaviour' (Geertz, 1973: 10). In this view, the work of the ethnographer is to 'ferret out' (Yanow, 2006) and record the use of language, symbols and artefacts within particular social groups to better understand their actions. Again, this is familiar to the action researcher for whom knowledge is co-constructed.

As discussed in earlier chapters of this book, ethnography has its origins in the hermeneutic and interpretivist traditions, arising out of the work of Durkheim, Weber, Dilthey, Gadamer, Schutz, Goffman and Taylor, and so reflects many similar theoretical and philosophical underpinnings to those of critical action research. Ethnography has developed from the early attempts to interpret cultural otherness, undertaken largely by British colonialists, whose accounts were often constructed using secondary documents describing other cultures that were assembled without the writer necessarily being directly involved in the culture being studied (Van Maanen, 1995). In the early twentieth century, Malinowski and others changed this approach to 'find out the typical ways of thinking and feeling, corresponding to the institutions and culture of a given community and formulate the results in the most convincing way' (Van Maanen, 1995: 6). In recent times, ethnographic approaches reflect both logical positivist and post-positivist approaches, as well as other more critical and interpretivist approaches that accentuate the social and discursive construction of knowledge (Berger and Luckmann, 1984; Foucault, 1972a). The latter emphasize social interaction and language use as the central components of human meaning-making, in ways not too dissimilar to critical action research ideas.

Social researchers have adapted ethnographic approaches to an expanding number of contexts and areas of study (Marcus, 1999). For example, Dorothy Smith describes her feminist, poststructural, institutional ethnography work as 'commit[ing] her to an exploration, description and analysis of such complex relations, not conceived in the abstract but from the entry point of some particular person or persons whose everyday world of working is organized thereby' (Smith, 2002: 19). In these ways Smith incorporates an ethnographic approach into her feminist poststructural theoretical framework.

Ethnography in organizations was for many years constrained by the dominant and institutionalized discourse in organizational research (particularly in the USA) that privileged functionalist and positivist approaches and dismissed critical and interpretivist works as mere subjectivism (Clegg, Courpasson and Phillips, 2007). Nevertheless, beginning with early works such as those from the Chicago school in the 1950s–1960s, others such as Collinson (1992), Orr (1996) and Yanow (1996) in the 1990s further developed the field. In recent times an increasing number of organizational researchers (such as those within this volume) are undertaking organizational ethnography in ways that create understandings of everyday meaning-making as a crucial component of organizing processes in organizations.

In our view, a critical action research approach may contribute to this emergent work in organizational ethnography. It is our contention that the researcher's active insider positioning within organizations facilitates both the drawing out of often overlooked and implicit knowing, as well as developing organizational knowledge. As such, insider positioning is particularly beneficial for examining critical issues relating to power/knowledge in organizations.

a critical approach to action research

Of the many approaches to action research, one of particular value to us in our work within organizations has been that broadly termed third-person action research. This term was initially introduced by Torbert (1991) and is developed from the earlier work of Marshall and Reason, who suggested that:

> All good research is for me, for us and for them: it speaks to three audiences … It is for them to the extent that it produces some kind of generalizable ideas and outcomes … It is for us to the extent that it responds to concerns for our praxis, is relevant and timely … [for] those who are struggling with problems in their field of action. It is for me to the extent that the process and outcomes respond directly to the individual researcher's being-in-the-world. (Marshall and Reason, 1994: 113)

Third-person action research refers to the relationship that the researcher has with these three audiences: self, participants and community. In first-person action research, the researcher describes his/her own experiences and reflections on the research as part of the research process itself; in second-person action research, the researcher relates to the group of participants in a reflective process that includes both participants and researcher. In contrast, third-person action research involves a two step process: initially, integrating and incorporating the first two levels of inquiry into some generalizable conclusions; and then, disseminating that knowledge in the wider community (Torbert, 2001). This type of inquiry also incorporates the action research spiral – plan, act, observe and reflect – in some form at each level of inquiry. The resulting engagement reflects, then, multiple spirals.

A range of qualitative research methods used widely in ethnography is employed iteratively to collect data throughout action research spirals. Interviews, focus groups, observation, meeting attendance, the collection of artefacts such as documents, videos, and images, as well as reflective journals, provide rich data for action research. These methods are employed both to collect background information about each organization and to collect texts for analysis that inform the reflection, theorizing and action phases of action research.

Five key characteristics are important to us in our work doing third-person action research. These characteristics necessarily overlap and inform both our approach to the research question/s and our application of the research methods within the fieldwork. First is our positioning as researchers. We engage in research with, rather than on, people. This is research that is for me, for you, and/or for them. It requires us to reflect on our multiple positions (as researchers and in other positions we may take up, such as organizational insiders) throughout the inquiry with an awareness of the ethical issues in research practices and the demands of researcher and research transparency. Second, our participative approach with people as co-researchers and partners in a shared inquiry includes a range of methods, often ethnographic. Third, we discuss reflexive research spirals of planning, acting, observing and reflecting with the multiple researcher positions such as those of 'insider' and 'co-researchers'. Fourth, we are committed to employing research processes that enable inquiry and emergence so as to construct new knowledge in action. Finally, we maintain an orientation toward social action within the research context, examining the social dynamics of knowledge and power within a context of organizational change.

Our adoption of third-person action research in organizations is located within a critical orientation that is useful for exploring power relations (Sykes, 2005; Treleaven, 2004; Treleaven and Sykes, 2005). In particular, we have sought to integrate the action research methodology with critical discourse analysis (such as that articulated by Fairclough, 2003; Wodak and Meyer, 2001) in order to identify and understand the production and operation of the powerful discourses driving competing political agendas within organizations.

distinctions between critical action research and ethnography

Using a critical action research approach in this way over many years, in a range of organizational contexts, we have adopted a knowledge-based approach to organizational research. In doing so, our research is able to address organizational complexity in terms of knowledge and power relations from a range of positions. On this basis we draw three important epistemological and methodological distinctions between our approach and that of traditional ethnography. These concern first, how participatory action researchers are positioned; second, how knowledge is co-constructed; and third, how attending to power/knowledge relations themselves forms the basis for inquiry. Such distinctions clarify features of social interaction, nuance and complexity that are often beyond the purview of participant observation but are crucial to understanding organizational complexity.

the positions of researchers

There are multiple positions from which the complexity of organizational life can be researched and represented. Using ethnography, researchers take care to maintain separation between their observations and actions called for by the context, while critical action researchers refuse to separate thought from action, laying claim to the view that in critical action research, knowing is inseparable from doing.

First-person action research: The insider-researcher First-person action research gives careful consideration to the orientation and position of the researcher within the research process itself. This orientation does not position the researcher as a somewhat detached outsider. Rather, identifying as an insider requires the adoption of a different positioning. For example, in one study working with a group of colleagues (Sykes, 2005), one of the authors positioned himself as a former employee, manager and board member of various community service organizations. A reflexive process was established, in which the researcher joined in a process of reflection within 'the community of practice' (Wenger, 1998) for the duration of the research. This insider positioning increased input from colleagues with respect to guidance, feedback and reflection, all necessary to rigorously develop the emergent processes of research.

The practical benefits of already being an organizational insider and research participant at the start of the inquiry are threefold. They facilitate, first, identifying initial issues of concern; second, locating suitable organizations and specific research sites; and third, gaining access to existing networks for study. Valuable time can be saved: there is no need to build new networks in pursuit of access to unfamiliar organizations. A rapport already exists. Furthermore, the benefits of insider positioning are not only pragmatic. The place of the self in social research has often been negated, overlooked or acknowledged with embarrassment (Harris, 2001). In much social research, the researcher is hidden in the background, behind the scenes of the research action, with any visibility of the researcher regarded as an unwanted intrusion or error. Such is the case in traditional, realist ethnography. In contrast, within first-person inquiry, the views, challenges, reflections and actions of the researcher are brought into the foreground and seen as being inextricably embedded in and constitutive of the research practices. Research is in some form for me and influenced by 'where I am coming from'.

First-person inquiry requires a commitment to action learning as a personal practice and way of being or ontology:

> First-person research/practice skills and methods address the ability of the researcher to foster an inquiring approach to his or her own life, to act awarely and choicefully, and to assess effects in the outside world while acting. (Reason and Torbert, 2001: 23)

Taking notes related to the research focus and activities, making journal entries, and undertaking reflective writing on the research processes are important aspects of first-person action research. The work of Argyris and Schön (1978) on espoused theory and theory-in-use, and Schön (1983) on the reflective practitioner, provides examples of the importance of understanding critical reflection on one's practice. More recently, the practice of using blogs on the internet provides a potential method for sharing personal reflections, particularly with those who have similar interests or share practices (journaling is done online and may include visual and audio representations).

First-person action research enables researchers to integrate relevant autobiographical accounts and influences with their records of the research process (Harris, 2001). The inclusion of the for-me dimension as first-person action research legitimates the use of the researcher's reflexive understandings within the research. Current ethnographic practices in organizational settings increasingly treat reflexivity, especially researcher positionality, as central to research design and reporting (see Chapter 3 in this volume). In this way, the distance between first-person action research and organizational ethnography is reduced.

Second-person action research: Co-researchers The second-person approach positions participants as co-researchers together with the researcher, beginning with co-establishing the inquiry. 'Second-person research/practice starts when we engage with others in a face-to-face group to enhance our respective first-person inquiries' (Reason and Torbert, 2001: 28). Various terms have been used for this idea of research for us: Reason and Bradbury (2001) include participatory action research and cooperative inquiry as ways of undertaking this research *for us* while others encourage the use of collaborative inquiry (Treleaven, 1994).

This approach contrasts strongly with much ethnography. The complex character of participation involves the emergent processes of forming a group, the ways in which research questions are developed together with participants so that there are benefits for those involved, and the expansion of the research inquiry through reflecting on the unfolding opportunities of action research (Treleaven, 1994). Contemporary ethnographic methodologies attend to the ways in which the ethnographer is not producing objective knowledge from a point outside of the organization being studied; but it has not yet taken up the active role of group-formation that characterizes second-person action research.

Third-person action research　Like ethnography, third-person inquiry is directed towards research 'for them', research participants. At the third-person level, the research approach is less focused on the processes of engaging the research participants and the fieldwork collection methods. Here, the orientation shifts toward action, representing and disseminating knowledge generated by the inquiry. Knowledge articulated by the participants and theorized from a range of other sources is drawn together by the researchers and shared with participants, thereby prompting further action responses within and beyond the inquiring community:

> Third-person research/practice aims to create a wider community of inquiry involving persons who, because they cannot be known to each other face-to-face (say, in a large, geographically dispersed corporation), have an impersonal quality. (Reason and Torbert, 2001: 33)

In many ways, all social research is 'for them'. However, distinctions may be drawn that are central to the way co-researchers are positioned in this third-person action research. Action researchers are committed to the inclusion and reflexive dissemination of knowledge constructed from both the researcher's reflection (at the first-person level) and her or his participants' insights (at the second-person level).

The third-person voice, the genre common for reporting most research, is also used in action research to report both the research conclusions and the inquiry methodology. This more distant voice is appropriate as new knowledge generated within the project may have a wider application in similar contexts. It is therefore important during the project to document the inquiry methodology, analyse the data and publicly disseminate the research findings. While the co-constructed knowledge is represented as findings, it has often already been taken up within the organization as part of the action research itself. Such integration of research findings into organizational practices is indicative of validity and legitimates the research at the third-person level for them.

A second epistemological and methodological distinction that features strongly in our critical action research approach relates to knowledge construction. Not only are there multiple positions from which to investigate the complexities of organizational life, there are also multiple, and at times conflicting, accounts represented in research conducted through a critical knowledge-based approach. The third-person approach to critical action research described above emphasizes and draws out this co-constructed character of knowledge.

The consideration and treatment of all participants as co-researchers in the research inquiry arise from an emphasis on the multi-vocality and plurality of knowledge. Knowledge is co-constructed within reflective dialogue and actions (Gaventa and Cornwall, 2001; Greenwood and Levin, 1998; Park, 2001). Such knowledge, generated reflectively, explicitly identifies and interprets both the meaning-making of organizational actors and the collective prioritizing of specific actions within the research itself. In this way, relevance and congruence are sustained beyond reporting and making sense of observations of everyday organizational life by engaging with people towards participant-led change and action.

Here is a central difference with organizational ethnography. A recurrent theme throughout this book is that a great deal of what happens every day in organizations may be regarded as commonplace, considered mundane, and therefore excluded from much non-ethnographic research. In its identification and engagement with participants' interests and actions, third-person action research, like organizational ethnography, is inclusive of everyday language and practices, opening up the meaning-making of the organizational actors. Both approaches are open-ended and inclusive of multi-vocality and heterogeneity, offering the possibility for the discussion of multiple interpretations, representations and discourses. But organizational ethnography in most of its forms does not seek to enable or foster change and action. Exceptions would include ethnography for social change (which might well share the values of action research; see Ghorashi and Wels, Chapter 12, this volume) or for management-led organizational change (which may well not share these values).

As critical action research relies on the co-construction of knowledge, it poses interesting challenges to traditional methodological concerns for rigour and validity. Whereas validity, in many traditional research approaches, derives from generalizability, validity for action research is achieved through the knowledge created in a particular context being taken up in action. Another yardstick is that action research theory reflexively incorporates the new knowledge it generates (Greenwood, 1998). This approach emphasizes identifying and understanding the operations of contextualized knowledge, with participants (as co-researchers) being involved in the sensemaking and analysis of data as part of the iterative spirals of action research. The success (or otherwise) of an action research project may well be judged by the community of practice in which the research is undertaken; and it ought, therefore, to be evaluated by 'whether a specific understanding is worth believing enough to act on it' (Greenwood and Levin, 1998: 80). This way of understanding validity accords with what Lather terms 'catalytic validity' (Lather, 1991): 'the degree to which the research process reorients, focuses and energizes participants toward knowing reality in order to transform it' (1991: 68). In other words, the extent to which the research catalyses change as the participants construct new knowledge within their practices (and thus actions) is an indicator of the 'validity' of the research producing that knowledge.

power relations

A third epistemological and methodological distinction developed in our critical action research attends to knowledge in organizations being constructed and employed within complex social relations of power. The extensive critical literature of organizational analysis (see, for example, Clegg et al., 2007) demonstrates that power relations within organizations develop and change through the complex entanglements with structures, identities, politics and, we would suggest, knowledge. For researchers to inquire critically within organizations, a number of key questions about power relations need to be raised for reflexive consideration throughout the research process. Which knowledge counts? Whose knowledge counts, and whose knowledge is privileged within organizational discourses? How is knowledge accorded such organizational status, and who decides the conditions of its possibility? Answers to such questions provide organizational researchers with alternative trajectories for critically examining and understanding organizational performance and management.

We contend that for such inquiry, critical action research is particularly useful. Not only does it make available multiple research positions and accounts from which to co-construct knowledge, but also, once constructed, knowledge and those involved in its construction are accorded different value in organizations. Some knowledge is taken up within dominant discourses, such as in policies and procedures, communities of practice or organizational systems (Sykes, 2006), while other knowledge may be marginalized, ignored or lost. For this reason, linking third-person action research to analysis of language through critical discourse analysis (Fairclough, 1995; 2003; Treleaven, 2004; Wodak and Meyer, 2001) has proved effective in investigating complex organizational change (Treleaven and Sykes, 2006) and organizational knowledge in community services organizations (Sykes, 2005).

Within critical action research, researchers generate questions, develop plans, and implement new knowledge with participants. The research processes themselves are therefore inextricably positioned within existing social relations of power within organizations, to influence and be influenced by organizational politics. While for some researchers such political positioning might be construed as a research deficit, within the critical action research described here, organizational research cannot conceivably be separated from organizational politics. Moreover, the specific engagement of strategic action within research projects is often a priority for organizational participants seeking to effect organizational change as a research outcome.

Accordingly, the range of participants and their organizational positioning strongly influences the research. Research participants may be positioned at different levels of an organization or they may come from different professional backgrounds or communities of practice. As such, participants may employ diverse practice-related terminology and conflicting politics. In our own research projects, for example, we have worked in partnership with networks of non-profit organizations and the government departments that fund them. Conflicting views and concerns involving power/knowledge issues arose in relation to the terms of research participation, actions, and findings that required careful and sensitive negotiation. While staff from non-profit organizations preferred the often time-consuming processes of gathering the perspectives of their service users, managers of government departments constrained by the need to deliver timely outcomes preferred more prescriptive, less consultative processes. Hence the effective engagement of participants required a sensitive consideration of organizational contexts and power relationships, as well as the application of different methods. More participative and reflexive engagements with multiple cycles were adopted with non-profit organizations, with project documentation being circulated for feedback. Shorter formal meetings with documentation were more effective in gaining the participation of government officials.

limitations of this approach to critical action research

Critical action research also has its limitations, both at a pragmatic and theoretical level. First, while action research (and ethnography) within organizations enable depth, both also require time to undertake quality research. However, organizations are often time-poor. Second, as researchers engage collaboratively, their research is embedded in the micro-relations of power in the organization. Such power relations necessarily shape research questions, processes and actions even though they may remain tacit. Third, we acknowledge explicitly our awareness and understanding that any intervention will change the phenomenon being studied. This would pose a problem for research that insists on the possibility of objectivity. For critical action research, however, the objective/subjective distinction is not a useful distinction though it may be problematic for those whose epistemology is imbued with such distinctions. Notwithstanding these limitations, we contend that critical action research may open up new possibilities for critical ethnographic studies of organizations.

conclusion

The three contrasts between critical action research and organizational ethnography presented in this chapter – those of researcher positioning, the co-construction of knowledge, and power relations – highlight the benefits of critical action research that traditionally have not been taken up by ethnographers. While these three epistemological and methodological differences from ethnography have been discussed individually, they are all mutually constituting. Further, as usefully represented by Foucault's (1972b) construct of the power/knowledge nexus, knowledge and power actively shape each other, as well as the positions taken up by researchers.

Our third-person action research is framed within a strong commitment to co-generating such values as trust, integrity and social justice to imbue a form of action that goes beyond the instrumental and strategic to a more deeply participative ethic. Such research can, at times, problematize hegemonic power relations within organizations and open up opportunities for participants and their organizations to adopt more inclusive ways of acting.

We contend that critical action research as a way of knowing may deepen traditional ethnographic research. Ethnographers undertaking research into the complexities of everyday organizational life may find that critical action research facilitates insights into the changing landscape of contemporary organizations. New forms of organization and organizing, such as networks and post-bureaucratic organizations, accentuate complexity and blur traditional organizational boundaries, structures and practices. As ethnographers explore these new organizational forms, engaging organizational actors in critical action research offers ways of inquiring that may be contextually appropriate for developing practical knowledge.

Finally, whereas the work of organizational ethnography, both epistemologically and methodologically, is often closely related to the work of action research, critical action research goes beyond it in offering research participants the opportunity to actively engage in processes of purposeful and reflective action in order to inquire into and change everyday issues of concern in organizations. In doing so, new knowledge is generated emergently from multiple realities, brought forward in multivocality, and enacted through participative inquiry into the complexities of everyday organizational life.

references

Argyris, C. and Schön, D.A. (1978) *Organizational learning: A theory of action approach.* Reading, MA: Addison Wesley.

Argyris, C., Putnam, R. and Smith, M.C. (1985) *Action science: Concepts, methods and skills for research and intervention.* San Francisco, CA: Jossey-Bass.

Berger, P.L. and Luckmann, T. (1984) *The social construction of reality: A treatise in the sociology of knowledge.* Harmondsworth: Penguin.

Braithwaite, R., Cockwill, S., O'Neill, M. and Rebane, D. (2007) 'Insider participatory action research in disadvantaged post-industrial areas: The experiences of community members as they become action researchers', *Action Research*, 5(1): 61–74. London: Sage.

Cairns, B., Harris, M. and Young, P. (2003) 'Building the capacity of the voluntary non-profit sector: Challenges of theory and practice'. Paper presented at the EGPA Workshop on Voluntary Action, Lisbon, Portugal.

Clegg, S., Courpasson, D. and Phillips, N. (2007) *Power and organizations.* London: Sage.

Clifford, J. and Marcus, G.E. (eds) (1986) *Writing culture: The poetics and politics of ethnography.* Berkeley: University of California Press.

Collinson, D. (1992) *Managing the shopfloor: Subjectivity, masculinity and workplace culture.* New York: De Gruyter.

Dick, B. (1991) *You want to do an action research thesis? How to conduct and report action research.* Brisbane: University of Queensland.

Fairclough, N. (1995) *Critical discourse analysis: The critical study of language.* London: Longman.

Fairclough, N. (2003) *Analysing discourse: Textual analysis for social research.* London: Routledge.

Foucault, M. (1972a) *The archaeology of knowledge.* London: Tavistock.

Foucault, M. (ed.) (1972b) *Power/knowledge: Selected interviews and other writings 1972–1977.* New York: Pantheon.

Freeman, M., Clarkeburn, H. and Treleaven, L. (2007) 'A collaborative approach to improving academic honesty', in A. Brew and J. Sachs (eds) *Transforming a university: The scholarship of teaching and learning in practice.* Sydney, NSW: Sydney University Press. pp. 153–61.

Freire, P. (1970) *Pedagogy of the oppressed.* New York: Herder and Herder.

Gaventa, J.C. and Cornwall, A. (2001) 'Power and knowledge', in P. Reason and H. Bradbury (eds) *Handbook of action research: Participative inquiry and practice.* London: Sage. pp. 70–80.

Geertz, C. (1973) *The interpretation of cultures.* New York: Basic Books.

Greenwood, D.J. and Levin, M. (1998) *Introduction to action research.* Thousand Oaks, CA: Sage.

Grundy, S. and Kemmis, S. (1982) 'Educational action research in Australia: The state of the art (an overview)', in C. Henry, C. Hook, S. Kemmis and R. McTaggart (eds) *The action research reader.* Geelong, Vic.: Deakin University Press. pp. 83–97.

Gutierrez, G. (1973) *A theology of liberation.* Maryknoll: Orbis Books.

Hammersley, M. and Atkinson, P. (1997) *Ethnography: Principles in practice* (2nd edn). London: Routledge.

Harris, M. (2001) 'The place of self and reflexivity in third sector scholarship: An exploration', *Nonprofit and Voluntary Quarterly*, 30(4): 747–60.

Heron, J. and Reason, P. (2001) 'The practice of co-operative inquiry: Research "with" rather than "on" people', in P.B. Reason and H. Brady (eds) *Handbook of action research: Participative inquiry and practice.* London: Sage. pp. 179–88.

Kemmis, S. and McTaggart, R. (2001) 'Participatory action research', in N. Denzin and Y. Lincoln (eds) *Handbook of qualitative research* (2nd edn). Thousand Oaks, CA: Sage. pp. 567–605.

Kindon, S., Pain, R. and Kesby, M. (eds) (2007) *Participatory action research approaches and methods: Connecting people, participation and place*. New York: Routledge.

Lather, P. (1986) 'Research as praxis', *Harvard Educational Review*, 56(3): 257–77.

Lather, P. (1991) *Getting smart: Feminist research and pedagogy with/in the postmodern*. New York: Routledge.

MacIntosh, R. and Bonnet, R. (eds) (2007) *Management Research News*, 30(5).

Marcus, G.E. (ed.) (1999) *Critical anthropology now: Unexpected contexts, shifting constituencies and changing agendas*. Santa Fe, NM: School of American Research Press.

Marshall, J. and Reason, P. (1994) 'Adult learning in collaborative action research: Reflections on the supervision process', *Studies in Continuing Education, Research and Scholarship in Adult Education*, 15(2): 117–32.

McTaggart, R. (1991) *Action research: A short modern history*. Geelong, Vic.: Deakin University.

Orr, J. (1996) *Talking about machines*. New York: ILR Press Cornell University.

Park, P. (2001) 'Knowledge and participatory research', in P.B. Reason and H. Brady (eds) *Handbook of action research: Participative inquiry and practice*. London: Sage. pp. 81–90.

Reason, P. and Bradbury, H. (2001) 'Introduction: Inquiry and participation in search of a world worthy of human aspiration', in P.B. Reason and H. Bradbury (eds) *Handbook of action research: Participative inquiry and practice*. Thousand Oaks, CA: Sage. pp. 1–15.

Reason, P.B. and Bradbury, H. (eds) (2001) *Handbook of action research: Participative inquiry and practice*. London: Sage.

Reason, P.B. and Torbert, W. (2001) 'The action turn: A further look at the scientific merits of action research', *Concepts and Transformation*, 6(1): 1–37.

Schön, D.A. (1983) *The reflective practitioner: How professionals think in action*. New York: Basic Books.

Senge, P.M. (1990) *The fifth discipline: The art and practice of the learning organisation*. New York: Doubleday Currency.

Smith, D. (2002) 'Institutional ethnography', in T. May (ed.) *Qualitative research in action*. London: Sage. pp. 17–52.

Stanley, L. (ed.) (1990) *Feminist praxis: Research, theory and epistemology in feminist sociology*. London: Routledge.

Sykes, C. (2006) (Unpublished PhD thesis) Efficient management wasted knowledge? A critical investigation of organisational knowledge in community service organizations. Sydney: University of Sydney.

Torbert, W. (1991) *The power of balance: Transforming self, society and scientific inquiry*. Newbury Park, CA: Sage.

Torbert, W. (2001) 'The practice of action inquiry', in P.B. Reason and H. Bradbury (eds) *Handbook inquiry and practice: Participatory inquiry and practice*. London: Sage. pp. 250–60.

Toulmin, S.E. (2001) *Return to reason*. Cambridge, MA: Harvard University Press.

Treleaven, L. (1994) 'Making a space: Collaborative inquiry as staff development', in P. Reason (ed.) *Participation in human inquiry*. London: Sage. pp. 138–62.

Treleaven, L. (2001) 'The turn to action and the linguistic turn: Towards an integrated methodology', in P.B. Reason and H. Bradbury (eds) *Handbook of action research: Participative inquiry and practice*. London: Sage. pp. 261–72.

Treleaven, L. (2004) 'A knowledge sharing approach to organisational change: A critical discourse analysis', in H. Tsoukas and N. Mylonopoulos (eds) *Organisations as knowledge systems: Knowledge learning and dynamic capabilities*. Basingstoke: Palgrave, Macmillan. pp. 154–80.

Treleaven, L. and Sykes, C. (2005) 'Loss of organizational knowledge: From supporting clients to serving head office', *Journal of Organizational Change Management*, 18(4): 353–68.

Van Maanen, J. (1995) 'An end to innocence: The ethnography of ethnography', in J. Van Maanen (ed.) *Representations in ethnography*. Thousand Oaks, CA: Sage. pp. 1–35.

Wadsworth, Y. (1991) *Everyday evaluation on the run*. Melbourne: Action Research Issues Association.

Wenger, E. (1998) *Communities of practice: Learning, meaning and identity*. Cambridge, UK: Cambridge University Press.

Wodak, R. and Meyer, M. (2001) *Methods of critical discourse analysis*. Thousand Oaks, CA: Sage.

Yanow, D. (1996) *How does a policy mean? Interpreting policy and organizational actions*. Washington, DC: Georgetown University Press.

Yanow, D. (2006) 'Thinking interpretively: Philosophical presuppositions and the human sciences', in D. Yanow and P. Schwartz-Shea (eds) *Interpretation and method: Empirical research methods and the interpretive turn*. London: M.E. Sharpe. pp. 5–26.

12

Beyond complicity: A plea for engaged ethnography

Halleh Ghorashi and Harry Wels

It seems that no one, including the organizational ethnographer, can escape complicity in contributing to and sustaining inequality and all sorts of injustices in the modern day global village and society. No matter the amount of good intentions towards social justice or ethical considerations about equal development or critical stances towards the inequities in the world today, complicity in the very things that are vehemently opposed or criticized even seems to tie the hands of the socially and politically engaged researcher. Engagement does not automatically make or break one free of complicity. Even the engaged researcher cannot escape complicity.

How, then, can engaged scholarship be legitimated, morally or politically, if everybody seems to be part and parcel of the same oppressive, disciplinary power configurations in society, including its organizations and their management, as postmodern authors such as Foucault, Deleuze and Guattari argue? How can Pontius Pilate ever have said that he washed his hands of guilt because he was 'not responsible' (according to Matthew 27:24, *Good News Edition*) for the death of Jesus? As Roman governor he could not escape complicity, no matter how much water he used for washing his hands or in what cleansing ritual he partook. So despite his engaged commitment to free Jesus and his resistance of the demands of the crowds in front of him, Pilate still has to be considered as complicit in the crucifixion as the rest of the people on the square ('and so are we', a devout Christian might add, implying that it is not 'presence' alone that makes one complicit). Is there anything to get us beyond complicity after Hannah Arendt's 'banality of evil', Derrida's 'contamination of oppositional pairs' or Foucault's attack on the autonomous subject? Is there anything beyond this hegemonic and suffocating sense of complicity-of-all agency?

In this chapter, we would like to argue that it is possible to develop an engagement with *all* players in the configurations of power, which goes beyond complicity in organizations and management practices, and that the practices and approaches in organizational ethnography might hold some promises for just that – promises that rise from the specific relations that organizational ethnographers are able to develop with and within the field while representing and reflecting on this field in their ethnographic writings.[1] However, if there is any chance of engagement, it cannot only be with the less-powerful, such as on the shop floor. Researchers should, as we already referred to above, also engage with the powerful, with those working at top managerial levels. The question to be answered then is basically how organizational ethnographic research can avoid or neutralize the divisions created in and through power and politics, between the dominant and the inferior. We want to show how the postmodern critique of power has created new opportunities for organizational ethnographers to engage with the less powerful. In order to avoid the antagonism between the powerful and less powerful, we also have to rethink and reflect on our own position as ethnographers in processes of identity politics, that is, our stake in modernist organizational power plays. In overviews of these issues, idealism still remains an essential ingredient of an active engagement through organizational ethnography. Because of his or her particular position in the field, the organizational ethnographer seems ideally suited to reconcile the inherent and persistent antagonisms between the powerful and the less powerful. How this works in detail is revealed towards the end of the chapter, as a logical final step in our argument.

After a more conceptual discussion of the role of engagement in anthropology in general and in organizational ethnography in particular and various approaches to the concept of power, we will illustrate our argument with examples in organization and management from two cases. The first case is a country-specific case of the struggle and search for equity in organization and management in South Africa. The second case concerns the general theme of the emancipation struggle of women in organizational and management practices worldwide. Both cases refer to power and emancipation struggles where it seemed clear who were the underdogs – that is – blacks and women who, almost automatically, deserved sympathy and support in their struggle against oppression and for a more equal distribution of power. Although both cases are based on the authors' earlier ethnographic work, for the purpose of this chapter we present them not as such, but as stepping stones in our suggestion that organizational ethnography can offer us glimpses of an engagement beyond complicity in organizational and management processes.

ethnographic fieldwork and engagement

The critical engagement of anthropological ethnographers with (economic) development issues and the less powerful in societies worldwide is considered a widespread phenomenon, if not a stereotype, in stories told about the discipline (Eriksen, 1995: 243–5 and 191–5; Eriksen, 2006). This stereotype is particularly based on the work of anthropologists from the 1950s onwards. Ethnographic work during those years led various anthropologists to become actively involved in power struggles against (colonial) government officials or in combating stereotyping and ethnocentrism and other forms of racism (Miles, 1989) in society in general (Pickering, 2001; for a concrete example in Asia see, for instance, Salemink, 1999) and in anthropology itself (see for example Asad, 1973; Fabian, 1983; Rigby, 1996).[2] This engagement most often had to do with a rather clear notion of what power was all about and, even more clearly, with a solid moral stance, usually backed by ethnographic work, concerning what it meant to abuse power and more specifically what it meant to be powerless.[3] These particular forms of engagement fitted in nicely and matched seamlessly with a modernist theoretical paradigm, in which the Cartesian subject was considered an autonomous, conscious and rational being: engagement in ethnographic work was grounded in the dominant academic critical discourses on power and power relations, based on assumptions brought by the Enlightenment.

But what happened to possibilities for engagement when this modernist endeavour was severely criticized and undermined – deconstructed – by the postmodern disposition also penetrating anthropological and organizational ethnographic discourses and analyses (Jeffcut, 1994), introduced by Marx, Freud and Nietzsche[4] and later elaborated upon by French philosophers like Lyotard and Foucault? What happened particularly to engagement in organizational ethnography when it became argued that power and its abuses were not rational or even conscious choices made by autonomous subjects, but were driven by the unconscious desires of men? Or that power and its abuse worked through human interactions through the 'banalities' of everyday life, as Hannah Arendt (1973) formulated it, through the inconspicuous, mundane rut of our everyday existence, instead of through recognizable malignant extravaganza? What room is left for engagement when every one of us is considered to be caught in and part of the structures and disciplines of power and its (ab)uses? What if the boundary between abuse and non-abuse of power becomes ever more blurred? What if full-blown complicity seems unavoidable for all of us (cf. Zimbardo, 2007)?

Although philosophical deliberations might have taken centre stage in the launch of postmodernism, it is in the fields of anthropology and organizational ethnography to the actual empirical research being done by (organizational) ethnographers that we now look for answers on how to cope with its consequences in terms of going beyond complicity. It is in the paradoxical situation of the ethnographer, at the same time being both part and not-part of the power configurations in organizations or in society, that complicity can be found (in observing as a participant), avoided perhaps in the rhetorics of writing but also experimented with (to transcend complicity). This latter is made possible precisely because the paradoxical (non-)position and temporality of the organizational ethnographer give room to manoeuvre in alliances being forged, sides taken and representations being constructed.

critical approaches to power

In the past decades, there have been diverse ways in approaching or defining power within the social sciences in general and in organizational studies in particular (for an overview see Phillips et al., 2006). For the purpose of this chapter we present a discussion on the ways that a postmodern approach to power has influenced the positioning of ethnographic research in the field of organization studies, influencing in particular the possibilities and room for organizational ethnographers to engage with the less powerful. But in order to understand the postmodern critique on conceptualizing power, we first need to explore briefly the critical approaches to power, inspired by Marx and later by Gramsci and, in his wake again, postcolonial theorists like Spivak.

In this critical body of literature power is seen and approached as domination (cf. Morgan, 1997: 301–44). Whereas Marx approached domination as a class-based, visible suppression related to the means of production, Gramsci's focus was on the invisible and taken for granted processes of domination or hegemonies (Hardy and Clegg, 1999). In this line of approach Steven Lukes' (1974) work on power and decision-making processes became especially popular within feminist studies (Brouns, 1993) and within organizational studies (Komter, 1992; Wilson and Thompson, 2001). The fundamental aspect of a critical approach is that power is seen as the cause of injustice and suppression – the latter being manifest or latent that calls for resistance. In this way critical theory became an essential basis for various kinds of emancipatory movements outside and inside organizations (Alvesson and Willmott, 2003: 15, 16).

The less-powerful or powerless in the postcolonial tradition were usually called the 'subaltern', a concept derived from Gramsci's 'Prison notebooks' (Hoare and Smith, 1978), which he wrote while in prison during Mussolini's fascist reign in Italy. Although perhaps a crude parallel and comparison, it could be argued that Gramsci was, in a way, an (organizational) ethnographer, who 'participated' (although forced to against his will) and 'observed' (although 'was subjected to' would maybe do more justice to his situation) for a long time in the 'field' (that is, prison). But through his writing he was also a distant observer and analyst, like any good organizational ethnographer. Through his 'extensive fieldwork' among the 'powerless' he could almost not do anything else but empathize with them in and through his description and analysis, in which the powerful were the 'significant Other' – and definitely the 'bad guys'.

In his work Gramsci used the term 'subaltern' interchangeably with 'subordinate': 'Gramsci used the term 'subaltern' to refer in particular to the unorganized groups of rural peasants based in southern Italy, who had no social or political consciousness as a group, and were therefore susceptible to the ruling class, culture and leadership of the state' (Morton, 2003: 48). And: 'Subaltern classes may include peasants, *workers* and other groups denied access to 'hegemonic' power' (Ashcroft et al., 2000: 215, emphasis added). Postcolonial theory later criticized Gramsci's notions, among other things, as male-biased in terms of considering who could be agents of change. Women were, in general, not considered as an option for Gramsci (Spivak, 1987). What is evident from this theoretical tradition is that it gives rather clear indices and ideas concerning changing things for the better, to empower the powerless and to have a clue of who the less powerful are. It also inspires visions and hopes for a better, more emancipated (future) world. It gives necessary mass and legitimation to critical engagement; it gives 'a theory of resistance' (Said, 1993).

What binds these approaches to power is their modernist base of departure. Where power is interpreted as domination, it is the belief in autonomous subjects who could use or abuse their power to dominate others, which makes it a modernist approach. One can clearly locate power and discern power structures. Power is seen as something that can be found, pinpointed and consciously manipulated. Power is considered to be a root of human behaviour, with a root system that can be traced among and related to individuals, and with a clearly traceable direction from powerful actors to less powerful actors. Engaged anthropologists at least knew where to start and to whom to direct their protests and emancipatory labour, i.e. power and its abuses were clearly located. But in this way, emancipatory movements also become modernist movements, since there is a belief in the possibility of reversing certain processes of domination through the act of conscious resistance.

The idea that power and its abuses could be located and countered and resisted made the critical approaches vulnerable to the postmodern critique on power. We come back to this discussion later on. We continue here to explore the specific dominant approaches to power in the anthropological discipline and their importance for analysing organizational processes from an ethnographic point of view.

anthropologists' positioning within organizational studies

Anthropology has often prided itself on its involvement with the less-powerful subjects of study (Lamphere, 2003). Through their ethnographic work anthropologists have done their best to become the voice of the voiceless within the societies they researched. This has partly to do with the history of anthropology: 'As a discipline that itself has often been considered to occupy a marginal voice in Western political theory, anthropology offers an ideal point of departure for the radical rethinking of the state that a view from the margins requires' (Das and Poole, 2004: 4). Following Das and Poole we go one step further by suggesting that, given its marginal position, anthropology has the ability to identify and empathize with the 'less-powerful' within the context of its dominant approach to research, 'doing ethnography' (Geertz, 1973). Being among the less-powerful for extensive periods of time during ethnographic fieldwork and trying to understand and describe their life world in ethnographic texts has led almost inevitably to contributions to the critical literature on power, with an emancipatory subtext.

Compared to anthropological ethnographic research in general, organizational ethnography is quite a new field of research (Kamsteeg and Wels, 2004). As such, its focus, compared to other organizational studies approaches, has been mainly on experiences on the work floor and in daily practices, rather than at the level of management (see, for instance, Kunda, 1992).[5] This bottom-up approach to organizations provides a unique entry point to observe the processes of inclusion and exclusion on daily bases. For organizational anthropologists and ethnographers it means giving due attention to empowering minorities in organizations, such as women and people of colour, who are often excluded from the core positions and major sources of power. In this way, by providing thick descriptions of processes of inclusion and exclusion within organizations, organizational ethnographies generate a better understanding of these processes, enabling and giving voice to certain forms of empowerment processes.

However, what perhaps makes the work of organizational ethnographers more difficult than that of other ethnographers is the matter of context and time. As a rather new discipline within the context of organization studies, organizational ethnography faces the dominant presence of functionalists and instrumentalists who pay little or no attention to power processes within organizations (Martin, 2002). In their attempt to join critical approaches to processes of organization and management (see for examples Forester, 1992; Hirsh and Gellner, 2001), organizational ethnographers have had to re-think the critical notions of approaches to power inspired by postmodern criticism (Crowther and Green, 2004: 129–48).

The postmodern 'Foucauldian attack on agency' (Hardy and Clegg, 1999: 381), in which the power of disciplinary processes involves *all* subjects, leaving little or no room for one subject to be more of 'an oppressor' than the rest, meant a blow to modernist approaches to power and especially the critical approach and emancipation related to it. Where could one start resisting structures of domination? How could one still discern power structures? If power was still metaphorically considered a root, it is certainly not in the modernist sense we described above, but more in the sense of a 'rhizome', as Deleuze and Guattari (1972) describe the postmodern condition (see also Deleuze and Guattari, 1987: 3). A rhizome has neither direction nor a single source: a rhizome is a 'botanical term for a root system that spreads across the ground (as in bamboo) rather than downwards, and grows from several points rather than a single tap root' (Ashcroft et al., 2000: 207: see also Chapter 6 in this volume). The rhizome metaphor was primarily introduced to sensitize people that imperial powers '… operate rhizomically rather than monolithically' (ibid.), as was often implicitly suggested or assumed in the modernist tradition. In this metaphor is the implication that power has no 'master plan' (ibid.), let alone a mastermind. The postmodern critique of the modernist concept of power virtually made engagement impossible. It left engaged ethnographers with empty hands and no particular power or mastermind to resist, except maybe themselves as part and parcel of the rhizome, leaving subjects to reflect on their own roles and positions of complicity in the rhizome.

Before we have a closer look to see if anything can be expected beyond complicity, i.e. engagement in a postmodern context, let us examine two different but related examples of engagement in the world of organization and management: the struggle for equity in organization and management in South Africa since 1994, when Mandela became the first democratically elected president of South Africa, and women's emancipation. Both cases revolve around issues of representing the professional potential of the Other in organizational practices and how this stereotyping negatively influences the power positions and potential of the Other in organization and management. The South African case is strongly bound to its particular historical contexts of imperialism and apartheid. It makes a clear point about racial or ethnic antagonism, but one might be inclined to dismiss the example as being 'out there' on the relatively isolated southern tip of the African continent. We therefore present a second case that comprises at least half of humanity, to show how fascinatingly similar, but at the same time also contextually different, power configurations affect the complicity and engagement nexus for the organizational ethnographer. The cases are meant to illustrate the following aspects of our argument so far: first, that much of the emancipatory rhetoric in the organization and management literature is still caught in modernist conceptions of power, with clear ideas of who is to blame and what needs to change in order to improve the situation; second, how difficult it is for the organizational ethnographer, within discourses of postmodern conceptions of power, to adhere to a strong and straightforward sense of engagement, doing justice to emancipatory ideals. On top of all this the cases illustrate how relatively easy it is to pay lip-service to these ideals, but how complicated it is to turn them into daily organizational realities.

in search of equity in employment opportunities and management in South Africa[6]

When Nelson Mandela became the first democratically elected president in 1994, he often referred to South Africa as the Rainbow Nation, celebrating the complementarities of racial/ethnic and cultural differences (Tutu, 1994; Woods, 2000). Until then South Africa had mainly been associated with its political ideology of apartheid, emphasizing the separateness of racial and cultural differences and, in its wake, policies towards 'separate development' (Sparks, 1990).[7] The notion of a Rainbow Nation could not be further from the basic assumptions of the apartheid ideology. The political bridge across this gap was sought in the creation of an extensive legal framework prescribing policies of equity and affirmative action in all spheres and types of organizations and management. But as we shall see in the description of the legislative process, this approach to redistributive justice is basically also about essentializing ethnic or particularistic traits. They tried to fight inequality by creating inequality (cf. Snijders, 2007). This means, among other things, that equity policies in South Africa could be interpreted in a way as a continuation of identity politics, firmly rooted in a modernist approach to power, just as we observe in the section below about women's sexual harassment.

In South Africa, the basis for legislation in support of equity policies was laid down in the constitution, which included the fundamental right to equality in the Bill of Rights. The Labour Relations Act (LRA) of 1995 was directed towards curbing discrimination and unfair labour practices in the workplace. The Bill of Rights formed the basis for the Employment Equity Act (EEA) of 1998. This Act was particularly meant for certain designated employers, mainly in the public domain, like municipalities and other state organs (with the exception of the security and defence services) and employers with 50 or more employees. Besides the issue of equity, the Act explicitly refers to implementing policies of affirmative action (Reddy and Choudree, cited in Holm, 2003: 32). For organizations that were considered non-designated in terms of the EEA, the Promotion of Equality and Prevention of Unfair Discrimination Act (PEPUDA) was introduced in 2000 (February and Abrahams, 2001). Naturally, in the wake of the demise of the apartheid system, much scholarly attention was geared towards racial issues addressed by these acts. However, race was not the only criterion in South Africa for holding a disadvantaged position. The disabled and women were also in a very disadvantaged position in terms of access to jobs and positions of power within organizations, and so were explicitly mentioned in the EEA (Orr and Goldman, 2001).

The reasons for this range of legislation can be interpreted as a mix of strategic and moral considerations. Most people would recognize the ethical demand for affirmative action. At the same time, the historical context of South Africa causes every system and procedure that is preferential on the basis of designated racial or any other socially constructed trait to be looked upon with suspicion, as a new guise for old practices. Such was the case with much of the equity legislation, especially the EEA with its emphasis on affirmative action. One could theoretically argue along the lines we presented above that this approach is rooted in the same modernist view of power as apartheid was. But that shouldn't close our eyes to the practical day-to-day problems policy-makers, HRM managers and politicians experience in trying to move an uneven distribution of jobs across ethnic groups (and between men and women, able and disabled persons) towards a more even situation. It is easier to give moral lip-service than to develop a policy that is practically applicable.

In the day-to-day practice of affirmative action in present day South Africa, processes of policy implementation can become rather complicated. Take, for example, the concept of 'equitable representation'. This is not a matter of aggregate numbers on a national level only, but at a regional and sectoral level as well. The outcomes on these different levels might well diverge. To complicate matters further, just human resources management is not only a matter of searching for equity, but also of finding people who are qualified for the jobs. For this purpose employers may make use of 'the pool of suitably qualified people from the designated groups' (Jeffery cited in Holm, 2003: 36). The Department of Labour can provide management with the numbers of suitably qualified personnel in the country, region or sector. If the particular skills that management is looking for are not available in the skills pool, employers have a valid reason not to employ someone from the designated groups recognized in the EEA: be they, for instance, a black person, disabled, female. It is not unlikely that management won't find the required skills in the designated groups, especially among black candidates, because they were usually denied a good education in South Africa under the apartheid regime and therefore today are not considered 'suitably qualified' (Human, 1996: 46). As a consequence, the pool of 'suitably qualified people' is not large, and there certainly was not a large pool immediately after 1994. Skills development is therefore an important issue for the Minister of Labour, which has been taken up in the Skills Development Act (Von Holdt, 2003: 304).

A rather recent example from the Western Cape shows just how unequal the situation still is. A provincial treasury macro-economic report from November 2003, presented and discussed at the Western Cape Growth and Development Summit, showed that nearly 500,000 people were unemployed in 2002, with the highest proportion among blacks (40 per cent). Furthermore, unemployment had been on the increase for the previous seven years, except among whites. 'Only 3.5 per cent of blacks found jobs, compared with 92 per cent of whites, 81 per cent of Asians and 54 per cent of coloureds'(*Cape Times*, 14 November 2003). Laurine Platzky, deputy director general of the Western Cape's Economic Development and Tourism Department, is quoted in the same newspaper article as having said, 'As the economy grows we will attract more people with and without skills. At the same time, *there are not enough skilled people for our new and growing industries*' (ibid., emphasis added).

Taken together, the various interpretations of what equitable representation exactly is and the limited pool of suitably qualified people make for a rather complicated practical implementation of affirmative action policies. When managers have to report on their 'reasonable progress' in implementing equity policies – another requirement of the EEA – these complications have to be answered for in a report legitimizing the course of action chosen with regard to affirmative action and equity. Such reporting requires a balancing act between morality, instrumentality and business sense.[8]

The October deadline for the annual employment equity reports always creates stress, both for the managers who have to write them and for the Department of Labour which has to monitor progress in the field. In 2003, a local newspaper in KwaZulu Natal quoted Snuki Zikalala, speaking on behalf of the Labour Minister Membathisi Mdladlana, as saying, 'Companies will be given no mercy at all. Those who did not submit [reports] will be liable to a minimum fine of R 500,000 and if they continue not complying with the law, we could even recommend prosecution of the company' (*The Witness*, 3 October 2003). By mid-October 2003, only some 30 per cent of South Africa's companies had submitted their employment equity reports (*This Day*, 17 October 2003). Despite the fact that black and white business organizations united on 11 October 2003 at a ceremony in Sun City under two bodies – the Chamber of Commerce and Industry of SA (Chamsa), and Business Unity SA – affirmative action and equity policies remain tough nuts to crack (*The Witness*, 13 October 2003). With the history of apartheid still fresh in their memory and the sheer size of the transformation in business that South Africa required, its bitterest opponents refer to affirmative action as 'apartheid-in-reverse' (Adam cited in Holm, 2003: 12) – that is – a continuation of apartheid with other people in power.

It seems that we can conclude with some confidence, even on the basis of this relatively short introduction to the theme of equity in South Africa, that the arena of the debates is highly politicized along modernist approaches to power: power and power abuses can be clearly detected and traced to a source. In terms of engagement this discussion and debate is modernist because it is 'easy' to distinguish between 'good' and 'evil', to fight the perpetrators and stand with the oppressed. Engagement is at least 'easy' in a moral sense that is abstracted from everyday realities, although it is highly complicated in the everyday routines of organizational and management life. But, all participants – freedom fighters, apartheid loyalists, intellectuals, politicians and so on – were at one stage part and parcel of the same apartheid system, the same configurations of power. Now that apartheid is officially abolished, South Africans in organization and management are all still in the same configuration together; all play their parts and were and are, in that sense, complicit. All are caught, as Derrida describes it, in the '"contamination" of oppositional pairs' (quoted in Sanders, 2002: 9): 'When opposition takes the form of a demarcation from something, it cannot ... be untouched by that to which it opposes itself'; and therefore '[o]pposition takes its first steps from a footing of complicity' (ibid.). In other words, all were participating in the same system and so are in a sense 'guilty' of the misdeeds of that system; all were caught in the apartheid system's Foucauldian disciplinary power configurations.

Fair enough, one could say, but this is such a specific case, in such a specific part of the world, that it cannot possibly serve as an example of similar patterns in other circumstances. Let us then complement this case with an example that is on the one hand completely different – women's emancipation in organizational and management settings – but on the other, strikingly similar in its effects in terms of power configurations and the paradoxical role of the organizational ethnographer in terms of engagement and complicity.

emancipation of women in organization and management

The great impact of modernist approaches to power within organizations has let us believe for a long time that 'natural' processes within modern organizations would result in selecting the most qualified person for the job. This selection of a perfect match for the organization was assumed to be neutral in the case of gender, race, ethnicity, or every other category. In this way, the notion of a 'norm employee' (that is, the employee who is considered to represent the norm) has often been related to the quality and availability of an assumed 'disembodied worker'; a worker without gender or ethnicity. Yet, Acker (1992) shows that this seemingly neutral notion of a 'disembodied worker' is anything but gender neutral. The claim of availability, for example, has a gendered layer to it, since the combination of work and homemaking and/or childcare typically means less availability for work and is, thus, a deviation from the assumed norm. Other scholars (Gowricharn, 1999; Hoetink, 1973) have shown that the notion of the norm worker, in addition to being gendered, also has ethnicity. The construction of the norm is influenced by cultural images of desired physical traits within organizations and their management. These images contribute to processes of inclusion and/or exclusion within organizations in which some have easier access to (more) powerful positions than others. Thus, it is not accidental that there are men of dominant ethnicities who occupy top positions, while women and ethnic minorities face glass ceilings in their careers within contemporary organizations.

It is in the context of the above described framework that the emancipation of women and later of minorities within organizations gained importance. It became clear that there is nothing neutral and 'natural' within organizations when it comes to power (see Benschop and Doorewaard, 1998; Kanter, 1977; Komter, 1990). In her book *The feminist case against bureaucracy* (1984), Ferguson shows that whereas 'bureaucracy' may seem to include difference (in this case women), its homogenizing and monopolizing language actually dominates all individual actions and perpetuates inequalities. Wilson (1996) argues that those considered as the 'founding fathers' of organization theory – Weber, Maslow and Taylor – have been gender blind in their work. The theories developed by these thinkers presented themselves as concerning generic workers, yet in reality they were about men, ignoring gender relations and women altogether. Workers were reduced to men only, yet neutrality was claimed at the same time. Some years later Stephen Linstead commented on Wilson's observation regarding the 'founding fathers' by claiming that it was not that these theoreticians were blind to gender issues but that they suppressed them consciously in line with the modernist- and rationalist-dominated frameworks of their time. So-called

> ... Scientific Management was, if anything, a theory of knowledge, part of a project of instrumental rationality, a means of appropriating knowledge wherever it was distributed. From this perspective, individual characteristics, including gender and ethnicity, are irrelevant to the function of management. (Linstead, 2000: 298)

Another possible argument is that to a certain extent, the biases of the founding fathers could be understood since the majority of workers at the time were male. But it is the representation of workers as male-only over the years since the 'founding fathers' published their works that is remarkable and maybe even shocking. What we can learn from this discussion is that power matters, be it the power of taken for granted or of conscious suppression, and that it is essential to realize that organizational processes are loaded with certain manifest and hidden forms of inclusion and exclusion, of which scholars need to be aware.

But realizing that power exists within organizations is one thing; approaching and dealing with (abuses of) power and powerlessness is another. Just to make clear how women's complicity in their own suppression seems to obstruct changes towards a more equal and fair treatment in organizations, we briefly look at the issue of sexual harassment in organizations. In her influential work, Kanter (1977) shows how certain manifestations of power – such as controlling, territorial, and other bureaucratic behaviours – are reactions to the feeling of powerlessness. Powerlessness corrupts, she states. In an interesting article, Wilson and Thompson (2001) link sexual harassment within organizations to the three dimensions of power discerned by Lukes (1974), of decision-making; the power that prevents conflict from becoming visible; and the deeply rooted notion of power through which the status quo appears as naturally given. With this last dimension of power, Lukes comes quite close to Gramsci's notions of hegemonic power. In Lukes' view power is about domination, and he notes different kinds of domination. In the first, power is about visible domination. From this perspective, sexual harassment is seen as yet another example in which men in power treat women (the powerless) as their objects. Women's fear of resistance to power is related to their vulnerable position within the organization. In the second kind of domination, power is present through defining and controlling agendas, in this case making sure that sexual harassment does not become an issue at all. Not having access to formal and informal centres of power, women do not dare to raise the issue, out of fear of not being taken seriously. The third dimension is the power of the broader patriarchal structures at work. It is the invisibility of this structure which makes the practice of sexual harassment acceptable and somewhat natural: 'At the interpersonal level it is not a conspiracy among men that they impose on women ... It is a complementary social process between women and men. Women are *complicit* in the social practices of their silence' (Smith, cited in Wilson et al., 2001: 72, emphasis added).

The example described above shows the importance of Lukes' dimensions of power for women's emancipation: when power is multidimensional, emancipation needs to be multidimensional as well. Formal and informal networks of power need to be developed to enable women to create strong collective identities and claim a voice against 'old boy networks'. Women also need to be empowered through an awareness of their position in order to oppose and resist the dominant patriarchal structures. In this way, emancipation has predominantly been about 'identity politics' in making gender identity the main point of a collective struggle of women as victims, against injustice and male dominance. Power and dominance were traceable and had a source that could be pinpointed – in short a modernist approach to power.

Recently, this approach has been criticized from a Foucauldian perspective. In this approach, power is not something to be possessed either by men or women, but it is present within social relations and incorporated into the practices of daily life. Power in a Foucauldian approach is not a zero-sum game in which some are powerful and others are only victims (Wilson and Thompson, 2001: 74). It is not so much the power of domination that deserves our attention, but the power of discourse. The power of discourse works through all human (inter)actions, which renders any kind of active opposition at the same time part of the dominant discourse, rather than something 'outside' of it. All are considered part and parcel of the same disciplinary power configuration that also leads to the unintended consequences of actions. Within the configuration of disciplinary power everybody is complicit in a way, which explains the backlash caused by certain organizational activities related to emancipation and emancipatory policies. In the case of affirmative action for women, it is not just 'angry white men' who reject it, but also the people who have been beneficiaries of affirmative actions themselves.

One unintended consequence of affirmative action programmes has been that they compromise or even negate a serious assessment of professional quality. For this reason, many women and people of colour in power themselves often deny that they owe their position to affirmative action, since stating this openly may seem their own disqualification. According to Acker (2006: 456), this unintended outcome has been on the rise ever since affirmative action policies became a prominent feature of organizational and managerial life in the 1980s; since then affirmative action programmes have increasingly become matters of bureaucratic paperwork, due to a decrease of activism against inequality, both inside and outside organizations.

Another backlash comes from the fact that the presence of women in power positions has not necessarily contributed to creating more inclusive organizations. Placing more women in management positions is not enough to break the patterns of domination, according to Ferguson (1984). What is required, in her view, is the rise of an alternative voice, one based on the experiences of women themselves; only that will challenge the patterns of power that dominate organizations and societies. According to Ferguson, the dominant discourse of today is not the language of women, even when women speak it. Adopting the same discursive practices, women often only reinforce the discourse of the dominant men. In a similar vein identity politics as a source of opposition seems to be ineffective since it builds upon the dominant form of essentializing practices, resulting in the reinforcement of boundaries between 'us' and 'them', instead of breaking them down.

What is left of emancipation and engagement for organizational ethnographers when our actions are solely to be understood within the power of discursive practices? Based on our two cases on South Africa and women, one might wonder if anybody can escape this prison of discursive discipline. Are we all trapped in an eternal and guilt-ridden condemnation? Has emancipation become an ideal of the past, only possible if linked to a modernist conceptualization of power in which 'good' and 'bad' can be clearly distinguished? What room to manoeuvre is still left for engagement in and through organizational ethnography?

_____ *engagement in or beyond complicity?* _____

If, as the postmodern critique of power suggests, everybody is part of the same disciplinary configuration up to his or her neck, and therefore considered complicit in its very existence, what room is left for the organizational ethnographer's engagement with the dominated? For us, complicity does not necessarily imply an end to an engagement with the less-powerful in organization and management; neither does it mean a sudden death for the ideals of emancipation in and through organizational ethnography. Nor does it have to imply or give organizational ethnographers the sense that every intervention and change in organization and management is *a priori* doomed to be drowned, so to speak, in the collective swamp of discursive practices within organizations. What is needed is a rethinking of the notions of agency, change and intervention within organizations.

Organizational ethnography could play a crucial role in the task of rethinking all this, given its status as a discipline in the margins of academia (cf. Das and Poole, 2004). Organizational ethnographers might be ideally positioned to accept complicity, rejecting the arrogance of 'being on the moral high ground' close to the less-powerful alone, and reflecting upon their positions through and within discursive practices. Embarking on this reflective journey might launch a contribution towards rethinking the consequences of the postmodern critique of modernist conceptualizations of the concept of power, along with reconceptualizing processes of engagement in organization and management. Let us explain how this could be done by returning to South Africa for a moment, before suggesting a direction towards moving beyond complicity in and through organizational ethnography.

On the basis of the notion of the 'banality of evil', the Truth and Reconciliation Commission (TRC) in South Africa argued, with an eye toward creating breathing space for those charged as accomplices, that the recognition of complicity implies 'not washing one's hands but actively affirming a complicity, or potential complicity', which then could lead to 'a heightening of personal responsibility' (Sanders, 2002: 3; cf. Judt, 1998). Not in any way referring to the example of South Africa, ironically enough, Janssens and Steyaert (2001) provide perfect examples for this perspective. From the context of organization and management practices, written in the spirit of the French postmodernists, these authors propose possible strategies and tactics for organizational ethnographers to translate their personal engagement and sense of responsibility in an unjust world, and move beyond complicity. In their conceptualization of what they call the 'praxis of difference', Janssens and Steyaert discern three levels (personal, interactional and societal), with three tactics related to each level (summarized on Janssens and Steyaert, 2001: 235–6). The first level concerns how to perceive the Other ('alterity', primarily based on French philosophers like Serres, Lyotard, Derrida, Deleuze and Guattari, and feminist writers like Kristeva and Hill Collins); the second, how to try to communicate with the Other ('dialogue', primarily based on Bakhtin's work); the third, how to fit multiculturality into a democratic framework within society and its organizations ('democracy', primarily based on the work of Giddens and Urry). We limit ourselves here to a discussion of those tactics in the context of organizational ethnography, related to answering the question of how people could perceive the Other, in order to suggest how engagement *beyond* complicity could be envisioned in ethnographies of organization and management. We add a fourth tactic to those of Janssen and Steyaert, drawing on the learning experiences of doing research in organization and management in the context of South Africa.

moving beyond complicity through organizational ethnography?

The first tactic Janssen and Steyaert suggest in relation to 'alterity' is, following Serres, 'to step aside', meaning to step into the margins of power in order to create space for one's own voice from the perspective of difference, rather than conforming to the dominant norm. This distance and distancing from 'the centre' could create novel ways of, and space for, relating to the other. By giving away one's position, one at the same time 'gives way' (ibid.: 106); one does not have to protect or defend one's space. Constantly 'giving way' creates a *perpetuum mobile* which prevents people from becoming 'tied' into positions of power (Serres in Janssen and Steyaert, 2001: 106). Constantly stepping aside is like dancing; and dance becomes the metaphor not only for giving way, but also for creating a new meeting ground that is devoid of the antagonisms of power.

This links to the second tactic – 'creating safe spaces' from where people can build their self esteem and self definition in order to be able to resist the power processes linked to Othering. Here, Janssen and Steyaert follow feminist writer Patricia Hill Collins, who argues that 'creating safe spaces' proposes a different kind of resistance, compared to identity politics. In Janssen and Steyaert's view, resistance through identity politics is always a reaction to 'the centre', automatically becoming part of the dominant power structure of 'the centre' itself (in the words of Derrida, opposition becomes 'contaminated' by the centre). 'Creating safe spaces' as resistance, by contrast, introduces a clear distance from 'the centre' (preventing 'contamination' through resistance), through which participants get the chance to position themselves through difference.

The third tactic is to develop yourself into someone able to listen to the Other, in terms of trying to 'becoming other' (Deleuze and Guattari, cited in Janssens and Steyaert, 2001: 122). The formulation has strong associations with Geertz's (1973) 'doing ethnography', which is also basically about developing a heightened sense of empathy for the Other. This parallel with the ethnographic approach is probably no coincidence. The ethnographic approach seems ideally positioned to reflect on the possibilities of engagement beyond complicity. What follows is why we think organizational ethnography can move beyond complicity.

The core notion of ethnographic work is to become engaged with the research setting. In this becoming-part-of, the research process and the researched enable the researcher to develop an in-depth, multi-layered understanding of processes of interaction in the field. The idea of being both a participant and an observer often makes researchers so much a part of the process that they even become contaminated with the complicities involved in that process. This is the risk posed by any kind of engaged research in which the balance of involvement and distance is constantly shifting. However, the organizational ethnographer's 'chosen' engagement also provides reflective space for researchers, almost forcing them to be challenged by the unexpected observations entailed in the research process itself. In this bottom-up, emic approach there is space for a deeper understanding of the views and experiences from the field because they are embedded in the connections and interactions in the field. In this way, the constructed binaries of otherness are not taken as a point of departure, but rather the situations and realms in which people actually meet and in which various forms of otherness intersect and have to be reconciled in the process and on the spot. Binary oppositions are situationally reconciled. The point of departure for the organizational ethnographer is the situational logic of acting, or 'the layered, complex and ambiguous configuration of rules that enter the game through the acting of actors in a specific (organizational) arena' (Glastra, 1999: 76; author's translation).

The bottom-up, engaged nature of ethnographies of organizations enables us to observe the complexities of the processes of inequality in organizations beyond modernist binaries like powerful versus powerless. Making complicity visible within the research process helps to spread the responsibilities for change, as the burden of complicity and the responsibilities that come with it are carried by all. In this, we are particularly inspired by postcolonial approaches in which the aim is not to deny 'the brute features of domination of power' but to provide 'a more sophisticated, nuanced, and complex reading' of power in organizations (Prasad, 1997: 288).

What is still missing, though, is an association with the powerful (cf. Koot, 1995), which we argue is a *sine qua non* condition for the development of an engagement beyond complicity. It is here that we want to add a fourth tactic, reconciliation. Without going into detail (for a critical reflection see, for instance, Soyinka, 1999), it can be argued that an active pursuit of reconciliation between the less-powerful and the dominant powers is an almost logical follow up to the three tactics described earlier. Engaging with alterity cannot come full circle without an active 'tactic', to stick to Janssen and Steyaert's wording, towards reconciling the two 'assumed' antagonists, i.e. the less-powerful and the powerful. When power is placed within the discourse, then the 'discourse produce[s] (and naturalize[s]) the subjectivities'[9] of both the powerful and the powerless. Reconciliation comes after a recognition and admission of complicity; reconciliation does not deny complicity. Through reconciliation all participants in the power configuration, both powerful and powerless, are able to move beyond complicity. In that way, reconciliation fits the postmodern discourse on power.

It is here that the example of South Africa's experiences with an active pursuit of reconciliation through the TRC is relevant. The dominant powers of this world all look in amazement and admiration to South Africa, where after so much antagonism under apartheid, reconciliation is propagated instead of revenge. Nelson Mandela and Bishop Tutu have become icons of the process. This is not to say that in South Africa the antagonism between the powerful and powerless is over, or that South Africa has become a multicultural utopia or the Rainbow Nation it was proclaimed to become (see for instance Sparks, 2003). But it did show the world how extreme antagonism, through an active policy of reconciliation in which admitting complicity was part of the process, has 'given way' to 'safe spaces' in which the (once) powerful and the (once) less-powerful created an opportunity to listen to the multivocality of the situation. It is therefore rather odd to observe that they haven't proceeded with this active pursuit of reconciliation on a state level in the sphere of equity policies in organizational and management practices, but have (re)turned to the old modernist stances of identity and power politics.

For the organizational ethnographer, engagement in and beyond complicity is possible through taking a more active responsibility for contributing to a more just world and trying to reconcile antagonisms in power configurations. The possibilities to do so can perhaps best be seen on a continuum reaching from the pole of an active mediating role in the power configurations in organizations and management, to the opposite pole of explicitly contextualizing ethnographic analysis in a reconciliatory discourse in the resulting ethnographic texts. Instead of using a combat-like discourse suggesting 'struggle', 'fight' and 'justice', organizational ethnographers could write their texts more explicitly in words that promote and evoke reconciliation. The organizational ethnographer is ideally positioned to do this because of his or her temporality in the field and paradoxical status between belonging and non-belonging. Temporality means that the ethnographer is not likely to become fixed in the power configurations; it gives the organizational ethnographer room to manoeuvre. The 'betwixt and between' (Turner, 1969) position of the organizational ethnographer results in a structural liminality,[10] which is a primary asset in the postmodern condition, as it enables manoeuvring within existing organizational power configurations and exploring and experimenting with possibilities for reconciliation (such as the 'safe spaces' discussed). The liminal position makes the organizational ethnographer just informed enough to be 'acceptable' to all stakeholders, without being associated permanently with one or another party within the power configuration.

In this fashion, engagement beyond complicity seems to be an option after all. It requires more ears than opinions; more ideals than solutions; more patience than activism; more humility than arrogance; more thinking than talking; more reading than writing; more doubt than certainties; and more feeling than rationality. Complicity requires engagement, and the latter can be informed by the specific characteristics and position of organizational ethnography.

notes

[1] What we argue in this chapter should not be confused with what is coined by Van de Ven (2007) as 'engaged scholarship'. Van de Ven defines this concept 'as a participative form of research for obtaining the different perspectives of key stakeholders (...) in studying complex problems. By involving others and leveraging their different kinds of knowledge, engaged scholarship can produce knowledge that is more penetrating and insightful than when scholars or practitioners work on the problems alone' (2007: 9). We argue that organizational ethnography offers possibilities for engagement that moves beyond complicity, instead of operationalizing 'engagement' as (multi- and interdisciplinary) participation.

[2] In this chapter we won't deal with the otherwise very informative debates and reflections around engagements (and complicities!) in the actual practice of ethnographic fieldwork in the context of changing 'zeitgeists' (especially the role of the anthropological discipline in the European colonial enterprise (complicity) and later decolonization (engagement). For a critical and reflective comment on Geertz's extensive fieldwork, particularly in the 1950s–60s in relation to the uses of complicity in 'doing ethnography', see Marcus, 1997.

[3] In this chapter we will not go into arguing, morally or otherwise, why organizational ethnographers should be engaged, or why (political) engagement in the social sciences matters at all. This falls outside the scope of this chapter. For this type of discussion see for instance Van der Stoep, 2005, on the work and engagement of Pierre Bourdieu (as we also base our argument in this chapter to a large extent on the influences and inspiration of French intellectuals).

[4] For more on this see Braidotti, 1994.

[5] Detailed ethnographic accounts of management have also been published, see for instance Watson, 1994; Koot and Sabelis, 2000.

[6] This section is based on earlier work presented in Spierenburg and Wels (2004), which condenses into an edited volume four extensive ethnographic accounts, based on students' ethnographic fieldwork in South Africa on issues in organization and management related to equity.

[7] We assume a general knowledge among our readers concerning the history of apartheid in South Africa, and we will therefore not go into that aspect of historical contextualization in this chapter. For those interested see Ross, 1999. For a largely political and economic contextualization of the promise and performance of post-apartheid South Africa, see for instance the trilogy by Allister Sparks (1990, 1994, 2003).

[8] Especially because the 'primary' and only criterion to be chosen into the illustrious *Business Times* (Top 100 Companies in South Africa) is the question of which companies 'have earned the most wealth for their shareholders (…). The winner is the company that earns the most for its shareholders in terms of share price growth, normal dividends, special dividends and bonus shares' (*Sunday Times*, 9 November 2003): equity is not even mentioned!

[9] The reference is to Prasad's sentence: 'The discourse of colonization needs to be seen as having worked simultaneously to produce (and naturalize) the subjectivities of both the colonizer and the colonized' (1997: 289).

[10] Victor Turner's work actually deserves closer scrutiny in the context of specifically organizational ethnography, as a follow up to the ideas in this chapter (especially his ideas on liminality in relation to some core concepts we explored briefly, like power relations in postmodern perspectives, complicity and reconciliation).

references

Acker, J. (1992) 'Gendering organizational theory', in A.J. Mills and P. Tancred (eds) *Gendering organizational analysis*. Newbury Park, CA: Sage.

Acker, J. (2006) 'Inequality regimes: Gender, class, and race in organizations', *Gender & Society*, 20: 441–64.

Alvesson, M. and H. Willmott (eds) (2003) *Critical management studies*. London: Sage.

Arendt, H. (1973) [1951] *The origins of totalitarianism*. San Diego, CA: Harcourt.

Asad, T. (ed.) (1973) *Anthropology and the colonial encounter*. London: Ithaca Press.

Ashcroft, B., Griffiths, G. and Tiffin, H. (2000) *Post-colonial studies: The key concepts*. London: Routledge.

Benschop Y. and Doorewaard, H. (1998) 'Covered by equality. The gender subtext of organizations', *Organization Studies*, 19(5): 787–805.

Braidotti, R. (1994) *Nomadic subjects: Embodiment and sexual difference in contemporary feminist theory*. New York: Columbia University Press.

Brouns, M. (1993) *De homo economicus als winkeldochter. Theorieën over arbeid, macht en sekse*. Amsterdam: SUA.

Cape Times (2003) 'Whites still take more Cape jobs', 14 November.

Crowther, D. and Green, M. (2004) *Organisational theory*. London: CIPD.

Das, V. and Poole, D. (2004) *Anthropology in the margins of the state*. Santa Fe/Oxford: School of American Research Press/James Curry.

Deleuze, G. and Guattari, F. (1972) *Anti-Oedipus: Capitalism and schizophrenia*. New York: Viking.

Deleuze, G. and Guattari, F. (1987) *A thousand plateaus: Capitalism and schizophrenia*. The Athlone Press.

Eriksen, Th.H. (1995) *Small places, large issues: An introduction to social and cultural anthropology*. London, New York: Pluto Press.

Eriksen, Th.H. (2006) *Engaging anthropology: The case for a public presence*. Oxford, New York: Berg.

Fabian, J. (1983) *Time and the other: How anthropology makes its object*. New York: Columbia University Press.

February, J. and Abrahams, L. (2001) 'Entrenching equality by countering racism in South Africa: a legislative brief'. Available online: www.uct.ac.za/depts/lrgru/equapaps/february.pdf. Accessed 29 September 2003.

Ferguson, K.E. (1984) *The feminist case against bureaucracy*. Philadelphia: Temple University Press.

Forester, J. (1992) 'Critical ethnography: On fieldwork in a Habermasian way', in M. Alvesson and H. Willmott (eds) *Critical management studies*. London: Sage.

Geertz, C. (1973) *The interpretation of cultures: Selected essays*. New York: Basic Books.

Glastra, F. (1999) *Organisaties en diversiteit: Naar een contextuele benadering van intercultureel management*. Utrecht: Lemma.

Gowricharn, R. (1999) 'De arbeidsmarkt, over driedeling en sociale cohesie', in F. Glastra (ed.) *Organisaties en diversiteit: Naar een contextuele benadering van intercultureel management*. Utrecht: Lemma.

Hardy, C. and Clegg, S.R. (1999) [1996] 'Some dare call it power', in S.R. Clegg and C. Hardy (eds) *Studying organization: Theory and method*. London: Sage. pp. 368–87.

Hirsch, E. and Gellner, D.N. (2001) 'Introduction: Ethnography of organizations and organizations of ethnography', in D.N. Gellner and E. Hirsch (eds) *Inside organizations: Anthropologists at work*. Oxford: Berg.

Hoare, Q. and Nowell Smith, G. (eds) (1978) *Selections from the Prison Notebooks of Antonio Gramsci*, translated by Q. Hoare and G. Nowell Smith. London: Lawrence and Wishart.

Hoetink, H. (1973) *Slavery and race relations in the Americas: Comparative notes on their nature and nexus*. San Francisco, CA: Harper & Row.

Holm, H. (2003) *Breaking the barriers to managing diversity: A case study of staff's perceptions on workforce diversity and relating policies at the University of Natal, South Africa*. Unpublished MA-thesis, Vrije Universiteit Amsterdam, the Netherlands.

Human, L. (1996) 'Managing workforce diversity: A critique and example from South Africa', *International Journal of Manpower*, 17(4/5): 46–65.

Janssen, M. and Steyaert, C. (2001) *Meerstemmigheid: Organiseren met verschil* ['Multivocality: Organising with a difference']. Leuven: Universitaire Pers; Assen: Koninklijke Van Gorcum.

Jeffcut, P. (1994) 'From interpretation to representation in organizational analysis: Postmodernism, ethnography and organizational symbolism', *Organization Studies*, 15(2): 241–74.

Judt, J. (1998) *The burden of responsibility*. Chicago, London: The University of Chicago Press.

Kamsteeg, F. and Wels, H. (2004) 'Anthropology, organizations and interventions: New territory or quicksand?', *Intervention Research. International Journal on Culture, Organization and Management*, 1(1): 7–25.

Kanter, R.M. (1977) *Men and women of the corporation*. New York: Basic Books.

Komter, A. (1990) *De macht van de dubbele moraal*. Amsterdam: Van Gennep.

Komter, A. (1992) 'Het "natuurlijk overwicht" van mannen. Over de macht van de vanzelfsprekendheid in arbeidsorganisaties', in M. Demenint and K. Disselen (eds) *Vrouwen, leiderschap en management*. Utrecht: Lemma. pp. 71–83.

Koot, W.C.J. (1995) *De complexiteit van het alledaagse: Een antropologisch perspectief op organisaties*. Bussum: Coutinho.

Koot, W.C.J. and Sabelis, I.H.J. (2000) *Overleven aan de top: Topmanagers in complexe tijden* [*Beyond complexity: Chief executives coping with complexity*]. Utrecht: Lemma.

Kunda, G. (1992) *Engineering culture: Control and commitment in a high-tech corporation*. Philadelphia: Temple University Press.

Lamphere, L. (2003) 'The perils and prospects for an engaged anthropology: A view from the United States', *Social Anthropology*, 11(2): 153–68.

Linstead, S. (2000) 'Comment: Gender blindness or gender suppression? A comment on Fiona Wilson's Research Note', *Organization Studies*, 21(1): 297–303.

Lukes, S. (1974) *Power: A radical view*. London: Macmillan.

Lyotard, J.F. (1984) *The postmodern condition: A report on knowledge*. Manchester: Manchester University Press.

Marcus, G.E. (1997) 'The uses of complicity in the changing mis-en-scène of anthropological fieldwork', *Representations*, 59 (Special Issue: 'The fate of "Culture": Geertz and beyond'): 85–108.

Martin, J. (2002) *Organizational culture: Mapping the terrain*. Foundations for Organizational Sciences Series. Newbury Park, CA: Sage Publications.

Martin, J., Frost, P. and O'Neill, O.A. (2005) 'Organizational culture: Beyond struggles for intellectual dominance', in S. Clegg, C. Hardy, T. Lawrence, and W. Nord (eds) *The handbook of organization studies*. (2nd edn). Thousand Oaks, CA: Sage.

Miles, R. (1989) *Racism*. London: Routledge.

Morgan, G. (1997) *Images of organizations*. Beverley Hills, CA: Sage.

Morton, S. (2003) *Gayatri Chakravorty Spivak*. London: Routledge.

Orr, L. and Goldman, T. (2001) 'Early experiences with the EEA', *Indicator SA*, 18(3): 13–23.

Phillips, N., Courpasson, D. and Clegg, S. (2006) *Power and organizations*. London: Sage.

Pickering, M. (2001) *Stereotyping: The politics of representation*. New York: Palgrave.

Prasad, A. (1997) 'The colonizing consciousness and representations of the other: A postcolonial critique of the discourse of oil', in P. Prasad, A.J. Mills, M. Elmes and A. Prasad (eds) *Managing the organizational melting pot: Dilemmas of workplace diversity*. Thousand Oaks, CA: Sage. pp. 285–312.

Rigby, P. (1996) *African images: Racism and the end of anthropology*. Oxford, Washinghton, DC: Berg.

Ross, R. (1999) *A concise history of South Africa*. Cambridge, MA: Cambridge University Press.

Said, E. (1993) *Culture and imperialism*. London: Chatto & Windus.

Salemink, O. (1999) 'Beyond complicity and naiveté: Contextualizing the ethnography of Vietnam's Central Highlanders, 1850–1990'. Unpublished PhD thesis, University of Amsterdam.

Sanders, M. (2002) *Complicities: The intellectual and apartheid*. Pietermaritzburg: University of Natal Press.

Snijders, D. (2007) 'Making haste slowly: Affirmative action and the South African labour market'. Unpublished MA thesis, VU University Amsterdam, the Netherlands.

Soyinka, W. (1999) *The burden of memory, the muse of forgiveness*. Oxford: Oxford University Press.

Sparks, A. (1990) *The mind of South Africa: The story of the rise and fall of apartheid*. London: Mandarin.

Sparks, A. (1994) *Tomorrow is another country: The inside story of South Africa's negotiated revolution*. Sandton: Struik Publishers.

Sparks, A. (2003) *Beyond the miracle: Inside the new South Africa*. Johannesburg, Cape Town: Jonathan Ball Publishers.

Spierenburg, M. and Wels, H. (2004) *Culture, organization and management in South Africa: In search of equity*. New York: Nova Science Publishers.

Spivak, G.C. (1987) *In other worlds: Essays in cultural politics*. New York: Methuen.

Sunday Independent (2003) 'Fostering a culture of high quality lifelong learning', 12 October.

Sunday Times (2003a) 'How the top 100 are picked', 9 November.

Sunday Times (2003b) 'The father of black business', 9 November.

This Day (2003a) 'Few businesses submit equity reports', 17 October.

This Day (2003b) 'Changing the pale face of corporate SA', 29 December.

Turner, V. (1969) *The ritual process: Structure and anti structure*. Chicago, IL: Aldine Publishers and London: Routledge & Kegan Paul.

Tutu, D. (1994) *The rainbow people of God: The making of a peaceful revolution*. New York: Doubleday.

Van de Ven, A.H. (2007) *Engaged scholarship: A guide for organizational and social research*. Oxford: Oxford University Press.

Von Holdt, K. (2003) *Transition from below: Forging trade unionism and workplace change in South Africa*. Pietermaritzburg: University of Natal Press.

Watson, T.J. (1994) *In search of management: Culture, chaos and control in managerial work*. London: Routledge.

Wilson, F. (1996) 'Research note: Organizational theory: blind and deaf to gender?', *Organization Studies,* 17(5): 825–42.

Wilson, F. and Thompson, P. (2001) 'Sexual harassment as an exercise of power', *Gender, Work and Organization,* 8(1): 61–83.

The Witness (2003) '"No mercy" for companies that failed to submit equity reports', 3 October.

The Witness (2003) 'Black and white business organisations unite', 13 October.

Van der Stoep, J. (2005) *Pierre Bourdieu en de politieke filosofie van het multiculturalisme.* Published PhD thesis. Kampen: Uitgeverij Kok.

Woods, D. (2000) *Rainbow nation revisited: South Africa's decade of democracy.* London: Deutsch.

Zimbardo, P.G. (2007) *The Lucifer effect: Understanding how good people turn evil.* New York: Random House.

Annotated Bibliography

defining 'organizational ethnography': selection criteria

Dvora Yanow and Karin Geuijen

On several occasions over the last few years, one organizational studies scholar or another has posted an inquiry to some listserve asking for references to organizational ethnographies. The replies have invariably implied the existence of only a few such works, naming the same handful over and again. With the intention, then, of helping to develop this field of study further, we set out to produce a list here. As we intend the book for a wide variety of organizational studies courses, both topical and methodological, it made sense to annotate the entries, by topical theme and by scope of method.

We are acutely aware that compiling a bibliography such as this is tantamount to 'worldmaking' (Goodman, 1978) within in a scholarly field. The ethnographic sensibility that informs our work therefore requires us to reflect on our processes for constructing the list. All such bibliographies must of necessity be incomplete. They are moving targets for several reasons, not least of which is that books are being published all the time, in this case worldwide, and it is difficult to keep up. At the same time, 'organizational ethnography' is a relatively new term, and older works would not have been marked with it, making identifying them harder and more subject to individual scholars' reading habits and evaluative criteria. Within these parameters, deciding what to include and what to exclude required us to engage a fundamental question. The field of organizational ethnography has, after all, no canon, unlike organizational theory, where such a compilation might begin with Max Weber, Henri Fayol, Frederick Winslow Taylor, Luther Gulick, Joan Woodward, Tom Burns and G.M. Stalker, and proceed from there. The list, then, is an artifact of the process that produced it. Others, with other resources, following other processes, might have produced a different list. Out criteria for inclusion (and exclusion) rested on methodological (ethnographic), substantive (organizational), and publication genre grounds, as follows.

To be counted methodologically as an organizational ethnography and included in this bibliography, a work had to meet the threefold criteria identified in the introduction to this book: methods, writing, and sensibility. This means it had to rely on ethnographic methods, or 'ethnographyies': observing (with whatever degree of participating), talking to people, and the close reading of research-relevant organizational documents, in some combination. The writing had to be in narrative form, with data details more or less thickly described (see Schwartz-Shea and Yanow, Chapter 3, this volume), rather than the more succinct textual form associated with presenting survey research or statistical analyses of various sorts. Finally, the text needed to express the ethnographic sensibility that would convince the reader of the trustworthiness of the author as well as of the findings s/he presented. Sensibility, as noted in the introduction to the book, is a diffuse concept, difficult to define. As it would be hard, in the end, to achieve an ethnographic sensibility in a manuscript without also engaging in the first two characteristics (methods and writing), this point was rendered something of a moot criterion, except in the following circumstance.

What these selection criteria ruled out methodologically were works relying on interviewing alone, even when their authors claimed to have produced an ethnography. At the same time, we did not rule out 'mixed methods' research per se (research combining surveys, for example, with ethnographic methods) as long as the ethnographic part of the research was clearly more than illustrative in the study. This meant that the third criterion – that elusive sensibility – would have to come into play throughout the work. Its presence in the narrative account as well as in the field is a key element in what demarcates an ethnography that *also* uses interviewing or surveys from an interview- or survey-based study. By comparison, many fictional works (e.g., Lodge, 1988) capture that ethnographic sensibility as they treat life in organizations; but they are based on imagination rather than on systematic, scientific inquiry and do not seek to examine theoretical arguments.

Other kinds of books presented other issues for our methodological decision-making. We decided to include books based on ethnographic methods containing a key chapter that is an organizational ethnography, but which otherwise would not qualify as fully ethnographic as they have more of a theoretical focus than a 'site' focus (for example, Goffman, 1961; Manning, 1977). In these choices, we were swayed once again by the presence of an ethnographic sensibility in parts of the books, even when the entire narrative did not take a strictly organizational ethnographic perspective as its point of departure. We did not, for example, include another study by Goffman (1959) whose focus is much more general-theoretical and is not directly based on ethnographic fieldwork within one or more organizations with a goal of telling the reader about these organizations as such. From a methodological perspective, works such as these raise key questions about the role of generalization in ethnographic research, as well as about the relationship between theorizing and data presentation. We also considered a few books that might be considered ethnographic in written form, but whose methods were not ethnographic, such as Martin (1992). While this work is considered by many to be an important cultural study of an organization, and it does reflect on problems associated with ethnographic writing, as it is based on interviews only rather than on 'being there', we have omitted it on methodological grounds.

Second, we needed to define organization in order to determine whether a work was an *organizational* ethnography. This proved to be far more difficult than one might guess. Should we, for instance, include studies that explored occupations, professions or other forms of work? This would open the door to a long list of 'sociology of work' (and, to a lesser extent, 'anthropology of work') research.[1] The question of what an organization is has long been the subject of debate, and we will not repeat it here in all its complexities (see, for example, Bolman and Deal, 1984; Fineman et al., 2005; Hatch and Cunliffe, 2006; McAuley et al., 2007; Morgan, 1986; Shafritz et al., 2005). Thinking this through, we decided to use as criteria those research topics that feature in organizational studies scholarship, ranging from structure to processes of organizing, from human relations to politics, from culture to economics (see, for example, Bolman and Deal, 1984; Morgan, 1986), involving various organizational levels, from shop floor workers to middle managers to chief executives, but also including external relations with clients and/or customers, governmental regulators, and other organizations, across a range of organizational types, from government agencies to corporations, health care to education, and so forth. If studies of work were situated in organizational contexts and engaged organizational studies topics such as these, we included them (for example, Abolafia, 1996; Zabusky, 1995). If they focused primarily on characteristics of work absent in an organizational context, we did not (for example, Kolb, 1983). The resulting bibliography reflects the breadth of the organizational studies field.

Furthermore, to make the research to produce it and its use more manageable, we needed to limit the size of the list, and so we decided to use the publication genre as the criterion. We have included only book length monographs: edited volumes, journal articles, and conference papers have been excluded. To make the list useful internationally, we have included only those works published by university or trade publishers and therefore likely to be publicly available and accessible, leaving out dissertations published by dissertation publishers. For the same reason, we have excluded books that are not written in English (for example, Ybema, 2003), it being today's academic lingua franca in most parts of the world. We recognize that the choice of language and publisher, together with biases embedded within the US-dominated field of organizational studies, have produced a list that is heavily slanted toward studies of Western organizations, from Western-influenced points of view. As the field of organizational ethnography grows, we look forward to a growing number of studies conducted of non-Western organizations and by non-Western-educated scholars (although language will continue to be a decisional Occam's razor).

Other interesting definitional challenges presented themselves along the way. 'Organization' has long referred to an entity with definable boundaries; but new technologies, new global work arrangements, and new types of 'political action' have led to new organizational forms that depart from traditional ones, with important consequences for the conduct of ethnography, itself prosecuted, historically, face to face within a geographically-located and bounded setting.

New kinds of organizations have come into being that are no longer territorially based in part or in whole. These include network organizations in which different combinations of people work together on a temporary basis to complete a particular project, or 'action nets' (interconnected nets of organizing; Czarniawska, 1997) with people working together but located in different places, sometimes even on different continents. Treating 'organizational studies' within the context of business, we would have to consider various forms of entrepreneurship; but if we include studies of two-person entrepreneurships (Down, 2006), should we also be considering the single entrepreneur? What about globalized cooperation in entrepreneurship and enterprise cultures based on relationships among business, ethnicity, religion, and nation-state policies such as ex-patriot Chinese doing business in Malaysia and other countries (for example, Dahles, 2007; Koning, 2007). There are also hybrid organizations that combine elements of geographically-based organizations with virtual ones; organizations based on (or at least that enable) tele-commuting, with employees working from home or at the client's or customer's organization or in the car. These sometimes result in what look like boundary-less organizations in which the lines between home and work are blurred, much as they were in pre-modern times. New technologies have also enabled new forms of political action and, with them, new forms of organizing, ranging from anti-globalization activism (which potentially links organizational studies to the social movement literature) to Al Qaeda.

And then there is the online world: is, for example, an online community an organization? Baym (2000) analyses a soap opera Usenet group, which consists of people who share neither a geographic location nor a set of artefacts, who are not all online simultaneously and who combine aspects of interpersonal communication with mass communication. These forms of communication provide structural resources with which members create practices, norms, relationships, and identities that come to define the group (Baym, 2000: 14). These kinds of activities can be defined as 'shared engagement in a project' (ibid., 2000: 22) or as 'organized institutions of interpretation' (ibid., 2000: 17).

Reviewing these studies, it becomes increasingly clear that organizing, in many cases, no longer necessarily takes place, as in our scholarly imaginary (we think) it used to, in one clearly demarcated space in which things are done one at a time. Instead, it is also fragmented, and sometimes done at a much faster pace than formerly: many things happen at the same time, and the people studied are constantly 'already elsewhere' (Czarniawska, 2007: 16). As Van Maanen (2001) has noted, developments like these problematize the traditional holistic perspective that organizational ethnographies inherited from anthropological forebears.

Under these circumstances, what does it mean to conduct an ethnography? Is it multi-sited ethnography (Marcus, 1995), 'fieldwork on the move' or 'moving ethnology' (Czarniawska, 2007), or is it a 'virtual ethnography' (Hine, 2000)? What does an ethnography of a distributed organization look like, or even more so, a virtual one? What would count as 'being there' in virtual organizations whose 'members' communicate by way of email, discussion forums, and other non-place-specific, non-face-to-face virtual modes, such as Second Life? What is the 'there-ness' of the organization, and what happens to 'observation', 'participation', and 'ethnographic interviewing' (Spradley, 1979) when these are mediated by computers, interactive web pages, Skype, instant messaging, and mobile phone messaging? Might there really be a place for relatively faster, shorter ethnographic research (although we continue to resist 'fly-through' studies), and how would this achieve the immersion of place-ness that is so central to an ethnographic sensibility? Some textbooks and articles treating these issues from a methods perspective are available (for example, Hakken, 1999), but very few book-length studies have been written showing what such new organizational ethnographies might look like (see, for example, Baym, 2000, for an exception).

And finally, what about forms of (re)presentation? Under contemporary organizational circumstances, perhaps ethnographic writing needs to expand to include multimedia technologies, either instead of or in addition to paper. We acknowledge Van Maanen's (2001: 239) plea for methodologically broadened, interdisciplinary ethnography: the legitimacy of social observation beyond what he calls 'the fetish of fieldwork', the tête à tête of interpersonal interaction. These fundamental shifts in the character of organizing make for interesting assessments of contemporary literature in light of both substantive and methodological definitions rooted in earlier times and their experiences and definitions.

In sum, then, this annotated bibliography includes often-classical works produced in the 1930s, 1940s, and 1950s as well as those reflecting a renewed interest since the 1990s. The works included here are wide-ranging both in empirical scope and in theoretical focus. They cover a variety of organizational settings, be these commercial or public (for example, corporations or police forces); political or bureaucratic (for example, members of parliament or the dynamics of bureaucracy); territorially-based or virtual; hierarchically-led or network-shaped. And they take very different theoretical perspectives:

examining power relations (for example, managerial or shop floor-focused), the role of agency and context, social or other identities, culture, gender, or interventions and organizational change. The list includes studies of single organizations as well as comparative studies of two or a small set of organizations.

a note on sources

Bibliography-making is an exercise in category-construction. One relies, first and foremost, on subject categories constructed by librarians using the latest in library science thinking, and categorizing systems proliferate, especially when searching across national boundaries: Library of Congresss (US), Dewey Decimal System (US), PiCarta (NL), Google or Google Scholar, and other internet search engines have made the task easier, on the one hand – one can control one's search terms oneself, generate new combinations of terms, and so forth – but harder, on the other, as the number of entries proliferates beyond control. Moreover, the choice of search terms and of criteria for inclusion/exclusion reflects the purposes for which a bibliography is being constructed, and these themselves reflect a membership of particular epistemic communities and professional networks.

Our sources included university library and other electronic databases, searching on 'organis(z)ational ethnography'. We also used a kind of 'snowball method' applied to the reference lists of our growing bibliography, supplemented by lists from methods articles, book chapters, and books (including, for example, Van Maanen, 2001). We were assisted by lists compiled by others, including Randy Hodson (although in the end we have used it mostly to clarify our thinking about what not to include; see note 1), and ourselves and colleagues for classroom and thesis teaching purposes in the Department of Culture, Organization, and Management at the Vrije Universiteit, Amsterdam.

[1] In a US National Science Foundation-funded project, sociologist Randy Hodson has compiled a list of workplace ethnographies (204 cases, drawn from 156 books), coded for 150 organizational, workforce, human relations, and management variables, each focusing on a specific group of workers within an organization (available at http://www.sociology. ohio-state.edu/rdh/Workplace-Ethnography-Project.html; last accessed 5 June 2008). While this provided an interesting resource, most of the entries did not meet our criteria for organizational studies. The Society for the Anthropology of Work (SAW) of the Amercian Anthropological Association has other resources (http://www.aaanet.org/saw/index.htm; last accessed 18 July 2008).

references

Abolafia, M. (1996) *Making markets: Opportunism and restraint on Wall Street.* Cambridge, MA: Harvard University Press.

Baym, N. (2000) *Tune in, log on: Soaps, fandom and online community.* Thousand Oaks, CA: Sage.

Bolman, L. and Deal, T. (1984) *Reframing organizations.* San Franciso, CA: Jossey-Bass.

Czarniawska, B. (1997) *Narrating organizations: Dramas of institutional identity.* Chicago: University of Chicago Press.

Czarniawska, B. (2007) *Shadowing and other techniques for doing fieldwork in modern societies.* Malmö: Liber AB.

Dahles, H. (2007) 'Creating social capital as competitive advantage in China: Singapore Chinese entrepreneurs venturing into China', in S. Clegg, Y. Wang and M. Barrell (eds) *Business networks and strategic alliances in China.* Cheltenham: Edward Elgar. pp. 182–208.

Down, S. (2006) *Narratives of enterprise: Crafting entrepreneurial self-identity in a small firm.* Cheltenham: Edward Elgar.

Fineman, S., Sims, D. and Gabriel, Y. (2005) *Organizing and organizations* (3rd edn). London: Sage.

Goffman, E. (1959) *The presentation of self in everyday life.* New York: Anchor Books.

Goffman, E. (1961) *Asylums: Essays on the social situation of mental patients and other inmates.* Harmondsworth: Penguin Books.

Goodman, N. (1978) *Ways of worldmaking.* Indianapolis, IN: Hackett Publishing Co.

Hakken, D. (1999) *Cyborgs@cyberspace? An ethnographer looks to the future.* New York: Routledge.

Hammersley, M. (1992) *What's wrong with ethnography? Methodological explorations.* London: Routledge.

Hatch, M.J. and Cunliffe, A.L. (2006) *Organization theory* (2nd edn). Oxford: Oxford University Press.

Hine, C. (2000) *Virtual ethnography.* Thousand Oaks, CA: Sage.

Kolb, D. (1983) *The mediators.* Cambridge, MA: MIT Press.

Koning, J. (2007) 'Chineseness and Chinese Indonesian business practices: A generational and discursive enquiry', in Can Seng Ooi and Juliette Koning (eds) 'The business of identity: To be or not to Chinese'. Special Issue, *East Asia: An International Quarterly* 24: 129–52.

Lodge, D. (1988) *Nice work.* London: Secker & Warburg.

Manning, P. (1977) *Police work: The social organization of policing.* Cambridge, MA: MIT Press.

Marcus, G. (1995) Ethnography in/of the world system: The emergence of multi-sited ethnography. *Annual Review of Anthropology* 24: 95–115.

Martin, J. (1992) *Cultures in organizations: Three perspectives.* Oxford: Oxford University Press.

McAuley, J., Duberley, J. and Johnson, P. (2007) *Organization theory: Challenges and perspectives.* Harlow: Pearson.

Morgan, G. (1986) *Images of organization.* Beverly Hills, CA: Sage.

Shafritz, J.M., Ott, J.S. and Jang, Y.S. (2005) *Classics of organization theory* (6th edn). Belmont, CA: Thomson Wadsworth.

Spradley, J.P. (1979) *The ethnographic interview.* New York: Holt, Rinehart and Winston.

Van Maanen, J. (2001) 'Afterword', in David Gellner and E. Hirsch (eds) *Inside organizations: Anthropologists at work.* Oxford: Berg. pp. 233–61.

Ybema, S. (2003) *De koers van de krant: Vertogen over identiteit bij Trouw en de Volkskrant* [Discourses on tradition and transition: Conflict about the newspaper's identity among editors of *Trouw and de Volkskrant*]. VU University, Amsterdam: published PhD dissertation.

Zabusky, S. (1995) *Launching Europe: An ethnography of European cooperation in space science.* Princeton: Princeton University Press.

Karin Geuijen

Abolafia, M. (1996) *Making markets: Opportunism and restraint on Wall Street.* **Cambridge, MA: Harvard University Press.**

Theme: Formal (rules and formal structures) and informal (norms) arrangements are constructed to avoid fraud and manipulation in three different kinds of financial market: futures, bonds, and stocks. Dynamic 'cycles of opportunism' are produced by the strategies that individuals and groups employ to handle the tension between individual self-interest and collective, institutional restraints.

Methods: Fieldwork (observation, interviews, and document analysis) on and near three trading floors between 1979 and 1992: futures market, five years, starting in1980; bond market traders at four of the ten largest Wall Street investment banks, October 1987–March 1989; New York Stock Exchange floor, 1990–1992.

Alvesson, M. (1995) *Management of knowledge-intensive firms.* **Berlin: De Gruyter.**

Theme: Management and control structures and processes and their consequences for employees at 'Enator', a Swedish computer consulting firm (a knowledge-intensive company) with about 500 employees across some 20 subsidiaries, each with one to 50 employees. Enator worked explicitly with culture as part of management and organizational operations. The study treats 11 corporate phenomena as symbols, among these the building, the business concept, and the project management philosophy course, perceived as 'keys' to the cultural understanding of the company.

Methods: Over a six-month period in 1987, three weeks of participant observation, plus interviews with 35 individuals, averaging 1.5 hours each, with an additional 15 brief conversations and some studies of corporate documents. Central was participation in the company's course on project management philosophy, attended by all employees. Chapter 4 on Qualitative Research and Philosophy of Science; section 4.6 on methods.

Barker, James R. (1999) *The discipline of teamwork: Participation and concertive control.* **Thousand Oaks, CA: Sage.**

Theme: The process of implementing self-directed work teams in a high-tech manufacturing company, the way team members discipline themselves and each other during this process ('concertive control'), and its consequences for the work experiences and identities of the team members.

Methods: Self-described ethnographic organizational culture study from a shop-floor perspective: observations of the manufacturing process, formal and informal meetings of teams, plus hundreds of interviews in day-to-day interactions during three years in the early 1990s at ISE Communications, a Colorado manufacturer of electronic circuit boards used for voice and data transmission equipment.

Barley, S. and Kunda, G. (2004) *Gurus, hired guns and warm bodies: Itinerant experts in a knowledge economy.* **Princeton, NJ: Princeton University Press.**

Theme: The shift from permanent employment to contract work for high-tech sector technicians brings them autonomy but also uncertainty, which they cope with by constantly maintaining and updating their human and social capital (their knowledge and networks). Focuses on the diverse reasons for contracting instead of hiring permanent staff and the implications of these new relationships for contractors, managers, and permanent employees.

Methods: One year of participant observation in three staffing agencies (starting November 1997), life histories with over 70 contractors (during 1998 and 1999), and studies of workers in some Silicon Valley firms that routinely employed technical contractors. Evidence consists of description of the perspectives and practices of people in different occupational groups: details of what the authors saw and heard, the patterns they found in the data, and the sense they made of those patterns.

Bartunek, J. (2003) *Organizational and educational change: The life and role of a change agent group.* **Mahwah, NJ: Lawrence Erlbaum Associates.**

Theme: The development of identities, actions, and stakeholder relations over seven years (from origin until fading) of a self-managed team, the Network Faculty Development Committee, an initiative to empower experienced teachers within a federated Catholic school system.

Methods: A longitudinal ethnographic study observing the meetings of the teachers' network from the mid-1980s to their ending in 1995. Each of the first seven years is described in a separate chapter.

Becker, H.S., Geer, B., Hughes, E. and Strauss, A. (1961) *Boys in white.* **Chicago: University of Chicago Press.**

Theme: Medical students' reactions to what they perceive as faculty's unrealistic demands, how they feel about their training in general, their teachers, and the profession that they are training to enter. The focus here is on the formal and informal aspects of the work environment.

Methods: Participant observation in classes, wards, laboratories, and operating theatres. Particular groups of students were observed intensively for periods ranging from one week to two months, supplemented with informal-casual and formal-structured interviews with 62 students plus faculty. Part I, 'Background and methods' (pp. 1–63); ethnographic methods detailed in Chapter 2, 'Design of the study' (pp. 17–32).

Bennett, W.L. and Feldman, M.S. (1981) *Reconstructing reality in the courtroom.* **London: Tavistock.**

Theme: Communication and judgment in trials. Criminal trial is not an objective process, but one organized around plausibility in story-telling and story-hearing which concerns the abilities of the actors involved. Accounts perceived as plausible are well-formed, containing many events that are relevant to the endpoint and numerous causal linkages among the story's elements.

Methods: An ethnographic study of more than 60 criminal trials in the Superior Court, King County (Seattle), Washington: observation's of court proceedings and in hallways; quasi-interviews and formal interviews. The initial video-taping of an actual trial; later, some communication experiments (with students testing researchers' theory development), and the analysis of transcripts of trials. Chapter 1 is on methods (pp. 3–18).

Blau, P. (1963) [1955] *The dynamics of bureaucracy: A study of interpersonal relations in two government agencies.* **Chicago: University of Chicago Press.**

Theme: Investigation of small groups of officials in two government agencies, a state employment agency and a federal law enforcement agency, on the processes of social interaction and the ways in which these relations influenced operations. Focuses on the conditions for change in government agencies and the role of internal tensions and cohesion.

Methods: Three months of observations of officials in both agencies (offices, field visits, lunches, etc.), but also of reviewers and stenographers, in 1948–49, followed by interviews. The Methodological Epilogue (pp. 269–305) contains a reflective chapter on 'Fieldwork in Bureaucracy' (pp. 269–86).

Bosk, C. (1979) *Forgive and remember: Managing medical failure.* **Chicago: University of Chicago Press.**

Theme: How the medical profession is interpreted, acted on, and defended by professionals as seen through a case study of a surgical training programme, including issues of deviance, medical failure, and social controls. Focus on how professional self-controls are instilled in trainees by the senior surgeons who train them, how privileges and responsibilities to patients and colleagues are conceptualized, and how the professional conscience gets structured.

Methods: Eighteen months of participant observation of the surgical training programme of Pacific Hospital, an elite medical institution affiliated with a major medical school and university. Observation of two different surgical services: one high research and low clinical-oriented, and the other low research and high clinical-oriented. Surgeons were followed through their daily activities and actively questioned; researchers attended faculty meetings, examined the written evaluations of house officers, and participated as 'an extra pair of hands', observing as a 'fly on the wall'. One-hour conversational interviews with key informants (house staff and attending physicians) followed on from fieldwork.

Burawoy, M. (1979) *Manufacturing consent: Changes in the labour process under monopoly capitalism.* **Chicago: University of Chicago Press.**

Theme: Shop-floor informal culture of 'playing the game' of 'making out' work practices studied from a Marxist perspective, focusing on the question, 'Why do workers work so hard?' Workers bend and break rules in order to maximize individual profits in the piece-work compensation system.

Methods: Participant observation while working as a miscellaneous machine operator at the engine division of a multinational corporation in Chicago for ten months (July 1974–May 1975) and analysis of managerial records and data, conducted with the explicit consent and knowledge of management.

Chetkovich, C. (1997) *Real heat: Gender and race in the urban fire service.* **New Brunswick: Rutgers University Press.**

Theme: A study of the role of informal structures in how new recruits to firefighting in Oakland, California gained opportunities from their colleagues and bosses to be where the action was, thereby demonstrating their capabilities and building confidence. Includes analysis of minority men and women in the hostile or offensive environment of a masculine 'culture'.

Methods: Eighteen months of ethnographic work at fire stations and during emergency calls (beginning March 1992), including interviews with veterans, members of the administration, etc., and repeated interviews with one class of 38 fire-fighters, including nine women. A subgroup of 26 were observed during their 18 month training period. Towards the end of the fieldwork, the researcher invited responses from members. Includes appendix on methods.

Cole, R.E. (1971) *Japanese blue collar: The changing tradition.* **Berkeley: University of California Press.**

Theme: The Japanese blue-collar worker's world and behaviour, in the context of Japanese tradition and contemporary industrial relations, including institutional and interpersonal commitments and the consequences these have for strengthening or weakening a Japanese corporate group consciousness.

Methods: Participant observation for three months as a machine expediter at Takei Diecast Joint Stock Company in Tokyo and for one month on the clutch assembly line at Gujo Auto Parts Company, supplemented by formal interviews with 15 workers in each location.

Collinson, D.L. (1992) *Managing the shopfloor: Subjectivity, masculinity and workplace culture*. Berlin: De Gruyter.

Theme: The construction of working-class masculinity on the shop-floor for male manual workers in a North-West England, heavy vehicle manufacturing company, 'Slavs', through resistance, compliance, and consent to organizational control.

Methods: Ethnographic research with groups and individuals on the shop-floor as well as on the workers' bus, the pub, and occasionally in people's homes, starting in 1979, supplemented by formal semi-structured interviews with 64 manual workers from every skilled trade represented in the top and bottom machine shops. Lasting between one and seven hours, and additional informal conversations. Includes appendix on methodology (pp. 233–7).

Crewe, E. (2005) *Lords of Parliament: Manners, rituals and politics*. Manchester: Manchester University Press.

Theme: Power, rules, symbols, rituals, hierarchies, and manners in the House of Lords: the way that Lords are socialized into the ways of the House, the way they establish their reputation, and the power relationships among them.

Methods: Fieldwork (1989–2000), including interviews [unstructured with 119 peers, 63 staff, 26 others; structured via two questionnaires, 177/1000 peers and 48/349 staff replied], participant observation [informal conversations in offices; observations of Chambers, meetings, commissions selecting staff; shadowing Inspector's interviews with staff; attending parliamentary ceremonies, social functions; visiting homes of three peers; working in jobs like personal assistant, etc.]). Appendix 2: 'Research methodology' (pp. 241–7).

Crozier, M. (1964) *The bureaucratic phenomenon*. Chicago: University of Chicago Press.

Theme: Vicious circles in bureaucratic organizations lead to rigidity, and periodic reorganizations and crises are potential motors for organizational change. Linking the meso level to the macro level and treating organizations in their contexts, Crozier finds not only organizational structures but also human activities and power relations as crucial for the outcomes of organizational processes.

Methods: Ethnographic fieldwork, as well as interviews and a survey (1955–59), in two large government-controlled organizations in France, one municipal administrative (clerical) and the other a state-owned manufacturing/production organization. The second case involved two successive studies: an intensive look at three plants in the Paris area, and a more superficial look at 20 (out of a total of 30) of Monopoly's plants throughout France.

Czarniawska, B. (1997) *Narrating the organization: Dramas of institutional identity.* **Chicago: University of Chicago Press.**

Theme: Case studies of the daily but hidden workings of public sector local administration and social insurance organizations in Sweden, using literary devices like metaphors.

Methods: An 'anthropologically inspired' study (p. 60) in which the author did 'observant participation' (p. 66) during 14 months, repeatedly asking her interlocutors, located in various parts of the organizations, to tell her what they had been doing at work over the past two or three weeks, visiting each organization ten to 20 times to observe selected events, plus extensive document analysis. Chapter 3: Interpretive studies of organizations: The logic of inquiry (pp. 54–72).

Dalton, M. (1959) *Men who manage: Fusions of feeling and theory in administration.* **New York: Wiley.**

Theme: Managers have to manage the lasting tension between official power and unofficial influences which characterizes intra-organizational conflict and compromise in three factories and one department store in a heavily industrialized area of the central United States. Official and unofficial rewards and punishment are resources for managers adapting to diverse circumstances involving formal and informal 'roles' and horizontal and vertical 'cliques'.

Methods: Formal interviewing, work diaries, participant observation as a member of staff in two of the firms before and during the research period, seeking understanding from a perspective 'as close as possible to the world of managers' (p. 1). Role as researcher was covert to management, overt to some of the staff. Appendix on methods (pp. 273–85).

Delbridge, R. (1998) *Life on the line in contemporary manufacturing: The workplace experience of lean production and the 'Japanese' model.* **Oxford: Oxford University Press.**

Theme: The influence that Japanese management techniques like 'just-in-time production' and 'total quality management' have had on the way work is organized in 'transplants' and other firms and sectors.

Methods: Ethnographic research: participant observation working on the shop-floor during four months' immersion. Chapter 2 on methods and methodology (pp. 13–39).

Down, S. (2006) *Narratives of enterprise: Crafting entrepreneurial self-identity in a small firm.* **Cheltenham: Edward Elgar.**

Theme: Two entrepreneurs – Paul and John – and their firm 'Fenderco' – a small joint venture firm based in a small market town in middle-England designing and selling fendering equipment that stops ship hulls and wharf sides from being damaged in berthing and manoeuvering procedures, with larger and corporate partners based in Europe and Australia – use narrative resources to construct their identity as entrepreneurs. The book also examines the social contexts in which self-identity narratives are spoken.

Methods: Ethnographic research (observations and interviews) conducted intermittently for two and a half years (1996–1998) hanging around for many hours in the office, on site, at Paul's home, and in the pub. The research depended on narrative accounts by the respondents of their pasts and the choices and decisions they made. Appendix on methods (pp. 118–28).

Feldman, M. (1989) *Order without design: Information production and policy making.* **Palo Alto: Stanford University Press.**

Theme: How bureaucrats generate information for reports for policy-makers and politicans, and how organizations develop cognitive understandings of issues and problems in their environments and of themselves through the interpretations constructed in these reports. The study focuses on analysts in the policy office of the US Department of Energy, which has to cooperate with the legal office and a programme office in order to create new policies.

Methods: Observing and participating during one and one-half years as an analyst in the policy office. Observations of meetings and discussions within the policy office and between them and other offices, complemented by interviews and analyses of analysts' written reports. Chapter 3: 'Method and data' (pp. 27–34).

Fine, G.A. (1996) *Kitchens: The culture of restaurant work.* **Berkeley: University of California Press.**

Theme: The organizational culture, structure, and working conditions in restaurant kitchens, both individually and as part of a larger culinary culture.

Methods: Participant observation in four restaurant kitchens for one month each (within an eight month period), complemented by interviews with all full-time cooks working in these restaurants. Appendix on methods: 'An ethnography in the kitchen' (pp. 233–53).

Foner, N. (1994) *The caregiving dilemma: Work in an American nursing home.* **Berkeley: University of California Press.**

Theme: Nursing aides in nursing homes are expected to provide care that is responsive to residents' needs, while at the same time structural or institutional characteristics (e.g., bureaucratic demands, the nursing hierarchy, pressures from patients' and their own families, ethnicity, gender relations) work against this kind of care. Their informal work culture makes their work life more bearable and also affects patients.

Methods: Observations of nursing aides and participation as a volunteer (coffee lady, wheeling patients to activities, making beds, etc.) on the patient floors of 'Crescent Nursing Home', a 200-bed non-profit skilled nursing facility in New York City, for eight months (1988–89); supplemented by 14 semi-structured in-depth interviews with nursing aides and others with administrative staff, nurses, and patients. Section in Introduction on methods: 'The field research' (pp. 4–8).

Geuijen, K., 't Hart, P., Princen, S. and Yesilkagit, K. (2008) *The new Eurocrats: National civil servants in EU policy-making.* **Amsterdam: Amsterdam University Press.**

Theme: Networks of national civil servants who prepare, take and implement decisions in Brussels and their home departments are studied as new modes of governance developing within the European Union. What do these civil servants do when they engage with the EU; how do they negotiate their dual roles as national civil servants and participants in European networks; and how do the ministries in which they are employed enhance or constrain their operations at the EU level?

Methods: A mixed method study drawing on a large-scale survey among Dutch civil servants; interviews with 49 middle-ranking and top officials in EU veterinary policy committees and police cooperating in local council working groups, and with 28 current and former national expert civil servants (SNEs) seconded by their government to the European Commission; observations of 16 meetings both in Brussels and The Hague; and participant observing of SNEs while working as a trainee at the European Commission. Methods section in Chapter 1 (pp. 24–7).

Goffman, E. (1961) *Asylums: Essays on the social situation of mental patients and other inmates.* **Harmondsworth: Penguin Books.**

Theme: An ethnographic study of and theoretical reflection on daily hospital life that seeks to describe how hospital inmates experience the social world in which they live.

Methods: Ethnographic fieldwork at St. Elizabeth's Hospital, Washington, DC (1955–56), additional brief field research of ward behaviour in the National Institutes of Health Clinical Center, Bethesda, Maryland (1954–1957).

Gouldner, A.W. (1954) *Patterns of industrial bureaucracy: A case study of modern factory administration.* **New York: Free Press.**

Theme: The formation and operation of industrial bureaucracy during changes in management resulting in a leadership succession crisis, developed through a case study of worker–management relations in a gypsum mine and processing plant.

Methods: Observations of the plant: walking around, observing workers and chatting with them as they worked, to contextualize 174 formal interviews of an hour and a half to two hours on average. One member of the research team – a skilled mechanic – spent a summer working in the mine, and documentary material was also used. Appendix on methods (pp. 247–69).

Gouldner, A.W. (1954) *Wildcat strike.* **Yellow Springs, OH: Antioch Press.**

Theme: A companion to the previous entry, this study focuses on group tensions during an industrial conflict – a wildcat strike – in a gypsum mine and processing plant.

Methods: See previous entry.

Hopgood, S. (2005) *Keepers of the flame: Understanding Amnesty International.* **Ithaca: Cornell University Press.**

Theme: Working life inside a major human rights organization, focusing on the moral and practical dilemmas faced by human rights activists, the decisions they make about the nature of the organization's mission, and the struggles over the implementation of that mission. Central to these dilemmas, decisions, and struggles are the tensions between 'moral authority' and 'political authority' and between 'the sacred' and 'the profane'.

Methods: Ethnographic fieldwork (2002–2003) at the International Secretariat of Amnesty International, London, drawing on more than 150 semi-structured interviews with staff members, archival research, and observations of day-to-day operations (for example, at internal meetings at all levels), governing meetings of the International Executive Committee, and the supreme policy-making forum of the International Council Meeting.

Ingersoll, V.H. and Adams, G.B. (1992) *The tacit organization.* **Greenwich, CT: JAI Press.**

Theme: A symbolic approach to the study of organizations that seeks to reveal what is 'omnipresent yet tacit' in organizational life, in the form of '(meta)patterns' and '(meta)myths'. The technology of data processing in the Washington State Ferry System – its formats and definitional constraints – can alter the way people conceptualize their work. The organization has roots in a small family business as well as in the state bureaucracy.

Methods: Observation at the ferry system and the state Department of Transportation, interviews with more than 50 people, and analysis of documents. Afterword on methodology: 'A symbolic approach to the study of organizations' (pp. 251–60).

Jackall, R. (1988) *Moral mazes: The world of corporate managers.* **Oxford: Oxford University Press.**

Theme: How corporate life within large bureaucracies, including internal political struggles and leadership at all levels, relates to questions of organizational and managerial morality.

Methods: Fieldwork in three companies – Fall 1980 to mid-1982 in one, Fall 1980 to mid-1983 in the second, and early 1982 through 1985 in the third – with 143 intensive semi-structured interviews and 40 re-interviews, often three or four times, with managers at every level. Findings were discussed with 12 managers during six meetings with each. Jackall also did non-participant and participant observation in formal and informal settings; he studied 13 cases of organizational dissenters, conducted interviews with 18 whistleblowers, and analysed relevant documents (company literature directed at managers and internal documents detailing organizational actions and stances on specific issues). Methods discussed in Chapter 1 and specified in author's note (pp. 205–6).

Jankowski, M.S. (1992) *Islands in the street: Gangs and American urban society.* **Berkeley: University of California Press**.

Theme: Jankowski finds an entrepreneurial spirit, not risk, turf or violence, to be the driving force behind urban gangs seen as quasi-rational business organizations. The first part of the book deals with the internal dynamics of gangs: individual decisions to join a gang; how gangs recruit and function and what factors influence their behaviours; how the organization supports itself through gang members' economic activities and what factors influence whether or not they are successful; the nature and causes of violence and how individual members and organizations cope with it; and gangs' relations with their local communities. The second part of the book turns to gangs' relations with the world outside the local community: urban politics, various government agencies, the criminal justice system, and the media.

Methods: Comparative ethnographic research on 37 gangs in a diversity of neighbourhoods in different cities – Los Angeles (13 gangs), New York City (20) and Boston (four) – ranging from working class to extremely poverty stricken, varying in size from 34 to more than 1000 members, and from different ethnic backgrounds (including Irish, African-American, Puerto Rican, Chicano, Dominican, Jamaican, and Central American, but not Asian). The researcher introduced himself to each gang leader as a professor who wanted to write a book comparing gangs over a period of ten years (1978–1989) and also interviewed people representing the official agencies or positions within society.

Jaques, E. (1970) *The changing culture of a factory: A study of authority and participation in an industrial setting.* **London: Routledge and Kegan Paul.**

Theme: A study commissioned by the Works Council explores the way a light engineering firm of 1500 employees tries to understand itself by interpreting how the large-scale problems of British industry are reflected in its own social development.

Methods: What the author calls a 'field theory approach,' in which researchers and their clients share responsibility for the research through a joint analysis of the problem, also sees the observer himself as one factor in determining his observations. The text of the report was subjected to rigorous criticism both by members of the firm and by the Works Council.

Johnson, K. (1998) *Deinstitutionalising women: An ethnographic study of institutional closure.* **Cambridge: Cambridge University Press.**

Theme: A study of deinstitutionalization's impacts on 21 women living in a closed unit in a large institution for people with mental disabilities. The author finds in this process a paradoxical discourse of rights and management.

Methods: Participant observation during 20 months of daily life and meetings at Hilltop's Unit N, interviews with staff, and analysis of documents and files.

Kamsteeg, F.H. (1998) *Prophetic Pentecostalism in Chile: A case study on religion and development policy.* **Lanham, MD: Scarecrow Press.**

Theme: A Chilean nongovernmental organization is analyzed as an instrument of Pentecostal politics whose goal is to produce religious change and raise Pentecostal social and political consciousness. The estrangement of NGO staff and ordinary church folk is an unintended outcome of the development discourse that increasingly separated development and religion.

Methods: Participant observation in three church congregations and a development-related nongovernmental organization in Santiago, Chile (1991–1992), with more than 100 visits to community activities (church services, Sunday School, youth group meetings, special occasions), plus 30 in-depth interviews with church leaders and members, as well as participant observation and interviews among NGO staff and the analysis of relevant policy documents. Chapter 2, 'Studying Latin American Pentecostalism', contains a section on methodology (pp. 37–42) and the methods applied (pp. 42–57).

Kanter, R.M. (1977) *Men and women of the corporation.* **New York: Basic Books.**

Theme: Corporate power in relation to the careers and self-images of people who are seeking upwardly mobile careers, focusing on managers (men) and secretaries, wives, and the occasional token manager (women) at the 'Industrial Supply Corporation'.

Methods: The author was a consultant, participant-observer, and researcher, conducting multiple research projects over a five year period: on site during 120 days consulting and doing participant observation in meetings and training programs, conducting 120 staff interviews, group discussions, and other conversations, plus 500 written surveys and content analysis of performance appraisal forms. Appendix on methodology (pp. 291–8).

Kaufman, H. (1960) *The forest ranger.* **Baltimore, MD: Published for Resources for the Future by Johns Hopkins Press.**

Theme: Top managers in the US Forest Service, a large, dispersed organization, are able to shape the behaviour of field officers into a coherent programme through unifying techniques, which are partly explicit and partly implicit.

Methods: The researcher immersed himself in the culture he proposed to describe, in an anthropological manner of gathering data doing field research in five districts (one week each), where he held conversations with the field officers, supplemented by observation.

Kondo, D. (1990) *Crafting selves: Power, gender and discourses of identity in a Japanese workplace.* **Chicago: University of Chicago Press.**

Theme: A Japanese-American studies work in Tokyo, comparing employees' self-construction with Western notions of the self.

Methods: Participant observation through living in a Tokyo neighbourhood, working in a beauty salon and in a small factory making goods to be sold in the bakery/confectionary across the street, supplemented with interviews with co-workers and people met elsewhere.

Kotter, J. (1983) *The general managers.* **New York: Free Press.**

Theme: Study of 15 'successful' male white executives in generalist or general-management jobs drawn from nine private corporations spread out across the United States in the late 1970s, focusing on questions about the nature of general-management jobs, the type of people who tend to be or become effective in such jobs, and what exactly it is that effective general managers do on a daily basis. He found that complexity was the central issue in their work lives.

Methods: An 'observational and self-report study' conducted between 1976 and 1981. Each individual was studied for almost a month's time, spread over the course of a year. Interviews (30–60 minutes) were done with the key people with whom each general manager worked, and several interviews of three to four hours total were done with each general manager. Each was also given a background questionnaire to fill out. A follow-up revisit took place four to seven months later, with observations over one-and-a-half to two days. Appendices on methods: Appendix A, The study (pp. 155–62); Appendix B, Interview guides (pp. 163–4); Appendix C, Questionnaires (pp. 165–74).

Kunda, G. (1992) *Engineering culture: Control and commitment in a high-tech corporation.* **Philadelphia: Temple University Press.**

Theme: A high tech engineering firm, the management of which explicitly tries to manage the organizational culture, is studied as an attempt at normative control of the employees, both engineers and staff. Research evidence shows that this attempt is met with ambivalence, ranging from enthusiasm to reluctant compliance to rebellious resistance. The final result of this 'cultural engineering' is a fragmented rather than a more integrated culture, with a considerable number of people dis-identifying with the official engineering culture.

Methods: A realist-style ethnography conducted in 1985: January to June in a staff group; June to December at 'SysCom': observations of daily work life, including meetings; interviews with staff. Kunda entered the organization as a management consultant, and later he became a full-time observer. Appendix on methods (pp. 229–40).

Latour, B. and Woolgar, S. (1979) *Laboratory life: The construction of scientific facts.* **London: Sage.**

Theme: Anaysis of day-to-day work in the Salk Institute for Biological Studies, California, looking at the production of scientific knowledge, specifically, the ways in which some stories come to be accepted as scientific knowledge and others do not.

Methods: Observations of the routine work carried out in a laboratory conducting scientific research (October 1975–August 1977), supplemented by formal interviews and the study of documents and literature produced by scientific staff at the laboratory.

Law, J. (1994) *Organizing modernity.* **Oxford: Blackwell.**

Theme: Processes of 'ordering' and organizing in formal organizations, and the role of social technologies of controlling, as distinct from the idea of a 'single social order', which Law perceives as the 'dream or nightmare' of modernity. Ethnography and writing are treated as yet another process of ordering, and Law invites the reader to watch him during his study.

Methods: Two years of ethnographic fieldwork at Daresbury Laboratory, a nuclear radiation research centre in Great Britain: interviewing, sitting in on meetings, and also observing experiments.

Leidner, R. (1993) *Fast food, fast talk: Service work and the routinization of everyday life.* **Berkeley: University of California Press.**

Theme: How routinization works in service jobs and the outcomes it produces, looking at the relations among routinization, skill, control, interaction, and self in two cases and exploring how they go about routinizing the work of employees who deal with the public. Both companies faced two basic challenges: to standardize the behaviour of employees, and to control the behaviour of customers. They differed on the extent of efforts to affect workers' personalities, the workers' gender, and the degree of supervision, as well as on how the interests of managers, workers, and service-recipients were to be aligned.

Methods: Interviewing and participant observation at McDonald's and Combined Insurance: attending corporate training programmes and interviewing executives to study the companies' goals and strategies for routinization, followed by doing or observing the work and interviewing interactive service workers to explore how the routines worked out in practice. Section on methods in Chapter 1, 'The research' (pp. 14–17). Two appendices with reflections on the research process: Appendix 1, Researching routinized work (pp. 233–48); Appendix 2, Revising the script at Combined Insurance (pp. 249–56).

Lutz, C. and Collier, J. (1992) *Reading National Geographic.* **Chicago: University of Chicago Press.**

Theme: An organizational ethnography of *National Geographic*, looking at the ways readers view photos, the structure and content of these images, and the organizations that produce them – the National Geographic Society, the photographers, the editors of the magazine, etc.

Methods: Twenty-five interviews were conducted with photographers, editors, and other staff members in the summers of 1989 and 1990. Observations of meetings of the National Geographic Society were done during that same time. In addition, an analysis was done of 600 randomly selected *National Geographic* photographs from 1950 to 1986 in relation to the larger wholes of the genre and its socio-cultural context. Interviews were conducted with and observations were done of the behaviour of readers of the magazine.

Manning, P. (1977) *Police work: The social organization of policing.* **Cambridge, MA: MIT Press.**

Theme: A 'dramaturgical perspective' on the dilemmas of policing, this study claims that the police have resorted to the dramatic management of the appearance of effectiveness, being faced with massive discrepancies between their claims (the police must dramatize the appearance of control of crime in order to gain public support) and their accomplishments (they cannot in fact control crime; they cannot possibly fulfill the ever-increasing public demand for an ever-higher level of public order and crime prevention).

Methods: Extensive fieldwork with a subdivision of the London Metropolitan Police (1973), with observation during 84 hours of walking home beats, riding in police cars, and sitting in the reserve room (the main information room of the station), the canteen, and in the office of the chief superintendent, supplemented by interviews, statistical analysis, and assistance to officers by collating phone and teleprinter messages received at the station. The researcher also drew on data from a study of two narcotics enforcement units in metropolitan Washington, DC.

Mayo, E. (1933) *The human problem of an industrial civilization.* **Boston: Harvard University Press.**

Theme: Mayo perceives organizations as 'social systems' in which informal rules and norms, mutual support within a work group, and other social-psychological factors are at least as important for motivating organizational performance as classical (Taylorist) individualist approaches. A classic study that paved the way for the Human Relations movement in organizational studies.

Methods: Experiments (Western Electronic Company: Hawthorne experiments in two experimental rooms), interviews and observations. During more than two years (1928–30), over 21,000 employees were personally interviewed (for one half to one and one-half hours) by 30 interviewers to find out their attitudes toward their work. During the last phase of the research project, one or two researchers made daily observations of the individuals in a department.

Moeran, B. (2006) *Ethnography at work*. Oxford: Berg Publishers.

Theme: How do advertisements come into being and why? Focusing on a case study of an advertising campaign made by Asatsu, a Japanese advertising agency, for the International Division of Frontier, a Japanese electronics manufacturing organization, the author looks at six central issues, among them 'follow the money', 'advertising talk', 'impression management', and 'creativity'. Comparing managers in professional settings to ethnographers, he suggests that while managers may fill roles common to ethnographers, they cannot be true ethnographers until they remove themselves from the situation.

Methods: A year of ethnographic fieldwork studying the day-to-day working life of people designing advertisement campaigns and trying to persuade clients to use their services.

Morrill, C. (1995) *The executive way: Conflict management in corporations*. Chicago: University of Chicago Press.

Theme: The causes of conflict among high level American corporate executives, and the multitude of covert and overt ways these executives dispute with one another.

Methods: A realist ethnography (1984–1986) consisting of interviews with over 200 executives and their support personnel at 13 companies (in the construction, manufacturing, professional, and services sectors), observations and informal interviews of executives and their staff; formal executive interviews; follow-up formal interviews with key informants; and analysis of historical data and documents. Appendix A: 'Anatomy of an ethnography of business elites' (pp. 229–55).

Ogasawara, Y. (1998) *Office ladies and salaried men: Power, gender, and work in Japanese companies*. Berkeley: University of California Press.

Theme: The complexities underlying the apparent dominance of men over women in Japanese offices, where female clerical workers ('office ladies') are seen by both men and women as utterly powerless. This book reveals the subtle and not-so-subtle ways in which these women manipulate men, subverting the power structure to their advantage by using informal means of control like gossip, outright work refusal, and public gift giving. The men must accede to these manipulative strategies in order to retain their power.

Methods: Six months of covert participant observation in a large bank in Tokyo, working as an 'office lady', including over 100 interviews with salaried men, their wives, and current and former office ladies. Appendix A: 'Data and methods' (pp. 169–77).

Ong, A. (1987) *Spirits of resistance and capitalist discipline: Factory women in Malaysia.* New York: State University of New York Press.

Theme: Disruptions, conflicts, and ambivalences in the lives of Malay women working in Japanese factories in Malaysia, caught between their Malay community culture and the culture of capitalism.

Methods: Over one year of participant observation living in post-colonial Malaysia.

Orr, J. (1996) *Talking about machines: An ethnography of a modern job.* New York: Cornell University Press.

Theme: The 'oral culture' of Xerox copy machine field service technicians repairing machines in their clients' offices and meeting together over lunch, where talk about the machines is instrumental to their success.

Methods: Participant observation of the day-to-day activities of copier repair technicians, after an initial training as a technician.

Parker, M. (2000) *Organizational culture and identity: Unity and division at work.* London: Sage.

Theme: Organizational culture is at the same time general and specific in that it always develops in relation to the local environment, organizational history, and macro developments. Specific attention is devoted to cultural identities and power relations between and within 'categories': dynamic groups which are constructed around different themes in organizations. As a result of these interplays, organizations tend to develop at least three categories: functional, generational, and geographically-based groups.

Methods: Three case studies of organizations in Britain – a manufacturing company (cookers), a financial sector organization (building society), and a hospital (within the UK's National Health Service) – between 1988 and 1998. Each case study took at least 18 months and involved document analysis; formal semi-structured interviews with higher status employees (managers, directors, and doctors); informal interviews and conversations; observations of day-to-day activities and meetings; and a month of 'shadowing' an employee at the hospital. Appendix on methods (pp. 235–41).

Perlow, L. (1997) *Finding time: How corporations, individuals, and families can benefit from new work practices.* Ithaca, NY: IRL Press (an imprint of Cornell University Press).

Theme: What is necessary for individual software engineers in a product development team to succeed in the existing work culture at 'Ditto', a Fortune 500 corporation, chosen because of its reputation as a leader in implementing flexible work policies to address employees' work/life conflicts. The 'vicious work time cycle' – a system of rewards that perpetuates crises and continuous interruptions, while discouraging cooperation – results in work practices that damage both organizational productivity and the quality of individuals' lives outside of work.

Methods: A nine-month participant observer study of the software group, with about four days per week on site, arriving early and leaving late, shadowing some of the engineers, attending meetings, and conducting formal interviews with each of the 17 members of the software team. Members of the team were also asked to write down their work and life activities during three randomly selected days. Perlow made home visits and interviewed spouses, as well as attending social events. Methodological Appendix: A research tale (pp. 141–8).

Pettigrew, A. (1973) *The politics of organizational decision-making.* **London: Tavistock.**

Theme: Power and conflict in the context of a series of innovative decisions concerning computer purchases in 'Brian Michaels'. The goal of the study was to map the historically developed power resources (e.g., information) of the participants in this process and the way they used these resources to promote their interests.

Methods: Participant observation four days a week (September 1966 to December 1969) beginning with the training programme in the systems department, where the team working on the computer decision was housed, including interviewing, diary keeping, questionnaires, and content analysis of documentary data. Interview data, which included an historical orientation, were checked with documentary material, such as company reports, correspondence, and internal memos. Chapter 4: The research process (pp. 52–75)

Ram, M. (1994) *Managing to survive: Working lives in small firms.* **Oxford: Blackwell.**

Theme: The day-to-day activities and dilemmas of managers and workers, including ethnic characteristics, in smaller Asian clothing firms in the UK Midlands. 'Negotiated paternalism' in management-labour relations is characterized 'neither by autocracy nor by harmony', but is a situation in which 'negotiated obligations are constructed and re-constructed'.

Methods: Ram worked for years in this industry as a manager and consultant before beginning the directed case study research, which is based on a year-long study of three clothing firms in the West Midlands. He began with semi-structured interviews with 16 owner-managers, followed by observational fieldwork over a four month period and then regular weekly visits for a year. Ram is reflexive about the 'messy' process of fieldwork, especially the role of 'exchange' between researcher and researched in 'managing fieldwork roles'. Chapter 2 on methodology (pp. 22–39).

Rosen, M. (2000) *Turning words, spinning worlds: Chapters in organizational ethnography.* **Amsterdam: Harwood Academic Publishers.**

Theme: A collection of previously published articles decoding market rules in the New York worlds of advertising (two chapters on 'Spiro's'), finance (three chapters on an insurance company and the New York Stock Exchange), and drug dealing.

Methods: Participant observer ethnography, in which the author reflects on the uses of ethnographic methods in organizational studies. The foreward and two chapters take up organizational ethnography.

Selznick, P. (1949) *TVA and the grass roots: A study in the sociology of formal organization*. **Berkeley: University of California Press**.

Theme: A study of the Tennessee Valley Authority (TVA) and the results of its policy of administering its programme, particularly in the agricultural field, through the use of local institutions. What price is paid in bureaucratic life when ideology becomes a resource in the struggle for power?

Methods: One year's observations in daily contact with personnel at TVA; a number of weeks in intensive contact with extension service personnel in the field; plus interviews with TVA personnel and an analysis of gossip channels and files.

Shore, C. (2000) *Building Europe: The cultural politics of European integration*. **London: Routledge.**

Theme: Study of the cultural politics of European integration and the organizational culture of the European Commission: how the European Commission attempted to create a single Europe and a single European identity by using culture – several instruments, among them Euro-symbols and statistics, European citizenship, and the single currency (the Euro) – as a tool for bringing about a sense of cohesion and belonging among Europeans. This study provides some interpretations for the 'seemingly endemic' fraud and corruption the Commission had to cope with at the time of the study.

Methods: Ethnographic fieldwork – immersion in daily activities, plus in-depth interviews and cross-check or follow-up interviews – carried out among European Union civil servants and politicians in Brussels between 1993 and 1997, including two periods of four and six months for intensive fieldwork. Methods section within the introductory chapter (pp. 7–11).

Smith, V. (1990) *Managing in the corporate interest: Control and resistance in an American bank*. **Berkeley: University of California Press.**

Theme: This case study of restructuring at the 'American Security Bank', a large multi-branch California bank, critiques management philosophies that blame middle-management rigidity for corporate problems. Middle-management behaviour is rational when perceived from the middle managers' own perspectives: they have their own goals (here, increasing productivity) that may differ from strategic management's goals ('cutting bureaucratic slack').

Methods: 'Involved observations' taking 75 hours in two week-long management training seminars (1985). Interviews were conducted with other managers about their seminar experiences, as well as with the corporate trainers; and open interviews were conducted with 60 bank-employees (operations middle managers, supervisors, and the management development personnel of three major divisions of the bank). Observations of the production process were done before, during, and after the interviews, and documentary sources were also analyzed. Section on methods (pp. 20–7); appendix on observations (pp. 201–3).

Tompkins, P. (1992) *Organizational communication imperatives: Lessons of the space program.* **Los Angeles, CA: Roxbury Press.**

Theme: 'Organizational forgetting' and effective communication strategies at NASA's Marshall Space Flight Centre, including an organizational failure in the Challenger Program.

Methods: Observations, interviews with principals, close readings of historical documents over a period of 25 years, starting in 1967 in the role of consultant, returning to interview top management in 1990, four years after the Challenger accident. A first-person narrative employing three points of view: 'first-person observer, first-person participant, and the objective point of view' (p. viii). Preface on methods (pp. vi–ix).

Watson, T.J. (1994) *In search of management: Culture, chaos & control in managerial work.* **London: International Thomson Business Press.**

Theme: The nature of managerial work at the British 'ZTC Ryland' plant (3000 employees), which develops, makes and sells telecommunications products. Insights into basic organizational activities and the processes that managers in the 1990s used as they coped with both traditional business pressures and the newer ideas of pursuing 'excellence' through changing cultures and 'empowering' employees. This study was arranged as a secondment from business school, with one of the key tasks to develop a scheme identifying and expressing the management competencies which ZTC Ryland would use in selecting and developing its managers for the future (see appendix, pp. 225–8).

Methods: One year of participant observation and conducting formal and informal interviews, working alongside managers while at the same time studying them and producing the scheme on the base of dialogues with them. He explicitly takes Melville Dalton's *Men who manage* as the study's predecessor in methods as well as theme. Reflective section on methods within the Introduction: 'Into the field: Revealing the ethnographer's hand' (pp. 6–8).

Wels, H. (2003) *Private wildlife conservation in Zimbabwe: Joint ventures and reciprocity.* **Leiden: Brill.**

Theme: This case study of the identifying processes of reciprocal exchange between joint venture partners in private wildlife conservation focuses on cooperation started in the 1990s, when the Land Question became crucial in the politically explosive situation in Zimbabwe, between the Savé Valley Conservancy (SVC, an organization established in June 1991 by 24 white commercial local cattle farmers) and its neighbouring black communities (communal farmers), represented through the Savé Valley Conservancy Trust

(SVCT). The SVC considered the Trust as its gift to the black communities and with that interpretation created an expectation for reciprocity: SVC would redistribute some of the economic benefits from its wildlife utilization programme, and in return the communities would respect the boundaries of the SVC instead of violating them through poaching.

Methods: Observations of the workings of SVC and its Conservancy Committee Meetings, interviews with its members and broad historical, socio-political and socio-cultural contextualizations.

Whyte, W.F. (1948) *Human relations in the restaurant industry.* **New York: McGraw Hill.**

Theme: Human relationships in the restaurant industry and the way these took shape under wartime conditions, comparing abnormal with normal situations and behaviours.

Methods: A one-year (1944–1945) intensive field study of 12 Chicago restaurants, with interviewing in 13 others, including seven in other cities. Whyte and three research assistants first conducted interviews with employees, supervisors, and executives concerning their human relations problems. Second, each of the researchers spent between one and six months performing various restaurant jobs (in some cases on the restaurant's payroll). Third, observations were done of the interactions among the various people who made up a restaurant. Appendix: A note on research (pp. 359–68).

Wolcott, H. (1973) *The man in the principal's office: An ethnography.* **Austin, TX: Holt, Rinehart and Winston.**

Theme: The day-to-day activities of a suburban elementary school principal, including the time devoted to various administrative activities, dilemmas faced, feelings, and how his many life roles affect and are affected by his role as principal, as reflected in his self-perceptions and others' perceptions of his behavior. Wolcott devotes particular attention to the principal's role as mediator among the various groups comprising the network of relationships that develop among his staff, parents, school system officials, and school-children, and himself.

Methods: An intensive case study shadowing 'Edward Bell' at all his work activities at the 'Taft School' in a middle-sized American city (1966–1968), supplemented by interviews with 15 members of the staff and written questionnaires. Wolcott was a teacher and a vice-principal at an elementary school himself before doing this study.

Yanow, D. (1996) *How does a policy mean? Interpreting policy and organizational actions.* **Washington, DC: Georgetown University Press.**

Theme: Organizational and public policy meanings are often expressed and communicated through symbolic language, objects, and acts. Analysis of these may explain unarticulated and sometimes conflicting meanings that characterize processes of devising and implementing policy by different actors.

Methods: Participating and observing in two government corporation community centers in Israel (November 1972–February 1973 and mid-March 1973–August 1975). Between September 1980 and February 1981 Yanow did follow-up interviews (including formal interviews with 37 people), document analysis, and further observations.

Young, M. (1991) *An inside job: Policing and police culture in Britain*. Oxford: Clarendon.

Theme: A study of British police practices as they occur on the ground in urban areas: how detectives in this insulated and conservative institution frequently assume sexist, racist and violent roles to play out their 'macho dramas', 'stage-managing the arbitrary and changing face of crime' by creating 'crime figures' and manipulating 'detection rates'.

Methods: 'Observing participation' by a career officer drawing on insider knowledge of Northumbria Police and West Mercia Police, having worked as a policeman in the Drugs Squad for ten years before being seconded in mid-career to the university, reading anthropology, and then writing this book. Chapter 1: Participant observation of police practice (pp. 1–56).

Zabusky, S. (1995) *Launching Europe: An ethnography of European cooperation in space science*. Princeton: Princeton University Press.

Theme: The complex processes involved in cooperation on space science missions in the contemporary context of European integration within the European Space Agency do not depend on a 'homogenizing of interests in a bland unity' but instead consist of 'ongoing negotiation of and conflict over often irreconcilable differences'. Some of these differences are technical (e.g., those of science), some political (e.g., European integration). Participants on space science missions make use of these differences, particularly those manifest in work and nationality identities, as they struggle together not only to produce space satellites but also to create European integration.

Methods: Fieldwork (September 1988–August 1989) at the Space Science Department of the European Space Research and Technology Center (part of the European Space Agency) at Noordwijk, The Netherlands, consisting of observations of day-to-day work practices – like engineering sessions at the laboratory – and meetings, doing semi-structured and unstructured interviews with cooperating staff scientists, and having informal conversations at social events. Published material and other written documents were also analysed. Section on methodology in Chapter 1 (pp. 41–6).

Zald, M. (1970) *Organizational change: The political economy of the YMCA*. Chicago: University of Chicago Press.

Theme: A sociological study of the adaptation of the Young Men's Christian Association (YMCA) to technological, ideological and social changes and the role of the organization's economic and political structures in this process.

The YMCA combines changes in policies, personnel, and power relations with maintaining and revitalizing what Zald terms their 'traditional political economy'.

Methods: Ethnographic fieldwork with a sociological disciplinary (rather than cultural) focus (1961–1964) at the metropolitan Chicago YMCA, in combination with historical analysis, observations of meetings, qualitative interviews, and a questionnaire administered to all professional staff and a sample of board members (1962). Several hundred hours of interviewing with board members, secretaries, professional staff members, and volunteers, plus observations of staff, the board of managers, the board of trustees, various committees, and the general secretaries' cabinet meetings. Participant-observation in the board of managers' planning committee (Fall 1963–Summer 1964), plus two weeks interviewing (1967) in the office and selected departments. Section on methods in Preface (pp. xiii–xvii).

Index

co-production/co-construction of knowledge 9, 83, 86–7, 192, 197, 198, 216, 218, 224–5
co-researchers 218, 220, 222–4
  see also co-production of knowledge
colonialism 218
collaboration 14, 84, 85, 117, 130, 206
Collinson, D. 112–13
computer database programs 36
constructivist approach *see* interpretivist approach
context 7, 10, 15, 24–5, 27,31–2, 34, 37–8, 56, 60, 62–3, 65, 69–70, 78, 95, 102, 104, 107, 120, 124–5, 127, 140, 148, 157, 160, 162, 164–6, 168–9, 192, 203, 220–1, 224, 235–6, 238, 241, 244, 245, 248–9
cultural scripts 157
contextualizing 35, 247, 251
conversational interviewing 23
convincing explanation 134
corporate culture change 83–97
covert studies 163
creating breakdowns 108, 167–9
culture 2, 3, 5, 7, 8, 13, 16–20, 24–6, 30, 38–9, 44, 54, 55, 79, 82, 89, 94, 96–7, 102–5, 108, 110, 113, 115, 117–19, 123, 137–8, 143, 155, 160–2, 167, 169, 170–4, 182–3, 187, 194, 213–14, 218, 228, 234, 250–1, 255–6, 258–61, 263–4, 266, 269, 271, 275, 277–8, 280
cultural change 83, 84, 91
Czarniawska, B. 4, 5, 111, 125, 130, 256–7
Czarniawska-Joerges, B. 105

Dalton, M. 111, 181
data details 64, 69, 70, 254
data observation 35
data types 34–6
  literature as data 34
'DDT' (dates, days and times of day) 66–7
deception 180–1, 192–3
defamiliarization
  creating breakdowns 168
  interpretation strategy 110
Delbridge 4, 17, 41, 54, 265
democratic proccess 215
Denzin, N. 163

Derrida, J. 231, 240
deskwork 56–7, 63
detachment 3, 88, 103, 105, 116, 148, 154
Dewey, J. 217
discourse analysis 173, 220, 225, 228, 229, 230
disengaged engaged ethnographer 106, 108
disengaged research 101–3, 115–16
  interpretation strategies 108–10
  involvement and detachment 103–6
  observation roles 111–15
distance
  engagement and distance phase in engaged research 202–3, 204, 207–8, 210–11
  friendship *vs* reflexive distance 111–12
  see also detachment; immersion/involvement
documents as data 34
double hermeneutic 57
Down, S. 83, 87, 95
  et al. 85
  and Garrety, K. 94
  and Hughes, M. 84
dual role (of researcher) 68

ecological validity 135, 137
emancipation 29, 81, 232, 236, 237, 240–4
emancipatory research 71, 234–5, 237, 243
emic *vs* etic understanding 103–4, 105
emotion / emotions 6, 7, 14, 18, 43, 47–8, 50–1, 81, 84–8, 94–8, 106, 113, 135, 167, 169, 173, 178, 181, 186, 189, 191, 198–200, 202, 211–12
empathy 246
employment
  South Africa 237–45
  women 240–4
empowerment 125
engaged ethnography *see* employment; engaged research; equity issues
engaged research 196–8
  ethical questions 203–5
  examples
    art 209–12
    science 205–8
  relationship phases 200–5, 212

Foucault, M. 217–19, 227, 231, 233, 236, 240, 243
Freire, P. 217
friendship 199–200
    critique of 181–4
    vs reflexive distance 111–12
frontstage and backstage perspectives 33, 112–13, 148

Gabriel, Y. 9, 94
Geertz, C. 41, 60, 97, 104–5, 146, 158–9, 163, 197, 218, 235
Gellner, D.
    and Hirsch, E. 153
    Hirsch, E. and 25–6, 27, 34
gender issues
    employment 240–4
    errors in surgical training study 190
    researcher–subject sexual relationships 188–9
getting in see access 29, 141–44, 154, 193
Glaser and Strauss 183
    see also grounded theory
Goffman, E. 3, 9, 148, 186, 188, 254
going native 78, 153, 154, 162, 171
graphic (re)presentation 70
Greenwood, D.J. and Levin, M. 59, 197, 215–17, 224–5
grounded theory 25–6, 35, 145–6, 183

Hammersley, M. and Atkinson, P. 101, 105–6, 110, 113
hermeneutics 57, 214
Hirsch, E.
    Gellner, D. and 153
    and Gellner, D.N. 25–6, 27, 34
humanity 88, 189
humour 17, 53, 114–15, 117
Humphreys, M. 45, 85–6, 95–6
    and Brown, A.D. 48–9
    et al. 41, 114

identity politics 242–3, 245–6
identification 54, 92, 97, 112, 198, 224
identity/ies
    and friendship 200
    of managers 87–8, 92–3, 95
    of newspaper editors 109
    see also self
ideology 93, 190, 237, 277
immersion/involvement
    and detachment 103–6

immersion/involvement cont.
    distancing by 112–13
    and intimacy 149
    see also participant observation
impression management 113, 153, 178, 181, 188, 192, 274
indigenous people 96, 98
informants 62, 141, 144–9, 153, 178, 180–1, 183, 185–91, 194, 263, 274
informed consent 180–1
'insider' perspective
    action research 221–2
    and outsider perspective 104–6, 107–8
    see also access
Institutional Review Board (I.R.B) 73, 82, 183
instrumentality 199, 239
integrity 72, 148, 170, 201, 227
intermediaries 130–1
interpretation strategies 108–10
interpreting 11, 16, 20, 26, 30, 81, 113, 119, 121, 157, 170, 174, 190, 194, 230, 269, 279
interpretivist approach 7–10, 57, 58, 157, 169, 218, 219
    vs 'objective'/positivist approach 72–5
intervention 186, 191
interviews
    as data 35
    problems with 157–8
involvement see immersion/involvement
'irrational'
    aspects of rational management 109–10
irony 91, 97, 103, 113–14, 116–18, 168, 174, 194

Jackall, R. 7, 110, 179–80
jester role 113–15
John Dewey 217
joint authorship 84, 88
justice 3, 13–14, 83, 158, 187, 190, 227, 231, 234, 237, 243, 247, 269

knowledge
    action research perspective 215–18
    co-production/co-construction of 9, 86–7, 192, 197–8, 216, 218, 224–5
    local 146–9
    and power 9, 217, 220–1, 225–6, 227
    prior 166–7
Kostera, M. 2, 4,109

silencing 198
Silverman, D. 4, 106, 127, 157, 158
sociological imagination 40, 55
socio-spatial exploration 31
South Africa 244, 247
  apartheid era 24–5
space/place dimension of organizations
  31, 65–6, 69
strangeness 13, 102, 105–6, 113–14, 116
stranger-ness 11–12, 99
strategy 4, 31, 34, 38, 51, 55, 93, 97, 102,
  109, 110, 111–13, 129, 131, 160, 168,
  180, 191, 203
studying up 5, 25, 145
subject–researcher relationships *see*
  co-production/co-construction; ethical
  issues; research relationships
'subjectivity'
  and prior knowledge 166–7
  see also engaged research; participant
  observation
surprise 11, 15, 33, 77, 103, 106–8, 112,
  113, 116, 165, 201, 206
symbolism
  and heritage 32–4
  and signs 218
symbols 8, 23, 27, 32, 45, 64, 70,
  158, 200, 218

tacit knowledge 58, 62
tales from the field 196, 205
telemonitoring project 123, 130–2
testability 59
textwork 9, 10, 13, 56–7, 59, 63–4, 70
theory
  data and 127
  and prior assumptions 24–7
thick description 41, 59–60, 69–70, 73, 166
third-person (critical) action research
  219–20, 223, 227
time dimensions 66–7, 69
translation, scientific 83, 94
transparency 27, 59, 61, 65, 69, 220
triangulation 60–1, 69
'triple hermeneutic' 57
trust 34, 36, 57–8
  in friendship 199, 200
trustworthiness of text 59–70

unexpected 29, 36, 103, 106–8, 109–10,
  124, 136, 149, 151, 165, 168, 201, 246
unstructured interviews 88

value statements 84
Van Maanen, J. 4, 6, 23, 25, 35, 42, 44, 56,
  68, 101, 102, 104, 158–9, 161, 182,
  189–90, 218, 257
virtual organizations 257
voice
  giving voice 2, 6, 71, 83, 236
  multivocality 8–9
  and silences 68–9

Watson, T.J. 40–1, 48, 51–2, 53
Whyte, W.F. 3, 112
Wittgenstein, L. 107
Wolcott, H.F. 85–6, 158
women *see* gender issues
work practices 120–1, 124, 134–6
writing
  enhanced: 'crossing the bridge' 45–8
  ethical issues 72–5, 191–2
  ethnography 10, 40–2, 106
  fictionalized 51–2
  perspective on member-checking
    70–2
  plain: 'entering the faculty' 44–5
  semi-fictionalized: 'charity begins at
    home' 48–51
  strategies 63–70
  typology and continuum 42–3
  writing-up to 40–1, 53

Yanow, D. 8–9, 56, 64, 134, 218

zooming in
  data and theory 127
  palette for 124–7
  telemedicine study 123–5, 127–8,
    130–3
zooming out
  comparing sites 132–3
  palette for 129–33
  relationships among practices
    131–2
  rhizome model 128–9, 133–4
  when to stop 133–4

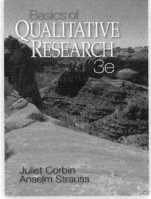

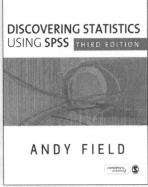
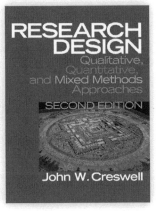

The Qualitative Research Kit

Edited by Uwe Flick

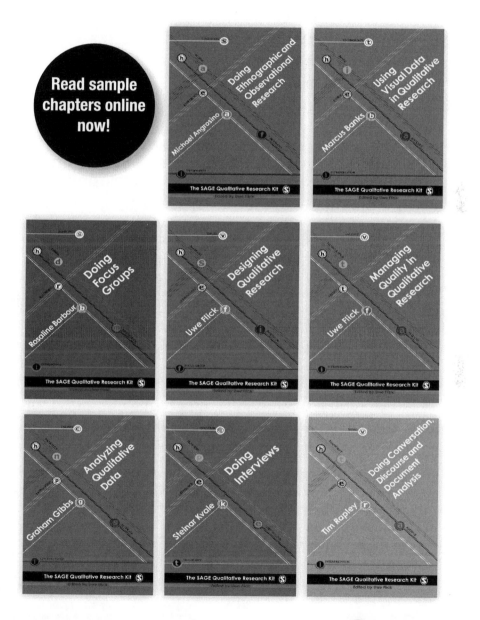

Read sample chapters online now!

Doing Ethnographic and Observational Research — Michael Angrosino

Using Visual Data in Qualitative Research — Marcus Banks

Doing Focus Groups — Rosaline Barbour

Designing Qualitative Research — Uwe Flick

Managing Quality in Qualitative Research — Uwe Flick

Analyzing Qualitative Data — Graham Gibbs

Doing Interviews — Steinar Kvale

Doing Conversation, Discourse and Document Analysis — Tim Rapley

The SAGE Qualitative Research Kit
Edited by Uwe Flick

www.sagepub.co.uk

SAGE

Supporting researchers for more than forty years

Research methods have always been at the core of SAGE's publishing. Sara Miller McCune founded SAGE in 1965 and soon after, she published SAGE's first methods book, *Public Policy Evaluation*. A few years later, she launched the Quantitative Applications in the Social Sciences series – affectionately known as the 'little green books'.

Always at the forefront of developing and supporting new approaches in methods, SAGE published early groundbreaking texts and journals in the fields of qualitative methods and evaluation.

Today, more than forty years and two million little green books later, SAGE continues to push the boundaries with a growing list of more than 1,200 research methods books, journals, and reference works across the social, behavioural, and health sciences.

From qualitative, quantitative and mixed methods to evaluation, SAGE is the essential resource for academics and practitioners looking for the latest in methods by leading scholars.

www.sagepublications.com